AF441967

A Textbook on
Fortran/2003

A Textbook on
Fortran/2003

Subrata Ray

Alpha Science International Ltd.
Oxford, U.K.

A Textbook on Fortran/2003
500 pgs | 37 tbls. | 201 figs.

Subrata Ray
Computer Centre
Indian Association for the Cultivation of Science
Jadavpur
Kolkata 700 032, India

ALPHA SCIENCE INTERNATIONAL LTD.

7200 The Quorum, Oxford Business Park North
Garsington Road, Oxford OX4 2JZ, U.K.

www.alphasci.com

Printed from the camera-ready copy provided by the Author.

ISBN 978-1-84265-479-8

Printed in India

This work is dedicated to

Minakshi Ghosh
and
Jayanta Kumar Bhattacharjee

PREFACE

This is a textbook on programming language Fortran/2003 based on the Fortran/2003 report (Working Draft J3/04-007, May 10, 2004). Though the book is written for beginners with very little knowledge about the earlier versions of Fortran, experienced programmers of earlier versions of Fortran may find this book useful if they want to learn the features of Fortran/2003. Such readers can directly look into the appropriate statements. It has been the endeavor of the author to avoid the "forward reference" as far as practicable. Therefore, when a particular statement is introduced, not all the options/attributes are given at one place – the options/attributes are sometimes scattered in different places of the book. This was necessary so that a beginner can start from the first page of the book and can proceed sequentially. A careful reader would find the complete statement after going through the book.

As Fortran is mainly used in solving problems related to science and engineering, standard numerical methods have been used as vehicle to illustrate the application of the language. However, knowledge beyond the level of elementary calculus is not required to understand the numerical examples given in the book. The emphasis of the book is on programming language, not on sophisticated numerical methods. The programming examples given in the book are simple and to keep the code readable, the code is not optimized. It is expected that a reader after proper understanding of the language would be able to write "much more efficient" codes.

Programming tips and programming style have been introduced at appropriate places. These are just guidelines. It is well known that every experienced programmer has his/her own programming style.

All the programs and program segments have been tested with the Fortran compiler provided by The Numerical Algorithms Group Ltd., Oxford, UK.

All the statements of the earlier versions of Fortran are expected to work with standard Fortran/2003 compilers. For example the declaration:

```
INTEGER A
```

is still a valid declaration under Fortran/2003. But the standard Fortran/2003 declaration:

```
INTEGER :: A
```

is used throughout the book. This is true for other Fortran instructions also. Usually Fortran/2003 instructions are more general and contain more attributes than the equivalent statements of earlier versions of Fortran (like Fortran 77).

Some of the instructions of the earlier versions of Fortran have been declared as obsolete though the present Fortran compilers support these features. These have been indicated at the appropriate places. Instructions like arithmetic IF, computed GOTO are normally not used now a days. Yet, these types of instruction are discussed as some of the old running programs may have these instructions and some times one has to read and modify these old programs.

Throughout the book Fortran stands for Fortran/2003 and any deviation from it has been mentioned whenever required.

Sections/chapters marked with asterisk may be skipped during the first reading of the book.

At the time of writing this book (October 2007), the author could not find a Fortran compiler that supports all the features of Fortran/2003 language.

The author may be contacted by e-mail (subratar@gmail.com). Some more information about the book will be made available at the website http://www. angelfire.com/sc3/subrata/F2003.

ACKNOWLEDGEMENTS

The author wishes to record his deep sense of gratitude to his colleagues, friends and associates who helped him prepare the manuscript during the various phases of this work.

Aditya Bagchi	Manika Banerjee	Satyabrata Roy
Atul Gurtu	Monika Mukherjee	Siddhartha Chaudhuri
Ajay Kumar Majhi	Prasanta Kumar Mukherjee	Siddhartha Ray
Debshankar Ray	Purnendu Das	Soumitra SenGupta
Debasis Sengupta	Ramaprasad De	Soumya Chakravarti
Indrajit Basu	Robert Holmes	Swapan Bhattacharjee
Indrani Bose	Sankar Chakravorty	Utpal Chattopadhyay
John Holden	Shankar Prasad Bhattacharyya	
Koushik Ray	Santosh Kumar Samaddar	

Sarbani Saha and Robert Dyson have gone through the entire manuscript. They located typos, errors of various nature and suggested several improvements.

Ardhendu Sekhar Dutta, Sudipta Dutta and Jayita Ghosh of SALIENCE have converted the raw manuscript into this decent form. They have drawn all the diagrams of this book.

The Numerical Algorithms Group Ltd., Oxford, UK provided with a free license to use their Fortran Compiler for one year.

Finally, the author wishes to thank his family — mother Prabha Ray, sister Uma Sen, brother Debabrata Ray, wife Sanghamitra Ray and daughter Sumitra Ray for their encouragement during the preparation of this manuscript.

Last but not least, the author wishes to thank the Laptop which he used almost 12 hours a day for months without a single breakdown during the preparation of this manuscript.

CONTENTS

Chapter 1

INTRODUCTION

A computer program is a set of instructions through which one instructs a computer to perform a specific job. A computer processor understands a single language – called the machine language. Machine languages are machine dependent and at the same time are difficult to learn. To circumvent this difficulty, several artificial languages (sometimes called high level languages) have been developed. These artificial languages are very easy to learn and are practically machine independent. However, this requires translation to the machine language of the processor. The translation is done by the computer itself through a system program – called a compiler. The compiler, while translating, checks the grammar of the language; if the source program is free from grammatical error, it generates the machine language version of the 'source program' called the 'object program' for the machine, which is subsequently linked (using a system program called the linker) with various libraries of the system (Fig 1.1). The resultant code, called the 'executable code', may be executed by the machine. As the machine languages of different machines are different, the compilers are naturally machine dependent. Therefore, that a particular machine can 'execute' a program written in high level language implies that the compiler for that high level language is available on that computer system.

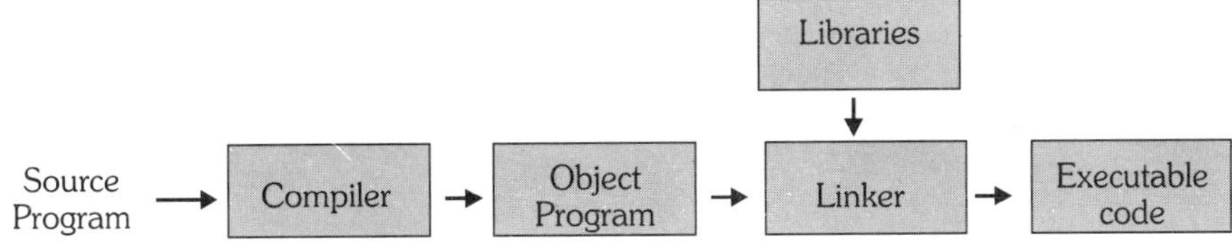

Fig 1.1 Block Diagram of Compilation and Linking

Fortran, one such programming language, is the abbreviation of FORmula TRANslation. It is widely used in solving scientific and engineering problems requiring a lot of numerical computation. In this book Fortran stands for the Fortran/2003, the present version of Fortran.

It must be mentioned at this point that no computer can execute directly any program written in Fortran or any other so called 'high level' language like Fortran. The compiler for the corresponding language must be available in the computer so that the translated version of the program written in a high level language may be executed by the computer. As this translation – Fortran to machine language of a particular machine – is transparent to the programmer, one may think as if computer is 'executing' Fortran program.

The compiler generates an object program only when the source is free from grammatical error. In case of any grammatical error being flagged by the compiler, the programmer has to go back to the source, make the necessary correction to the source, and recompile to get the object program. Object program will not be generated until all grammatical errors are removed from the source program.

A program, free from grammatical error, may not give a correct result. The program must be free from 'logical error'. Logical error means the error in the program logic at the source level. For example, a particular program may require addition of two numbers – but the programmer, by mistake, has performed subtraction instead of addition. 'Run time error' may occur during the execution of a program. Suppose a program requires division by two numbers. The division process is valid so long as the second number (denominator) is not zero. Division by zero is not a valid arithmetic operation. This error will show up during the execution of program should the denominator become zero. The program behaves normally so long as the denominator remains non-zero.

Therefore, to obtain a correct result from a program the following three conditions must be satisfied:

- Program must be free from grammatical errors,
- Program must be free from logical errors,
- There should not be any runtime error.

1.1 Character Set

The programming language and its syntax are described by a set of characters. The character set that is available to a Fortran programmer consists of:

- All letters of English alphabets, both the upper case (A-Z) and the lower case (a-z).
- Underscore character (_).
- All digits (0-9).
- Several special characters like bracket, colon, full stop etc.
- Several unprintable characters like tab, linefeed, new line characters etc.

Table 1.1 List of Special Characters

Character	Name	Character	Name
	Blank	;	Semicolon
=	Equal (assignment)	!	Exclamation sign
+	Plus	"	Quote
-	Minus	%	Percent
*	Asterisk	&	Ampersand
/	Slash	~	Tilde
\	Backslash	<	Less than
(	Left parenthesis	>	Greater than
)	Right parenthesis	?	Question mark
[	Left square bracket	'	Apostrophe
]	Right square bracket	`	Grave accent
{	Left curly bracket	^	Circumflex accent
}	Right curly bracket	|	Vertical line
,	Comma	$	Currency sign
.	Decimal point	#	Number sign
:	Colon	@	Commercial at

Normally, Fortran is case insensitive, i.e. it does not distinguish between the upper and the lower case letters. There is, however, one exception. This will be discussed at the appropriate place. Table 1.1 shows the list of special characters.

1.2 Identifiers

Identifiers are used to specify various objects as permitted by the language. An identifier,
- must start with a letter of alphabet,
- may contain other digits and letters or underscore character,
- must not contain any special character or blank,
- must have a length not exceeding 63 characters.

It is obvious that the length of the identifier must be at least one and in that case it must be a letter of alphabet only. It is obvious that the first character cannot be an underscore character.

The following are valid identifiers:

```
XMAX            COUNTER         BASIC_PAY        I            VOLT
```

The following are invalid identifiers:

```
1XY             (starts with a digit)
A(B             (contains special character)
X MIN           (contains a blank character).
```

The following identifiers are equivalent:

```
ABC             Abc               aBC                abC
```

or any combinations of upper and lower case A, B and C since Fortran does not distinguish between the upper and the lower case letters.

Usually, identifiers are so chosen that they have some relation with the actual objects they refer to. For example, the identifier VOLT is a natural choice for denoting the voltage of an electrical circuit. One can equally choose Q78BM to represent voltage; however it appears to be a poor choice since the readability of the program is diminished once such choice is made. It is needless to mention that the length of the identifier must be of reasonable size. Though the language permits 63 characters to represent an identifier, rarely more than 8 or 10 characters are used to represent an identifier. Unnecessarily long identifiers will invite typing errors and will perhaps reduce the readability.

Several characters like (2 and Z), (1 and I), (O and 0) look similar. So care should be taken while using similar characters within the same identifier. For example, identifier like O0 ("oh zero") should be avoided. One may invite further trouble if one chooses another identifier OO ("oh oh") in the same program unit. It must be understood that for the Fortran compiler both O0 ("oh zero") and OO ("oh oh") are valid, but different identifiers; it is the human programmer who may mix up these two similar looking identifiers.

1.3 Constant and Variable

In any programming language we normally use two types of objects – constants and variables. Several types of constants and variables are available in the Fortran language. For the present, we shall discuss only the types: integer and real.

1.4 Constants

A quantity whose value remains fixed during the execution of a program is called a constant. The compiler identifies the constant – its type and the value – from its appearance. In other words, the constant conveys both its type and its value to the compiler.

1.5 Integer Constants

An integer constant is a whole number, i.e., it does not contain any decimal point. It contains only digits and a leading sign, if necessary. An integer constant may be positive, negative or zero. Negative constants are prefixed by a minus sign and the positive constant may optionally be prefixed by a plus sign. Unsigned integer constants are assumed to be positive. The constants 10 and +10 are equivalent. Normally, a leading positive sign is not used, as it is optional. The integer constant, say 127, tells the compiler its type, in this case it is an integer and its magnitude, which is 127. The maximum and minimum values, that an integer constant may assume, are machine dependent. The typical values are 2147483647 (maximum: 2 to the power 31 minus 1) and -2147483648 (minimum: minus 2 to the power 31).

Valid integer constants are:

```
2              35              -7432              12345          0              -4321
```

Invalid integer constants are:

```
2.0                  (contains decimal point)
37-                  (negative sign is not prefixed)
1234567891234        (most probably exceeds the capacity of the
                      processor but might not at some point in future)
2a3                  (contains non-digit character)
```

Leading zeros of an integer constant is ignored. For example,

```
01                   001                   00001                        1
```

are all equivalent.

1.6 Real Constants

A real constant is a real number containing one and only one decimal point. The decimal point may be explicit or implicit (possible in scientific notation – to be discussed shortly). A real constant may be positive, negative or zero. A real negative constant is prefixed by a negative sign. An unsigned real constant is assumed to be positive. Like the integer constant, a leading plus sign for the positive real constant is optional. A real constant, in the standard form, contains digits, one decimal point and prefixed by a plus or minus sign, if necessary. Valid real constants are:

```
3.1415926          -25.3456          12345.678              0.0
```

Invalid real constants are:

```
36                      (contains no decimal point)
35.3.2                  (contains more than one decimal point)
3a3563.25               (contains a letter 'a')
45.2(2)                 (contains special character)
5  6.0                  (contains a blank).
```

If there is no digit before or after the decimal point, zero is assumed. For example 2. is treated as 2.0. Similarly, .25 is a valid real constant which is same as 0.25. It is needless to mention that just a decimal point does not represent any real constant, i.e. not 0.0. The maximum and minimum value and also the precision of the real number is machine dependent.

The use of real constants like 2. and .25 are strongly discouraged. This reduces the readability of the program. This should be written as 2.0 and 0.25 respectively.

Real constants may also be represented by powers of 10, known as scientific form. This makes it very convenient to express very small or very large numbers. In this form, a real constant consists of two parts: an integer or real number followed by an exponent. The exponent is denoted by the letter 'E' or 'e'. The number 1.24E4 is actually 1.24×10^4, 'E4' stands for ten to the power of four. There is no space between 'E' and the real or integer part (also called fractional part). The exponent must be an integer and may be signed. The sign is placed after the exponent symbol. Unsigned exponent is assumed to be positive.

Valid real constants in scientific notation are:

```
1.24E4        -111.90E10        77.345E-3          -123.345E-5
```

The values of the above real constants are respectively:

$$1.24 \times 10^4 \qquad -111.90 \times 10^{10} \qquad 77.345 \times 10^{-3} \qquad -123.345 \times 10^{-5}$$

Invalid real constants are:

```
1.24E4-                 (wrong position of minus sign)
3.25   E5               (space between fraction and the exponent symbol)
777.24E2.5              (exponent must be an integer)
6.935E500               (probably excceds the capacity of the processor).
```

As mentioned earlier, the decimal point in a real constant may be implicit. For example, 123E4 is a real constant though it does not contain any decimal point. The default decimal point is assumed between '3' and 'E'. It is, thus equivalent to, 123.0×10^4. Leading zeros of the fraction are ignored. For example,

```
0123.24E4              00123.24E4              123.24E4
```

are all equivalent. Similarly, leading zeros in the exponent are also ignored. The following real constants are equivalent:

```
2.345E+2          2.345E+02          2.345E02          2.345E2
```

1.7 Literal Constants

The constants mentioned above are also known as literal constants. Literal constants do not have names attached to them.

1.8 Variables

An object whose value may vary during the execution of a program is called a variable. A variable can store only one value at a time and which may change during the execution of the program. A variable must have a name attached to it. A variable is identified by its name, its type and its value. If no value is assigned to it, it remains unassigned or undefined. Note the word 'may' in the definition. The variable may or may not change its value during the execution of the program. Constants, on the other hand, cannot change its value during the execution of the program.

By default, if the variable name starts with I, J, K, L, M or N, it is an integer variable. All other variables that start with letter other than I – N are real variables. An integer variable can store only an integer quantity and similarly, a real variable can store only a real quantity. In spite of the above default rule, it is a good programming practice to explicitly define each and every variable. This default feature, i.e., I – N rule, can be switched off by appropriate declaration and in that case it is mandatory to declare each and every variable.

1.9 Integer Variables

An integer variable can store only an integer quantity. This is declared in the following manner:

```
INTEGER :: A
INTEGER :: B
INTEGER :: C, D
```

In the above declarations A, B, C and D are declared as integer variables and therefore these variables can store only integer quantities. It is apparent from the above declarations that more than one variable may be declared by a single declaration – in that case the variables are separated by a comma. The first two declarations may be combined as shown below:

```
INTEGER :: A, B
```

Blanks between INTEGER and '::' and between '::' and the variable name are introduced to increase the readability.

An identifier (variable name) may be treated like a box. The name of the box is the name of the variable. The content of the box is undefined. When a value is assigned to a variable, the content of the box is the value of the variable.

1.10 Real Variables

A real variable can store only a real quantity (Real numbers are also called floating point numbers).

Real variables are declared as follows:

```
REAL :: X
REAL :: Y
REAL :: P, Q
```

In the above declarations X, Y, P and Q are declared as real variables.

1.11 Assignment Operator

Assignment operator (=) is used to assign a value to a variable. For example, if a variable FIRST is declared as integer, the variable FIRST is assigned to a value in the following manner:

```
INTEGER :: FIRST
      .
      .
FIRST = 10
```

Subsequently, if 20 is assigned to FIRST, the old value 10 will be lost and now FIRST will contain 20. The instruction is:

```
FIRST = 20
```

We shall discuss this assignment operator in great details in chapter 2. Already it was mentioned that an integer variable can store only an integer quantity and the real variable can store only a real quantity. Consider the following:

```
INTEGER :: A
      .
A = 2.6
```

The variable 'A' has been declared as integer, so it can store only integer. However, 2.6 is a real number and therefore truncation will take place and 2 will be stored in A. Similarly,

```
REAL :: R
      .
R = 10
```

will store 10.0 in R. Numerical value of 10 and 10.0 are same but integer and real numbers are stored in a different fashion inside the computer.

1.12 Meaning of a Declaration

A declaration is a placeholder for a variable, i.e., it merely reserves location(s) for a variable and defines the type of the variable. No value is assigned to the variable. A suitable Fortran statement must be used to assign a value to a variable. A variable can store only one value at a time. The same variable cannot be declared more than once in a program unit. For example, the declarations:

```
INTEGER :: A
REAL :: A
```

will give rise to Fortran error because the variable A cannot be an integer and a real variable at the same time.

Unassigned variables should not be used, as the result of such computation is unpredictable.

1.13 Named Constants

The constants introduced in sections 1.5 – 1.7 are called literal constants. A symbolic name may be attached to a constant. The symbolic name becomes an alias to the constant. The alias behaves just like literal constant and it cannot be modified during the execution of the program. A true constant, say, PI, may thus be used in this manner.

```
REAL, PARAMETER :: PI=3.1415926
```

In the above declaration PI is the symbolic name of 3.1415926 because of the presence of the attribute PARAMETER with the REAL declaration. REAL and PARAMETER are separated by a comma. In the above declaration, PI is NOT a real variable – it is just another name of 3.1415926. During compilation each occurrence of PI will be replaced by 3.1415926. Since PI is alias of 3.1415926, PI cannot be assigned to a different value.

```
PI = 4.25
```

is not allowed as named constants by definition cannot be modified. The reason is not difficult to guess. During compilation PI will be replaced by 3.1415926, so the statement PI=4.25 will become:

```
3.1415926 = 4.25
```

which is clearly not a valid Fortran statement.

Moreover, the program unit cannot have any variable named PI as already PI has been made an alias of 3.1415926. The following will generate error:

```
REAL, PARAMETER :: PI = 3.1415926
INTEGER :: PI
```

We shall now try to understand the difference between a named constant and a variable. We consider the following program segments identified as Left and Right respectively:

```
Left                                          Right

REAL, PARAMETER :: PI=3.1415926               REAL:: PI
                                              .
                                              PI=3.1415926
                                              .
                                              PI=6.257
```

In the program Left, PI is symbolic constant, its value being 3.1415926. It cannot be modified. In the program Right, PI is a real variable – it can assume any real value. It can be modified during the execution of the program. It is good programming practice to assign a symbolic name to a true constant like PI so that even by mistake the constant cannot be modified during the execution of the program. We shall revisit the named constant again in chapter 2.

An alternative way to represent a named constant is through the parameter statement:

```
PARAMETER (named constant=value,...)
```
Example:
```
PARAMETER (PI=3.1415926)
```

The type of the named constant declared by the parameter statement is either declared or it follows the default I – N rule. For example, in case of

```
PARAMETER (IP=2.3)
```

each occurrence of IP is substituted by 2 and not 2.3 since, without any declaration, IP being an integer, can store only an integer quantity. More than one named constant may be defined by a single parameter statement as shown below:

```
PARAMETER (PI=3.1415926, E=2.303, LPT=6)
```

Named constants are assigned values at the time of compilation. Therefore, it cannot contain anything whose value is not known during compilation.

1.14 Keywords (*)

The Fortran language contains several keywords. Already we have encountered two such keywords – INTEGER and REAL. However, the keywords are not reserved words and may be used as identifiers. This is strongly discouraged. For example, DO is a Fortran statement and also a Fortran keyword. It is permitted to have an identifier named DO. The compiler will identify the DO statement from its appearance; it will also correctly treat the DO identifier. But for the sake of readability this should be avoided.

A keyword cannot have embedded space. The keyword, say, READ cannot be written as RE AD. If a name follows a keyword, the keyword and the name must be separated by a blank. Blank is optional for some 'single' keywords which consists of two keywords like END DO. In this case ENDDO and END DO are the same. However, blank is mandatory for keywords like DO WHILE, IMPLICIT NONE etc. Table 1.2 is a list of such adjacent keywords where blanks are optional and mandatory. There is no need to memorize the table. The table may be referred to, if the compiler complains about a keyword during compilation. We shall come back to this topic again in chapter 19 in connection with the discussion of subprogram.

Table 1.2 Adjacent Keywords

Blank Optional	Blank Mandatory
BLOCK DATA	CASE DEFAULT
DOUBLE PRECISION	DO WHILE
ELSE IF	IMPLICIT *type-spec*
END BLOCKDATA	IMPLICIT NONE
END DO	INTERFACE ASSIGNMENT
END FILE	INTERFACE OPARATOR
END FUNCTION	MODULE PROCEDURE
END IF	RECURSIVE FUNCTION
END INTERFACE	RECURSIVE SUBROUTINE
END MODULE	RECURSIVE *type-spec*
END PROGRAM	*type-spec* FUNCTION
END SELECT	*type-spec* RECURSIVE
END SUBROUTINE	
END TYPE	
END WHERE	
GO TO	
IN OUT	
SELECT CASE	
END FORALL	
END ASSOCIATE	
SELECT TYPE	
END ENUM	
ELSE WHERE (*)	
DOUBLE COMPLEX	

(*) NAG compiler gives error. It wants ELSEWHERE.

1.15 Source Form

A Fortran source program consists of one or more lines. A line may contain zero or more characters. Fortran statements may be written in two different forms:
- Fixed form
- Free form

These two forms cannot be mixed in a single program unit. The current trend is to write program in free form.

1.16 Fixed Form (*)

In this form a line is divided into several fields:

Position: 1–5	Statement number field
Position: 6	Continuation field
Position: 7–72	Statement field
Position: 73–80	Identification field (normally not used)

In fixed form, a line can have maximum 72 (80 if identification field is available) characters including blanks.

Positions 1–5 are used for typing the statement number. A statement number must be an unsigned integer between (and including) 1 and 99999. Zero is not a valid statement number. A statement number may be typed anywhere within the field. It is usually typed either left or right adjusted within the field. Leading blanks, zeros and trailing blanks are ignored. Space within the digits, as long as it is within the field, is ignored. A statement number is used to refer to a particular statement. The field may be left blank, if necessary. No two statements can have same statement number within a single program unit. Statement numbers are arbitrary. It is not necessary to select the statements in any particular order. A blank line cannot have a statement number; at least one non-blank character must be present in a labeled statement.

Position 6 is used as a continuation field. If a statement cannot be accommodated in a particular line or if is necessary to split a statement, the statement may be continued to the next line by typing any character other than blank or zero in position 6 of the next line. A maximum 19 continuation lines can be used for a statement. Thus,

1	2	3	4	5	6	7	8	9	10	11	12	13	14	15	16
						A	=	B	+						
					1	C									

is same as A=B+C. Arithmetic operator will be formally introduced in chapter 2. A continuation line cannot have a statement number. Though any character other than blank or zero may be used as a continuation character, some programmers prefer to use sequential number 1, 2, 3, ... etc. to indicate continuation as shown below:

1	2	3	4	5	6	7	8	9	10	11	12	13	14	15	16
						A	=	B							
					1	+	C								
					2	+	D								

The above is same as A=B+C+D. The same can be written as

1	2	3	4	5	6	7	8	9	10	11	12	13	14	15	16
						A	=	B							
					*	+	C								
					*	+	D								

where asterisk is used as continuation character.

The continuation statement cannot have a statement number, only the first line of a continued statement may have a statement number.

Positions 7 – 72 are used as statement field. In this field Fortran statements are typed. Normally blanks are ignored. Sometimes one or more blanks are added to increase readability.

Positions 73 – 80 are used as identification field. It is not used now a days. In this field any thing can be typed. Years ago these positions were usually used to type sequence number. At that time the inputs were from punched cards.

Comment: If 'C' or 'c' or '*' appears in the first position of a line, the whole line is treated as comment. The compiler ignores this line, although the line is included in the listing of the program. Comments are used for documentation. In addition to this, if a '!' sign is typed anywhere other than position 6, the rest of the line is treated as comment. Comments cannot be continued. If a multiple line comment is desired, each of the commented line must have a comment character in the first position as shown below:

1	2	3	4	5	6	7	8	9	10	11	12	13	14	15	16	17	18	19	20	21
C	-	-		T	H	I	S		I	S		A		C	O	M	M	E	N	T
C	-	-		A	P	R		2	0	0	7									
*			A	N	O	T	H	E	R		C	O	M	M	E	N	T			
!			A	L	S	O		A		C	O	M	M	E	N	T				
						I	=	2	!	I	N		L	I	N	E				

If the first character between positions 7 and 72 is '!', this line cannot have any statement number.

1.17 Free Form

In free form, a Fortran statement can be extended to 132 characters per line. The statement may start anywhere within this field. If the last non-blank character of a particular line is '&', the next line is considered as the continuation of the previous line. A total number of 255 continuation lines is allowed (per statement).

1	2	3	4	5	6	7	8	9	10	11	12	13	14	15	16
						X	=	Y	+		&				
						Z									

is equivalent to X=Y+Z. No line can contain a single '&' as the only non-blank character. Also no line can contain one '&' character followed by '!' character. A statement number, if any, should be placed at the beginning of the line. There must be a blank or a tab character after the statement number.

1	2	3	4	5	6	7	8	9	10	11	12	13	14	15	16
1	4	7				X	=	Y	+	Z					

There may be any number of blanks before the statement number.

1	2	3	4	5	6	7	8	9	10	11	12	13	14	15	16
			1	0	5	X	=	Y	+	Z					

There cannot be any blank within the statement number. The following is not allowed.

1	2	3	4	5	6	7	8	9	10	11	12	13	14	15	16
		1		2	5		X	=	Y	+	Z				

If the character '!' is typed anywhere in a line the rest of the line is treated as comment.

1	2	3	4	5	6	7	8	9	10	11	12	13	14	15	16
1	4		X	=	Y	+	Z	!	C	O	M	M	E	N	T

A comment line cannot have a statement number.

```
100    ! This is a comment
```

is not a valid statement.

A blank line is treated as comment both in the free and the fixed form. In fact, judicious use of blank lines increases the readability of the program.

If the continuation symbol '&' is typed after the comment character '!', the character '&' becomes a part of the comment and is not considered as continuation character.

1	2	3	4	5	6	7	8	9	10	11	12	13	14	15	16
						X	=	Y	+	!	&				
						Z									

The above will generate compilation error as '&' is not considered as the continuation character in this case so the next line is not treated as continuation of the previous line.

Normally, continuation starts from the first character of the next non-commented line. However, if it necessary to start the continuation from a particular position of the next line, the '&' character must also be typed just before the desired character of the next line. This will be discussed in detail in chapter 8.

		X		=	Y	+	&
	Z						

The above will be treated as:

```
X=Y+ Z (one blank between '+' and Z)
```

On the other hand,

		X		=	Y	+	&
&	Z						

will be treated as:

```
X=Y+Z (No blank between '+' and 'Z')
```

In these situations both mean the same as Fortran ignores the blank. This effect will be felt when we discuss character strings in chapter 8 where the presence or absence of blank within a character string may result in a different meaning.

1.18 IMPLICIT NONE

It was mentioned earlier that if the variables are not declared explicitly, Fortran allows certain default rule (I – N rule) in selecting the variable type. This can be switched off by placing:

```
IMPLICIT NONE
```

at the beginning of the program unit. In this case all variables are to be declared explicitly. For example, if a variable I1 (I and one) is declared as integer and if it is typed as II (I and I) in the body of the program (typing error), IMPLICIT NONE will force the compiler to a generate Fortran error (undefined variable). On the other hand, if IMPLICIT NONE is absent, it will be treated as another integer variable following the default I – N rule and since it is undefined (no value is possibly assigned), the result is unpredictable. The modern trend of programming is to use IMPLICIT NONE in every program unit so the programmer is forced to declare all the variables explicitly. Any typing error, similar to that shown above, will be flagged as an error at the compilation stage. The IMPLICIT statement will be discussed in chapter 9.

1.19 PROGRAM Statement

The optional PROGRAM statement is the first statement of a program. It supplies the name of the program.

```
PROGRAM FIRST
```

where FIRST is the name of the program.

1.20 END Statement

END statement signifies the end of the program unit. END may contain PROGRAM and the name of the program. However, this is optional.

A typical Fortran program will be of following form:

```
PROGRAM FIRST
         .

         .
END PROGRAM FIRST
```

Between the PROGRAM and END statements, declarations and Fortran statements are placed.

The END statement cannot be continued. Also the statement like END FILE 10 (chapter 24) cannot be continued. For example,

```
END
1FILE 10
```

is not allowed. A variable name (say ENDRUN) containing END as the first three letters cannot be broken across the line boundary with END in one line and the rest in the other.

```
END
1RUN=27
```

is not allowed.

Once the END statement is reached the compiler starts compiling that particular unit without looking at the continuation character of the next line and this is bound to generate a compilation error.

1.21 Executable and Non-executable Statements

Fortran statements are basically of two types – executable and non-executable statements. The first one means some action. For example A=10 is an executable statement where the variable A is assigned to a value 10.

The statement INTEGER :: A is an non-executable statement. This is a declaration and this merely passes information to the compiler to reserve locations for an integer variable A. Appendix B contains a list of executable and non-executable statements. Non-executable statements cannot be the targets of any branch statement (chapter 3).

1.22 Initialization

A variable may be initialized to a value along with its declaration. In this case when the execution begins, the corresponding variable is not undefined; it has an initial value.

```
INTEGER :: A=10
REAL :: X=1.34
INTEGER :: B=10, C=20
```

In the first case not only A is declared as integer, it is initialized to 10 also. Similarly, X, B and C are also initialized to 1.34, 10 and 20 respectively.

In case more than one variable is declared by a single declaration, all the variables are to be initialized individually. For example,

```
INTEGER :: D, E=200
```

will initialize E to 200 but D will remain un-initialized. If it is necessary to initialize both the variables, it is done as shown:

```
INTEGER :: D=200, E=200
```

that is, both the variables are initialized separately.

1.23 INCLUDE

Strictly speaking INCLUDE is not a Fortran statement; it is a directive to the compiler. The syntax of INCLUDE is:

```
INCLUDE char-constant
```

where the *character-constant* is usually a file name. The compiler replaces the INCLUDE statement by the content of the file. The INCLUDE statement cannot be labeled; it may be nested, that is, it may contain another include statement; it cannot 'include' itself directly or indirectly. In other words, INCLUDE 'A' may contain INCLUDE 'B', but the file B cannot contain INCLUDE 'A' (a recursive 'call'). The INCLUDE statement must be typed on a separate line.

```
INCLUDE 'myfile.f95'
```

The content of 'myfile.f95' is included at the point of inclusion. INCLUDE statement cannot be continued.

Chapter 2

ARITHMETIC OPERATORS

A computer is a machine that can perform basic arithmetic operations at a high speed. Naturally, the Fortran language provides arithmetic operators to perform these operations.

2.1 Binary and Unary Operators

Two types of arithmetic operators are available to a Fortran programmer – binary and unary operators.

Binary operators require two operands. The following are the binary arithmetic operators:

Symbol	Meaning
**	Exponentiation (to the power)
/	Division
*	Multiplication
+	Addition
-	Subtraction

Examples of binary operators are:

```
A + B    (Add A to B)
A * B    (A multiplied by B)
A - B    (Subtract B from A)
A / B    (A divided by B)
A ** 2   (A raised to the power 2)
```

Unary operators require a single operand. The following are the unary arithmetic operators:

Symbol	Meaning
+	Unary plus
-	Unary minus

As unsigned integer or real constants are treated as positive number, unary plus is rarely used, $+5$ is same as 5. Unary minus changes the sign of a variable or a constant. Example of unary minus is -5, where the sign of 5 is changed. Similarly, the magnitude of – A is the value of A with its sign reversed. It may be noted that the same symbol '+' and '–' are used to indicate both the unary and the binary operations. The compiler from the context can determine the meaning of the operators – whether it is a binary or a unary operator.

2.2 Arithmetic Expression

Arithmetic expressions are formed using constants, variables, other objects as permitted by the language and arithmetic operators discussed in the previous section. Examples are:

```
X + Y + Z
2 * I + K
A + B - C**2 / D + 7.9
```

2.3 Assignment

The symbol '=' is used to assign a value to a variable. The general form of assignment statement is:

```
variable = expression
```

The *expression* on the right hand side of the assignment sign is evaluated and the value thus obtained is stored in the variable. As a variable can store only one value at a time, current value of the variable is lost and a new value is stored in its place. Examples of assignment are:

```
I = 2
AREA = LENGTH * WIDTH
S = U * T + 0.5 * F * T**2
```

Consider the following expression:

```
C = A + B
```

Let us assume that the values of A and B are 2 and 3 respectively. The value of C is not our concern at this moment. Before the expression is evaluated, the contents of A, B and C are as shown below:

C	A	B
?	2	3

When A is added to B, result is 5 and the result is stored in the location C. However, A and B will retain their old values. So, at the end of the operation, the picture looks as shown below:

C	A	B
5	2	3

The symbol for the assignment sign i.e., '=' must not be confused with the equal sign used in algebra. For example,

```
I = I + 1
```

is a valid Fortran statement – this is not an algebraic equation. Had it been so, canceling I from both sides would give us,

```
0 = 1
```

which is clearly not acceptable. The proper meaning of I = I + 1 is to increment I by 1. To be more specific, in this case the current value of I is taken, 1 is added to it and the result is stored in the same location I. If, for example, the value of I is 10 before the execution of the statement, it is 11 at the end of the operation and the result is stored in the location I. The content of I before and after the statement is executed is depicted below:

One can write similar statements:

```
I = I - 1
I = I * J
```

In an assignment operation, unless the same variable appears on both sides of the assignment sign, the variables appearing on the right hand side of the assignment sign are not modified – they retain their old values and the variable on the left hand side of the assignment sign gets a new value.

2.4 Rules for Arithmetic Expression

The following rules must be followed while writing arithmetic expression:
Rule1: Arithmetic operations are not allowed on the left hand side of the assignment sign. For example,

```
A + B = C
```

is not a valid arithmetic expression. The left hand side of the assignment sign must be a variable. Arithmetic operation on the left hand side of assignment sign is allowed only to calculate the address of a variable. This will be discussed in chapter 11 when we shall discuss array.
Rule 2: No arithmetic operation is assumed like algebra.

```
(A + B) (A - B)
```

is not taken as (A + B) * (A - B) – the multiplication operator in this case must be specified explicitly.

Rule 3: No two arithmetic operators may appear side be side.

$$C = A * \quad -B$$

is not a valid Fortran statement. Should such situation arise, it must be enclosed within parenthesis as shown:

$$C = A * (-B)$$

This rule appears to have been violated in case of exponentiation operator '**'. However, it must be remembered that the exponentiation operator is a single entry – it is not two successive multiplication operators.

Rule 4: Arithmetic expressions may contain parenthesis. It may contain nested parenthesis i.e., parenthesis within parenthesis also. In case of nested parentheses, nearest left and right parenthesis form a pair. If an expression contains parenthesis, the number of left parentheses must be equal to the number of right parentheses. The Fortran statement:

$$F = A + (B + C * (D + E)$$

will be rejected by the compiler because of unmatched parenthesis.

Rule 5: If both A and B are real numbers, A ** B can be evaluated only if A is a positive quantity. This is because when both A and B are real numbers, A ** B is calculated as $e^{\ln A}$ where ln is log base e. If A is negative, ln(A) is not defined.

2.5 Multiple Statement

Two or more Fortran statements, separated by a semicolon, may be placed in a line.

$$C = A + B; \quad D = 10$$

This is same as:

```
C = A + B
D = 10
```

In this case only the first statement may have a statement number. As multiple statements decrease the program readability, this is not encouraged.

2.6 Priority Rules

An arithmetic expression may contain different kind of operators. So it is necessary to specify a rule regarding how the following expression like:

$$D = A / B * C$$

is going to be evaluated. If the division is performed before the multiplication the expression becomes algebraically:

$$D = (A / B) \quad . \; C$$

If, on the other hand, the multiplication is performed before the division, the expression becomes:

$$D = A \quad / \quad (B.C)$$

It is needless to mention that the results of the two sets of calculations are different. This may be verified by assuming the values of A, B and C as 6, 3 and 2 respectively. In the first case,

$$D = (6 / 3) \; . \; 2 = 4$$

and in the second case:

$$D = 6 / (3 \; . \; 2) = 1$$

Arithmetic operators have been assigned different priorities as shown below:

High		Exponentiation	**
		Multiplication & Division	/, *
	↓	Unary Minus and Plus	-, +
		Addition and Subtraction	+, -
Low		Assignment	=

The priority of the exponentiation operator is the highest and that of the assignment operator is the lowest. The priority of the multiplication and the division operators are same, and they are less than that of the exponentiation operator. Also, the priority of the addition and the subtraction operators are same and lower than that of the multiplication and the division operators. The priority of unary plus and minus operator is in between the multiplication / division and the addition / subtraction operators.

In any arithmetic expression, the high priority operators are evaluated before the low priority operators. For example, in case of the following expression:

$$E = A + B * D$$

multiplication, B * D is calculated first and than A is added to get the final result. If an arithmetic expression contains operators having same priority, computation proceeds from left to right. In case of

$$D = A + B - C$$

the addition will be performed before the subtraction.

There is one exception to the above-mentioned rule. For exponentiation, the evaluation proceeds from right to left. A ** B ** C is evaluated from right to left i.e., B ** C is performed first and then the result is used as the power of A. If brackets are used to indicate the order of evaluation, the two expressions shown below are not equivalent:

$$(A ** B) ** C$$

and

$$A ** (B ** C)$$

This may be verified by assuming $A = 2$, $B = 3$ and $C = 4$. Substituting these values $(A ** B) ** C$ becomes 2^{12} and $A ** (B ** C) = 2^{81}$.

Parenthesis has the highest priority. Inside the parenthesis the above rules are followed. $A / (B * C)$ and $A / B * C$ are not the same. In the first case $B * C$ is evaluated first and then A is divided by the result. In the second case, without the parenthesis, computation proceeds according to the default priority rules. The priority of the division and the multiplication being equal, computation proceeds from the left to the right and the division is performed before the multiplication; the result is multiplied by C.

In the case of nested parenthesis, computation starts from the innermost one.

$$A + (B * (C * (D + E / F)))$$

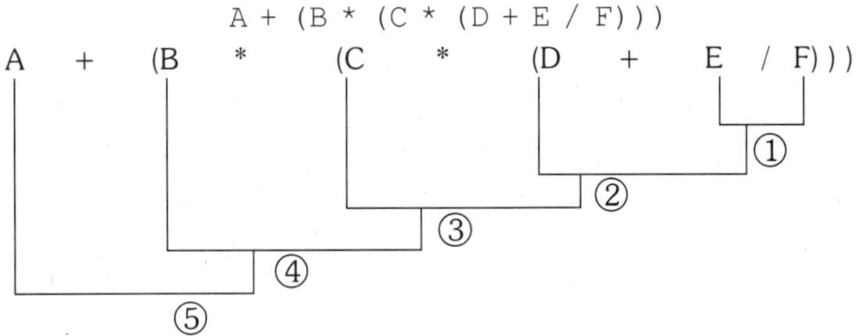

The innermost parenthesis containing expressions involving the division and the addition are evaluated first, the default priority rules being used (division before addition); this result is then multiplied by C; this is then multiplied by B and the result is added to A. In the above diagram the numbers indicate the order of evaluation, the first one is indicated by 1 and the second one by 2 and so on.

The rule of thumb is that in case of any doubt, parenthesis may be used to indicate the intention. Extra balanced parentheses do not cause any harm.

$$D = A / B * C$$

is same as

$$D = (A / B) * C$$

Sometimes compilers are smart enough to change the order of the evaluation of the arithmetic expressions to make it more efficient. In Table 2.1, expressions and allowable alternative forms are shown. In these expressions, X, Y, Z are any type of numeric operands and A, B and C represent any arbitrary real or complex (chapter 6) operands.

Table 2.1 Allowable Alternative Form

Expression	Alternative Form
X + Y	Y + X
X * Y	Y * X
-X + Y	Y - X
X + Y + Z	X + (Y + Z)
X - Y + Z	X - (Y - Z)
X * A / Z	X * (A / Z)
X * Y - X * Z	X * (Y - Z)
A / B / C	A * (B * C)
A / 5.0	0.2 * A

Table 2.2 shows the non-allowable alternative form of expressions. In this case I and J are integers.

Table 2.2 Non-allowable Alternative Form

Expression	Non-allowable Alternative Form
I / 2	I * 0.5
X * I / J	X * (I / J)
I / J / A	I / (J * A)
(X + Y) + Z	X + (Y + Z)
(X * Y) - (X * Z)	X * (Y - Z)
X * (Y - Z)	X * Y - X * Z

2.7 Mixed Mode Operation

For an expression involving variables or constants of different types, conversion takes place before the expression is evaluated. For the present, we shall consider expressions involving reals and integers only.

In an expression involving a real and an integer constant or variable on the two sides of the binary arithmetic operator, the integer is converted into a real before the calculation takes place. For example, the expression A+2 will be calculated as follows (A is a real variable):

The integer 2 will be converted to the real 2.0 by the processor and 2.0 will be added to A. The result of (A+2) will be real.

Similarly, during the assignment operation, if the type of the variable (or the result) on the right hand side of the assignment side is different from the type of the variable on the left hand side, an automatic type conversion takes place. An integer is converted to a real, keeping the magnitude same – integer 2 is converted to real 2.0. On the other hand, a real is converted to an integer by truncating the fractional part – real 4.56 is converted to integer 4.

One important point may be noted: the operands determine the type of the operation and accordingly type conversion takes place. Consider the following expression:

```
I = J + A * 2
```

where I and J are integers and A is real number. The steps required to perform this computation are listed below:

- Integer 2 is converted to real and stored in a temporary location;
- Priority of multiplication operator is more than that of addition;
- 2.0 is multiplied by A – the result of the computation is real and is stored in a temporary location within the system;
- J is converted to real because the result of the computation A * 2 is real and is stored in a temporary location;
- The addition is performed in the real mode. The result of addition is stored in a temporary location;
- As the left hand side of the assignment operator is an integer, the result of the computation is converted to an integer and is stored in the location I.

The process is depicted below (Fig 2.1):

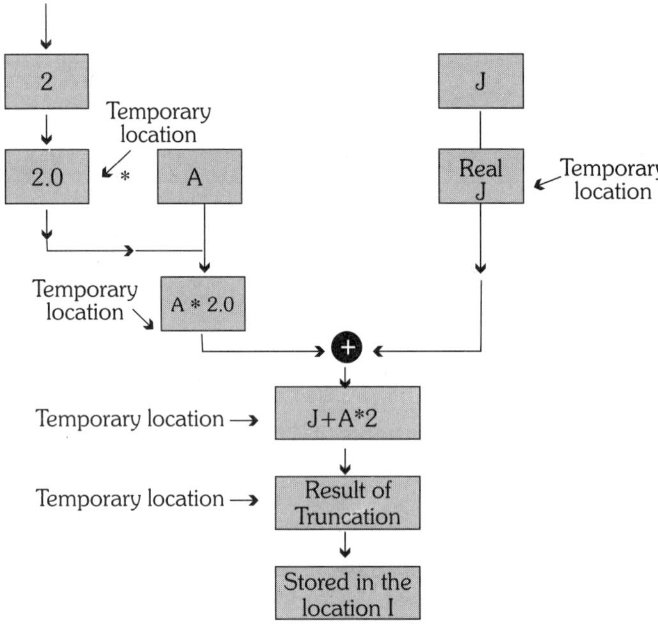

Fig 2.1 Mixed Mode Arithmetic

2.8 Integer Division

Integer division deserves special attention. Improper use of integer division may invite serious problem.

If I and J are integers, I divided J is calculated in the integer mode and the result of the computation is an integer (whole number). Following this logic, 3 / 2 is 1 and 2 / 3 is 0. If A is a real variable, the expression A = 5 / 2 is calculated in the integer mode; the result is 2 and since A is real, the result of the computation is converted to 2.0 and 2.0 is stored in A. The conversion is done by the computer itself.

Now, consider this expression:

$$I = 5.0 / 2.0$$

and

$$J = 5 / 2$$

In the first case, 5.0/2.0 is a real number and it is 2.5. Since I is an integer, 2.5 is truncated to 2 before it is stored in I. In the second case, 2 is stored in J and no type conversion takes place as all the operands and the variable are of the same type.

It may be noted the final result of the computation in the above two cases are same; however the way they are evaluated is different.

Consider the following expression:

$$X = Y * 10 ** (-2)$$

The value of X is zero, irrespective of the value of Y. This is because 10 ** (-2) is evaluated as 1 / 100. Since both 1 and 100 are integers, computation is performed in the integer mode and the result is zero. One should be extremely careful while translating algebraic expressions like:

$$A = 4 / 3 \text{ x } \pi \text{ x } R^3$$
$$S = U \text{ x } T + 1 / 2 \text{ x } F \text{ x } T^2$$

in Fortran. 4/3 is 1 and 1/2 is 0. It is necessary to write at least one integer constant as a real number or better both as real numbers:

$$A = 4.0 / 3.0 * 3.1415926 * R ** 3$$
$$S = U * T + 1.0 / 2.0 * F * T ** 2$$

Often the result of computation unexpectedly turns out to be zero. In such a situation one should look for an integer division similar to shown above.

2.9 List Directed Input Output Statement

We now introduce the free formatted input/output statement. This is also called list directed input/output statement. Detailed discussion on formatted input/output statement is postponed till chapter 16.

An input statement reads a value of a variable from external device, say, the keyboard. Similarly, an output statement displays the value of a variable or result of a computation or some message on some output device, say, screen.

Various kinds of input-output devices are available. Some devices are used as input only, some devices are used as output only, while some devices are used both for input as well as output devices. Table 2.2 lists some of these devices. The list is not exhaustive.

Table 2.3 Input Output Device

Name	Input/output
Keyboard	Input
Screen	Output
Disk	Both input and output
Printer	Output

Free formatted input/output states are:

```
READ *, list
PRINT *, list
```

respectively, where '*list*' is a list of items to be read or written. If the '*list*' contains more than one element, the elements are separated by comma.

```
READ *, A, B, C
PRINT *, A, B, C
```

Therefore,

```
READ *, A
```

will read data from the keyboard and store in the location A erasing the existing value of A. Similarly,

```
PRINT *, A
```

will display the current value of A on the screen. When a READ statement is encountered, the computer waits till the required input is supplied through the keyboard.

Normally, for numbers, blank or any number of blanks are used as delimiters.

```
READ *, I, J, K
```

will have the corresponding data from the keyboard as:

```
10     20     30
```

so that 10, 20 and 30 will be stored in the location I, J and K respectively. Normally, while supplying inputs, list items are separated by one or more blanks. However, characters like comma, tab or carriage return etc. may also be used as delimiter. For example, in the above case data may be entered in the following manner also:

```
                    10, 20, 30 <enter>
```

or

```
                    10 <enter>
                    20 <enter>
                    30 <enter>
```

or

```
                    10, 20 <enter>
                    30 <enter>
```

or various such combinations where *<enter>* indicates the 'enter' key of the keyboard.

For real number, normally the decimal point is typed. If the decimal point is absent, it is assumed just before the delimiter. If X, Y and Z are declared as real, and the data corresponding to the READ statement is entered as:

```
                    10      20      30
```

it is taken as 10.0, 20.0 and 30.0 for X, Y and Z respectively.

Real number may be input in scientific notation also for the above mentioned case:

```
        1.4E2           1.245E-4              3.25
```

In this case X, Y and Z are assigned to 1.4×10^2, 1.245×10^{-4} and 3.25 and respectively.

To display a message on the screen, the message is to be enclosed within apostrophes.

```
            PRINT *, 'The result is = ', R
```

If the value of R is, say, 2.5, this PRINT statement will display:

```
            The result is = 2.5
```

on the screen. Within apostrophes, blank is also treated as a character and the number of blanks between '=' and 2.5 on the screen depends on the number of blanks between '=' and the closing apostrophe within the PRINT statement.

List directed input/output statements are very convenient. However, the programmer has practically no control over its appearance on the screen. For example, while using the PRINT statement the programmer has very little control where the value will appear on the screen and how many digits will be displayed after the decimal point for a real number. A programmer can gain more control over input/output statement through Format statement discussed in chapter 16.

2.10 Programing Examples

A sample program using arithmetic operators is given below:

```
PROGRAM ARITHOP
IMPLICIT NONE
INTEGER :: A,B,RES
A=100
B=20
PRINT *, 'A = ', A
PRINT *, 'B = ', B
RES=A+B
PRINT *, 'A+B = ', RES
RES=A-B
PRINT *, 'A-B = ', RES
RES=A*B
PRINT *, 'A*B = ', RES
RES=A/B
PRINT *, 'A/B = ', RES
END PROGRAM ARITHOP
```

It may be noted that same variable RES is used to store the results of computation and the PRINT statement is the next statement after the computation is done. Thus, this program cannot print all the results after all the computations are over, because same variable is used to store all the results. If, however, it is necessary to print the results after all the computations are performed, four such variables, not just one, are required to store the results as shown in the next program:

```
PROGRAM MODIARITHOP
IMPLICIT NONE
INTEGER :: A,B
INTEGER :: R1,R2,R3,R4
A=100
B=20
PRINT *, 'A = ', A
PRINT *, 'B = ', B
R1=A+B
R2=A-B
R3=A*B
R4=A/B

PRINT *, 'A+B = ', R1
PRINT *, 'A-B = ', R2
PRINT *, 'A*B = ', R3
PRINT *, 'A/B = ', R4

END PROGRAM MODIARITHOP
```

The following example converts miles to kilometers.

```
      PROGRAM MILETOKM
      REAL, PARAMETER :: FACTOR=1.609

!        Mile to KM conversion factor

      INTEGER :: MILE, YARD
      REAL :: KM

!        Marathon distance - 26 miles 385 yards

      MILE=26
      YARD=385
      KM=FACTOR*(MILE+YARD/1760.0)

!        1 mile=1760 yards
      PRINT *, MILE, ' Mile and ', YARD, ' yards = ',  &
                    KM, ' Kilometers'

      END PROGRAM MILETOKM
```

In this program YARD / 1760.0 is very crucial. YARD is an integer and if 1760 is written in place of 1760.0, the result of division would be zero.

The next program converts Fahrenheit to Centigrade.

```
       PROGRAM FAHREN

!        Converts Fahrenheit to Centigrade

      REAL :: CENT, FAHR
      FAHR=100.0
      CENT=5.0/9.0*(FAHR-32.0)
      PRINT *, FAHR, 'degree Fahrenheit = ',CENT, &
       ' degree Centigrade'
      END PROGRAM FAHREN
```

2.11 Variable Assignment – Comparative Study

We have just seen that a variable may be assigned in three different ways – through initialization, through assignment and through the READ statement:

```
        INTEGER :: X=20      ! initialization

        INTEGER :: X

        X = 20               ! assignment

        READ *, X            ! data from the keyboard
                             ! 20 is supplied as data
```

Let us consider the first statement: INTEGER :: X=20. The declaration reserves location(s) for X and initializes the variable to 20. This is done before the execution begins. Therefore, when the execution begins, X has a value of 20. Subsequently, X may be set to some other value if necessary.

In the second program segment, the declaration reserves locations for X and the statement X=20 sets the value of X. This value is assigned during execution. In absence of any other assignment statement the value of X remains 20. If it is desired to set the value of X to 200, the corresponding line is to be changed; the program is to be compiled again.

The third program segment READ *, X also sets the value of X during the execution. In this case, the value is supplied through external device (keyboard). Therefore, same program can be executed with different values of X say 20 or 200. Recompilation of the source is not necessary since no Fortran statement needs to be changed. A guideline may be prescribed as follows:

(a) True constants like PI (3.1415926) and E (2.303) etc. should be declared as named constants.
(b) If the initial value is required for a variable, it should be initialized along with the declaration.
(c) If the same program is to be executed for different set of values, corresponding variables should be read from outside, i.e., READ statement should be used.
(d) Other variables may be assigned by the assignment statement.

2.12 Library Function

Several commonly used functions are available in the system as library functions to calculate, say, square root, absolute value, trigonometric functions etc. A library function is 'called' by its name and correct number and type of argument(s) is (are) supplied within parenthesis. The library function SQRT calculates square root of a real quantity and takes one argument (constant, variable or expression). The library function will be discussed in details in chapter 15.

The time period of a simple pendulum is:

$$T = 2\pi\sqrt{(l/g)}$$

where T is the time period, l is the length of the pendulum and g is the acceleration due to gravity. We shall now write a program to calculate the time period of a simple pendulum where the length of the pendulum is 100 cm and the acceleration due to gravity is 979.55 cm/sec^2.

```
PROGRAM PENDULUM
REAL, PARAMETER :: PI=3.1415926
REAL, PARAMETER :: G=979.55
REAL :: LENGTH, PERIOD

LENGTH=100.0
PERIOD=2.0*PI*SQRT(LENGTH/G)

PRINT *, 'LENGTH = ', LENGTH
PRINT *, 'ACCELERATION DUE TO GRAVITY = ',G
PRINT *, 'TIME PERIOD OF THE PENDULUM = ',PERIOD

END PROGRAM PENDULUM
```

The argument of SQRT needs some clarification. It was mentioned that it has to be real. If the argument is an expression, the expression is evaluated and the square root of the result is calculated. It may be noted that the result of computation LENGTH / G is a real number.

2.13 Initialization and Library Function

A variable may be initialized with standard library functions which can be evaluated at the compilation time.

```
REAL :: A=SQRT(3.0)
```

NAG compiler does not support this feature.

Chapter 3

BRANCH STATEMENTS

The computer executes instructions sequentially, i.e., one after another. Normally programming logic is not so simple and the flow of program is not always linear. Branch statements allow branching or jumping to a particular statement as demanded by the program logic.

There are two types of branch statements – unconditional and conditional. Unconditional branch statement, when executed, allows branching to a particular statement without any condition; on the other hand a conditional branch statement transfers the control to a particular statement after testing a certain condition – the branch is executed depending upon the state of the condition.

3.1 Relational Operators

A relational operator tests a relation. It returns either true or false. For example, if a question is asked: "Is A greater than B?" The answer is either yes (true) or no (false). The relational operators are:

Symbol	Alternative Symbol	Meaning
.LT.	<	Less than
.LE.	<=	Less than or equal to
.GT.	>	Greater than
.GE.	>=	Greater than or equal to
.EQ.	==	Equal to
.NE.	/=	Not Equal to

It may be noted that either the symbolic notation or the equivalent mathematical notation may be used. In symbolic notation the symbol is bound by periods.

3.2 Priority Rule of Relational Operators

The priority of all the relational operators is same, and it is less than the priority of arithmetic operators. In an expression involving arithmetic and relational operators, the arithmetic operators are evaluated first and then the relations are tested (see diagram below). Table 3.1 is a list of operators encountered till now according to their priority.

$$B**2 - 4.0 * A*C \ .GT. \ 0$$

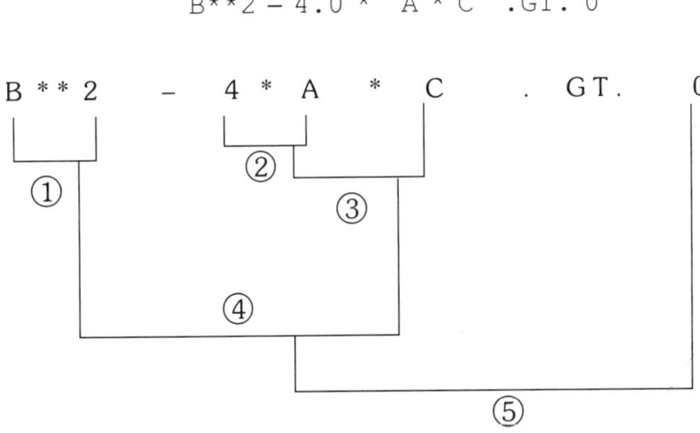

Table 3.1 Priority of Operators

Priority	Symbol	Meaning
High	**	Exponentiation
	*, /	Multiplication, Division
	+, -	Unary plus, Unary minus
	+, -	Binary Addition and Subtraction
	.LT., .LE., .GT., .GE., .EQ., .NE.	Relational operator
Low	=	Assignment

3.3 The GOTO Statement

GOTO is an unconditional branch statement. The syntax of GO TO is:

```
GOTO nnn
```

where *nnn*, a statement number, which must refer to an executable statement present in the same (scoping) unit as GOTO.

When GOTO statement is encountered, the control is unconditionally passed to a statement having the statement number mentioned in the GOTO statement. The statement where the control is transferred may be before or after the GOTO statement.

```
GOTO 20
```

will transfer the control to the statement number 20 unconditionally. There may be space between GO and TO and 20 is the statement number of an executable statement present in the same unit as GOTO. The following program, though not an elegant one, demonstrates the use of GOTO.

```
        PROGRAM NOTELEGANT

!          A very stupid program

        REAL :: NUM,SQNUM
10      PRINT *, ' Type a real positive number '
        READ *, NUM
        SQNUM = SQRT(NUM)
        PRINT *, 'Square Root of  ',NUM,' is ',SQNUM
        GOTO 10
        END
```

This program will read the value of NUM from the keyboard again and again; it will calculate and print the number and its square root. Note that the program will *never terminate because there is no exit point* – the unconditional GOTO will transfer the control to the statement number 10 after printing the result. Hopefully, the 'break key' at the terminal will terminate the program. If the GOTO is removed, the program will terminate after reading the first set of data. Indiscriminate use of GOTO makes a program very unstructured and should be avoided as far as practicable. In fact, there are schools, which advocate GOTO-less programming. There are other schools, who feel that it is still possible to write structured program with restricted use of GOTO, especially when the jumps are very small (say a few lines). However, the present version of Fortran provides several other statements, which facilitates writing a GOTO-less program with ease.

3.4 Block IF

The syntax of block IF is

```
        IF (cond) THEN
         stmt
        ENDIF
```

In all subsequent discussions, whenever we refer to *stmt* or *stmt-1* or the like we mean either a single Fortran statement, called a simple statement or a group of Fortran statements, called the compound statement. The block may not contain any statement; it may be empty.

Block IF works as follows:

The IF statement tests a condition. If the condition is true, all the statements as permitted by the program logic upto ENDIF are executed (Fig 3.1). If the condition is false, the statements upto ENDIF are skipped and the statement following ENDIF is executed. It is, perhaps, clear that the statement mentioned above may be a single statement (simple statement) or a number of Fortran statements (compound statement).

Fig 3.1 Block IF

```
IF (A > B) THEN
   I=I+1           ! Single statement
ENDIF

IF (P .LT. Q) THEN
   I=I-1           ! statement 1
   PRINT *, I      ! statement 2
ENDIF
```

In the above case if the condition is true, both the statements are executed.
Block IF may be labeled. However, this is optional.

```
CHECK:    IF(X.EQ.Y) THEN
            C=A+B
            D=SQRT(C)
          ENDIF CHECK
```

There is a colon between the label and the block IF. It is needless to mention that when IF has a label the ENDIF must have the same label.

3.5 IF-THEN-ELSE

This construct allows the execution of a group of instructions (or a single instruction) if a condition is true and another group of instructions (or a single instruction) if the condition is false (Fig 3.2).

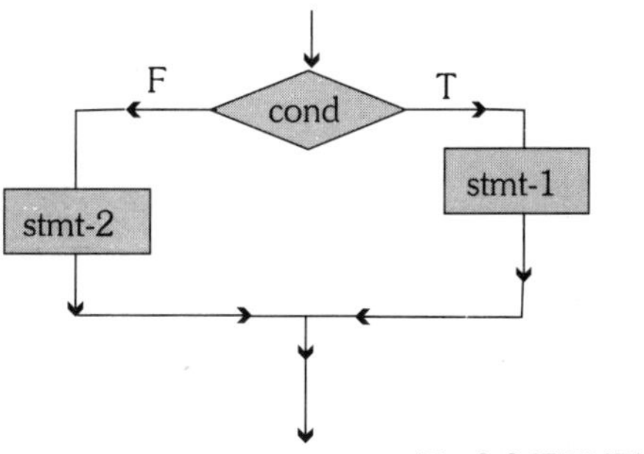

Fig 3.2 IF-THEN-ELSE

```
IF (cond) then
   stmt-1
ELSE
   stmt-2
ENDIF

IF (A>B) THEN
   I=I+1                 ! True path
ELSE
   I=I-1                 ! False path
ENDIF
```

In the above program segment, if the condition is true, i.e., A is greater than B, I is incremented by 1 and if the condition is false, I is decremented by 1. As already mentioned, there can be any number of statements between THEN and ELSE and between ELSE and ENDIF. The most important point to be noted is that depending upon the condition either the "THEN" path or the "ELSE" path is chosen – both are never chosen. These two paths are insulated from each other. Usually, the statement following the ENDIF is executed provided there is no branch statement (say GOTO) within THEN ... ELSE or ELSE ... ENDIF. Normally, such a statement is not present. The following program tests a number, whether it is even or odd.

```fortran
PROGRAM EVENODD
INTEGER :: NUM
PRINT *,  'Type a positive Integer '
READ *,NUM
IF(NUM/2*2-NUM .EQ. 0) THEN
    PRINT *, NUM, ' is an even number '
ELSE
    PRINT *, NUM, ' is an odd number '
ENDIF

END
```

Since NUM is an integer, NUM/2 (2 is also an integer) will be calculated in integer mode. Let us consider two cases: N=4 and 3. NUM/2*2 - NUM is 0 and -1 when N=4 and N=3 respectively (4/2 is 2 and 3/2 is 1). So the property of the integer division is used to distinguish between the even and the odd number.

The condition decides the position of 'even' and 'odd' PRINT statements. For example, if the condition is modified to:

```fortran
IF (NUM/2*2 – NUM .NE.0)
```

the same program is to be modified as shown below:

```fortran
IF(NUM/2*2-NUM .NE. 0) THEN
   PRINT *, NUM, ' is an odd number '
ELSE
   PRINT *, NUM, ' is an even number '
ENDIF
```

IF-THEN-ELSE may be labeled provided the corresponding IF and ENDIF are labeled.

```
CHECK:          IF(A>B) THEN
                   I=I+1
                ELSE CHECK
                   I=I-1
                ENDIF CHECK
```

or

```
CHECK:          IF(A>B) THEN
                   I=I+1
                ELSE
                   I=I-1
                ENDIF CHECK
```

Moreover, all of them must have the same label as shown above.

3.6 ELSE-IF

The ELSE part of the IF-THEN-ELSE can be another IF statement.

```
IF (cond-1) THEN
  stmt-1
ELSE IF (cond-2) THEN
      stmt-2
    ELSE IF (cond-3) THEN
      stmt-3

          .

          .

    ELSE IF (cond-n) THEN
        stmt-n
ELSE
   stmt
ENDIF
```

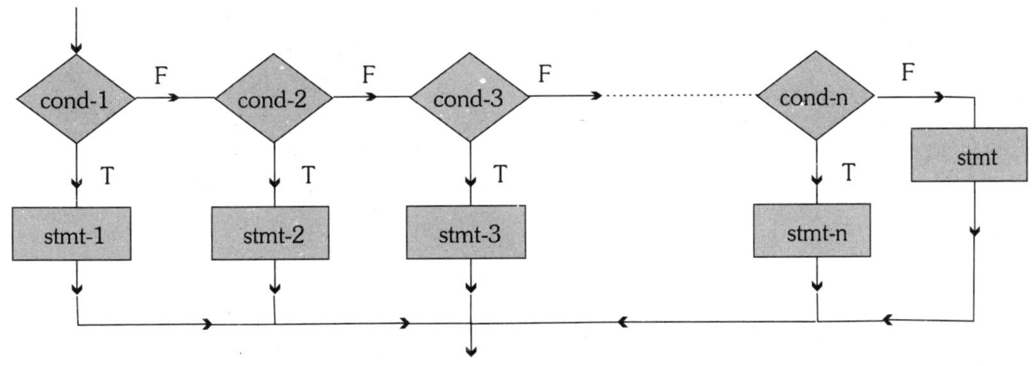

Fig 3.3 ELSE-IF

If the condition *cond-1* is true, the statement *stmt-1* is executed and the next statement is the statement following ENDIF. If the condition *cond-1* is false, condition *cond-2* is tested. If the condition is true, *stmt-2* is executed and like the previous condition, the next statement is the statement following ENDIF. If all the conditions are false, statement *stmt* is executed. Note that there is only one ENDIF in the sequence (Fig 3.3). The statements *stmt-1*, *stmt-2* .. may be a single statement or may be a group of statements. The process is illustrated by means of a few examples:

```fortran
      PROGRAM MAXMIN
!              Maximum between two numbers
      INTEGER :: NUM1,NUM2
!              NUM1 and NUM2 are assigned to some value

      PRINT *, 'Type two integers  '
      READ *,NUM1,NUM2
      IF(NUM1>NUM2) THEN
         PRINT *,'NUM1 is greater than NUM2 ', NUM1,NUM2
      ELSE IF (NUM1 <NUM2) THEN
              PRINT *,'NUM1 is less than NUM2 ',NUM1,NUM2
          ELSE
              PRINT *,'NUM1 is equal to NUM2 ', NUM1,NUM2
      ENDIF
      END
```

The next program calculates the roots of a quadratic equation:

```fortran
      PROGRAM ROOTS
!              Roots of quadratic equation
      REAL ::   X1,X2,A,B,C,TEMP,DISCR,TWOA
!              A*X**2+B*X+C=0
      PRINT *, 'Type the values of A, B and C '
      READ *, A,B,C
      DISCR=B*B-4.0*A*C
      IF(DISCR > 0.0) THEN
         TEMP=SQRT(DISCR)
         TWOA=1.0/(2.0*A)
         X1=(-B+TEMP)*TWOA
         X2=(-B-TEMP)*TWOA
         PRINT *, 'Roots are : ', X1,X2
      ELSE IF (DISCR .EQ.0) THEN
!        Such test should be avoided, see chapter 17 & 18
             X1 = -B/(2.0*A)
             X2 = X1
             PRINT *, 'Root are equal ', X1,X2
           ELSE
             PRINT *, 'Roots are complex number'
      ENDIF
      END
```

A few important points may be noted here. The expression 1.0/(2.0*A) is required for calculating both X1 and X2. It is better to define a temporary variable for 1.0/(2.0*A) so that the calculation is done only once. There is no need to calculate the same expression twice. Moreover, normally multiplication is a faster operation than division and therefore TWOA is defined as 1.0/(2.0*A) so that two divisions are replaced by multiplication. An optimizing compiler may do the same thing.

The next program converts marks of an examination to a remark like 'excellent', 'very good' etc. according to the table shown below:

Mark	Remark
>90	Excellent
>80 and <=90	Very good
>70 and <=80	Good
>60 and <=70	Fair
<=60	Repeat

```
PROGRAM MARKTOREM
INTEGER :: MARK
        SET MARKS TO SOME VALUE
!

PRINT *, 'Enter Marks ... '
READ *, MARK
IF(MARK > 90) THEN
   PRINT *, 'Excellent, ', 'Mark = ',MARK
ELSE IF (MARK > 80) THEN
        PRINT *, 'Very Good, ','Mark = ',MARK
ELSE IF (MARK > 70) THEN
        PRINT *, 'Good, ','Mark = ',MARK
ELSE IF(MARK > 60) THEN
        PRINT *, 'Fair, ','Mark = ', MARK
ELSE
    PRINT *,'Repeat, ','Mark = ',MARK
ENDIF

END
```

ELSE IF can be labeled provided the corresponding IF and ENDIF are also labeled.

```
LAB:   IF(N.EQ.0) THEN
          N=1
       ELSE IF (N.EQ.1) THEN LAB
             N=-1
          ELSE LAB
             N=0
       ENDIF LAB
```

3.7 Nested IF

IF statement may be nested; there can be an IF statement within another IF statement.

```
IF (cond-1) THEN
    IF (cond-2) THEN
        stmt-1
    ELSE
        stmt-2
    ENDIF
ELSE
    stmt-3
.ENDIF
```

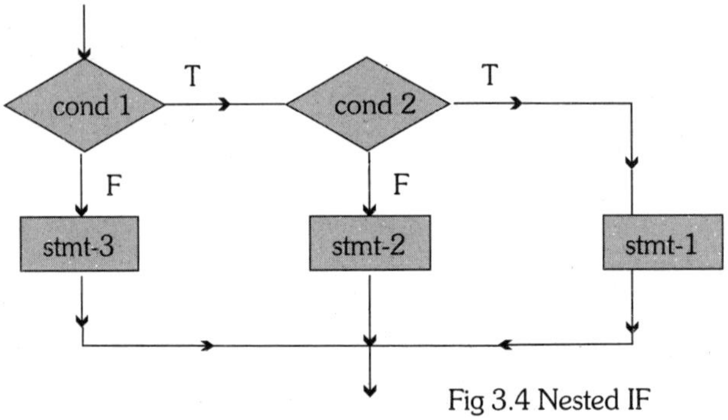

Fig 3.4 Nested IF

If *cond-1* is true, *cond-2* is tested. If *cond-2* is true, *stmt-1* is executed and if it is false then *stmt-2* is executed. If *cond-1* is false, *stmt-3* is executed. The statements *stmt-1*, *stmt-2* and *stmt-3* may be either a single or a compound statement. It may be noted that the condition *cond-2* is checked only when *cond-1* is true. If *cond-1* is false, *stmt-3* is executed – *cond-2* is not checked (Fig 3.4).

```
IF(A>B) THEN
IF(P<Q) THEN
  I=I+1          ! Both the conditions are true
ELSE
  I=I-1          ! A>B is true, P<Q is false
ENDIF
ELSE
  I=0            ! A>B is false
ENDIF
```

IF statement can be nested to any level.

3.8 Nested IF without ELSE

As an IF statement might not have an ELSE, the number of ELSE in a nested IF is always less than or equal to number of THEN. However, the reverse is not true, the number of THEN cannot be less than the number of ELSE – compiler will flag that as an error.

```
IF (cond-1) THEN
   IF (cond-2) THEN
       stmt-1
   ELSE
       stmt-2
   ENDIF
ENDIF
```

In this case the ELSE is associated with the inner IF – the outer IF does not have any ELSE. If the condition *cond-1* is false, control is passed to the statement following the outer ENDIF.

```
IF (A>B) THEN     ! No ELSE with this IF
   IF(P>Q) THEN
       I=I+1
   ELSE
       I=I-1
   ENDIF
ENDIF
```

If A>B is false, the value of I will not be changed and the next statement is the statement following the second ENDIF (outer ENDIF).

Consider the following program segment:

```
IF (A>B) THEN
   IF(P<Q) THEN      ! No ELSE for this IF
   I=I+1
   ENDIF
ELSE
   I=I-1
ENDIF
```

If A>B is true but P<Q is false, the value of I will not be changed. If A>B is false, I is decremented by 1.

3.9 Rules of Block IF

(a) It is possible to come out of the block IF by means of a GOTO statement.

```
       IF (A>B) THEN
          .

          .
       GOTO 10
          .

          .
       ENDIF
10     . . . . .
```

(b) However, it is not permitted to enter into block IF from outside (without touching the IF statement)

```
                GO TO 100      ! not allowed
                .

                .
                IF(P<Q) THEN
                   .

                   .
100                .  .  .  .
                   .
                ENDIF

                GOTO 20        ! not allowed
                IF(A>B) THEN
                   .
                ELSE
                   .
20              . . . .

                   .
                ENDIF
```

Similarly, it is not permitted to jump into "ELSE" path from "THEN" path and vice-versa.

```
                IF (A<B) THEN
                   .
                GOTO 30   ! not permitted
                   .
                ELSE
                   .
30              . . . . . .
                ENDIF
```

(c) It is perfectly legal if such transfer is caused within the "THEN" or "ELSE" block:

```
                IF (A>B) THEN
                   .
                GO TO 10      ! allowed
                   .
10              . . . . . .

                   .
                ELSE
                   .
                GOTO 30       ! allowed
                   .
30              . . . .
                   .
                ENDIF
```

(d) If labels are used for nested IF, the inner label must terminate before the outer label as shown below:

```
OUTER:        IF(cond-1) THEN
                   .
INNER:           IF(cond-2) then
                     .
                 ENDIF INNER
                 .
              ENDIF OUTER
```

(e) ELSE IF statement cannot appear after the ELSE statement.
(f) One can jump on to the ENDIF statement either from the "THEN" or "ELSE" path.

3.10 CASE Statement

CASE statement allows multi-way branching. The syntax of CASE statement is shown below.

```
SELECT CASE (expr)
   CASE(low-1:high-1)
       stmt-1
   CASE(low-2:high-2)
       stmt-2
       .
END SELECT
```

The low and high are the lower and the upper bounds of the selected expression respectively. Both the high and the low or one of them must be present. The CASE statement works as follows (Fig 3.5). The expression *expr* is evaluated. It should return an integer (logical and character will be considered later). A particular path is chosen depending on the value of the expression. If the value of the expression is between (and including) *low-1* and *high-1*, *stmt-1* is executed and the next statement is the statement following END SELECT. Similarly, if the value of the expression lies between *low-2* and *high-2*, *stmt-2* is executed. The statements *stmt-1*, *stmt-2* may be a simple statement or a compound statement.

A particular path is automatically insulated from the other paths – CASE does not fall through. If the value of the expression does not match with any of the CASEs, the CASE statement is ignored (CASE DEFAULT is discussed in 3.11) and the executable statement following the END SELECT is the next statement executed. If *stmt-1*, *stmt-2* etc do not contain any branch statement (say GOTO), the next executable statement following the END SELECT is always executed.

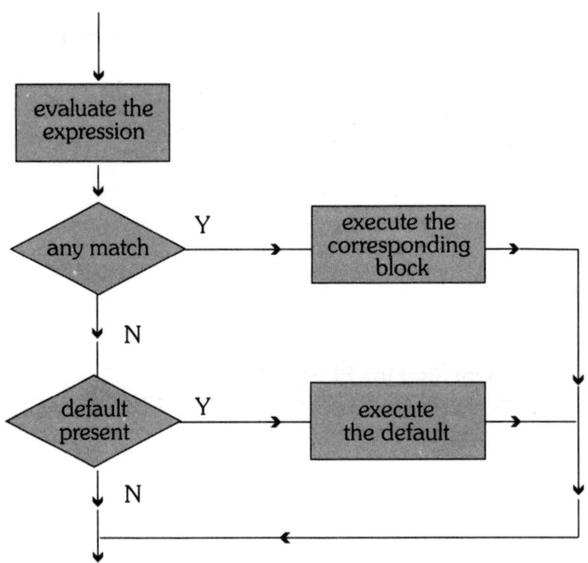

Fig 3.5 CASE Statement

The CASE statement may have a label. However, this is optional.

```
LAB:    SELECT CASE (expr)

        .

        .

        END SELECT LAB
```

There are several types of CASE statements.
(a) Type I: When only one integer (or expression) is present, the CASE is selected for that particular value.

```
SELECT CASE (INDEX)
 CASE(1)
  N=N+1
 CASE(2)
  N=N-1
 CASE(3)
  N=N+2
 CASE(4)
  N=N-2
 END SELECT
```

When the value of INDEX is 1, N is incremented by 1 and the next statement is the statement following END SELECT. Similarly, for INDEX = 2, 3 and 4 respective paths are chosen. Note that, after choosing a particular path and exhausting the statements in the path, control is passed to the statement following END SELECT.

(b) Type II: If the upper and lower bounds are specified, a particular path is chosen when the value of the expression falls within the range.

```
SELECT CASE (INDEX)
  CASE(1:3)
!        index=1 or 2 or 3
     N=N+1
  CASE(4:6)
!        index=4 or 5 or 6
     N=N-1
  CASE(7:14)
!        index=7 or 8 or 9... or 14
     N=N+2
  CASE(15:20)
!        index=15 or 16 or 17 ... 20
     N=N-2
END SELECT
```

In the above example, when the value of the INDEX is 1 or 2 or 3, N is incremented by 1; when the INDEX is 4 or 5 or 6, N is decremented by 1 and similarly for other paths.

(c) Type III: When either the upper or the lower bound is missing, but the colon is present, upper or lower bound is respectively assumed to be all the permissible values. For example, (20:) indicates all values greater than or equal to 20. In a similar way, (:1) indicates 1, 0 and all the negative integers (all values less than or equal to 1).

```
SELECT CASE (INDEX)
   CASE ( :0)
!          index less than or equal to 0
      N=N+1
   CASE (1:3)
      N=N-1
   CASE (4:10)
      N=N+2
   CASE (11: )
!       index greater than or equal to 11
      N=N-2
   END SELECT
```

In case of CASE(:0), the lower bound is missing; for all values of the INDEX less than or equal to zero, N is incremented by 1. Similarly, for all values of the INDEX greater than or equal to 11, N is decremented by 2.

(d) Type IV: It is possible to specify discrete as well as continuous values for the expressions provided they do not overlap.

```
SELECT CASE(INDEX)
   CASE(1,3,5,9:12,14)
       stmt-1
       .
       .
       .
END SELECT
```

stmt-1 will be executed if the value of the control variable (in this case INDEX) is 1 or 3 or 5 or any value between 9 and 12 or 14. Similarly, for

```
SELECT CASE(INDEX)
   CASE(1:3, 5: )
      stmt-2
      .
      .
END SELECT
```

the *stmt-2* will be executed if the value of the control variable is 1 or 2 or 3 or any value greater than or equal to 5. Also for,

```
SELECT CASE(INDEX)
   CASE( :0,2,3,7: )
       stmt-3
       .
       .
END SELECT
```

the *stmt-3* will be executed when the control variable has a value less than or equal to zero or 2 or 3 or any value greater than or equal to 7.

3.11 CASE DEFAULT

If the value of the expression does not match with any of the CASE, the SELECT CASE statement is ignored. However, if it is necessary to choose a default, should there be no match, CASE DEFAULT may be used (Fig 3.5).

```
SELECT CASE (INDEX)
   CASE(1,2)         ! 1 and 2
      N=N+1
   CASE(3:6)         ! 3, 4, 5 ,6
      N=N-1
   CASE(7:10)        ! 7, 8, 9, 10
      N=N+2
   CASE(11:20)       ! 11 to 20
      N=N-2
   CASE DEFAULT      ! none of the above
      N=0
END SELECT
```

The CASE DEFAULT is chosen in the above case when the INDEX is less than 1 or greater than 20. In that case, N is set to zero. CASE DEFAULT does not have to be the last item of the list of CASEs and there must be a space between CASE and DEFAULT.

3.12 Nested CASE

CASE can be nested, that is, there can be one CASE within another. This is illustrated by means of an example:

```
SELECT CASE(I)
   CASE(1)
   SELECT CASE(J)
      CASE (1)      ! I=1, J=1
         .
      CASE(2:3)     ! I=1, J=2 or 3
         .
      CASE(4: )     !I=1,J=4,5,6,....
   END SELECT
   CASE(2)          ! I=2
      .
END SELECT
```

The values of I and J for different paths are shown through inline comments.

3.13 Rules of CASE

(a) There should not be any overlap among the various paths while specifying the CASE. The following is not acceptable:

```
SELECT CASE (INDEX)
   CASE(1:2)
      N=N+1
   CASE(2:3)
      N=N-1                ! not allowed
END SELECT

SELECT CASE(INDEX)
   CASE (1,2:10,8:13)      ! overlap not allowed
      N=N+1
      .
END SELECT
```

(b) A statement within a particular CASE may have a statement number. It is possible to jump to a statement by GOTO or IF within the same path. But such jump is not allowed from one path to another. Also a jump is not allowed from outside the CASE to inside the CASE.

```fortran
              GOTO 10                    ! not allowed
              .
              SELECT CASE (INDEX)
                 CASE (1:2)
                    .
   10            I=I+1
                    .
              END SELECT

!             allowed

              SELECT CASE (INDEX)
                 CASE (1:2)
                    N=N+1
                    IF (N>20) THEN
                       GOTO 20           ! This is allowed
                    ENDIF
   20            .....
                 CASE (3:4)
                    .
              END SELECT

!             Not allowed
              SELECT CASE (INDEX)
                 CASE (1:2)
                    N=N+1
                    .
                 IF (N>20) THEN
                       GOTO 30           ! not allowed
                 ENDIF
                    .
                 CASE (3:4)
                    N=N-1
                    .
   30            .

              END SELECT
```

(c) CASE statement may be labeled. In case of nested CASE, the inner one must terminate before the outer one.

(d) Block IF may contain CASE. However, the terminal point of CASE must be before the block IF.

```fortran
   OUTER:        IF (cond-1) THEN
                    .
   INNER:           SELECT CASE (expr)
                       .
                    END SELECT INNER
                    .
                 ENDIF OUTER
```

(e) It is possible to jump to the END SELECT statement from within the CASE construct. The NAG compiler flags this as error. The GFORTRAN compiler issues warning. The g95 compiler compiles without any warning. However this is strongly discouraged.

3.14 Programming Examples

The following program using CASE converts marks to grade:

```
PROGRAM MARKTOGR
INTEGER :: MARK
!    Read Mark
PRINT *,'Type a positive integer between 0 and 100'
READ *, MARK
SELECT CASE (MARK)
   CASE(91:100)
       PRINT *, 'Excellent ', MARK
   CASE(81:90)
       PRINT *, 'Very Good ', MARK
   CASE(71:80)
       PRINT *, 'Good ', MARK
   CASE(61:70)
       PRINT *, 'Fair ', MARK
   CASE(0:60)
       PRINT *, 'Repeat ', MARK
   CASE DEFAULT
       PRINT *, 'Bad Data ', MARK
  END SELECT

  END

!      Number of days in a month (not a leap year)

PROGRAM NOOFDAYS
INTEGER :: MONTH, DAY
!      Input month
READ *, MONTH       ! 1=Jan, 2=Feb, ....
      SELECT CASE(MONTH)
      CASE (4,6,9,11)
         DAY=30
      CASE (2)
         DAY=28
      CASE(1,3,5,7:8,10,12)
         DAY=31
      END SELECT
PRINT *, 'No of days in month ',MONTH, ' is' ,DAY
END
```

3.15 Obsolete Branch Statements (*)

Several conditional branch statements have been declared as obsolete. These are now a days rarely used. Compilers still accept these statements as valid Fortran statement. In future there is a possibility that these might be de-implemented. These are: arithmetic IF, logical IF, computed GOTO and assigned GOTO.

3.16 Arithmetic IF(*)

The arithmetic IF allows three-way branching depending on the value of an expression. The syntax of arithmetic IF is

```
IF(expn) n1,n2,n3
```

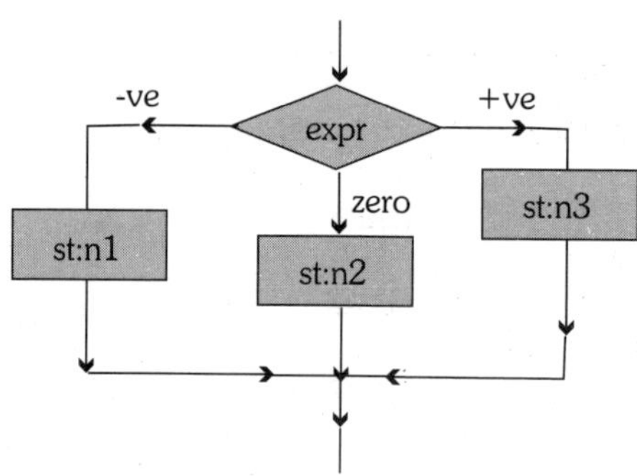

Fig 3.6 Arithmetic IF

The expression within the bracket is evaluated. If it is negative, control is passed to the statement having statement number $n1$; if it is zero, control is passed to the statement having statement number $n2$ and if it is positive, control is passed to the statement having statement number $n3$ (Fig 3.6). The statement number must refer to executable statement present within the same unit as arithmetic IF (statement must be in the same scoping unit). For example, in case of

```
IF (X+Y) 10, 20, 30
```

the value of the expression X+Y will determine the label where the branching would take place.

Value of X+Y	Statement to be executed
X+Y < 0	Statement number 10
X+Y = 0	Statement number 20
X+Y > 0	Statement number 30

The statement numbers present along with arithmetic IF might not be all different.

```
IF (A + B / C) 10, 10, 20
```

If the expression A+B/C is either zero of negative, control is passed to the statement number 10; otherwise control is passed to the statement number 20. The following are valid usage of arithmetic IF.

```
IF(A) 10, 20, 20
IF(A+B) 10, 20, 10
```

If all the three numbers are identical arithmetic IF becomes equivalent to GOTO:

```
IF (A) 100, 100, 100
```

and in such a case the conditional branch statement which is independent of the condition should be replaced by,

```
GOTO 100
```

as this is much more elegant and faster too. The following algebraic expression may be represented by arithmetic IF as:

$$
\begin{aligned}
B&=A/2, &&\text{when } R<0 \\
B&=0, &&\text{when } R=0 \\
B&=2*A, &&\text{when } R>0
\end{aligned}
$$

```
      IF(R) 11, 12, 13
11    B=0.5*A
      GOTO 20
12    B=0.0
      GOTO 20
13    B=2.0*A
20    ...
```

Note that GOTO 20 statements insulate a path from another.

3.17 Logical IF (*)

In the case of a logical IF, a condition is tested and if it is true, the statement after the logical IF is executed. If the condition is false, the statement after logical IF is ignored. The syntax of the logical IF is given below:

```
IF (cond) stmt
```

where *cond* is the condition to be tested. If the condition is true, the statement *stmt*, which is a single statement, is executed; if the condition is false, the statement *stmt* is not executed – it is skipped. The statement (*stmt*) cannot be an ASSOCIATE construct, another logical IF, block IF, CASE, DO, DO WHILE, ELSE, ELSE IF, ELSE WHERE, END, END DO, END IF, END SELECT, END FORALL, END WHERE, END FUNCTION, END SUBROUTINE, FORALL, SELECT CASE or WHERE statement. It may be noted at this point that all the statements mentioned above have not yet been introduced. These will be discussed at the appropriate places. The statement following the logical IF is always executed unless the statement after logical IF is a branch or jump statement or any such statement, which terminates the program at that point. A few examples of logical IF are given below:

```
      IF(A>B) I=I+1
!         if A is greater than B, I is incremented
      IF(P.LE.Q) A=2.0 ! if P<=Q, set A to 2
      IF(A+B .LT. C+D) X=Y+Z
!         if A+B < C+D execute the statement X=Y+Z
```

The last statement needs some clarification. The arithmetic operators are evaluated (A+B and C+D) and then the results are compared as the priority of arithmetic operators is greater than the priority of relational operators. If the condition is true, X is set to Y+Z. Otherwise X is not altered. The next statement following the logical IF (not shown in the program segment) is executed in both the cases.

   If it is necessary to execute a group of instructions depending upon a condition, logical IF and GOTO may be combined (Fig 3.7).

```
      IF(A<=B) GOTO 30
         I=I+1
         PRINT *, I
            .

            .
         GOTO 20
30       I=I-1
            .

            .
20       ...
```

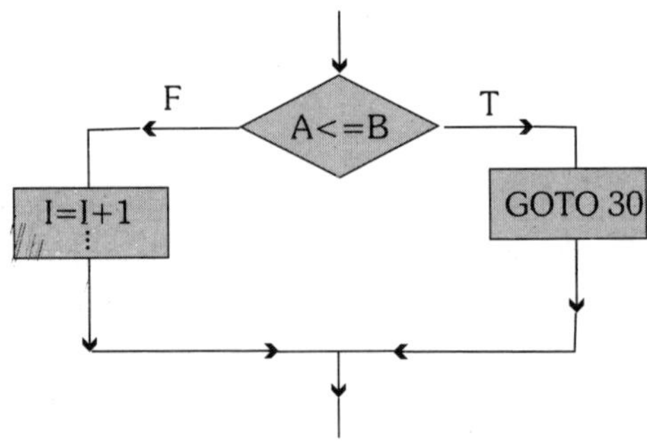

Fig 3.7 Logical IF

When the condition is true, all the statements from statement number 30 (as permitted by the programming logic) to statement number 20 are executed. If the condition is false, all statements after the IF up to GOTO 20 are executed. It may be noted that block IF with IF-THEN-ELSE feature is much more elegant compared to logical IF and as such its use is rather limited.

3.18 Computed GOTO(*)

Computed GOTO allows multi-way branching. Though computed GOTO was heavily used in early versions of Fortran, it has now become almost obsolete, as the better, powerful and more general CASE statement has been introduced. The syntax of computed GOTO is:

```
GOTO (n1,n2,n3,....,nN), expr
```

The expression *expr* is evaluated, if it is not an integer it is truncated to an integer. If the value of the expression is 1, control is passed to the statement having statement number *n1*, if the value of the *expr* is 2, the control is passed to the statement having statement number *n2* and so on. The argument of computed GOTO may contain any number of statement numbers. All the statement numbers must refer to executable statement numbers present in the same unit as computed GOTO. If the value of the *expr* is less than 1 or greater than N, where N is the total number of statements present within the computed GOTO, the computed GOTO is totally ignored. The control is passed to the statement following the computed GOTO (Fig 3.8).

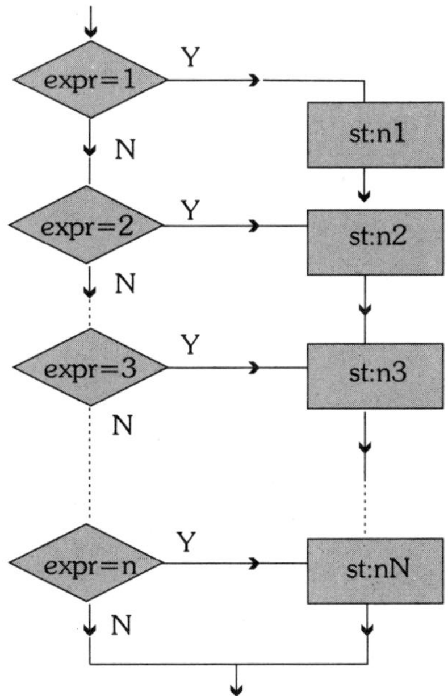

Fig 3.8 Computed GO TO

```
GOTO (10, 40, 100, 90), I
```

In the example shown above, if the value of I is 1, control is passed to the statement having statement number 10; if the value of I is 2, control is passed to the statement having statement number 40 and so on. Note that in this case, if the value of I is less than 1 or greater than 4 (as there are four statement numbers present as argument of computed GOTO), computed GOTO is ignored. It is possible to repeat the statement numbers within computed GOTO, that is, all the statement numbers within the computed GOTO need not be different.

```
GO TO (10, 20, 20, 35, 30), I
```

In the above example, control is passed to the statement having statement number 20 when I is 2 or 3. Computed GOTO transfers the control to a particular statement depending upon the value of the control variable (or expression) and then the execution proceeds sequentially. The paths are not insulated from each other like CASE statement. It becomes the responsibility of the programmer to insulate one path from the other, if necessary.

Assume that the income tax of different categories (1, 2, 3 and 4) is respectively 20%, 30%, 35% and 40%.

```
           !         Use of computed GOTO
                     REAL :: INCOME, TAX
                     INTEGER :: CATEGORY

                     .

                     .
                     GOTO (10, 20, 30, 40), CATEGORY
      10             TAX=0.2*INCOME
                     GOTO 100
      20             TAX=0.3*INCOME
                     GOTO 100
      30             TAX=0.35*INCOME
                     GOTO 100
      40             TAX=0.4*INCOME
     100             . . . . . .
```

The GOTO 100 in the above program needs some explanation. If GOTO 100 statements were not present, the TAX, calculated above would have been always 0.4*INCOME irrespective of the value of the category. Suppose the value of CATEGORY is 1. When the computed GOTO is executed, control is transferred to the statement number 10 and the TAX is calculated as 20% of the income. Now, if GOTO 100 is not present, the next statement will be executed and this will wrongly re-calculate the TAX as 30% of the income. Following this logic, we come to the conclusion that if GOTO 100 statements are not present, TAX will always be 0.4*INCOME irrespective of the value of the category, as 0.4*INCOME is the last statement in the sequence. If the individual paths are not "insulated" from each other, the calculation would be correct only for the CATEGORY equal to 4. We now redraw the diagram 3.8 where all the paths are insulated from each other (Fig 3.9).

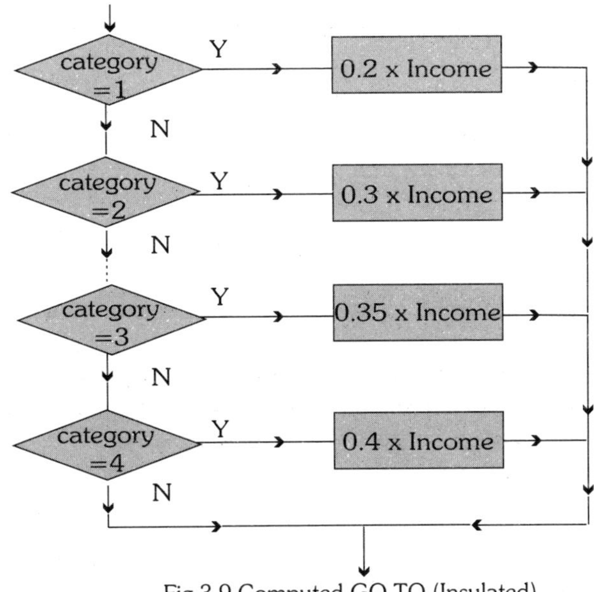

Fig 3.9 Computed GO TO (Insulated)

The diagram also shows that when the value of the CATEGORY is not 1 or 2 or 3 or 4, computed GOTO is skipped (ignored).

3.19 Assigned GOTO(*)

Assigned GOTO consists of two parts. First a statement label (number) is assigned to an integer variable and then GOTO statement with the integer variable as statement label is executed. The value of the integer variable is the statement number to be executed next. Therefore, by assigning different statement numbers to the control variable, same GOTO statement may be used to branch to different statement. In other words, the current value of the control variable determines the statement to which control will be passed.

```
     !       Assigned GOTO
             INTEGER :: LAB

             .
             ASSIGN 10 TO LAB
             .
     10      .....
             .
             GOTO LAB              ! jump to statement 10
             .
             ASSIGN 15 TO LAB
             .
             GOTO LAB              ! jump to statement 15

             .
     15      .....
```

Optionally, the assigned GOTO may contain the list of statement numbers where the control may be transferred.

```
          .
          .
    ASSIGN 10 TO I
          .
    GOTO I (10, 15, 20)
```

The statement number must correspond to executable statements present in the same unit as the assigned GOTO statement.

It is illegal to assign a statement number to a variable, which is not present in the unit.

Assigned GOTO has never been popular since the early days of Fortran and will be de-implemented from the future release of Fortran. The use of Assigned GOTO is strongly discouraged as this makes a program very unstructured.

Chapter 4

LOOP

Programming logic often requires executing a group of instructions repeatedly depending on certain condition. For example, if one tries to add the series $1+2+3+ \ldots + 1000$, it is not practicable to sum the series directly assuming that one will not use the formula $n(a+1)/2$. Fortran provides instructions to execute statements repeatedly depending on some condition. These instructions are collectively called "loop instruction". Two instructions, DO and DO WHILE are used to perform "loop" operation.

4.1 DO Statement

There are several forms of the DO statement. The most popular form of DO statement is:

```
DO int-var=m1, m2, m3
    .
    .
END DO
```

where *int-var* is an integer variable and *m1*, *m2* and *m3* are usually integer constants or integer expressions. If *m1*, *m2* and *m3* are expressions, they are evaluated before the DO loop is entered. Space between END and DO is optional.

```
DO I=1, 10, 1
    .
ENDDO
```

The above DO statement works as follows – the integer variable I, also called the control variable or loop index, is initialized to 1 (*m1*), a check is made whether I is less than or equal to 10 (*m2*). If the answer is yes, the statement following the DO, as permitted by the program logic upto ENDDO are executed. The control variable is then incremented by 1(*m3*) on reaching ENDDO and the control is passed to the top of the loop. The check is once again done whether I is less than or equal to 10 (*m2*) or not. This process continues till the value of I exceeds 10 (*m2*). In that case the control is passed to the statement following the ENDDO. Note that, each time program control comes to ENDDO, the control variable I is incremented by 1 (*m3*). It is perhaps clear that following the above logic, the loop shown above will be executed 10 times and the loop will be exited when the control variable I exceeds 10 (Fig 4.1).

If the increment is 1, the increment (*m3*) may be omitted.

```
DO I=1, 10    ! increment 1
  .
ENDDO
```

A DO statement may have a label. However, it is optional.

```
LABEL:   DO int-var=m1, m2, m3
  .
ENDDO LABEL
```

DO and ENDDO must have same label as shown below:

```
LOOP:    DO I= 1, 10
  .

  .
ENDDO LOOP
```

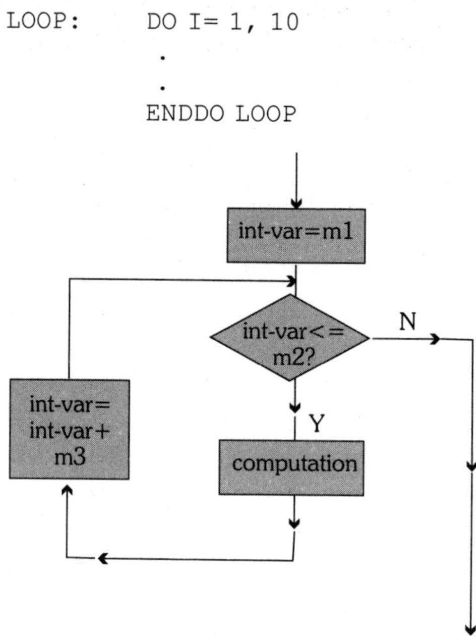

Fig 4.1 DO Statement

The use of DO statement is illustrated by means of several examples.

```
PROGRAM NUMSQ
!   Print a number, square of number, cube of number and
!   square root of the number

INTEGER :: NUM, SQNUM, CUBENUM
REAL :: XNUM, SQRTNUM
INTEGER, PARAMETER :: LIMIT=10
DO NUM=1, LIMIT
```

```fortran
      XNUM=NUM ! convert to real
      SQNUM=NUM*NUM
      CUBENUM=SQNUM*NUM
      SQRTNUM=SQRT(XNUM)
      PRINT *, NUM, SQNUM,CUBENUM,SQRTNUM
    ENDDO
    END


    PROGRAM ADD
!      S=1+2+3+... +100
    INTEGER, PARAMETER :: LIMIT=100
    INTEGER :: SUM=0, I
    DO I=1, LIMIT
     SUM=SUM+I
    ENDDO
    PRINT *, SUM
    END


    PROGRAM FACTORIAL
!      P=1x2x3...x6
    INTEGER, PARAMETER :: LIMIT=6
    INTEGER :: PROD=1, I
    DO I=1, LIMIT
     PROD=PROD*I
    ENDDO
    PRINT *, PROD
    END


    PROGRAM EOADD
!      S1=1+3+5...+99
!      S2=2+4+6...+100
    INTEGER, PARAMETER :: LAST=100
    INTEGER :: SUM1=0, SUM2=0,I

    DO I=1, LAST, 2
     SUM1=SUM1+I
    ENDDO

    DO I=2, LAST, 2
     SUM2=SUM2+I
    ENDDO

    PRINT *, 'Sum of the odd series ', SUM1
    PRINT *, 'Sum of the even series ', SUM2
    PRINT *, 'Sum of even and odd series ', SUM1+SUM2

    END
```

We shall now try to solve a slightly difficult problem using the DO statement. The problem is to find all numbers between 100 and 999 such that the number is equal to the sum of the cubes of the digits. For example, $153 = 1^3 + 5^3 + 3^3$. The algorithm to solve the problem is to extract the individual digits from all the numbers between 100 and 999 and check whether they satisfy the above mentioned condition.

```fortran
PROGRAM NUMCUBE
INTEGER :: NUM, I1, I2, I3, IT
PRINT *, 'The numbers are:'

DO NUM=100, 999
!       Extract digits

        I1=NUM/100        ! integer division
        IT=MOD(NUM,100)

!       The library function MOD returns the remainder
!       of the division of the first argument by the
!       second argument.

        I2=IT/10
!       Extract the third digit
        I3=MOD(IT,10)

!       Now apply the condition
        IF(I1**3+I2**3+I3**3 .EQ. NUM) THEN
           PRINT *, NUM
        ENDIF

    ENDDO

    END
```

It may be verified that there are four such numbers between 100 and 999, which satisfy the condition. They are 153, 370, 371 and 407.

4.2 Negative Increment

The increment of DO loop ($m3$) may be negative. However, in that case the initial value of the control variable ($m1$) should be greater than or equal to the final value ($m2$).

```fortran
!               S=100+99+98+... +1
              SUM=0
              DO I=100, 1, -1
               SUM=SUM+I
              ENDDO
```

4.3 Numbered DO

The DO statement can have a statement number attached to it; in that case the same number should be the statement number of the ENDDO statement.

```
                DO 100 J=1,25
                .
    100     ENDDO
```

In the earlier versions of Fortran there was a restriction that the last statement of DO cannot be certain statements like, DO, IF, PAUSE, STOP, CALL EXIT etc. The difficulty could be avoided by terminating the DO statement by a statement called CONTINUE. The statement CONTINUE, an executable statement, does nothing and can be used at other places of the program also.

```
                SUM=0
                DO 100 I=1, 100
                   SUM=SUM+I
    100     CONTINUE
```

In this book we shall always use DO-ENDDO combination and never attach a statement number to the DO statement to avoid the above-mentioned complications.

4.4 Infinite Loop

Another form of DO is possible when no control variable is required. This forms an infinite loop and unless there is some mechanism to come out of the loop, the loop will never terminate.

```
                DO
                .
                ENDDO
```

The statements between DO and ENDDO are repeatedly executed.

4.5 EXIT

When the EXIT statement is executed within a DO loop, control is passed to the statement following the ENDDO. The following program segment adds 1 to 100.

```
                SUM=0
                I=1
                DO
                   SUM=SUM+I
                   I=I+1
                   IF(I>100) THEN
                      EXIT
                   ENDIF
                ENDDO
                PRINT *, SUM
```

When I exceeds 100, the EXIT statement is executed and control is passed to the statement following the ENDDO, that is, the PRINT statement.

The next program is another example of infinite loop. The loop is exited when the input is zero or negative – otherwise it takes input from the keyboard repeatedly.

```
        PROGRAM AVER
!          Average calculation
        INTEGER :: NUM=0, NUMBER
        REAL :: SUM=0.0, AVERAGE
        DO
           PRINT *, 'Type a positive integer '
           READ *, NUMBER
           IF(NUMBER .LE. 0) THEN          ! exit when <=0
              EXIT        ! division by zero occurs if the first number is 0
           ENDIF

           PRINT *, NUMBER
           NUM=NUM+1
           SUM=SUM+NUMBER
        ENDDO

        AVERAGE=SUM/NUM
        PRINT *, 'Average =', AVERAGE
        END
```

4.6 CYCLE

When a CYCLE statement is executed within a loop, all instructions following the CYCLE statement upto ENDDO (terminal statement) are skipped and a fresh cycle for the DO loop begins. The difference between EXIT and CYCLE statements may be noted at this stage. The former, when executed, transfers the control outside the current loop. On the other hand, the later initiates, after skipping all instructions up to the terminal statement of the loop, a new cycle from that point. The following, though not an elegant program, shows how to add all the even numbers between 1 and 100 using CYCLE.

```
        SUM=0
        DO I=1, 100
          IF(MOD(I,2) /=0) THEN
             CYCLE  ! skip for odd numbers
          ENDIF
          SUM=SUM+I
        ENDDO
```

MOD is a library function. MOD (I, J) is the remainder of I/J.

This is for demonstrating the CYCLE statement. An elegant way to do the same job is to use DO statement with 2 as increment.

```
SUM=0
DO I=2, 100, 2
 SUM=SUM+I
ENDDO
```

4.7 DO WHILE

The syntax of DO WHILE is:

```
DO WHILE (cond)
   .
ENDDO
```

The space between DO and WHILE is mandatory. The condition *cond* is tested; if it is true all the statements as permitted by the program logic following DO WHILE upto ENDDO are executed. The control is then passed to the top of the loop and a fresh cycle begins. The condition is tested at the beginning of each cycle. The process continues till the condition is false and in that case control is passed to the statement following ENDDO.

DO WHILE is illustrated with the help of a few examples.

Any positive number can be reduced to 1 by the following algorithm. If the number is odd multiply the number by 3 and add 1; if the number is even divide the number by 2. Continue till the number reduces to 1.

```
       PROGRAM REDUCE
       INTEGER :: NUM, COUNT=0
!        Read the number
       PRINT *, 'Type one positive integer '
       READ *, NUM
       DO WHILE (NUM /= 1)
         IF (MOD(NUM,2) /= 0) THEN
           NUM = 3*NUM + 1       ! odd
         ELSE
           NUM = NUM/2
         ENDIF
         COUNT=COUNT+1
       ENDDO
       PRINT *, 'Convergence achieved in ', &
        COUNT,' cycles:', ' Num = ',NUM
       END
```

The next program calculates the GCD between two numbers.

```
        PROGRAM GCD
!          Calculation of GCD
        INTEGER :: FIRST, SECOND, NUM1, NUM2, TEMP
        FIRST=81
        SECOND=45                ! GCD of 81 and 45 required
        NUM1=FIRST
        NUM2=SECOND
        TEMP=MOD(NUM1,NUM2)
        IF (TEMP .EQ. 0) THEN
          PRINT *, 'The GCD of ',FIRST, ' and ', &
           SECOND, ' is = ', NUM2
          STOP
        ENDIF

        DO WHILE(TEMP .NE. 0)
          NUM1=NUM2
          NUM2=TEMP
          TEMP=MOD(NUM1,NUM2)
        ENDDO
        PRINT *, 'The GCD of ',FIRST, ' and ', &
           SECOND, ' is = ', NUM2

        END
```

The statement STOP terminates the job at that point. The STOP statement may contain a number or a character string. These are displayed when the STOP statement is executed. This helps to identify the STOP statement if there is more than one STOP statements within the program.

```
        STOP 10
        STOP 'End of Data'
```

In this case the STOP statement is necessary if the GCD is obtained before entering the DO WHILE loop (say when FIRST=12, SECOND=4).

The next example shows a round about way of multiplying two positive integers N1 and N2. The algorithm is, if N1 is odd add N2 to a counter, divide N1 by 2 and multiply N2 by 2. Continue till N1 becomes 1.

```
        PROGRAM ROUNDMUL
        INTEGER :: N1, N2, SUM=0, NUM1, NUM2
        PRINT *, 'Type two positive integers '
        READ *, N1, N2
        NUM1=N1
        NUM2=N2
        IF(MOD(N1,2) /= 0) THEN
          SUM=SUM+N2
        ENDIF
```

```
DO WHILE (N1 /= 1)
   N1=N1/2
   N2=2*N2
   IF(MOD(N1,2) /= 0) THEN
      SUM=SUM+N2
   ENDIF
ENDDO

PRINT *, NUM1,'*',NUM2,'=',SUM
END
```

The Trapezoidal rule can be used to integrate a function numerically:

$$\int f(x)\,dx = h[(f(a)+f(b)/2+ f(a+h)+f(a+2h)\ldots. + f(a+nh)]$$

where a and b are the limits of integration and $h=(b-a)/n$, n is an even number. We shall now integrate a function $f(x)=x**3*exp(-x**3)$ and the limits of integration are 1 and 4, EXP is a library function which calculates the "e to the power" its argument (real).

```
PROGRAM TRAP
INTEGER :: I, N=100
REAL :: A=1.0, B=4.0
REAL :: SUM=0.0, H, X
H=(B-A)/N
SUM=SUM+0.5*(A**3*EXP(-A**3) + &
         B**3*EXP(-B**3))

X=A+H
DO I=2,N
  SUM=SUM+(X**3*EXP(-X**3))
  X=X+H
ENDDO
SUM=SUM*H
PRINT *, 'The result of integration is ', SUM
END
```

A better method to integrate a function numerically is the Simpson's one-third rule. In this method:

$$\int f(x)\,dx=h/3[(y_1+y_{n+1})+4(y_2+y_4+y_6+.. +y_n) + 2(y_3+y_5+y_7+... +y_{n-1})]$$

where, $h=(b-a)/n$, n is an even number, a and b are the limits of integration.

```
PROGRAM SIMPSON
INTEGER :: I, N=100
REAL :: A=1.0, B=4.0, H, SUM=0.0, X, CS=2.0
H=(B-A)/N
```

```
        SUM=SUM+(A**3*EXP(-A**3)+ &
                 B**3*EXP(-B**3))
        X=A+H
        DO I=2,N
          CS=6.0-CS
          SUM=SUM+CS*(X**3*EXP(-X**3))
          X=X+H
        ENDDO
        SUM=H/3.0*SUM
        PRINT *, 'The result of Integration ', SUM
        END
```

Another way of writing the same program is shown below:

```
        PROGRAM SIMPSON1
        INTEGER :: I, N=100
        REAL :: A=1.0, B=4.0, H, SUM=0.0, X
        H=(B-A)/N
!            Terminal points
        SUM=SUM+(A**3*EXP(-A**3)+ &
                 B**3*EXP(-B**3))
        X=A+H
        DO I=2,N,2        ! Note the increment

        SUM=SUM+4.0*(X**3*EXP(-X**3))
        X=X+H
        SUM=SUM+2.0*(X**3*EXP(-X**3))
        X=X+H
        ENDDO

        SUM=H/3.0*SUM
        PRINT *, 'The result of Integration ', SUM
        END
```

It would be interesting to observe the changes of the final result by varying the value of N i.e., the number of strips between the limits A and B.

4.8 Nested DO

The DO statement may be nested; there can be a DO within another DO. These are respectively called the inner and the other loops (Fig 4.2).

```
        DO I=1, 10
          .
            DO J=1, 100

            ENDDO
          .
        ENDDO
```

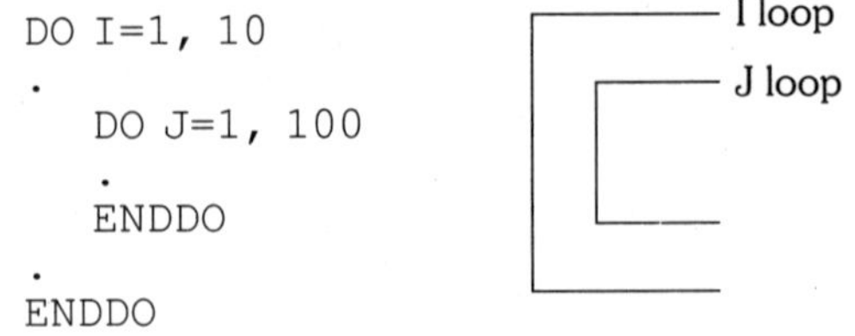

Fig. 4.2 Nested DO

During the execution, for each value of the control variable of the outer loop, all values of the control variable of the inner loop are taken. This means that the control variable of the inner loop varies more rapidly than that of the outer loop. This is illustrated by the following program segment:

```
DO I=1,2
   DO J=1,2
      PRINT *, 'I = ', I, 'J = ', J
   ENDDO
ENDDO
```

The output of the program will be:

```
I = 1           J = 1
I = 1           J = 2
I = 2           J = 1
I = 2           J = 2
```

Following the property of the DO loop the whole process may be summarized:
When the nested loop is entered from the top, I is initialized to 1 and since I<=2, I loop is entered. The next statement is another DO statement with J as its control variable. When this inner loop is entered, J is initialized to 1 and since J<=2, the PRINT statement is executed with the current value of I and J (both 1). After printing the values of I and J, control comes to ENDDO of the inner loop (J-loop). J is incremented by 1 and the J loop is executed once again with I=1 and J=2. Now when control comes to the ENDDO of the inner loop, J loop is exited because J is no longer less than or equal to 2. Now the control comes to the ENDDO of the outer loop (I-loop). This brings the control to the top of the outer loop, I is incremented by 1 and the J loop is entered once again. So the process is repeated with I=2 and J=1 and 2. Having completed the J loop the control is passed to the ENDDO statement of the outer loop. Now when I is incremented by 1, I is no longer less than or equal to 2. So I-loop is exited and the control is passed to the next statement following the ENDDO of the outer loop. Fig 4.3 illustrates this point.

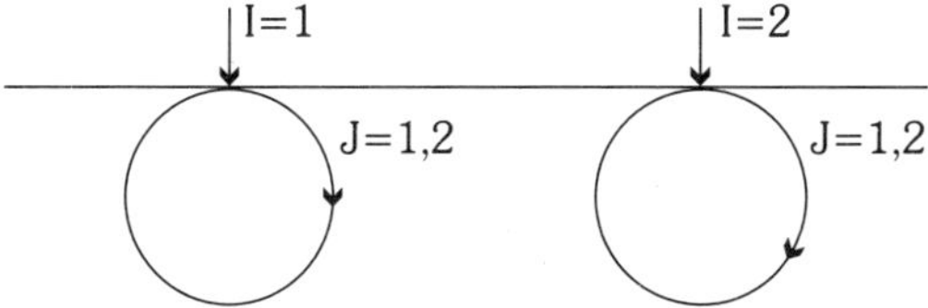

Fig 4.3 Nested DO

The figure 4.3 shows that for a given value of the outer index, in this case I, all the permissible values of the inner loop index, in this case J, are taken. The same concept may be extended for a nested loop having depth greater than 2.

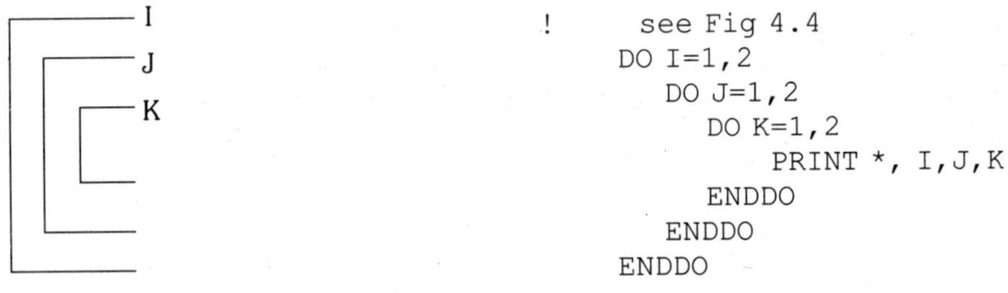

```
                      !       see Fig 4.4
                      DO I=1,2
                         DO J=1,2
                            DO K=1,2
                               PRINT *, I,J,K
                            ENDDO
                         ENDDO
                      ENDDO
```

Fig. 4.4 Nested DO (Depth=3)

The readers may verify that the output of the program segment are:

```
        1        1        1
        1        1        2
        1        2        1
        1        2        2
        2        1        1
        2        1        2
        2        2        1
        2        2        2
```

The digit program (number is equal to sum of the cubes of the digits) shown earlier with a single DO statement may be written with the help of nested DO also.

```
PROGRAM DIGIT
INTEGER :: I,J,K,IC,JC,IH,JT
DO I=1,9            ! first digit
  IC=I**3
  IH=100*I
  DO J=0,9         ! second digit
    JC=J**3
    JT=10*J
    DO K=0,9       ! third digit
      IF(IC+JC+K**3 .EQ. &
          IH+JT+K) THEN
      PRINT *,I,J,K
      ENDIF

    ENDDO
  ENDDO
ENDDO

END
```

IC+JC+K**3 is the sum of the cube of the digits and IH+JT+K is the number where the digits from the left are respectively, I, J and K.

It may be noted that in the earlier case (section 4.1) digits were extracted from the number and in this case the number is constructed from the digits.

4.9 CYCLE, EXIT and the Nested Loop

When a CYCLE or an EXIT is executed within a loop, it acts on that particular loop only. For example, if the EXIT statement is executed within an inner loop, control is transferred to the statement following the corresponding ENDDO.

```
DO I=1, 50
   .
   DO J=1, 100
      .
      IF( I+J .LT. 100) THEN
          EXIT
      ENDIF
   ENDDO     <-------
   .
   .
ENDDO
```

Here when EXIT is executed within the inner loop, control is passed to the next statement following the ENDDO of the inner loop. Similarly, if CYCLE is executed within a loop, a fresh cycle for that loop starts.

```
DO I=1, 50
  .
  .
  IF(A+B>C+D) THEN ! some condition
     CYCLE
  ENDIF
  DO J=1, 100
     .
  ENDDO
  .
------> ENDDO
```

If loops are labeled it is possible for an inner loop to transfer the control to the outside of the outer loop.

```
OUTER:          DO I=1, 25
                  .
INNER:             DO J=1, 125
                     .
                     IF(I+J .EQ. 70) THEN
                          EXIT OUTER
                     ENDIF
                     .
                   ENDDO INNER
                 .
                ENDDO OUTER  ←————————
```

Similarly, a CYCLE statement executed within an inner loop may begin a fresh cycle for the outer loop.

```
OUTER:          DO I=1, 25
                  .
INNER:             DO J=1, 125
                     .
                     IF(I+J .EQ. 70) THEN
                          CYCLE OUTER
                     ENDIF
                     .
                   ENDDO INNER
                 .
                ENDDO OUTER ←————————
```

4.10 Rules of DO Statement

Some of the rules of a DO loop were introduced in earlier sections. Here all the rules of the DO loop are summarized. It may be noted that the compiler may not complain if some of the rules are violated; but such violation of rule may lead to undesirable results.

(a) The loop index cannot be modified inside the loop.

(b) $m1$, $m2$ and $m3$ are integer constants or integer expressions. Earlier versions of Fortran allowed real numbers. This used to create problems. (This may be omitted during the first reading of this book.)

```
REAL :: AC
DO AC=0.1, 1.0, 0.1
  .
ENDDO
```

Since all the decimal numbers may not have exact binary representation (chapter 17, 18), 0.1 when added ten times may not give 1.0 but most likely it will return a number slightly less than 1.0, say 0.9999998. Naturally, the loop will be executed 11 times instead of 10 times and will, thus, invite logical error. If it is desired to have the value between 0.1 and 1.0 with a step 0.1, the better way to do the job would be as shown below.

```
            DO I=1, 10    ! I is an integer
              .
              AC=I/10.0 ! AC is real
!             Should be 10.0 to avoid integer division
              .
            ENDDO
```

As integers have exact binary representation, the integer control variable I will ensure that the loop will be executed exactly 10 times and AC will vary between 0.1 and 1.0 with a step 0.1.
(c) If the increment $m3$ is absent, it is assumed to be equal to 1.

```
            DO I=1, 10, 1
```

and

```
            DO I=1,10
```

are equivalent.
(d) The number of times the DO loop is executed is determined by the following expression.

```
         T=MAX((m2-m1)/m3+1,0)
```

The library function MAX returns the maximum of its arguments. The minimum value of the expression is zero. If the value of T is zero, the loop is skipped. The following DO loop is skipped, as T is zero.

```
            DO I=10, 1
              .
            ENDDO
```

(e) If $m1$, $m2$ and $m3$ are (all or any one of them) variables or expressions involving variables, the variables may be modified inside the DO loop. This modification does not change the number of iterations as this is calculated when the loop is entered for the first time using the formula mentioned in Rule (d).
(f) The increment may be negative; in that case $m1$ should be greater than or equal to $m2$ to make T greater than zero. The iteration count is zero when $m1 > m2$ and $m3 > 0$ or $m1 < m2$ and $m3 < 0$.
(g) It is prohibited to jump into a DO loop without touching the DO statement.

```
            GOTO 100      ! not allowed
              .
              .
            DO I=1, 80
              .
100         CONTINUE
              .
            ENDDO
```

The reason being that unless the DO statement is touched, proper initialization of the control variable is not performed.

(h) Jumping into the top of the DO loop from within the loop without touching the ENDDO is prohibited.

```
200          DO J=1, 100
             .
             IF(SUM.GT.100) THEN
                GOTO 200           ! not allowed
             ENDIF
             .

             .
             ENDDO
```

The control variable is modified when ENDDO is reached, which is not done in the above case.
(i) However, it is possible to jump to the top of the loop from outside the loop.

```
             GOTO 90        ! allowed
             .
90           DO K=10, 20
             .
             ENDDO
```

(j) It is not possible to jump to the terminal statement of DO from outside the DO loop.

```
             GOTO 501
             .
             DO K=1, 25
             .
501          ENDDO
```

(k) It is permissible to jump to the terminal statement of DO loop from inside the DO loop. In that case ENDDO must have a statement number; but it is really not necessary as the same thing can be done with CYCLE statement.
(l) Premature exit i.e., exit from the DO loop before exhausting all the cycles is possible.

```
             DO K=1, 75
             .
             IF (A>B) THEN      !  some condition
                GOTO 20
             .
             ENDDO
20           CONTINUE
```

On premature exit from the loop, the loop index retains its last value. For example, if in the above program segment the value of K is, say, 37 when A>B becomes true, the value of K will retain this value outside the DO loop. But on normal exit from the DO loop, loop index is considered to be undefined.

```
SUM=0
DO I=1, 100
 SUM=SUM+I
ENDDO
```

The loop index, just outside the DO loop after normal exit, should not be used without redefining the same after ENDDO.

(m) The nested loop must have different loop index (Fig 4.5), otherwise it will violate rule (a).

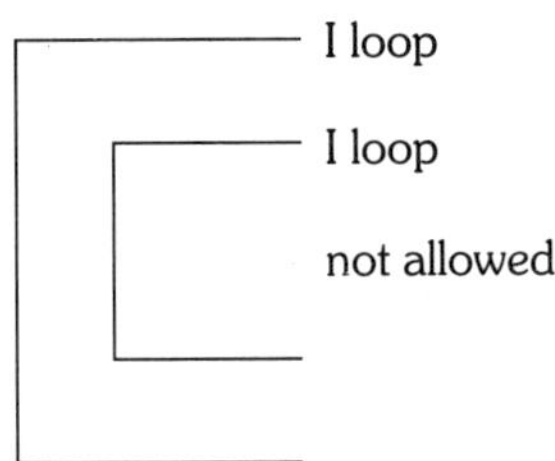

Fig. 4.5 Nested Loop (not allowed)

(n) For nested loops, the inner loop must terminate before the outer loop.

```
OUTER:        DO I=1, 20
                .
INNER:          DO J=1, 100, 2
                  .
                ENDDO OUTER      ! not allowed
              ENDDO INNER        ! not allowed

              DO 70 K=1, 45
                .
                DO 75 L=1, 40
                  .
70            CONTINUE      ! not allowed
                .
75              CONTINUE    ! not allowed
```

(o) For a numbered DO loop, the inner and outer loop may terminate at the same point (Fig 4.6).

```
              DO 10 I=1,4
                DO 10 J=1,10
                  .
                  .
10            CONTINUE
```

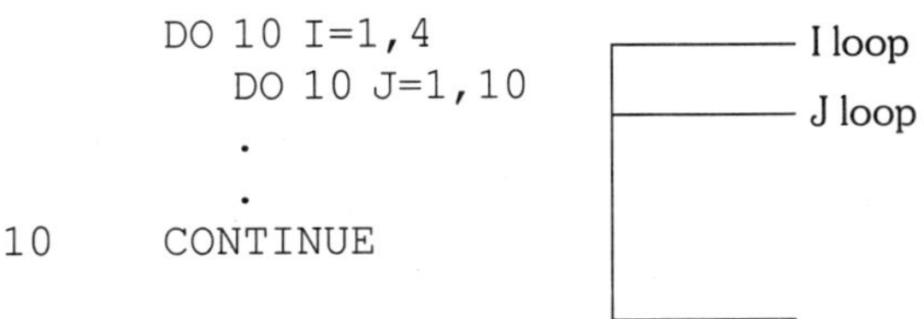

Fig 4.6 Nested DO (same terminal point)

This is not recommended. Each loop should have a separate terminal statement. The following program may invite trouble.

```
                        DO 10 I=1, 10
                         .
                         IF(I.EQ.5) GO TO 10
                         .
                        DO 10 J=1, 10
                         .
            10          CONTINUE
```

It is not clear whether the GOTO statement will transfer control to the terminal statement of inner of the outer loop – such a statement should be avoided. Some of the present day compilers do not allow such a statement.

(p) It is possible to jump from the inner loop to the outer loop and jump back to the inner loop.

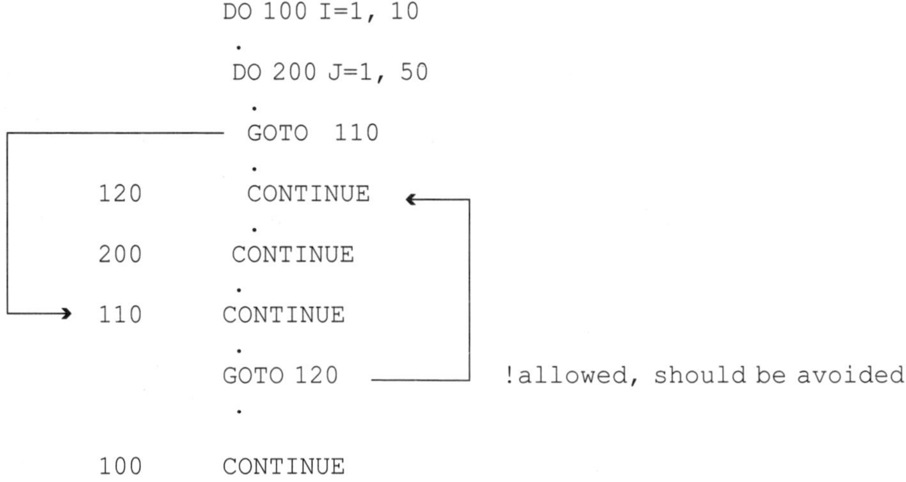

This is strongly discouraged. This is totally against the modern concept of structured programming.

(q) If a DO loop contains a CASE statement, the CASE statement must end before the ENDDO. Also if a CASE statement contains a DO, the ENDDO must come before the END SELECT.

(r) If the DO loop contains an IF statement, the IF statement must terminate before the ENDDO.

(s) If the DO statement is inside an IF statement, the DO loop must terminate before the IF statement.

4.11 Remark About Loop Statements

Since there are basically two forms of loop instruction, DO and DO WHILE, a rule of thumb may be suggested regarding the usage of these two statements. If the number of times the loop is to be executed is known before hand, DO ENDDO is used. For example, to sum the series $S=1+2+3+..+100$, it is preciously known that the loop is to be executed 100 times and therefore DO ENDDO is preferred. However, when it is not known how many times the loop is to be executed before hand,

DO WHILE is preferred. Such examples are given in section 4.7 (calculation of GCD). The number of cycles required to achieve the result is dependent on the inputs. It may be noted that the program logic can always be modified such that DO WHILE may be replaced by DO and vice versa. Moreover it is better to avoid numbered DO statements.

Chapter 5

DOUBLE PRECISION NUMBERS

Double precision quantities are real numbers but are more precise compared to their single precision counterpart. It is well known that a computer internally uses binary numbers and all decimal numbers do not have an exact binary representation. For example, when 0.1 is converted to binary, the binary number may not be exactly 0.1 – it is probably 0.09999.. . A computer is finite bit (binary digit) machine and the number of bits used determines how close the binary number is to the decimal counterpart (chapter 17,18 and 20). For infinite precision arithmetic, the two numbers would have been identical. By increasing number of bits to store a real number, the binary counterpart can be made closer to the decimal value. Double Precision numbers take more memory than the single precision numbers and consume more CPU time to perform any arithmetic operations compared to the single precision numbers.

5.1 Double Precision Constant

Double Precision constants are more precise than the corresponding single precision value. Such a constant is expressed in scientific notation. To indicate "ten to the power" for double precision constant, 'D' or 'd' is used. For example, PI, correct up to 13 decimal places, is written as:

```
3.1415926589793D0
```

The rules discussed in connection with the single precision real numbers (in scientific notation) are equally valid for the double precision quantities.

5.2 Named Double Precision Constant

A symbolic name may be attached to a double precision constant.

```
DOUBLE PRECISION, PARAMETER :: PI=3.1415926589793D0
```

In this declaration PI is a named constant whose value is a double precision quantity.

5.3 Double Precision Variable

A double precision variable can store a double precision quantity. It is declared as shown below:

```
DOUBLE PRECISION :: D1
DOUBLE PRECISION :: D3, D4
```

5.4 Initialization

A double precision variable may be initialized along with its declaration in the usual manner.

```
DOUBLE PRECISION :: PI=3.1415926589793D0
```

5.5 Arithmetic Operators

Standard arithmetic operators introduced in chapter 2 can be used to handle double precision quantities. For example, if D1, D2 and D3 are double precision variables, the following are arithmetic expressions using double precision quantities:

```
D1 = D2 + D3
D1 = 3.1415926589793D0*D2/D3
```

5.6 Mixed Mode Operation

Operations involving an integer or a real quantity with a double precision variable or constant are performed by first converting integer or real quantity into double precision. However, it must be noted that the real number, thus converted, does not become more "precise". The digits after the normal precision are meaningless. If single precision PI (3.1415927) is converted to double precision, the digits after the last digits on the right, that is, say 6 are not correct. Similarly, when a single precision expression is equated to a double precision variable, the single precision number is converted into double precision before it is stored. Again, extra digits so added to make it double precision do not have any significance. Thus, by equating a single precision number to a double precision variable, the resulted double precision number does not become more "precise" compared to the single precision number.

The precision may be illustrated by considering this program:

```
PROGRAM TESTDBL
DOUBLE PRECISION :: D1,D2
D1=2.0/3.0
D2=2.0D0/3.0D0
PRINT *, D1,D2
END
```

It is known that the result of the arithmetic operation is 0.666666666666.... . The outputs of the program (using NAG Fortran compiler) are 0.6666666861348816 and 0.66666666666666 respectively. Note that the displayed value of D1 is correct up to 7 significant figures. Consider the following program:

```
PROGRAM TESTDBL
DOUBLE PRECISION :: D1,D2
D1=3.1415926535897932
D2=3.1415926535897932D0
PRINT *, D1,D2
END
```

In absence of 'D0', 3.1415926535897932 is treated as single precision constant and additional digits after, say, 6 significant digits are removed to make it single precision constant. Again, this single precision constant, when equated to a double precision variable D1, is converted to double precision constant – but the digits so added do not have any significance. The outputs of the program are respectively: 3.1415927410125732 and 3.1415926535897931.

5.7 Input and Output

The READ and PRINT statements discussed in connection with the ordinary real variables are equally valid for double precision variables as well.

```
DOUBLE PRECISION :: D1
        .
READ *, D1
        .
PRINT *, D1
```

5.8 Double Precision Library Function

Library functions introduced in chapter 2 have their double precision counterpart. The library function SQRT may be called with a single double precision argument to calculate the square root of a double precision quantity. The name SQRT is the generic name of the square root family. Depending upon the type of the argument the compiler will generate appropriate call to the proper routine DSQRT. In fact, one can directly use DSQRT in place of SQRT when the argument is a double precision quantity. The disadvantage of this method is that if the argument is changed to real (single precision), the name of the library function is to be changed. If the generic name is used the compiler will call the appropriate routine depending upon the type of the argument. In this book we shall always use only generic names.

5.9 Programming Examples

In this section we shall calculate sin(x) using Taylor series.

$$\text{SIN}(X) = X - (X^3/3!) + (X^5/5!) - (X^7/7!) \ldots$$

From the second term onwards, the successive terms can be generated from the previous terms by multiplying the previous terms by:

$$(-X^2/2K(2K+1))$$

where K is 1 for the second term, 2 for the third term and so on. All calculations will be done in double precision mode.

```fortran
PROGRAM CALCSINE
DOUBLE PRECISION, PARAMETER :: PI=3.1415926589793D0
DOUBLE PRECISION :: SUM=0.0D0, TEMP, RAD, DEG
INTEGER:: LIMIT=20, K, INDEX=0
DOUBLE PRECISION, PARAMETER :: EPS=1.0D-8
PRINT *, 'Type the angle in Degree '
READ *, DEG
!     Convert to Radian
RAD=DEG*PI/180.0D0
SUM=RAD                          ! first term
TEMP=RAD                         ! individual term
DO K=1,LIMIT                     ! maximum 21 terms
   IF (ABS(TEMP) <= EPS) THEN
     INDEX=1                     ! converged
     EXIT
   ENDIF
   TEMP=-TEMP*RAD*RAD/(2*K*(2*K+1))
   SUM=SUM+TEMP
ENDDO
IF (INDEX.EQ.1) THEN
   PRINT *, 'Convergence achieved in ',K, &
    ' cycle ','sin(',DEG,') = ',SUM
ELSE
   PRINT *, 'Convergence not achieved '
ENDIF

END
```

The next program uses Newton-Raphson method to find the root of an equation:

$$f(x)=0$$

The technique is to start with a guess value xg. Obviously, f(xg) is not equal to zero as xg is not a root of the equation. However, one can choose a 'h' such that

$$f(xg+h)=0$$

with,
$$h = -f(xg)/fp(xg)$$

where, fp(xg) is derivative of f(xg) with respect to xg. The new value of x (actually xg), which is xg+h is then used and the whole process is repeated. This process continues till the absolute value of h becomes very small and in that case xg is the root of the equation to within EPS.

We choose,

$$f(x) = \sin(x)/x$$

so,
$$fp(x) = 1/x(\cos(x) - \sin(x)/x)$$

```
PROGRAM NEWTON
DOUBLE PRECISION:: F, FP, H=1.0D0
DOUBLE PRECISION:: XG=2.0D0, EPS=1.0E-8
DO WHILE (ABS(H)>EPS)
 F=SIN(XG)/XG
 FP=1.0D0/XG*(COS(XG)-SIN(XG)/XG)
 H=-F/FP
 XG=XG+H
ENDDO

PRINT *, 'The root is = ', XG
END
```

The library function ABS returns the absolute value (magnitude) of its argument. ABS(-5) is 5, ABS(5) is also 5. The root of the equation is the value of π or some multiple of π depending on the guess value,

Chapter 6

COMPLEX NUMBERS

Complex numbers are widely used in science and engineering. A complex number consists of two parts – real and imaginary. The Fortran compiler can handle complex numbers according to the rules of the complex algebra. The real and the imaginary parts may separately be positive, negative or zero.

6.1 Complex Constant

A complex constant consists of an ordered pair of numbers, the real and the imaginary part respectively. Both the real and the imaginary parts are integers or real numbers. The real and the imaginary pair are enclosed within brackets. The real and imaginary parts are stored as real number.

Valid complex constants are:

```
(2.0, 5.0)            (-3.373, 5.397)    (-4467.23, 891.45)
(3.124E2, -4.935E-7)  (33,25)            (-15.72, -21)
```

Since the real and the imaginary parts are real numbers, the discussions regarding real numbers are equally valid for the real and the imaginary parts respectively.

6.2 Complex Named Constant

A symbolic name may be defined in place of a complex constant.

```
COMPLEX, PARAMETER :: ZPAR=(10.0,30.0)
```

The named constant ZPAR is synonymous with the complex constant $(10.0+30.0i)$.

6.3 Complex Variable

Complex variables are defined as shown below:

```
COMPLEX :: C
COMPLEX :: X, Y
```

A complex variable can store only complex numbers. The declaration instructs the compiler to reserve locations for the variable. However, no value is assigned to the variable. Storage requirement of a complex variable is twice than that of the corresponding real variable. Either or both the real part or the imaginary part may be zero. The real and the imaginary part of a complex variable may be a double precision quantity also.

```
DOUBLE COMPLEX :: DC1
DOUBLE COMPLEX :: DC2, DC3
```

The space between DOUBLE and COMPLEX is optional. Double Complex variables will be discussed in details in chapter 10.

6.4 Assignment

A complex constant may be assigned to a complex variable through the library function CMPLX. This library function takes two arguments – the first one becomes the real part and the second one becomes the imaginary part of the complex variable.

```
COMPLEX :: C
     .
C=CMPLX(2.0,3.0)
```

This assigns 2.0 and 3.0 to the real and the imaginary parts of C respectively (C=2.0+3.0i).

6.5 Initialization

A complex number may be initialized along with its declaration in the usual manner.

```
COMPLEX :: Z1=(10.0, 20.0)
```

This initializes the real part of Z1 to 10.0 and the imaginary part to 20.0.
    The library function CMPLX may also be used to initialize a complex variable.

```
COMPLEX ::C=CMPLX(3.0,4.0)
```

It is also possible to use named constants as real or imaginary part.

```
REAL, PARAMETER :: RE=4.0
REAL, PARAMETER :: IM=5.0
COMPLEX :: C=(RE, IM)
```

    The NAG Fortran compiler does not support this feature.

6.6 Arithmetic Operators

All the arithmetic operators defined in chapter 2 are applicable to complex numbers as well. However, arithmetic operations follow the rules of complex algebra. For example, if C1, C2 and C3 are complex variables with

```
C1=CMPLX(2.0, 3.0)
C2=CMPLX(4.0, 5.0)
```

then,

$$C3=C1+C2$$

would yield the real part of C3 as 6.0 and the imaginary part of C3 as 8.0.

In mixed mode operation involving an integer or a real with a complex quantity, the integer or the real is converted to a complex number with the imaginary part set to zero. Thus, C*2.0 where C is complex variable will be calculated as C * CMPLX(2.0, 0.0). In a similar way, when a real or an integer is equated to a complex variable, the real or the integer becomes the real part of the complex variable with zero as the imaginary part.

In arithmetic operations involving a double precision real and a complex variable, the double precision variable is first converted into a double complex number (both the real and the imaginary parts are double precision quantity). Subsequently, the complex variable is converted into double complex number. The result is a double complex number.

The may be verified with the help of the following program:

```
DOUBLE PRECISION :: D=2.1234567891234D0
COMPLEX :: C=(2.0, 3.0)
PRINT *, D+C
END
```

6.7 Relational Operators

The relational operators .LT., .LE., .GT., .GE. cannot be used for comparison between two complex numbers or variables. Only .EQ. (equal) and .NE. (not equal) may be used to compare two complex numbers or variables.

Two complex numbers are said to be equal if both the real and the imaginary parts are separately equal. If Z1 and Z2 are complex variables with,

```
Z1=CMPLX(2.0, 3.0)
Z2=CMPLX(2.0, 3.0)
```

then Z1 and Z2 are equal since their real and imaginary parts are separately equal. However, the following complex variables C1 and C2 where,

```
C1=CMPLX(3.0, 4.0)
C2=CMPLX(4.0, 3.0)
```

are not equal since their real and imaginary parts are separately not equal.

6.8 Input Output

The READ and PRINT statements can be used for complex variables also. As the complex number consists of two parts, two numbers are to be supplied during the input operation for each complex variable. Similarly, two numbers are displayed in the output operation. The first and the second numbers correspond to the real and the imaginary parts respectively. The data in response to the

READ statement is supplied as (r, i), where r is the real part and i is the imaginary part.

```
COMPLEX :: C1
    .
READ *, C1
```

If the data supplied from the terminal is (2.0, 3.0), 2.0+3.0i will be assigned to C1. Similarly,

```
PRINT *, C1
```

will display the real and the imaginary parts within brackets.

6.9 Library Functions

The library function REAL can be used to extract the real part of a complex variable.

```
COMPLEX :: Z, W
REAL :: R, IM
Z=CMPLX(10.0, 20.0)
R=REAL(Z)      !      R=10.0
```

The library function AIMAG can extract the imaginary part of the complex number.

```
IM=AIMAG(Z)   !      IM=20.0
```

The library function CONJG takes a complex variable as its argument and returns the complex conjugate of its argument.

```
W=CONJG(Z)
```

The real part of W is the same as the real part of Z, but the imaginary part is equal to the negative of the imaginary part of Z. Thus, in the above example the real part of W is 10.0 and the imaginary part of W is - 20.0.

6.10 Programming Example

The following program calculates the roots of a quadratic equation. The problem is so chosen that the roots are complex numbers. The library function SQRT is called by its generic name, so that the compiler will substitute the exact name CSQRT to calculate the square root of the complex number.

```
PROGRAM COMQUARD
COMPLEX:: ROOT1, ROOT2, DISCR
REAL :: A, B, C, TWOA
A=1.0
B=-4.0
C=13.0
DISCR=CMPLX(B*B-4.0*A*C, 0.0)
TWOA=1.0/(2.0*A)
DISCR=SQRT(DISCR)
ROOT1=(-B+DISCR)*TWOA
ROOT2=(-B-DISCR)*TWOA
PRINT *, 'The roots are :', ROOT1, ROOT2
END
```

The roots of the equation are (2 + 3i) and (2- 3i) respectively.

Chapter 7

LOGICALS

This chapter deals with logical constants, variables and expressions. Integer and real quantities can assume innumerable values. Logical quantities, on the other hand, can assume only two values – true and false.

7.1 Logical Constant

There are only two logical constants – .TRUE. and .FALSE.. These constants are bound by two periods. Lower case letters may also be used like .true. and .false..

7.2 Logical Variable

A logical variable can store only logical quantity having either true of false value. A logical variable is declared as shown below:

```
LOGICAL :: L1
LOGICAL :: L2
LOGICAL :: L3, L4
```

The declaration, like other type declarations, merely reserves location for a variable. No value is assigned to the variable.

7.3 Named Constant

A symbolic name may be attached to a logical constant. This has been discussed in details in chapter 1 for the real and the integer constants.

```
LOGICAL, PARAMETER :: L3=.TRUE.
LOGICAL, PARAMETER :: L4=.FALSE.
```

L3 and L4 are named logical constants which are synonymous to logical constants .TRUE. and .FALSE. respectively.

7.4 Logical Expression

A logical expression is formed by using constants, variables, arithmetic, relational and logical operators (to be discussed in the next section).

A logical variable may be assigned to a value by means of logical expression:

```
L = .TRUE.
X = .FALSE.
!           L and X are logical variables.
L = A>B        !      A and B are integers
X = P==Q       !      P and Q are integers
```

The meaning of the first two expressions is obvious. For the third expressions, if A is greater than B, true value will be assigned to L. It not, false value will be assigned to L. Similarly, X is set to true or false, depending on whether P is equal to Q or not. Note that neither A nor B are logical – the result A>B is logical.

7.5 Logical Operator

There are five logical operators. All these logical operator are bound by periods.

Table 7.1. Logical Operators

Operator	Meaning
.NOT.	Logical negation
.AND.	Logical conjunction
.OR.	Logical inclusive disjunction
.EQV.	Logical equivalence
.NEQV.	Logical non-equivalence

The logical operator .NOT. is logical negation. It changes true to false and vice versa.

```
.NOT. (A>B)
```

is true if A is not greater than B, that is, A>B is false. It is false if A is greater that B, that is, A>B is true.

```
L = .NOT. (A>B)
```

true value is assigned to L if A is not greater than B.

The logical operator .AND. is logical conjunction. If L1 and L2 are logical,

```
L1 .AND. L2
```

is true if both L1 and L2 are true. It is false if one of them or both are false.

```
L = A>B .AND. P<Q
```

L is true if A is greater than B and at the same time P is less than Q. Otherwise it is false.
The operator for the logical inclusive disjunction is .OR.. If L1 and L2 are logical variable,

```
L1 .OR. L2
```

is true if either L1 or L2 or both are true. It is false, if both of them are false.

```
L = A<=B .OR. P==Q
```

L is true if either A is less than or equal to B or P is equal to Q, that is, one or both the relations are true. It is false only when both are false.
The logical operator .EQV. stands for logical equivalence. If L1 and L2 are logical,

```
L1 .EQV. L2
```

is true if both L1 and L2 are true or both L1 and L2 are false.

```
L = A .EQ. B .EQV. P.NE.Q
```

is true if both the logical expressions are true or both the logical expressions are false.
Finally, the logical operator .NEQV. is logical non-equivalence. If both L1 and L2 are logical,

```
L1 .NEQV. L2
```

is true if either L1 or L2 is true. It is false if both L1 and L2 are true or both L1 and L2 are false.

```
L = A>B .NEQV. P<=Q
```

is true if one of the logical expression is true. It is false otherwise.
If L1 and L2 are logical, the Table 7.2 shows the results of various logical operations.

Table 7.2 Truth Table

L1	L2	.NOT. L2	L1 .AND. L2	L1 .OR. L2	L1 .EQV. L2	L1 .NEQV. L2
T	T	F	T	T	T	F
T	F	T	F	T	F	T
F	T	F	F	T	F	T
F	F	T	F	F	T	F

[T stands for True and F stands for False]

A logical expression may contain any number of logical operators.

7.6 Priority Rule

The priority of the logical operators is lower than that of the relational operators. Among the logical operators, the priority, high to low, is shown below:

High	.NOT.
↓	.AND.
↓	.OR.
Low	.EQV., .NEQV.

The priority of .EQV. and .NEQV. is same. We now include the logical operators and redraw the priority table (Table 7.3).

Consider the expression:

```
L = A .GT. B .OR. P .LE. Q .AND. R .EQ. S
```

The expression is evaluated as,

```
L = A .GT. B .OR. (P. LE. Q .AND. R. EQ. S)
```

as the priority of AND is greater than that of OR. Thus L is true if either A is greater than B or both the conditions P<=Q and R==S are true.

Table 7.3 Priority of Operators

Priority	Symbol	Meaning
High	**	Exponentiation
	*, /	Multiplication, Division
	+, -	Unary plus, Unary minus
	+, -	Binary Addition and Subtraction
	.LT., .LE., .GT., .GE., .EQ., .NE.	Relational operator
	.NOT.	Logical negation
↓	.AND.	Logical conjunction
	.OR.	Logical inclusive disjunction
	.EQV., .NEQV.	Logical equivalence, non-equivalence
Low	=	Assignment

7.7 Input

To read a logical variable from the keyboard,

```
READ *, L    !        L is a logical variable
```

is to be used. The data must be of the following type:

.TRUE. or TRUE for the true value and .FALSE. or FALSE (small letters are also allowed) for the false value. In addition to this if, the first non-blank character is T or F (upper or lower case) or a period followed by T or F (upper or lower case), true or false value are respectively, read in. Note that, if TREU (intentional spelling mistake) is typed in place of TRUE, true value is assumed because the first non-blank character is T.

7.8 Output

PRINT *, L where L is a logical quantity or expression displays either T or F depending on whether L is true of false. Examples of PRINT statements are:

```
LOGICAL :: L
INTEGER :: A, B, C, D, E, F
.
PRINT *, L
PRINT *, A>B
PRINT *, (C .LE. D .AND. E .GT. F)
.
```

7.9 IF, DO and the Logical Operator

The relational operators and the logical operators may be combined to form a complicated condition, which can be used with IF and DO statements:

```
.
IF (A>B .AND. P<Q) THEN
.
ENDIF
.
IF (A==B .OR. (P<Q  .AND. R .LE. S)) THEN
.
ENDIF
.
DO WHILE (I/=1 .AND. COUNT <=100)
.
END DO
```

It may be noted that,

```
IF (A>B) THEN
.
ENDIF
```

and

```
L = A>B        !      L  is a logical variable
IF(L) THEN
.
ENDIF
```

are equivalent.

The time period of rotation of the Earth around the Sun is not exactly 365 days (1 year). Therefore, a correction in the form of increasing a day for the month of February once in four years is required. This particular year is called a leap year. However, the centennial years (like 1900) are not leap years but centennial years divisible by 400 (like 2000) are leap years.

```fortran
INTEGER :: YEAR
READ *, YEAR
IF (MOD(YEAR,4).EQ.0 .AND. (MOD(YEAR,100) .NE.0 .OR. &
        MOD(YEAR,400).EQ.0)) THEN
  PRINT *, YEAR, " is a leap year"
ELSE
  PRINT *, YEAR, " is not a leap year"
ENDIF
END
```

Note that in this case the brackets within the IF statement is required as the priority of AND is more than the priority of OR.

We shall now rewrite the program of reducing any positive integer to 1 given in chapter 4. The defect of the previous program was that in case the program failed to converge for some reason, the loop would become infinite. It is always desirable to have a check on the iteration process so that after a reasonable number of iterations, the program stops if it fails to converge. It is desirable that similar DO WHILE loops should always have a check so that it always terminates after a finite number of cycles. The program, given below, would stop after 200 iterations, if it fails to converge.

```fortran
PROGRAM REDUCE
INTEGER :: NUM, COUNT= 1
INTEGER, PARAMETER :: LIMIT=200

!       Read the number
PRINT *, 'Type one positive integer '
READ *, NUM
DO WHILE (NUM /= 1.AND. COUNT <=LIMIT)
  IF(MOD(NUM,2) /=0) THEN
    NUM = 3*NUM + 1      !        odd
  ELSE
    NUM = NUM/2
  ENDIF
  COUNT=COUNT+1
  PRINT *,NUM
ENDDO
!       Come here if NUM=1 or COUNT >LIMIT
IF (NUM == 1) THEN
  PRINT *, 'Convergence achieved in ', &
```

```
      COUNT,' cycles:', ' Num = ',NUM
   ELSE
    PRINT *, 'Convergence not achieved in ', &
      COUNT, ' cycles -- ',' Num = ',NUM
   ENDIF


   END
```

The program fails to converge if either there is a logical error in the program or more cycles are required. In the first case the logical error is to be removed and in the second case, it would be necessary to increase the value of the variable LIMIT.

7.10 CASE and Logical Variable

The control variable of a CASE statement may a logical variable. In this case different paths may be chosen according to the value of the logical variable (true or false).

```
      LOGICAL :: L1
        .
      SELECT CASE (L1)
         CASE(.TRUE.)
    !          This path if L1 is true

           .

           .
         CASE (.FALSE.)
    !          This path if L1 is false

           .

           .
      END SELECT
```

7.11 Ordering of Logical Operator

Consider this expression:

```
      A > B .AND. P < Q
```

Some compilers are smart enough to return this result false if the first expression is false without evaluating the second expression. Similarly, there is no need to evaluate the second logical expression:

```
      A > B .OR. P < Q
```

if the first logical expression is true. Similar could be the cases for other logical operators.

When two conditions are connected by AND, and if it is known that the frequency of one condition being false is more than the other, this condition should be placed as the first condition to be tested to increase the execution speed (no need to check the second condition if the first is false). Similarly, when two conditions are connected by OR and if it is known that the frequency of one condition being true is more than the other, this condition should be placed as the first condition to be tested (the need to test the second condition does not arise when the first condition is true).

Chapter 8

CHARACTER HANDLING

The ASCII character set was introduced in chapter 1. In fact, Fortran supports other character sets thereby permitting the use of characters from other 'languages'. However, in this book we shall stick only to the ASCII character set.

8.1 Character Constant

Character constants are zero or more characters enclosed within quotes or apostrophes. Examples of character constants are:

```
'A'
'ABC'
' '
"West Bengal"
```

Note that blank is also a character (blank between West and Bengal). The character 'A' and 'a' are not same. It is case sensitive. Also character '1' and number 1 are different and they are stored in different ways inside the machine. Conventional arithmetic operations are not permitted with the character constant like '1'. To represent apostrophe as a character constant either two successive apostrophes are used or it is enclosed within quotes:

```
'don''t'
"don't"
```

Similarly, to represent quote as a character constant either two successive quotes are used or it is enclosed within apostrophes:

```
""""
'"'
```

Null is represented as two successive apostrophes (or quotes) with nothing in between.

8.2 Character Variable

Character variables are declared as shown below:

```
CHARACTER :: C
CHARACTER :: E, F
```

By default, the number of characters that a character variable can store is 1, that is, the length is 1. A character variable may store more than one character if it is declared in an appropriate manner.

```
CHARACTER (LEN=10) :: C
```

The variable C can store 10 characters. The length can also be specified as:

```
CHARACTER *10 C
```

but this type of declaration is expected to be de-implemented in the future version of Fortran. So this will not be used in this book.

8.3 Named Constants

A character named constant is defined using parameter attribute:

```
CHARACTER, PARAMETER :: START= 'A'
```

For a character named constant, an asterisk may be used as the length of the named constant; the compiler from the declaration can find out the length of the named constant (allocates locations to store the constant).

```
CHARACTER (LEN=*), PARAMETER :: CITY= 'KOLKATA'
```

From the declaration the compiler can ascertain that the named constant CITY should have a length 7 to accommodate the string 'KOLKATA' and allocates locations accordingly. The above declaration is equivalent to:

```
CHARACTER (LEN=7), PARAMETER :: CITY= 'KOLKATA'
```

8.4 Initialization

A character variable may be initialized along with its declaration.

```
CHARACTER (LEN=4) :: INST= 'IACS'
```

The variable INST is a character variable of size 4. It is initialized to 'IACS'

8.5 Continuation of Character Strings

It was mentioned in chapter 1 that if the last non-blank character in a normal line is '&', the next line is treated as the continuation of the previous line. Normally, Fortran ignores blanks. Blank is considered as a character within a character string. So special consideration is needed for continuing a character string to the next line. For this purpose, an ampersand character ('&') must be the last non-blank character of the first line of the character string and each continuation line must have an ampersand character. Continuation begins form the character following the ampersand of the continuation line. Consider the following:

C	H	A	R	A	C	T	E	R	(		L	E	N		=		8	0	)		:		:		C	H		=		&			
"	A	S	S	O	C	I	A	T	I		O	N			O	F			V	O	L	U	N	T	A	R	Y		&				
&						B	L	O	O	D			D	O	N	O	R	S	"														

The variable CH is initialized along with its declaration. Line 2 and 3 are continuation of line 1. We consider lines 2 and 3. As the continuation starts from the first character of a line (in this case line 3), six blanks will be added before the string "BLOOD DONORS". The character variable CH will be initialized to:

```
"ASSOCIATION OF VOLUNTARY^^^^^^BLOOD DONORS"
```

where ' ^ ' represents blank. However, if the intention of the programmer to initialize the variable to:

```
"ASSOCIATION OF VOLUNTARY BLOOD DONORS"
```

that is, only one blank between 'VOLUNTARY' and 'BLOOD', the third line should also have an ampersand character as shown below:

C	H	A	R	A	C	T	E	R	(L	E	N		=		8	0	)		:		:		C	H		=		&				
"	A	S	S	O	C	I	A	T	I	O	N			O	F			V	O	L	U	N	T	A	R	Y		&				
			&		B	L	O	O	D		D	O	N	O	R	S		"														

The ampersand in the third line ensures that continuation starts from the character following the ampersand which is just a blank in this case.

If a keyword or other attributes of the language (technically called token) is split across the line for which no embedded blank is allowed, there should not be any space between the ampersand and the rest of the token in the continued line as shown below.

```
RE&
&AD *, A
```

The above is treated as READ *, A. Note that the position of the ampersand in this case ensures that there is no space between 'RE' and 'AD'

8.6 Assignment

The general rules for assignment are applicable to characters also. A character variable may be assigned to a character expression:

```
CHARACTER (LEN=6) :: CH
          .
CH= 'ABCDEF'
```

| A | B | C | D | E | F |

If the number of characters on the right hand side of the assignment sign is less than the number of characters that the variable can accommodate, blanks are added to the right.

```
CH = 'ABCD'
```

| A | B | C | D | | |

If there are more characters on the right hand side of the assignment sign than the variable can store, it is truncated from the right.

```
CH = 'PQRSTUVW'
```

| P | Q | R | S | T | U |

is stored as 'PQRSTU' as the variable can store only 6 characters. The next program is a slight modification of a similar program discussed in chapter 3. It converts marks to grade.

```
PROGRAM MARK2GRADE
INTEGER :: MARK
CHARACTER :: GRADE
PRINT *,'Type a positive number between 0 and 100 '
READ *, MARK
IF (MARK > 90) THEN
   GRADE= 'A'
ELSE IF (MARK >=80) THEN
      GRADE='B'
ELSE IF (MARK >= 70) THEN
      GRADE='C'
ELSE IF (MARK >= 60) THEN
      GRADE='D'
ELSE
   GRADE='F'
ENDIF
PRINT *, 'Mark = ', MARK, 'Grade = ', GRADE

END
```

8.7 Concatenation

Two or more character variables or constants or their combinations may be concatenated (joined) by the concatenation operator, which is denoted by two successive division sign (//).

```
'abc' // 'def'
```

would become 'abcdef'.

Some more examples of concatenation are given below:

```
CHARACTER (LEN=10) :: FULLNAME
CHARACTER (LEN=5) :: NAME
    .
NAME= 'Piku'
FULLNAME=NAME // 'Ray'
```

The maximum number of characters that a variable can store is fixed and is governed by the declaration. Therefore, when characters are appended as shown above, care must be taken so that truncation on the right does not occur. In the above example the variable NAME is assigned to 'Piku' (system has added one blank at the end). Subsequently, when 'Ray' is appended with NAME the value of the variable FULLNAME becomes 'Piku ^ Ray ^ ^' with two blanks at the end. The priority of the concatenation operator is lower than that of addition or subtraction (binary) operator but is higher than that of the relational operator.

```
CHARACTER (LEN=2) :: CH= 'pq'

IF ('a' // 'b' .EQ. CH) THEN
    .
ENDIF
```

Since the priority of the concatenation operator is more than the relational operator, 'a' and 'b' are joined to form 'ab' and subsequently it is compared with the character variable CH. We now update the priority table by incorporating the concatenation operator (Table 8.1).

Table 8.1 Priority of Operators

Priority		Symbol	Meaning
High		**	Exponentiation
		*, /	Multiplication, Division
		+, -	Unary plus, Unary minus
		+, -	Binary Addition and Subtraction
		//	Concatenation
		.LT., .LE., .GT., .GE., .EQ., .NE.	Relational operator
		.NOT.	Logical negation
		.AND.	Logical conjunction
		.OR.	Logical inclusive disjunction
		.EQV., .NEQV.	Logical equivalence, non-equivalence
Low		=	Assignment

8.8 Input / Output

The READ and PRINT statements discussed in the earlier chapters can also be used for characters also. It is necessary to enclose the data with apostrophes (or quotes) when the data contains leading or trailing or embedded blanks. If the data does not contain leading or trailing or embedded blanks, apostrophes are optional. To be on the safe side, it is always better to enclose the data within apostrophes.

```
CHARACTER (LEN=20) :: CH
.
READ *, CH
PRINT *, CH
.
```

If the data is Indian ^ Association, 'Indian' is stored in CH because blank between 'Indian' and 'Association' prevents reading the data beyond 'Indian'. Here blank acts as a separator. So the PRINT statement will print 'Indian' (without the apostrophe). If the data is enclosed within apostrophes, CH becomes 'Indian ^ Association'. If the data corresponding to READ statement is:

^ ^ ^ Indian

where, as usual ' ^ ' stands for blank, the variable CH will be assigned to blank as the second blank acts a separator. However, if it is desired that CH should be assigned exactly like the data, the data must be enclosed with apostrophes.

8.9 Collating Sequence

The question whether a particular character is 'greater than' or 'less than' another character is determined by the collating sequence. In the ASCII character set, the sequence number starts with zero and goes up to 127. A character, which has a sequence number 65, is 'less' than a character having sequence number 66. The sequence number is actually the internal representation of the character in integer. Generally speaking, character 'A' is less than character 'B'. If the characters are arranged in ascending order, the character 'A' will come before the character 'B'. Also character '0' is less than character '1'. The following sequence is always maintained.

$$'A' < 'B' < 'C' \dots \qquad \dots < 'Z'$$
$$'a' < 'b' < 'c' \dots \qquad \dots < 'z'$$
$$'0' < '1' < '2' \dots \qquad \dots < '9'$$

Appendix A contains a list of all characters in the ASCII character set and their collating sequence. Characters having collating sequence number greater than 127 are processor dependent. Fortran supports other types of characters (Unicode). A discussion on other character sets is outside the scope of this book. If the program depends on the absolute value of a character in the collating sequence, the program may not behave properly in a machine that uses a character set other than ASCII.

8.10 Character Comparison

Characters can be compared by means of relational operators:

```
CHARACTER:: C1, C2
      .

C1 = 'X'
C2 = 'A'
IF (C1 > C2) THEN
      .
ELSE
      .
ENDIF
```

In the above example, since 'X' appears later than 'A' in the collating sequence, C1 is greater than C2 and 'THEN' path is chosen.

8.11 Comparison of Character Strings

Two character strings may be lexically compared. If they are not of equal length blanks are added at the end of the shorter string to make the length of the two strings equal. Two strings are said to be 'equal' if each of the characters of the first string is exactly identical to the corresponding character of the second string. For example, the following pair of strings are 'equal'.

'ABCD' and 'ABCD'

'pq^ ^' and 'pq'

where '^' indicates blank. In the second case the second string is shorter than the first string and therefore, it is extended by adding two blanks at the tail. The first unmatched character of the two strings determines the question of whether one string is greater or less than the other string. The string having the first unmatched character less in the collating sequence is less than the other string.

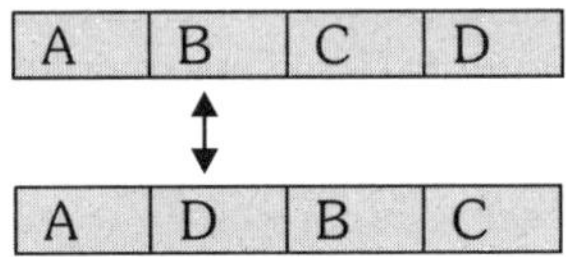

For example, 'ABCD' is less than 'ADBC' as the first unmatched character (second character) of the first string is ('B') is less than the corresponding character ('D') of the second string. Note that 'less' or 'greater' is determined by the first unmatched character. Characters beyond the first unmatched character are not considered.

8.12 Lexical Comparison Functions

Fortran provides four lexical comparison functions. All these functions take two strings as arguments. They are LLT, LLE, LGT and LGE. In subsequent discussions of this section, $str-1$ and $str-2$ refer to two different strings.

LLT($str-1$, $str-2$) returns true if $str-1$ is less than $str-2$; otherwise it returns false.

LLE(*str-1*, *str-2*) returns true if *str-1* is less than or equal to *str-2*; otherwise it returns false.

LGT(*str-1*, *str-2*) returns true if *str-1* is greater than *str-2*; otherwise it returns false.

LGE(*str-1*, *str-2*) returns true if *str-1* is greater than or equal to *str-2*; otherwise it returns false.

The IF statement may be used along with the lexical comparison function.

```
LOGICAL :: L1
CHARACTER (LEN=6) :: C1, C2
.
IF (LLT(C1, C2)) THEN
  .
ELSE
  .
ENDIF
.
L1 = LLT(C1, C2)
IF (L1) THEN
  .
ENDIF
```

8.13 Length of a String

The library function LEN takes one string as its argument and returns an integer as the length of the string.

```
INTEGER :: LENGTH
LENGTH=LEN ('abcd')              ! length is 4
LENGTH=LEN ('UVWX^^^^')          ! length is 8
```

LEN can return the length of a character variable even if it is not defined. In that case the length is the number of characters the variable can store.

```
INTEGER :: I
CHARACTER (LEN=10) :: CH
I=LEN(CH)    ! I=10
```

Even before the character variable is initialized, the LEN function returns 10 as the length of the string because by definition the variable CH can hold 10 characters.

The library function LEN_TRIM takes one character string or a character variable as its argument and returns an integer as the length of the string without the trailing blanks.

```
INTEGER :: I
.
I = LEN_TRIM ('ABCD')            ! I=4
I = LEN_TRIM ('ABCDE^^^')        ! I=5
```

In the second example LEN_TRIM returns 5 as the length of the string since trailing blanks are not considered while calculating the length of the string. However, it is obvious that embedded blanks are considered while calculating the length of the string using LEN_TRIM.

```
I = LEN_TRIM ('ABCD^^EF^^^^')            ! I=8
```

In this case LEN_TRIM returns 8 – the embedded blanks are included for the calculation of the length of the string.

8.14 Trimming and Adjusting a String

Three library functions are available to trim a string. They are TRIM, ADJUSTL and ADJUSTR.

TRIM takes a string or character variable as its argument and returns a string without the trailing blanks. This function is especially useful when it is necessary to join two strings after removing trailing blanks.

```
CHARACTER (LEN=15) :: NAME, TITLE
CHARACTER (LEN=20) :: FNAME
NAME = 'Soumya'
TITLE = 'Chakravarti'
FNAME = TRIM (NAME) // ' ' // TRIM (TITLE)
```

NAME:

TITLE:

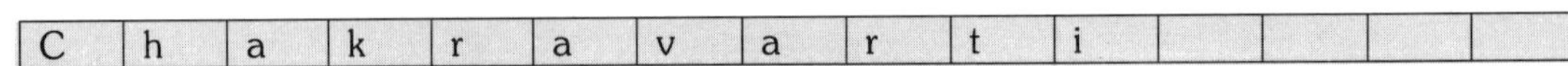

FNAME:

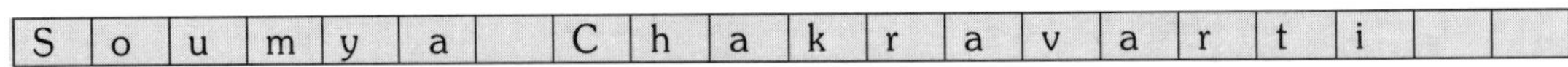

The TRIM function will remove all the trailing blanks after "Soumya". This is then concatenated with a blank and then with the string "Chakravarti". The variable FNAME will have two blanks at the end because FNAME can accommodate 20 characters and the total length of the string on the right hand side of assignment sign is 18.

The library function ADJUSTL takes an identical argument as above. It removes the leading blanks and adds these blanks at the end.

```
CHARACTER (LEN=10) :: NAME
NAME = '^^^^Soumya'        ! 4 blanks at the beginning
NAME =  ADJUSTL (NAME)     ! NAME = 'Soumya^^^^'
```

Before:

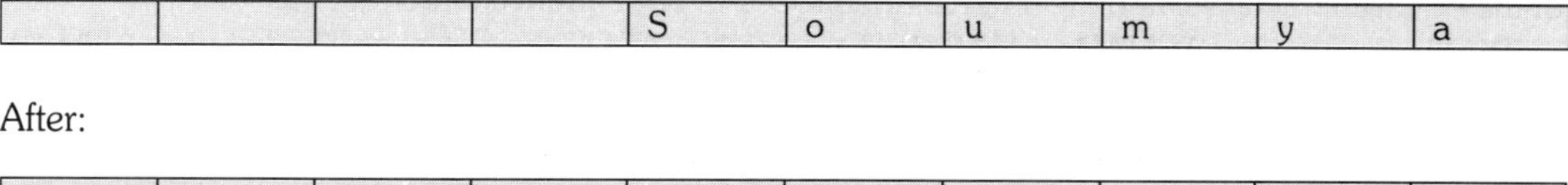

After:

This function, therefore, makes a string left adjusted keeping the length of the string same.

The function ADJUSTR makes a string right adjusted, that is, it removes the trailing blanks and adds the same in front of the string.

```
NAME = 'Subrata^^^'          ! 3 blanks at the end
NAME = ADJUSTR (NAME)        ! NAME='^^^Subrata'
```

Before:

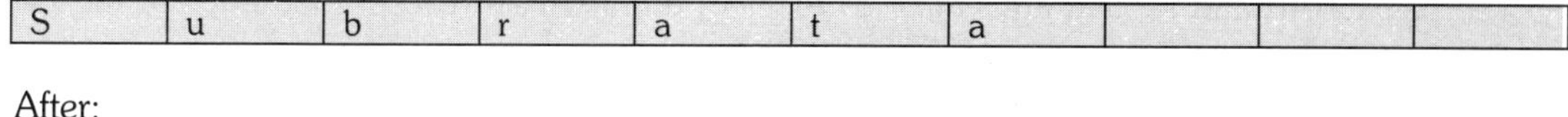

After:

The variable NAME now contains "^ ^ ^Subrata".

8.15 REPEAT

The library function REPEAT takes two arguments, a string or character variable and an integer count. It returns a string with the input string concatenated repeat count times. If the repeat count is zero, it returns a null string.

```
REPEAT ('pqr', 3)
```

returns 'pqrpqrpqr'.

Before   After

The repeat count must be positive.

8.16 Character – Integer Conversion

In character–integer conversion, an integer may be "converted" into a character according to its position in the collating sequence. Similarly, a character may be converted into an integer where its position in the collating sequence is returned as an integer. There are two sets of these functions – one for the ASCII character set and the other for the processor dependent character set.

The library function ACHAR and IACHAR are used for ASCII character set. The function ACHAR takes one integer between 0 and 127 as its argument and returns the corresponding character (len=1) in the collating sequence.

```
CHARACTER :: CH
INTEGER :: IC=99
CH=ACHAR(IC)
```

The value returned is 'X'.

Similarly, if Ch='A'

```
IC = IACHAR(CH)
```

will return 65.

The pair CHAR and ICHAR are similar to ACHAR and IACHAR except that they are for the processor dependent character set.

If the system is using the ASCII character set, these two pairs are same.

8.17 Character Substring

A single or a group of contiguous characters may be referenced from a character string using character substring representation by providing the start and end positions of the substring within the string. The positions are indicated by integers or integer expressions. A colon separates the start and the end positions. The lower bound must be greater than or equal to 1 and the upper bound must be less than or equal to the length of the character string.

```
CHARACTER (LEN=15):: C1,C2,C3
CHARACTER(LEN=49):: C= &
&"Indian Association for the Cultivation of Science"
```

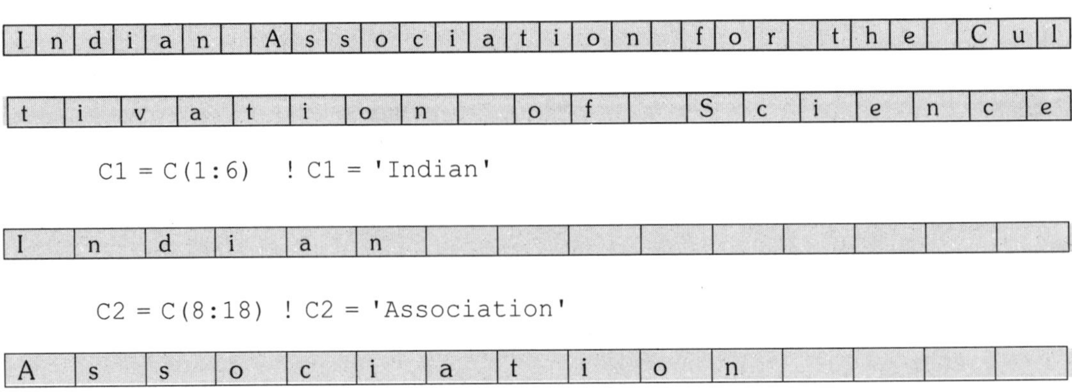

```
C1 = C(1:6)   ! C1 = 'Indian'
```

```
C2 = C(8:18)  ! C2 = 'Association'
```

```
C3 = C(20:30)        !C3 = 'for the Cul'
```

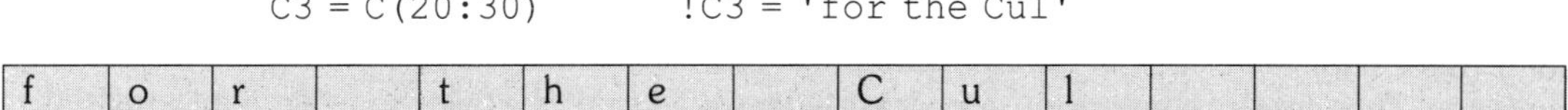

If the lower bound is not supplied, it is assumed to be 1, that is, the beginning of the string.

```
        C1 = C ( : 6)        !C1 = 'Indian'
and,    C1 = C (1: 6)
```

are equivalent.

It the upper bound is not supplied, it is assumed to be the end of the string.

```
        C3 = C (40:  )       ! C3 ='of Science'
```

It is perhaps obvious that C(:) refers to the entire string. Also C (I : I) refers to the Ith character of the string.

If the starting value is greater than the end value, a null string is returned.

```
        I = 10
        J = 8
        C1 = C (I : J)
```

will return a null string.

The substring may appear on the left hand side of assignment sign also.

```
        CHARACTER (LEN=13) :: BLD = "Blood Volume^"
        .
        BLD (7:13) = 'Storage'
```

Before:

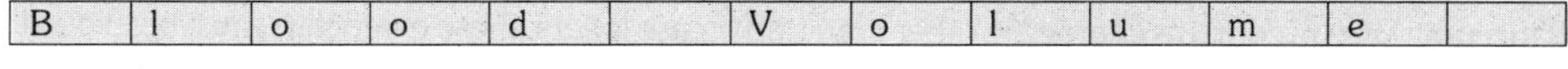

After:

The character positions 7 to 13 of BLD have been replaced. Note that character positions 1 to 6 remain unchanged.

8.18 Programming Examples

The following program reads a character string and converts all the upper case letters to the corresponding lower case letters. The programming trick is that we know:

```
        'A' < 'B' < 'C' .....        ..... < 'Z'
        'a' < 'b' < 'c' .....        ..... < 'z'
```

and the relative position of any upper case letter with respect to 'A' in the collating sequence is the same as the relative position of the corresponding lower case letter with respect to 'a' in the collating sequence. Therefore, to convert any upper case letter say 'D' to 'd', the following statement is utilized.

```
ACHAR (IACHAR ('D') - IACHAR ('A') + IACHAR ('a'))
```

IACHAR('D') - IACHAR('A') will give the relative position of 'D' with respect to 'A', which is 3. This, when added to IACHAR('a') and converted to character by ACHAR, gives the character 'd'. Note that, the absolute value of 'D', 'A' and 'a' in the collating sequence nor the numerical value of the difference between 'A' and 'a' in the collating sequence (actually 32) are not required.

```
PROGRAM UP2LOW
CHARACTER (LEN=1) :: ASMALL= 'a', ACAP = 'A'
CHARACTER (LEN=80) :: BUF
INTEGER :: SIZ, I
READ *, BUF
!    Assume for simplicity that it contains only
!    upper case letters
SIZ = LEN_TRIM (BUF)
PRINT *,BUF(1:SIZ)
DO I=1, SIZ
BUF(I:I)=ACHAR(IACHAR(BUF(I:I)) - IACHAR(ACAP)+ &
     IACHAR(ASMALL)) ! see table below
ENDDO
PRINT *,BUF(1:SIZ)
END
```

1	2	3	4
A	B	C	D
a	b	c	d

If the input stream contains characters other than upper case letters, these characters must be allowed to pass through and only upper case letters are to be changed. For this purpose, it would be necessary to modify the DO loop slightly.

```
PROGRAM UP2LOW
CHARACTER (LEN=1) :: ASMALL= 'a', ACAP = 'A',CT
CHARACTER (LEN=80) :: BUF
INTEGER :: SIZ, I
READ *, BUF
SIZ = LEN_TRIM (BUF)
PRINT *,BUF(1:SIZ)
DO I=1, SIZ
CT=BUF(I:I)
!    Convert if it is an upper case letter
IF (CT >= 'A' .AND. CT <= 'Z') THEN
   BUF(I:I)=ACHAR(IACHAR(CT) - IACHAR(ACAP)+ &
```

```
      IACHAR(ASMALL))
ENDIF
ENDDO
PRINT *,BUF(1:SIZ)
END
```

All the upper case characters are greater than or equal to 'A' and less than or equal to 'Z'. The IF statement in the above program segment allows characters other than upper case letters to pass through test. One should calculate IACHAR (ASMALL) and IACHAR (ACAP) outside the DO Loop.

The next program determines whether a string is a palindrome of not. A palindrome is a string of characters which, when written in the reverse order, remains the same as the original string. For example, 'MADAM' or 'madam' is a palindrome ('Madam' is not a palindrome as the lower case letters are not same as the upper case letter within a string). The program will check the first character with the last character, second with the last but one and so on. Any mismatch indicates that the string is not a palindrome.

```
PROGRAM PALIN
INTEGER :: IT, SIZ, I
CHARACTER (LEN=80) :: BUF
LOGICAL :: L=.TRUE.
READ *, BUF
SIZ=LEN_TRIM(BUF)
DO I=1, SIZ/2   ! Integer division
IT=SIZ-I+1
IF(BUF(I:I) .NE. BUF(IT:IT)) THEN
  PRINT *, 'Not a palindrome : ',BUF
  L=.FALSE.
  EXIT
ENDIF
ENDDO

IF (L) THEN
!  L remains true if there is no mismatch
  PRINT *, 'The string is a palindrome : ', &
    BUF(1:SIZ)
ENDIF

END
```

8.19 Some More Library Functions

Fortran provides a few more useful library functions to handle strings – INDEX, SCAN and VERIFY.

INDEX: The INDEX function takes three arguments, a string, a substring and an optional logical parameter. The logical parameter, if not present, is assumed to be false. If the logical parameter is either absent or false, INDEX returns the starting position (as an integer value) of the substring within the string. If the substring is not present it returns zero.

           INDEX ('Subrata', 'a')

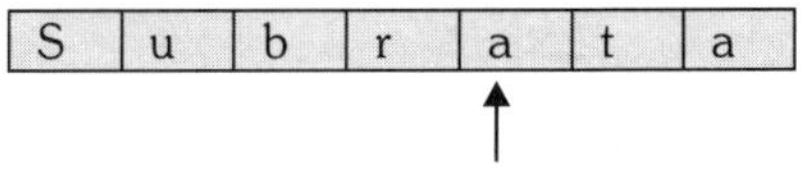

or,   INDEX ('Subrata', 'a', .FALSE.)

will return 5.

If the logical parameter is true, INDEX returns the starting position of the substring from the end.

           INDEX ('Subrata', 'a', .TRUE.)

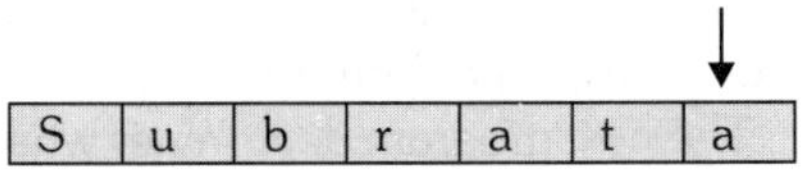

returns 7.

If the substring is the null string and either the third parameter is absent of false, INDEX returns 1. However, if the third parameter is true, it returns an integer equal to the length of the string + 1.

           INDEX ('Subrata', '')

returns 1 and

           INDEX ('Subrata', '', .TRUE.)

returns 8.

SCAN: This intrinsic also takes three arguments – a string, a set of characters and an optional logical parameter. If the logical parameter is absent it is assumed to be false.

If the logical parameter is absent or false, the first position of first occurrence of any character from the set of characters is returned. If none of the members of the set is present in the first string, zero is returned.

           SCAN ('Subrata', 'ab')

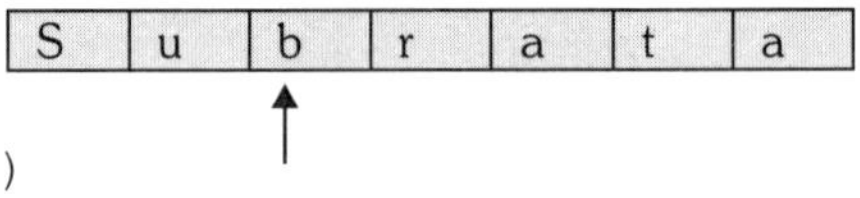

or,   SCAN ('Subrata', 'ab', .FALSE.)

will return 3.

If the logical parameter is true, the position of the last character from the (that is scanning starts from the end) string that matches with any member from the set is returned.

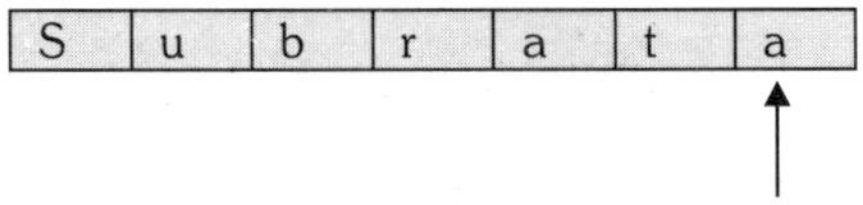

           SCAN ('Subrata', 'ab', .TRUE.)

returns 7.

           SCAN ('Subra', 'xyz')

returns zero as no character from the second is present in the first string.

VERIFY: Like SCAN, VERIFY also takes three arguments – a string, a set of characters and an optional logical parameter. If the logical parameter is absent, it is assumed to be false. If the logical parameter is absent or false the function returns zero if all the characters in the string are members of the set (second argument); otherwise it returns the position of the first left most character, which is not present in the set.

```
VERIFY ('Subrata', 'abrstu')
```

or,
```
VERIFY ('Subrata', 'abrstu', .FALSE.)
```

returns zero. However,

```
VERIFY ('Subrata', 'Suba')
```

returns 4 as 'r' is not present in the set.

If the logical parameter is true, the position of the right most character of the string which is not a member of the set is returned.

```
VERIFY ('Subrata', 'Suba', .TRUE.)
```

returns 6 as 't' is not a member of the set.

8.20 CASE and Character

The CASE statement was introduced in chapter 3. Only integer variables were used as the control variable for CASE. In fact, the control variable of CASE can be characters as well. The following program counts the number of vowels from a given character string.

```
PROGRAM COUNTV
CHARACTER (LEN=80) :: CH
INTEGER :: SIZ, I, VC=0, OC=0
READ *, CH
SIZ=LEN_TRIM(CH)
DO I=1,SIZ
SELECT CASE (CH(I:I))
!      Examine each character one by one
    CASE('A','E','I','O','U','a','e','i','o','u')
       VC=VC+1 !   increment the counter for vowel
    CASE DEFAULT
       OC=OC+1 !   increment the counter for other
END SELECT
ENDDO
PRINT *, 'No of vowels : ', VC

END
```

For all characters other than vowel, the default path will be chosen and the counter OC will be incremented.

A colon may be used to specify a range of characters in the collating sequence, 'b' :'d' is equivalent to 'b', 'c' and 'd'.

```
      PROGRAM COUNTV
      CHARACTER (LEN=80) :: CH
      INTEGER :: SIZ, I, CONS=0, OTHER=0
      READ *, CH
!        assume all the inputs are in lower case
      SIZ=LEN_TRIM(CH)
      DO I=1,SIZ
      SELECT CASE (CH(I:I))
!        Examine each character one by one
         CASE('b':'d','f':'h','j':'n','p':'t','v':'z')
           CONS=CONS+1
!            increment the counter for consonant
         CASE DEFAULT
           OTHER=OTHER+1
!            increment the counter for other
         END SELECT
      ENDDO
      PRINT *, 'No of consonant : ', CONS

      END
```

The above program counts the number of consonants.

The CASE statement may be of the following form:

```
            CASE ('ME': 'YOU')
```

For example,

```
            CHARACTER(LEN=4) :: CH='SHE'
            SELECT CASE (CH)
              CASE('ME' : 'YOU')
                PRINT *, CH
            END SELECT
```

The PRINT statement will be executed, as 'SHE' is between 'ME' and 'YOU'.

8.21 NEW_LINE

This function returns the new line character. The argument is of type character. For the default character type (ASCII)

```
            PRINT *, IACHAR(NEW_LINE('A'))
```

returns 10.

Chapter 9

IMPLICIT STATEMENT

It was mentioned in chapter 1 that if the variables are not declared explicitly, the default rule of Fortran comes into play. Variables that start I, J, K, L, M or N are treated as integers and the rest are treated as real. If the program contains only reals and integers, it is possible to write a program by following the above rule without any declaration of variables. However, modern programming practice is to define each and every variable and also to switch off the default behavior of the Fortran compiler.

9.1 IMPLICIT NONE

The IMPLICIT NONE statement was introduced in chapter 1. It is here briefly mentioned for the sake of completeness. The default rule of Fortran to associate variables starting with a particular character from a certain set of characters as integer and the rest as real can be switched off by placing a statement,

```
IMPLICIT NONE
```

at the beginning of the program unit. In this case all variables are to be declared explicitly.

9.2 IMPLICIT

In this section we shall discuss IMPLICIT statement, which goes against the argument mentioned in the previous section. This statement is used to treat variables that start with certain letter to be of a particular type.

9.3 IMPLICIT INTEGER

The statement is

```
IMPLICIT INTEGER (A)              ! (1)
IMPLICIT INTEGER (A, C)           ! (2)
IMPLICIT INTEGER (A-C)            ! (3)
IMPLICIT INTEGER (A-C, X-Z)       ! (4)
```

Statement (1) directs the compiler to treat all variables that start with 'A' as integers. That is, the compiler will treat AM, AX1, AP etc. as integers.

The statement (2) tells the compiler to assume that the variables that starts with 'A' or 'C' to be integers. The statement (3) contains A-C, which is equivalent to A, B and C. This is same as

```
IMPLICIT INTEGER (A, B, C)
```

The statement (4) states that all variables that start with A, B, C, X, Y and Z are integers. It is, perhaps, needless to mention that 'dash' sign (minus sign) indicates a set of contiguous letters, the first and the last letter in the set are placed on the left and the right of the 'dash' sign. The discussion of this section is equally applicable to the subsequent sections. So these will not be repeated there.

9.4 IMPLICIT REAL

The statement is:

```
IMPLICIT REAL (X)
IMPLICIT REAL (X-Z)
IMPLICIT REAL (A-H, O-Z)
```

9.5 IMPLICIT DOUBLE PRECISION

This statement is:

```
IMPLICIT DOUBLE PRECISION (A-H, O-Z)
IMPLICIT DOUBLE PRECISION (D)
IMPLICIT DOUBLE PRECISION (E, F)
```

9.6 IMPLICIT COMPLEX

The statement is:

```
IMPLICIT COMPLEX (C)
IMPLICIT COMPLEX (D, E)
IMPLICIT COMPLEX (P-Q)
```

9.7 IMPLICIT LOGICAL

The statement is:

```
IMPLICIT LOGICAL (L)
IMPLICIT LOGICAL (M-N)
IMPLICIT LOGICAL (A,C)
```

9.8 IMPLICIT DOUBLE COMPLEX

The statement is:

```
IMPLICIT DOUBLE COMPLEX (S)
IMPLICIT DOUBLE COMPLEX (T, U)
IMPLICIT DOUBLE COMPLEX (X-Z)
```

9.9 IMPLICIT CHARACTER

The statement is:

```
IMPLICIT CHARACTER (C)
IMPLICIT CHARACTER (A,B)
IMPLICIT CHARACTER (X-Z)
```

For a character variable, if the length parameter is not present along with the IMPLICIT declaration, the length is assumed to be equal to 1. The length parameter may be specified along with the IMPLICIT declaration:

```
IMPLICIT CHARACTER (LEN=4) (P-Q)
```

This declaration needs some explanation. It states that variables that start with P or Q are character variables of length 4, that is, they can store 4 characters.

9.10 Rules of IMPLICIT

If the program unit contains:

```
IMPLICIT NONE
IMPLICIT INTEGER (I-J)
```

the compiler will treat variables that start with I and J as integers and all other variables are to be defined.

A program unit cannot contain two IMPLICIT statements with the same letter.

```
IMPLICIT INTEGER (C)
IMPLICIT REAL (C)
```

or,

```
IMPLICIT INTEGER (C-F)    ! this includes D
IMPLICIT REAL (D)
```

are not legal.

Explicit declaration overrides an IMPLICIT declaration:

```
IMPLICIT INTEGER (I)
REAL :: I
.
I=2
PRINT *, I
END
```

The output is 2.0 as 'I' was treated as real variable because of explicit real declaration.

9.11 Comment on IMPLICIT

Readers may be wondering why the discussion related to IMPLICIT NONE goes against the declaration IMPLICIT INTEGER / REAL / DOUBLE PRECISION / COMPLEX / CHARACTER. A guideline may be formulated. IMPLICIT NONE is certainly very safe; it isolates all the undefined variables and helps to eliminate most of the typing errors related to variable names. On the other hand, IMPLICIT INTEGER etc. saves lot of typing, especially if the program unit contains many variables. Some programmers use the first letter of variables to indicate the type of variables. For example, one may choose 'C' as the first letter for all the complex variables and 'D' as the first letter for all the double precision variables. In such a situation IMPLICIT DOUBLE PRECISION (D) and IMPLICIT COMPLEX(C) are convenient. In such a case, the compromise formula could be to include an IMPLICIT NONE at the beginning of the program so that this unit requires explicit declarations for variables other than complex and double precision (like real, integer etc.). So it is a matter of choice. The present author prefers IMPLICIT NONE and he feels that if more time is spent during the development phase of the program (that is coding and typing), debugging time is substantially reduced and the problems mentioned related to the undefined variables never crop up.

Chapter 10

KIND (*)

One of the main features of the Fortran language is the portability of the source code. When a variable or a constant is declared, the compiler allocates storage locations for the variable or the constant with default machine dependent range and precision. Fortran allows the programmer to specify the precision and the range of a variable through the KIND attribute. This makes the program machine independent. Fortran provides library functions or intrinsics, SELECTED_INT_KIND and SELECTED_REAL_KIND to specify the range and precision of the variable or the constant. If the KIND is not specified, default KIND, which is compiler dependent, is assumed by the compiler.

A word of caution: beginners are advised to use the default KIND (i.e., precision and range) for the constants and the variables; this concept of KIND looks attractive but in reality the present compilers support basically two types of real variables, the so called standard precision and the double precision.

10.1 SELECTED_INT_KIND

This intrinsic, SELECTED_INT_KIND, takes one integer, say x, as its argument. The argument determines the range of the integer variable or constant corresponding to this KIND, it is $-10^x < n < 10^x$, where n is the integer.

```
INTEGER, PARAMETER :: SIZ=SELECTED_INT_KIND(2)
INTEGER(SIZ) :: A
```

The integer variable A of KIND 'SIZ' may assume values between -99 and $+99$. The argument of SELECTED_INT_KIND in this case is 2 and therefore the variable of KIND=SIZ should be able to handle integers between (and including) -99 and $+99$. The intrinsic returns -1 if it fails to allocate an integer in the range with the specified argument.

```
INTEGER, PARAMETER :: BIG=SELECTED_INT_KIND(9)
INTEGER (BIG) :: B
```

The integer variable B may assume values between -10^9 and $+10^9$. Based on the declaration it is the responsibility of the compiler to allocate the required number of bytes (of storage) for the variable to store the integer having this range of values.

Coming back to the declaration, SELECTED_INT_KIND(2), one must not think that there will be integer overflow if the value of the stored number exceeds 99, say, 100. The declaration merely guarantees that the compiler will allocate enough storage location for the variable such that it can accommodate any number from -99 to +99. Memory is allocated in terms of bytes. Eight binary digits make one byte. One byte of storage can accommodate any integer from -128 to +127. Though the variable created using SELECTED_INT_KIND (2) is supposed to accommodate any integer between -99 and +99, it is, in fact, will accommodate any integer between -128 and +127. In an identical way, SELECTED_INT_KIND(3) tells the compiler to assign storage such that it can accommodate any integer between -999 and +999. Actually, the compiler will allocate 2 bytes (16 bits) and this amount of memory can actually accommodate integers between (and including) -32768 and 32767. The compiler allocates the minimum amount of storage to cover the range specified in the SELECTED_INT_KIND intrinsic. Since the memory is allocated in terms of bytes, normally the memory allocated by the compiler would cover a range beyond the range specified in the declaration. This, however, does not go against the declaration. The declaration merely ensures the upper and lower limit of the variable. The table 10.1 illustrates this for the NAG Fortran compiler. Note that the table is compiler dependent as different people (compiler designers) used different integers to represent KIND values internally.

Table 10.1 Kind Parameters of NAG Fortran Compiler (Integer)

Argument of SELECTED_INT_KIND	Range of integer desired	No bytes allocated	Value of the KIND parameter	Maximum value permitted
1	$-10^1 < N < 10^1$	1	1	127
2	$-10^2 < N < 10^2$	1	1	127
3	$-10^3 < N < 10^3$	2	2	32767
4	$-10^4 < N < 10^4$	2	2	32767
5	$-10^5 < N < 10^5$	4	3	21474883647
6	$-10^6 < N < 10^6$	4	3	21474883647
7	$-10^7 < N < 10^7$	4	3	21474883647
8	$-10^8 < N < 10^8$	4	3	21474883647
9	$-10^9 < N < 10^9$	4	3	21474883647
10	$-10^{10} < N < 10^{10}$	8	4	9223372036854775807
11	$-10^{11} < N < 10^{11}$	8	4	9223372036854775807
12	$-10^{12} < N < 10^{12}$	8	4	9223372036854775807
13	$-10^{13} < N < 10^{13}$	8	4	9223372036854775807
14	$-10^{14} < N < 10^{14}$	8	4	9223372036854775807
15	$-10^{15} < N < 10^{15}$	8	4	9223372036854775807
16	$-10^{16} < N < 10^{16}$	8	4	9223372036854775807
17	$-10^{17} < N < 10^{17}$	8	4	9223372036854775807
18	$-10^{18} < N < 10^{18}$	8	4	9223372036854775807
19	$-10^{19} < N < 10^{19}$		NOT	SUPPORTED

Actually, SELECTED_INT_KIND returns a compiler dependent integer parameter called KIND, which is subsequently used to define a variable or a constant. From the table 10.1, it is apparent that the present compiler supports 4 types of integer having the KIND parameter as 1, 2, 3 and 4. In fact, one can define a variable through these numbers directly:

```
INTEGER (KIND=1) :: K1
INTEGER (KIND=2) :: K2
INTEGER (KIND=3) :: K3
INTEGER (KIND=4) :: K4
```

The constants may also refer to these KIND parameters directly, where the constant and the KIND value are separated by underscore character (_).

```
2_1
3456_2
423456_3
123456789123_4
```

However, use of these compiler dependent KIND values is discouraged because the numerical value of the KIND parameters may be different for another compiler. If used, such program becomes compiler dependent. A better way is not to use numerical value for the KIND parameters directly:

```
INTEGER, PARAMETER :: S1=SELECTED_INT_KIND(1)
INTEGER, PARAMETER :: S2=SELECTED_INT_KIND(2)
INTEGER, PARAMETER :: S3=SELECTED_INT_KIND(6)
INTEGER, PARAMETER :: S4=SELECTED_INT_KIND(12)
INTEGER(KIND=S1) :: K1
INTEGER(KIND=S2) :: K2
INTEGER(KIND=S3) :: K3
INTEGER(KIND=S4) :: K4
```

The constants may also be defined in terms of S1, S2, S3 and S4.

```
2_S1
3456_S2
423456_S3
123456789123_S4
```

It is apparent that if the above mentioned procedures are followed, the program becomes compiler independent as the program does not use numerical value of KIND for a particular compiler directly.

It may appear from the definition of SELECTED_INT_KIND, as if compiler allocates memory in a continuous fashion to accommodate different ranges. In practice, as memory is allocated in the unit of bytes and so long as a particular chunk of memory can accommodate different ranges, change of KIND does not take place. For example, one byte of memory can accommodate integers from -128 to 127. Therefore, SELECTED_INT_KIND (1) and SELECTED_INT_KIND (2) will have same KIND parameter. The former wants a range between -9 and +9 while the later requires a range between -99 and +99. However, SELECTED_INT_KIND (3) requires a range between -999 and +999 and one byte of memory cannot accommodate such a range. So a new KIND parameter is required which needs two bytes of memory. These two bytes cannot accommodate integers between 10^{-5} and 10^{+5}.

So again, a change of KIND takes place for this range. In short, several ranges may have identical KIND value.

10.2 Precision and Range of Real Numbers

The precision of a real number is a measure of "exactness" of the number. It is specified in terms of the number of digits that are used to express the number reliably. When a real number is stored in a computer, the number of bits used for the fractional part determines the precision of the number. Though real numbers are stored as binary digits, precision is expressed both in binary and in decimal. For "standard" precision, precision of a real number is approximately 6 (decimal places) and for double precision it is 15 (decimal places).

The range for real numbers is a measure of the biggest number that can be processed and is the maximum exponent (power of ten) that the processor can handle. For standard precision it is 37.

10.3 SELECTED_REAL_KIND

This intrinsic returns an integer value of the KIND parameter corresponding to the precision P and range R (power of ten), where both P and R are integers and the first and second parameters of the function respectively.

```
INTEGER, PARAMETER :: RN=SELECTED_REAL_KIND (6,37)
INTEGER, PARAMETER :: RD=SELECTED_REAL_KIND (15, 307)
REAL (KIND=RN) :: X
REAL (KIND=RD) :: Y
```

Like the intrinsic function SELECTED_INT_KIND, the compiler dependent KIND values are not used directly. In this case the variable X has a precision 6 and range 37, that is, ten to the power 37. Similarly, the variable Y has a precision 15 and range 307, that is, ten to the power 307. The intrinsic returns -1 if support from the processor for precision greater than or equal to P is not available but support for range greater than or equal to R is available.

```
INTEGER, PARAMETER :: S=SELECTED_REAL_KIND (16,37) ! S=-1
```

Similarly, the intrinsic returns -2 if support from the processor for precision P is available but for the R is not available.

```
INTEGER, PARAMETER :: S=SELECTED_REAL_KIND (6,400) ! S=-2
```

The intrinsic returns -3 if support from the processor is simultaneously not available for precision P and range R.

```
INTEGER, PARAMETER :: S=SELECTED_REAL_KIND (16,400)! S=-3
```

The intrinsic returns -4 if the processor supports the precision P and the range R individually but not simultaneously. If more than one KIND is available for the precision P and range R, the intrinsic returns the one with the smallest decimal precision.

Table 10.2 shows precision, range and KIND parameter of real numbers for NAG Fortran compiler.

Table 10.2 Kind Parameters of NAG Fortran Compiler (Real)

Argument of SELLECTED_ REAL_ KIND		No of Bytes allocated	Value of KIND parameter	Precision allocated	Highest Exponent	Maximum permitted value
P	R					
1	1	4	1	6	37	3.402828235E+38
6	37	4	1	6	37	3.402828235E+38
7	37	8	2	15	307	1.7976931348623157E+308
1	38	8	2	15	307	1.7976931348623157E+308
15	37	8	2	15	307	1.7976931348623157E+308
15	307	8	2	15	307	1.7976931348623157E+308

From the table 10.2 it is observed that the present NAG compiler supports two types of real variable or constant – the so-called standard precision and double precision. The precision and the range for standard precision are 6 and 37 respectively. The precision and range for double precision are 15 and 307 respectively. One interesting point may be observed from the Table 10.2. When the desired precision is 1 and the range is 38, compiler allocates locations for precision 15 and range 307 because to accommodate range greater than 37, next available range for this compiler is 307 and for which the precision is 15. To be more precise, there is no exact KIND corresponding to precision 1 and range 38 – the nearest one (in this case only one) available to the compiler has a precision 15 and range 307. Therefore, to accommodate the range 38, compiler chooses a KIND, which in this case has a range 307. This particular KIND will not only increase the range to 307 but at the same time the precision 1 to 15 as well. The requirement was of precision 1 and range 38, but to accommodate this range and precision the compiler is forced to choose a KIND, which has a precision 15 and range 307.

10.4 SELECTED_CHAR_KIND

This intrinsic takes one character string as its argument and the returns the kind parameter corresponding to its argument. The character string can be one of the following:
- DEFAULT
- ASCII
- ISO_10646

```
INTEGER, PARAMETER::S=SELECTED_CHAR_KIND('ASCII')
CHARACTER(KIND=S):: CH
```

The intrinsic returns -1 if the argument is not supported.

10.5 KIND Intrinsic

The KIND intrinsic takes one real or integer constant or variable as its argument and returns the KIND (a compiler dependent integer) of its argument. The NAG compiler returns 1 and 2 when the KIND intrinsic has argument 0.0 and 0.0D0.

```
PRINT *, KIND(0.0)
PRINT *, KIND(0.0D0)
```

will print 1 and 2 respectively. These numbers, 1 and 2, are compiler dependent. The output will be same if the following program is executed:

```
REAL :: R1
DOUBLE PRECISION :: R2
PRINT *, KIND(R1)
PRINT *, KIND(R2)
END
```

Also,

```
2.0_KIND(0.0D0)
```

or,

```
2.0_2
```

is equivalent to 2.0D0, that is, a double precision constant.
   However,

```
PRINT *, KIND(0)
```

will display 3 (NAG compiler) because this is default KIND for an integer.
   Consider the following program:

```
INTEGER, PARAMETER :: VSMALL=SELECTED_INT_KIND(2)
INTEGER, PARAMETER :: SMALL=SELECTED_INT_KIND(3)
INTEGER, PARAMETER :: MEDIUM=SELECTED_INT_KIND(5)
INTEGER, PARAMETER :: BIG=SELECTED_INT_KIND(10)
INTEGER (VSMALL) :: A
INTEGER (SMALL) :: B
INTEGER (MEDIUM) :: C
INTEGER (BIG) :: D

PRINT *, KIND(A)          ! 1
PRINT *, KIND(B)          ! 2
PRINT *, KIND(C)          ! 3
PRINT *, KIND(D)          ! 4
END
```

The outputs are 1, 2, 3 and 4 respectively. The result follows from the numbers given in table 10.1. For g95 compiler they are 1, 2, 4 and 8 respectively.
   Normally, these compiler dependent "kind parameters" are not used because that would make

the program compiler dependent. Though discussion in this section is general in nature, some examples of "kind numbers" are compiler dependent. Using the property of the intrinsic SELECTED_INT_KIND that the intrinsic returns -1 for non-existence kind, the following program prints the available "kind number" of a particular compiler.

```
INTEGER :: KOLD=0, KNEW=0, I=0
DO WHILE (.TRUE.)
   I=I+1
   KNEW=SELECTED_INT_KIND(I)
   IF(KNEW < 0) THEN
      EXIT            ! non-existent kind
   ENDIF
   IF(KNEW .NE. KOLD) THEN
      KOLD=KNEW    ! change of kind
      PRINT *, KNEW, I
   ENDIF
ENDDO
END
```

The outputs of this program are:

```
1       1
2       3
3       5
4       10
```

This again demonstrates that NAG compiler supports four types (kind) of integers having KIND=1, 2, 3 and 4. Other compilers may or may not support four kinds of integers. Even if they support, the "kind number" may be different.

Real and double precision variables may be defined with the help of KIND also.

```
REAL (KIND=KIND(0.0)) :: R5
REAL (KIND=KIND(0.0D0)) ::R6
REAL (KIND=1) :: R7        ! compiler dependent
REAL (KIND=2) :: R8        ! compiler dependent
```

Some explanation is perhaps required for the above mentioned declarations – KIND=KIND (0.0) and KIND=KIND(0.0D0). KIND (0.0) returns the kind parameter corresponding to the constant 0.0 (single precision real number), which is 1 for the NAG compiler. This "KIND" is KIND intrinsic. This when equated to the KIND attribute, declares R5 as a single precision real variable. Therefore, the first KIND is the attribute of the declaration and the second KIND is a "call" to the intrinsic KIND which returns the "kind number" corresponding to its argument. The argument is same for KIND=KIND(0.0D0). The last two declarations are compiler dependent and therefore should be avoided.

10.6 DOUBLE COMPLEX

DOUBLE COMPLEX, whose both real and imaginary parts are double precision quantities, was introduced in chapter 6. The COMPLEX declaration with proper KIND is required to declare a DOUBLE COMPLEX variable.

```
COMPLEX (KIND=KIND(0.0D0)) ::C1
```

The library function CMPLX, introduced in chapter 6, takes a third optional argument, KIND. The double complex variable C1 is equated to double precision real and imaginary part with this parameter of KIND.

```
C1=CMPLX(1.23456789123456D0,2.34567891234567D0,&
    KIND=KIND(0.0D0))
```

It is to be noted that without the correct argument of KIND, C1 will not be double complex in the true sense as without proper KIND, the real and the imaginary part (inspite of the presence of D0) will be truncated to 'normal' real quantities first and then converted to double precision before storing as the real and imaginary parts of C1 as C1 has been declared as DOUBLE COMPLEX. As a result, the digits, say, after 6 places of decimal are meaningless when a single precision is converted to double precision by adding additional digits at the end. These additional digits do not have any significance. One can gain more insight into problem by executing the following program segment and comparing the results:

```
COMPLEX (KIND=KIND(0.0D0)) ::C1
C1=CMPLX(1.23456789123456D0,2.34567891234567D0,&
  KIND=KIND(0.0D0))
PRINT *, C1
C1=CMPLX(1.23456789123456D0,2.34567891234567D0)
PRINT *, C1
END
```

10.7 Quadruple (Quad) Precision

Some compilers like Intel's IFORT support quadruple precision real numbers. These numbers are more precise than the corresponding double precision real number. Quad precision variable is defined as:

```
REAL (KIND=KIND(0.0Q0)) :: Q, R
```

Note that 0.0Q0 stands for quadruple precision real number having magnitude 0.0. The precision of such numbers may be verified by executing the following program:

```
PRINT *, 2.0Q0/3.0Q0
END
```

The result is 0.6666666666666666....6 (approximately 34 places). The present NAG Fortran compiler does not support quadruple precision.

Chapter 11

ARRAYS

Fortran programs often require handling of vectors and matrices. It is practically impossible to name each and every element of the vectors or the matrices. For example, a 100 by 100 matrix has 10000 elements. To access each element, 10000 different variable names would be required in such a naming scheme, which is clearly unacceptable.

An array is a built-in data structure of Fortran where all the elements are of same type. An array is referred to by its name and usually accessed by subscript(s). An array may be accessed in four different ways:

- the array as a whole,
- element by element,
- a portion of the array,
- by means of vector subscripts.

An array may be of single dimension or it may have more than one dimension. A single dimensional array is called a vector and a two-dimensional array is called a matrix. Fortran allows an array to have a maximum dimension of seven.

11.1 Array Declaration

An integer single dimensional array of size 10 is declared as:

```
INTEGER, DIMENSION (10):: A
```

The array A is referred to by its name and its elements are accessed by A(1), A(2), ... , A(10) or in general A(I), where I is usually an integer constant or expression. Depending upon the current value of I, a particular element of an array is accessed. The lower bound of the array is, by default, 1 and the upper bound is specified along with the array declaration; in this case it is 10. Therefore, the subscript of the array, in this case, must have a value between 1 and 10. For an integer array the individual elements of the array can consist of only integer quantities. The dimension of the array is an integer constant or could be a symbolic name associated with a constant (allocatable array is discussed in chapter 21).

```
INTEGER, PARAMETER :: S=10
REAL, DIMENSION(S) :: A
```

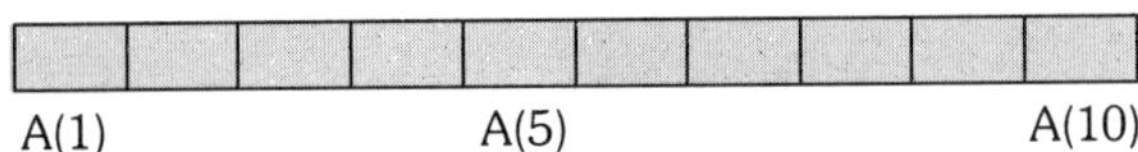

In the declaration, first the item is the type of the array, that is, type of its content is specified – like INTEGER, REAL, COMPLEX, DOUBLE PRECISION, LOGICAL, CHARACTER, DOUBLE COMPLEX. Next the dimension of the array followed by name of the array is specified. The array declaration merely reserves locations for the variable.

```
      REAL, DIMENSION (100):: C, D
!        C & D are real arrays of dimension 100
      COMPLEX, DIMENSION (50):: Z1, Z2
!        Z1 & Z2 are complex arrays of dimension 50
```

The keyword dimension may be omitted if the upper bound is given within brackets as shown below:

```
      INTEGER :: A(10)
```

Again,

```
      INTEGER, DIMENSION(100) :: X, Y(40)
```

declares array X with dimension 100 and Y with dimension 40. If Y(40) is replaced by just Y, both X and Y will have upper bound of 100.

A character array may also be declared in an identical manner. However, if the individual elements are expected to store more than one character, the size of each of the elements must be specified. Obviously, the size of all the array elements must be same.

```
      CHARACTER(LEN=20),DIMENSION (200)::CH
```

This defines a character array CH of dimension 200 having a length equal to 20 characters per element. It is also possible to specify the lower bound also.

```
      REAL, DIMENSION(-5 : 5):: X
```

A colon separates the upper and the lower bounds. In the above case, the lower bound of X is -5 and the upper bound is 5. The permissible subscripts for the array are -5, -4, -3, -2, -1, 0, 1, 2, 3, 4, 5. The upper bound must be greater than or equal to the lower bound. If the upper bound is less than the lower bound a 'zero' sized array is created.

Just like scalars, the precision and the range of the array elements may be specified. It is obvious, that in such a case, all the elements of the array must be of same precision and range as specified in the declaration. In the absence of the precision and the range, the array will assume the default precision and range.

```
INTEGER, PARAMETER :: S=SELECTED_INT_KIND(9)
INTEGER(KIND=S), DIMENSION (100) :: A

INTEGER,PARAMETER::P=SELECTED_REAL_KIND(15, 307)
REAL(KIND=P),DIMENSION(200):: B
```

11.2 Multi-dimensional Array

An array can have more than one dimension.

```
REAL, DIMENSION(3,3)::X
```

X – array elements

1,1	1,2	1,3
2,1	2,2	2,3
3,1	3,2	3,3

where the upper bounds of the two dimensions are separated by a comma. Again, by default, the lower bound in each dimension is 1. In this case X is a two-dimensional array having 3 rows and 3 columns. As in the case of single dimension, the lower bounds may be other than 1. To access a single element, two subscripts are required for two-dimensional array.

```
REAL, DIMENSION(-1:1, -2:0)::P
```

P – array elements

-1, -2	-1, -1	-1, 0
0, -2	0, -1	0, 0
1, -2	1, -1	1, 0

Upper and lower bounds are separated by a colon and each dimension is separated by a comma. The array elements are (column wise):

P(-1, -2), P(0, -2), P(1, -2), P(-1, -1), P(0, -1), P(1, -1), P(-1, 0), P(0, 0) and P(1, 0).

Similarly, arrays having more than two dimensions may be declared:

```
        INTEGER,DIMENSION(3, 4, 5)::R
!         3-D array
        REAL,DIMENSION(1 : 2, -1 : 5, 3)::T
!           lower bound of third dimension is 1 (default value)
        LOGICAL, DIMENSION(3, 3, 3)::L
        CHARACTER,DIMENSION(4, 4, 3)::CH
```

11.3 Storage Arrangement of 2-D Array (*)

All the multi-dimensional arrays have to be mapped into the single dimension of memory addresses.

A two dimensional array is stored column wise. A two dimensional array of dimension 2 by 2 is mapped into single dimension as shown below:

Element	Location
A (1, 1)	1
A (2, 1)	2
A (1, 2)	3
A (2, 2)	4

1	2	3	4
A(1, 1)	A(2, 1)	A(1, 2)	A(2, 2)

Similarly, for a three-dimensional array B of dimension 2x2x2, relations between the array elements and the locations are indicated below.

Element	Location	Element	Location
B (1,1,1)	1	B (1,1,2)	5
B (2,1,1)	2	B (2,1,2)	6
B (1,2,1)	3	B (1,2,2)	7
B (2,2,1)	4	B (2,2,2)	8

1	2	3	4	5	6	7	8
B(1,1,1)	B(2,1,1)			B(1,1,2)			B(2,2,2)

The same concept may be extended for arrays of higher dimensions. Fortran compilers arrange storage so that successive array elements can be accessed by the very fast machine code increment operator.

We shall now discuss how a two dimensional array is mapped into a single dimension. Consider one 3 by 3 two-dimensional array:

```
REAL, DIMENSION (3,3)::D
```

Symbolically, if the dimension of the array is (I, J) [in this case it 3x3], the (i, j)th element can be computed by the formula:

$$(i, j)\text{th element} = i + (j-1) * I$$

This may be verified for D (1, 2). Substituting, we get

$$1 + (2-1) * 3 = 4$$

1, 1	**1, 2**	1, 3
2, 1	2, 2	2, 3
3, 1	3, 2	3, 3

As the elements are stored column wise, (1, 2)th element is stored in the 4th location and that is what we get from the formula.

For a three dimensional array of dimension (I, J, K), the (i, j, k)th element is mapped as:

$$i + (j-1) * I + (k-1) * I * J$$

Similar formula can be derived for arrays having dimensions greater than 3. For a seven dimensional array of dimension (I, J, K, L, M, N, O) the (i, j, k, l, m, n, o)th location is mapped into single dimension as:

$$i + (j-1)*I + (k-1)*I*J + (l-1)*I*J*K + (m-1)*I*J*K*L + (n-1)*I*J*K*L*M + (o-1)*I*J*K*L*M*N$$
$$= i + (I*((j-1) + J*((k-1) + K*((l-1) + L*((m-1) + M*((n-1) + N*((o-1)))))))))$$

It has already been mentioned that all multi-dimensional arrays are mapped into single dimension in the memory. To access an element of a seven-dimensional array, processor has to perform a calculation similar to above which involves several additions, subtractions and multiplications. This will reduce the execution speed. The rule of thumb is that unless it is absolutely essential, higher dimensional arrays should be avoided.

11.4 Characteristics of Array

An array is characterized by three attributes – Rank, Size and Shape.
Rank: The rank of an array is defined as the number of dimensions of the array, a single dimensioned array has a rank 1, a two dimensional array has a rank 2 and so on. Fortran supports arrays up to rank 7.

An ordinary variable, also called a scalar, has a rank zero.

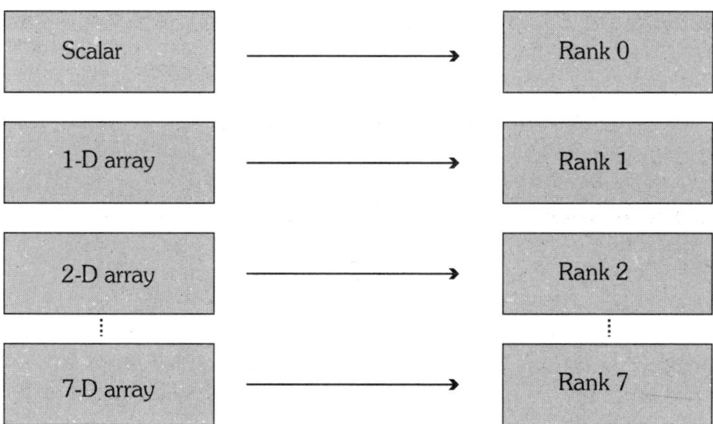

Size: The size of an array is defined as the total number of elements of an array or the number of elements in a particular direction. First we consider a two dimensional array. The total size of the array as well as the size of the row or column separately can be determined by the SIZE intrinsic.

```
INTEGER, DIMENSION(4,3) :: A
.
PRINT *, SIZE(A)           ! total size is 4*3 =12
PRINT *, SIZE(A, DIM=1)    ! total no of rows 4
PRINT *, SIZE(A, DIM=2)    ! total no columns 3
```

1,1	1,2	1,2
2,1	2,2	2,3
3,1	3,2	3,3
4,1	4,2	4,3

DIM=1 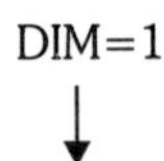

DIM=2 ⟶

SIZE (A) returns 12, the total number of elements of A (4x3). SIZE (A, DIM=1) returns 4, the number of rows and SIZE (A, DIM=2) returns 3, the number of columns. Readers may verify that for an array X having a dimension 4x5x6,

```
PRINT *, SIZE (X, DIM=1)
PRINT *, SIZE (X, DIM=2)
PRINT *, SIZE (X, DIM=3)
```

will display 4, 5 and 6.

Shape: The extent of an array is defined as the number of elements in a particular dimension. The shape of an array is the set of all the extents of the array. The SHAPE intrinsic returns a single dimension array of size equal to the rank of the input array to the intrinsic (SHAPE).

```
INTEGER, DIMENSION (4, 5, 6) :: A
```

The extents of the array A are 4, 5 and 6 and the shape of the array is (4 5 6). Now consider the following:

```
INTEGER, DIMENSION (-10:10,20) :: A
INTEGER, DIMENSION(2):: SZ
!         The size of SZ must be at least 2
!         as the rank of A is 2.
SZ=SHAPE (A)
PRINT *, SZ
END
```

Since A is a rank 2 array (2-D array), the size of rank 1 array SZ must be at least 2. The PRINT statement will display two numbers, 21 and 20, which are the number of elements (extents) in the first and second dimensions respectively.

Two arrays are said to be conformable if the shapes of the two arrays are identical.

```
INTEGER, DIMENSION(3,3):: A,B
```

The array A and B are conformable.

```
INTEGER, DIMENSION(3,3)::C
INTEGER, DIMENSION(0:2, 2:4)::D
```

In this case also, since the shape of the arrays, C and D are same – they are conformable. This may be verified by executing the statements:

```
PRINT *, SHAPE (C)
PRINT *, SHAPE (D)
```

Both the print statements will print (3 3)[without bracket].

Two zero sized arrays may have same rank but shapes may be different. One of the array may have shape (0 5) and the other (5 0) or (0 4). These types of arrays are not conformable. But a scalar is always conformable with any array and thus,

$$zero\text{-}sized\text{-}array = scalar$$

is a valid statement; it does not do anything.

A zero sized array is always considered as 'defined'.

11.5 Array Constant

Array constant of rank one in Fortran can be constructed by enclosing the constants between '(/' and '/)' or '[' and ']'. For example,

```
         (/ 1, 2, 3, 4 /)
or,      [ 1, 2, 3, 4 ]
```

defines an array constant of size 4 with individual elements as 1, 2, 3 and 4. This is also called array constructor. Implied DO loop can be used to define the above-mentioned array constant.

```
         (/ (I, I=1,4) /)
or,      [ (I, I=1,4) ]
```

The value of I starts from 1 goes up to 4 with a step of 1 (default step, if the step is not explicitly mentioned). The step can be other than 1.

```
         (/ (I, I=2, 10, 2) /)
or,      [ (I, I=2, 10, 2) ]
```

is equivalent to:

```
         (/ 2, 4, 6, 8, 10 /)
or,      [2, 4, 6, 8, 10]
```

In this book we shall use the square bracket notation to indicate array constants. Some old compilers may not support this notation – in that case the notation ' (/ ' and ' /) ' must be used.

It is needless to mention that array constants may be of data type other than integers.

```
[10.0, 20.0, 30.0, 40.0, 50.0]
[.TRUE., .FALSE., .FALSE., .TRUE.]
[1.2E2, 9.23E-1, -25.73E4, 33.75]
[(1.0, 2.0),(3.0, 4.0),(5.0, 6.0),(7.0, 8.0)]
```

The last one is complex array constant. A few other array constants using the implied DO are shown:

```
[(I*10,I=1,5)]
```

results in an array constant:

```
[10, 20, 30, 40, 50]
```

Similarly,

```
[(I*10, I=1, 10, 2)]
```

is equivalent to:

```
[10, 30, 50, 70, 90]
```

11.6 Initialization

As mentioned earlier, the dimension statement merely reserves locations for variables – no value is assigned to them: they are undefined. The dimensioned variables may be assigned along with the dimension statement.

```
INTEGER, DIMENSION(4)::INP = 100
```

```
INP(1)  INP(2)  INP(3)  INP(4)
```

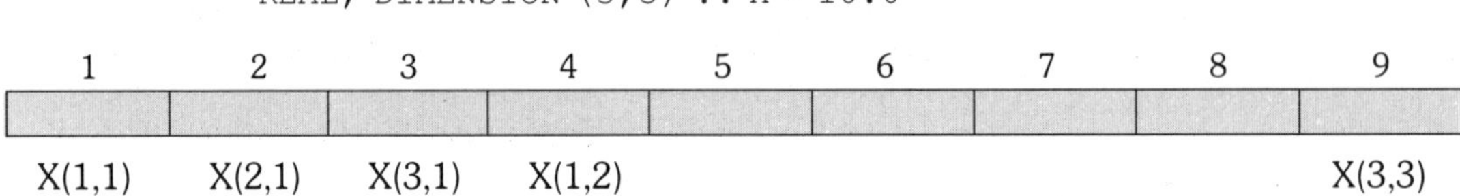

All the elements of INP are initialized to 100.

```
REAL, DIMENSION (3,3) :: X = 10.0
```

All the elements of X are set to 10.0.

```
INTEGER, DIMENSION (4) :: B = [ 10, 20, 30, 40 ]
```

10	20	30	40
B(1)	B(2)	B(3)	B(4)

B (1) is initialized to 10, B (2) to 20, B(3) to 30 and B(4) to 40.
   An array may be initialized by implied DO also.

```
REAL,DIMENSION(10)::A = [(I, I=1,10)]
```

This sets:

```
A (1)      ⟶      1
A (2)      ⟶      2
A (3)      ⟶      3
      .
A (10)     ⟶     10
```

The implied DO loop may be of following type:

```
INTEGER, DIMENSION (5):: Z = [(3*I, I=1,5)]
```

In this case Z(1) to Z(5) are initialized to 3, 6, 9, 12 and 15. The implied DO loop, like the ordinary DO loop, can have an increment not equal to 1.

```
INTEGER, DIMENSION (5):: W=[(3*I, I=2, 10, 2)]
```

This initialization results in setting W(1) to 6, W(2) to 12, ... W(5) to 30. The initialization of array using the DATA statement is discussed in chapter 13.

11.7 Named Array Constant

A named array constant is a rank one array constant having a name attached to it. A named array constant is declared with the PARAMETER attribute and cannot be modified during the execution of the program.

```
INTEGER, PARAMETER, DIMENSION(4) :: IA=[25, 50, 75, 100]
```

The elements of IA may be accessed in the usual manner through subscript. However IA, being a named constant, cannot be modified and therefore cannot appear on the left hand side of the assignment sign.

11.8 Array Element

One of the methods of accessing array elements is through subscripts. The subscript must be an integer or an array expression. The expression is evaluated before accessing the array element. The number of subscripts must be same as the rank of the array.

Rank 1 array : It is accessed by a single subscript:

```
A (1)
A (I)
A (3*I)
A (3*I+3)
```

Rank 2 array: It is accessed by two subscripts. The subscripts are separated by a comma. Some examples are given below:

```
B (1, 2)
B (I, 3)
B (I, J)
B (2, J)
B (2*I, 4)
B (2*I, 3*J+2)
```

For an array of rank 3, three subscripts are required. An array can have maximum 7 subscripts, as the rank of an array cannot exceed 7.

The subscript(s) must be the within the bounds of the array. If the lower and the upper bounds of an array are 1 and 100 respectively, the subscripts should not be less than 1 and greater than 100. If the subscript is out of bounds the result is unpredictable.

11.9 Array Assignment and Array Arithmetic

An array element may be used like a scalar variable.

```
!                       A, B, C are 1-D array
!                       I, J, K are defined

                A(1) = 0
                A(3) = A(1) + A(2)
                B(2) = A(2) * C(3)
                B(I) = A(J) - B(K)
                B(I+2) = A(3*J) * B(3)
!                  P, Q, R are 2-D array
                P(1, 2) = 110.0
                P(I, J) = Q(I, K) * R(K, J)
```

An array may be assigned as a whole, that is, the same value to all its elements.

```
INTEGER, DIMENSION(10) :: A, B
A = 100
B = 200
```

The statement $A = 100$ sets all the elements of A to 100 and similarly $B = 200$ sets all the elements of B to 200.

A rank 1 array may be equated to an array constructor.

```
INTEGER, DIMENSION (4) :: IA
  .
IA = [50, 60, 70, 80]
```

The above statement assigns IA(1), IA(2), IA(3) and IA(4) respectively to 50, 60, 70 and 80 respectively.

Arithmetic operations are allowed involving the whole array. A scalar, when it operates on an array, modifies each of the array elements identically according to the arithmetic operator.

```
IA = IA*10
```

is equivalent to:

```
IA(1) = 10 * IA(1)
IA(2) = 10 * IA(2)
IA(3) = 10 * IA(3)
IA(4) = 10 * IA(4)
```

Now, consider the following program segment where the arrays IA and IB are conformable (identical shape).

```
INTEGER, DIMENSION (5)::IA, IB
  .

  .
IB = IB + IA
```

The above statement is equivalent to:

```
IB(1) = IB(1) + IA(1)
IB(2) = IB(2) + IA(2)
  .
IB(5) = IB(5) + IA(5)
```

The following program segment demonstrates arithmetic operations involving the array as a whole.

```
INTEGER, DIMENSION (4):: A, B, T
     .
A = [10, 20, 30, 40]
B = [100, 200, 300, 400]
T= A + B
     .
     .
T= A - B
     .
     .
T= A * B
     .
     .
T= B / A
     .
     .
END
```

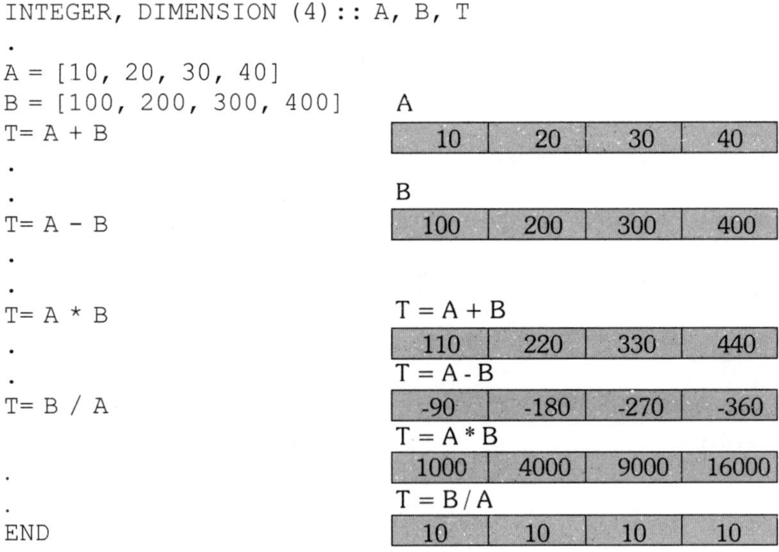

We shall discuss the addition operation. The rest follows the same logic.

```
T = A + B
```

is equivalent to,

```
T (1) = A (1) + B (1)
T (2) = A (2) + B (2)
T (3) = A (3) + B (3)
T (4) = A (4) + B (4)
```

We shall now illustrate the use of array through an example. The next program swaps the contents of two arrays.

```
PROGRAM SWAP
INTEGER, DIMENSION (4):: A=[10, 20, 30, 40]
INTEGER, DIMENSION (4):: B=[100, 200, 300, 400]
INTEGER, DIMENSION (4):: T
T = A
A = B
B = T
PRINT *, A
PRINT *, B
END
```

Now, suppose C, D and X are 2x2 matrices of the following form.

$$C$$

1	3
2	4

$$D$$

100	300
200	400

$$X$$

100	900
400	1600

If X is a 2x2 matrix,

$$X = C * D$$

will return the matrix X as the product of the corresponding matrix elements of C and D. Note that, this type of operations is possible provided arrays are conformable.

11.10 Array Section

A portion of the array can be accessed in Fortran. The following program segments define various arrays for this section.

```
INTEGER, DIMENSION (4, 4):: A
INTEGER, DIMENSION (2, 2):: B
INTEGER, DIMENSION (4):: C, D
INTEGER :: I, J
     .
     .
DO  I = 1, 4
  DO J = 1, 4
    A(I, J) = 100*I+J
  ENDDO
ENDDO
```

This results in the array:

A=

101	102	103	104
201	202	203	204
301	302	303	304
401	402	403	404

Now the statement

```
C (:) = A (1,  : )
```

will assign C(1), C(2), C(3) and C(4) with the respective elements of the first row of A, that is, 101, 102, 103 and 104 respectively.

C(:) $\longrightarrow$ | 101 | 102 | 103 | 104 |

In other words, the above statement is equivalent to:

```
DO  I = 1, 4
 C(I) = A(1, I)
 ENDDO
```

Similarly,

```
D(:) = A(:,2 )
```

will copy the second column of A to D. The elements of D's are now:

```
D(1) = 102
D(2) = 202
D(3) = 302
D(4) = 402
```

101	**102**	103	104
201	**202**	203	204
301	**302**	303	304
401	**402**	403	404

A(:,2)

$\downarrow$

102
202
302
402

Using the same notation, a portion of contiguous elements of an array may be assigned to a value without affecting other array elements not present in the statement.

```
C(1:3) = [10,20,30]
```

The element C(4), not present in the statement, is not affected. Here C(1: 3) refers to C(1), C(2) and C(3). The array index could be a triplet consisting of starting location, end location and an increment (stride). Hence, (1 : 10 : 3) refers to the elements 1, 4, 7 and 10. The index triplet may be used for higher dimension also. Somewhat similar to implied DO statement, one can specify the increment (default is 1). Thus,

```
C(1:4:2) = [100,200]
```

will only modify C(1) and C(3) and set these elements to 100 and 200 respectively. C(2) and C(4) are not affected. The diagonal element of a matrix may be extracted if the two dimensional array A is made equivalent (section 13.7) to a single dimensional array E (size 16) then,

```
D(:) = E(1:16:5)
```

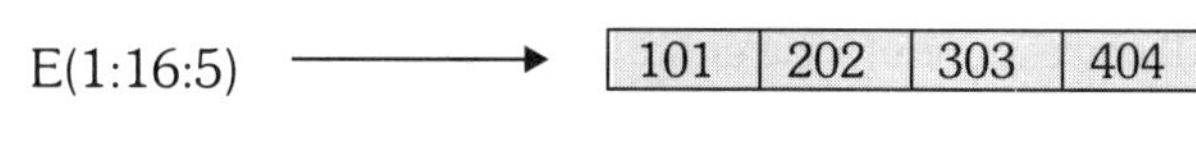

A portion of the array can be extracted by using array section:

```
B(:,:) = A (2:3,2:3)
```

The 2x2 B array will have elements as shown below:

101	102	103	104
201	**202**	**203**	204
301	**302**	**303**	304
401	402	403	404

```
B(1,1)          202
B(1,2)          203
B(2,1)          302
B(2,2)          303
```

Both the sides of the assignment statement may contain array sections from the same array. In fact, there can be even overlapping elements. But the right hand side always uses the unmodified (existing) array elements for the overlapping portions.

```
INTEGER, DIMENSION (10):: A=[(I,I=1,10)]
A(6:8) = A (5:7)
PRINT *, A
```

A (before)

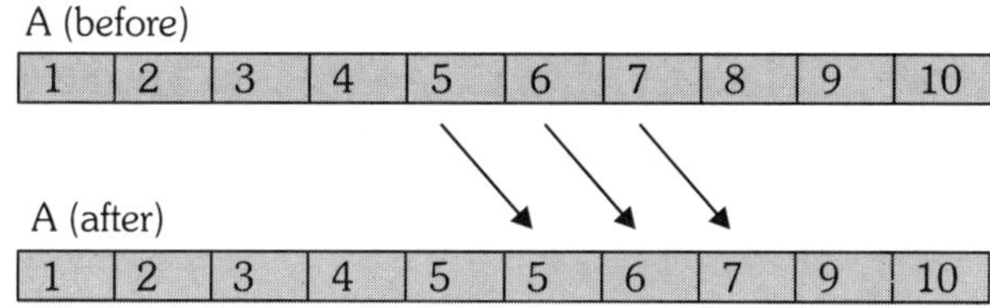

This instruction when expanded results:

```
A(6) = A(5)
A(7) = A(6)
A(8) = A(7)
```

with the assumption that the unmodified values of A(5), A(6) and A(7) are used on the right hand side of the assignment sign. Though A(6)=A(5) will modify A(6) to 5, yet this value of A(6) will not be used in the next statement, A(7)=A(6), the old unmodified value of A(6), which is 6, will be used instead.

The PRINT statement will display the A array as:

```
1     2     3     4     5     5     6     7     9     10
```

In general X(I, 1:J) corresponds to 1 to Jth elements of the Ith row.
X(I :) corresponds to the entire Ith row.
X(: J) corresponds to the entire Jth column
X(I, 1:J:K) corresponds to the 1, (1+K)th, (1+2K)th, ... elements of Ith row.
X(1:I:K, J) corresponds to 1, (1+K)th, (1+2K)th ... elements of Jth column.

Finally, for an array of characters, it is possible to access a substring within a particular element of character array.

```
CHARACTER (LEN=20), DIMENSION (100) ::CH
CH (4)(3:6) = 'SINP'
```

will store 'SINP' in the character positions 3 to 6 of the fourth element of the character array CH.

11.11 Input

The READ statement is used to input either the individual elements or the array as a whole or selected elements using the implied DO loop.

```
INTEGER, DIMENSION(10):: A
READ *, A(1), A(2), A(4)
!               only A(1), A(2) and A(4) are read
READ *, A
!               read all the elements of A
READ *, (A(K), K=1, 8)
!               read A(1) to A(8)
READ *, (A(K), K=1, 10, 2)
!               read A(1), A(3), A(5), A(7) and A(9)
READ *, A(1 : 3)
!               read A(1), A(2) and A(3)
READ *, A(1 : 10 : 2)
!               read A(1), A(3), A(5), A(7) and A(9)
```

Similarly for two-dimensional arrays either the individual elements or the whole array or some elements using the implied DO may be read.

```
REAL, DIMENSION (2, 2) :: B
READ *, B(1, 1), B(2, 2)
!           only two elements are read
READ *, B
!           elements are read column wise
!           B(1, 1), B(2, 1), B(1, 2), B(2, 2)
READ *, ((B(I, J), J=1, 2), I=1, 2)
!           using implied DO loop elements
!           are read row wise
```

The last two READ statements need some clarification. As the array is stored column wise, READ *, B will assign data in the following order – the first item will be stored in B(1, 1), the second item will be stored in B(2, 1) and so on. If the supplied data are 10, 20, 30 and 40, READ *, B will create the matrix B as:

$$B = \begin{array}{|c|c|} \hline 10 & 30 \\ \hline 20 & 40 \\ \hline \end{array}$$

However, the last statement uses implied DO loop and because the inner index J takes all values before a change in the outer index I, this READ statement will assign data in the following order – B(1,1), B(1, 2), B(2,1) and B(2, 2) so the matrix with the same set of input will be:

$$B = \begin{array}{|c|c|} \hline 10 & 20 \\ \hline 30 & 40 \\ \hline \end{array}$$

11.12 Output

The PRINT statement can display a particular element or a whole array or a selected portion of the array using implied DO statement.

```
!           declaration of the previous section is used
PRINT *, A(1), A(3)
!           only A(1), A(3)
PRINT *, A
!           prints the complete array
PRINT *, (A(I), I=1, J)
!           prints A(1), A(2), ..... A(J)
PRINT *, A(1:3)
!           prints A(1), A(2), A(3)
PRINT *, A(1 : 10 : 2)
!           prints A(1), A(3), A(5), A(7) and A(9)
PRINT *, B(1, 1), B(2, 2)
!           prints only B(1, 1) and B(2, 2)
PRINT *, B
!           prints the complete array column wise
PRINT ((B(I, J), J=1, 2), I=1, 2)
!           prints the complete array row wise
```

The next few programs illustrate the use of arrays. Later we shall see that Fortran contains several very useful intrinsics which are much more convenient to handle similar kind of tasks.

```fortran
PROGRAM MAXVAL
INTEGER, PARAMETER:: SZ=10
REAL, DIMENSION(SZ) :: A
REAL :: AM
INTEGER :: MLOC, I
A = [-40.0, 23.97, 0.0, 37.25, 11.92, -17.1, &
        100.0, -123.25, 36.25, 22.12]
!     To find the largest value from an array
MLOC=1
!        Let maximum=first element
!        compare and redefine AM if necessary
AM=A(1)
DO I= 2, SZ
  IF(AM .LT. A(I)) THEN
    AM=A(I)
    MLOC=I
  ENDIF
ENDDO
!        AM contains the maximum of A
!        MLOC is the corresponding array location
PRINT *, 'Location ', MLOC, ' contains ', AM, &
            ' (highest value)'
END
```

By changing the IF statement, it is easy to find the minimum of A and in this case MLOC is the corresponding array location.

```fortran
PROGRAM MINVAL
INTEGER, PARAMETER:: SZ=10
REAL, DIMENSION(SZ) :: A
REAL :: AM
INTEGER :: MLOC, I
A = [-40.0, 23.97, 0.0, 37.25, 11.92, -17.1, &
        100.0, -123.25, 36.25, 22.12]
!     To find the smallest value from an array
MLOC=1
AM=A(1)
DO I= 2, SZ
  IF(AM .GT. A(I)) THEN
    AM=A(I)
    MLOC=I
  ENDIF
ENDDO
PRINT *, 'Location ', MLOC, ' contains ', AM, &
            ' (lowest value)'
END
```

Next program shows how to multiply two matrices. Two matrices A and B may be multiplied if the number of rows of matrix A is same as the number of columns of matrix B. The C(I, J)th elements of the product is given by:

$$c_{ij} = \sum a_{ik} * b_{kj} \text{ [sum over all k]}$$

```
PROGRAM MATRIXMUL
INTEGER, PARAMETER :: SZ =3
REAL, DIMENSION(SZ,SZ) :: A, B, C
!    square matrix for simplicity
INTEGER :: I, J, K
REAL :: SUM, X
DO I =1, SZ
  DO J= 1, SZ
  CALL RANDOM_NUMBER(X)  !        initialize the matrices
                         !        using random number
  A(I,J)=X*100.0         !        library function
  CALL RANDOM_NUMBER(X)
  B(I,J)=X*10.0
  ENDDO
ENDDO
PRINT *, A
PRINT *, B
DO I=1, SZ
  DO J=1, SZ
  SUM=0.0
    DO K=1, SZ
    SUM=SUM+A(I,K)*B(K,J)
    ENDDO
  C(I,J)=SUM
  ENDDO
ENDDO
PRINT *, C
END
```

The library function RANDOM_NUMBER generates pseudo random number between 0 and 1. In the following example the variable X returns such a random number. The random number generator is used to fill in the array with some value. RANDOM_NUMBER is discussed in chapter 26.

We now use a very inefficient algorithm to sort an array in ascending order.

```
PROGRAM SORT
INTEGER, PARAMETER :: SZ=10
REAL, DIMENSION(SZ) :: A
INTEGER :: I,J
REAL :: X, TEMP
!        A array is initialized with some random value
```

```
     DO I=1,SZ
      CALL RANDOM_NUMBER(X)
      A(I)=X*100.0
     ENDDO

     PRINT *, A

     DO I=1, SZ-1
      DO J=I, SZ
!          interchange if not in order
       IF (A(I) > A(J)) THEN
         TEMP=A(I)
         A(I)=A(J)
         A(J)=TEMP
       ENDIF
      ENDDO
     ENDDO
     PRINT *, A

     END
```

The program compares the first element of the array with the rest (second to SZ); at the end of J loop, A(1) contains the smallest value among all the array elements. Next the second element of the array is compared with third to SZ elements. At the end of the J loop A(2) would contain the second smallest value among all the array elements. This process continues and at the end of I-loop, the array A becomes a sorted array.

The following program merges two sorted arrays (ascending order) into a single array.

```
     PROGRAM MERGE_LIST
     INTEGER, DIMENSION(10)::A=[-7,20,40,51,79,105,127,190,207,315]
     INTEGER, DIMENSION(8)::B=[-1,36,42,81,112,136,167,328]
     INTEGER::I,J,K,SA,SB
     INTEGER,DIMENSION(50)::C
!    the size of C array must be at least SA+SB
     SA=SIZE(A)
     SB=SIZE(B)
     PRINT *,A
     PRINT *,B
     I=1
     J=1
     K=1
     DO WHILE(I<=SA .AND. J<=SB)
!    Exit from the loop if one of the array (or both) is exhausted
       IF(A(I)<B(J)) THEN
         C(K)=A(I)
         I=I+1
         K=K+1
       ELSE
```

```
      C(K)=B(J)
      J=J+1
      K=K+1
    ENDIF
  ENDDO
!   Add  the elements from A array if available
  DO WHILE(I<=SA)
    C(K)=A(I)
    I=I+1
    K=K+1
  ENDDO
!   Add  the elements from B array if available
  DO WHILE(J<=SB)
    C(K)=B(J)
    J=J+1
    K=K+1
  ENDDO
  PRINT *,C(1:SA+SB)
  END
```

The next program searches an element from an already sorted array using the technique known as binary search.

```
PROGRAM BINARY_SEARCH
INTEGER, DIMENSION(10):: A=[1,33,45,96,107,109,127,145, &
                                205,300]
INTEGER::LOW, HIGH, MID, D, LOC
LOGICAL:: FOUND=.FALSE.
PRINT *, 'Type an integer ... '
READ *, D   ! element to be searched
LOW=1
HIGH=10
MID=(LOW+HIGH)/2
DO WHILE (LOW < MID .AND. MID < HIGH)
 IF(A(MID) .EQ. D) THEN
  LOC=MID  ! found, print the result
  FOUND=.TRUE.
  EXIT
 ENDIF

 IF(A(MID) .GT. D) THEN
  HIGH=MID
 ELSE
  LOW=MID
 ENDIF
 MID=(LOW+HIGH)/2
 ENDDO
 IF(.NOT. FOUND) THEN  ! if already found skip
```

```fortran
      IF(A(LOW).EQ.D) THEN
        LOC=LOW
      ELSE IF(A(HIGH).EQ.D) THEN
            LOC=HIGH
      ELSE
        LOC=0    ! not found
      ENDIF
    ENDIF
    IF (LOC.EQ.0) THEN
      PRINT *, D, ' is not in the list'
    ELSE
      PRINT *, D, ' is at the position ', LOC
    ENDIF
    END
```

The method is to locate the mid-point (MID) and to check whether the number (D) is less than or equal to or greater than the corresponding array element (A(MID)). If D is equal to A(MID), then D is present in the array at the location MID. If D is not equal to A(MID), the LOW or the HIGH variable is adjusted and again the same procedure is repeated till either the element is found within the array or it is not found within the array. If the number is present, the corresponding position is displayed. If it is not present, zero is displayed. Note that this method can be applied on a sorted array. The algorithm may be found in any standard textbook on Data Structures.

11.13 Array Bound

As mentioned earlier, each dimension of the array has a lower bound and an upper bound. Fortran provides two intrinsics to find out the lower and upper bounds.

11.14 LBOUND

This intrinsic LBOUND returns an integer array of rank 1 and size equal to the rank of the input array containing the lower bounds in each dimension.

```fortran
        REAL, DIMENSION(-10:10,0:35)::A
        INTEGER, DIMENSION(2)::LB
        .
        LB=LBOUND (A)
        PRINT *, LB
        END
```

The program sets LB(1) to -10 and LB(2) to 0. They are respectively, the lower bounds of the input array in each dimension. LBOUND returns a scalar, if the lower bound of an array in a particular direction is desired through DIM argument.

```fortran
        J=LBOUND(A, DIM=1)
!          J is an integer (scalar), it is -10
        K=LBOUND(A, DIM=2)
!          K is an integer (scalar), it is 0
```

DIM=1 returns the lower bound of the first dimension and DIM=2 returns the lower bound of the second dimension.

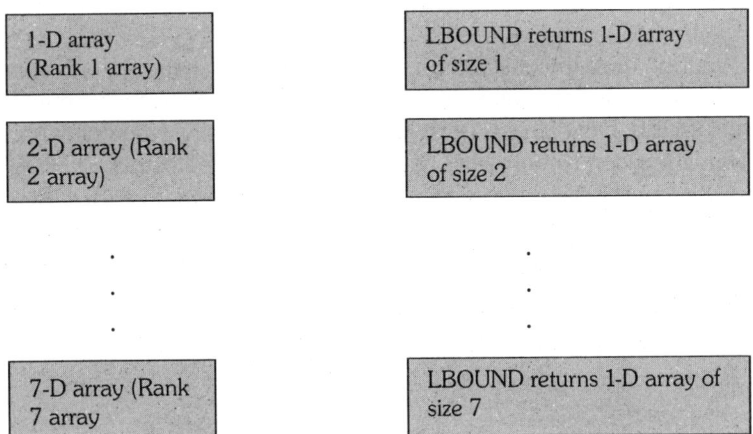

An interesting case arises if the input to LBOUND is a single dimension array, say Z. Both LBOUND(Z) and LBOUND(Z, DIM=1) will return same value but the type of the returned value are different – the former returns a single dimension integer array of size 1 and the later returns an integer (scalar).

11.15 UBOUND

The intrinsic UBOUND is exactly identical to its sister intrinsic LBOUND, except that it returns the upper bound. Using the declaration of the previous section and defining

```
INTEGER, DIMENSION(2) :: UB
```

this program segment returns the upper bounds in the respective dimensions.

```
UB=UBOUND (A)
!           UB(1) = 10, UB(2) = 35
J=UBOUND(A, DIM=1)
!             J is a scalar, it is 10
K=UBOUND(A, DIM=2)
!             K is a scalar, it is 35.
```

The discussions related to the input of a single dimension array to LBOUND are equally valid for UBOUND.

UBOUND (Z) where Z is single dimension array returns a rank 1 integer array of size 1, but UBOUND (Z, DIM=1) returns an integer. Both will contain the upper bound of Z in a particular direction.

It may be noted that though the examples were given using single and two-dimensioned arrays, the same can be extended to arrays having more dimensions as permitted by the language.

11.16 RESHAPE

RESHAPE is an intrinsic used to construct an array of specified shape (i.e. number of elements in each dimension) from the elements of a given array. RESHAPE takes four arguments – SOURCE, SHAPE, PAD and ORDER. Out of these, last two are optional. The first argument is the array with the values you want and the second argument is an array of rank 1. We illustrate RESHAPE with the help of examples. In these examples if the arguments are supplied in order i.e. SOURCE, SHAPE, PAD and ORDER – it is not necessary to write SOURCE= *array-name*, SHAPE= .. etc. On the other hand, SOURCE= , SHAPE=   , must be used when the arguments are supplied in any order.
Type I argument:

```
INTEGER, DIMENSION(3,3):: B
INTEGER, DIMENSION(9):: X
INTEGER, DIMENSION(2):: S
X = [10, 20, 30, 40, 50, 60, 70, 80, 90]
S =[3,3]
B=RESHAPE(SOURCE=X,SHAPE=[3,3])
```

This will construct a 3x3 array B whose elements are assigned column wise:

B – array

```
B(1,1) = 10
B(2,1) = 20
B(3,1) = 30
B(1,2) = 40
B(2,2) = 50
B(3,2) = 60
B(1,3) = 70
B(2,3) = 80
B(3,3) = 90
```

10	40	70
20	50	80
30	60	90

The above RESHAPE instruction may also be written in the following forms:

```
        B=RESHAPE(X, [3, 3])
or,     B=RESHAPE([10,20,30,40,50,60,70,80,90], &
            [3,3])
or,     B=RESHAPE(SHAPE=[3,3],SOURCE=X)
or,     B=RESHAPE(X,S)
or,     B=RESHAPE(SHAPE=S,SOURCE=X)
or,     B=RESHAPE (SHAPE[3,3],SOURCE = &
            [10,20,30,40,50,60,70,80,90])
```

or any combination of above as permitted by the language (see also 19.22). All the above mentioned forms are equivalent. The number of elements in SOURCE (in this case it is 9) must be greater than or equal to the product of the elements of the SHAPE array (in this case it is 3x3=9). For example,

```
B=RESHAPE([1,2,3,4,5,6,7,8,9,10],[3,3])
```

is acceptable, but the following

```
B=RESHAPE([1,2,3,4,5,6,7,8],[3,3])
```

is not because the number of elements in SOURCE is less than the product of extents (in this case 9) of the input array.

Type II argument: RESHAPE can have a third optional array valued parameter PAD. If the number of elements in SOURCE is less than the product of the elements of the SHAPE array (3x3=9 in this case), the unfilled elements are padded with PAD.

```
B=RESHAPE(SOURCE=[1,2,3,4,5,6,7],SHAPE=[3,3],PAD=[99])
```

will create a B array as:

$$B = \begin{array}{|c|c|c|} \hline 1 & 4 & 7 \\ \hline 2 & 5 & 99 \\ \hline 3 & 6 & 99 \\ \hline \end{array}$$

It is to be noted that if the elements to be filled is more than the number of elements in PAD, the elements of PAD is used repeatedly till all the elements are filled. In the above case 99 is used twice to fill in elements (2, 3) and (3, 3). In the case of

```
B=RESHAPE(SOURCE=[1,2,3,4,5,6],SHAPE=[3,3],PAD=[88,99])
```

the resultant B array becomes:

$$B = \begin{array}{|c|c|c|} \hline 1 & 4 & 88 \\ \hline 2 & 5 & 99 \\ \hline 3 & 6 & 88 \\ \hline \end{array}$$

88 and 99 are used repeatedly to fill in all the elements of B array.

Type III argument: RESHAPE accepts a fourth optional array valued parameter ORDER. The order array is of shape same as SHAPE and the elements are permutations of 1, 2, ... n, where n is the size of SHAPE. If the parameter ORDER is absent, it is assumed to be 1, 2, 3 ... n. The argument ORDER tells the order in which the index will vary during storing. The use of ORDER is illustrated with the help of examples:

```
INTEGER, DIMENSION (2, 2, 2)::B
    .
B=RESHAPE(SOURCE=[1,2,3,4,5,6,7,8],SHAPE=[2,2,2], &
      ORDER=[1,2,3])
```

In this case ORDER=[1, 2, 3] is the natural order, so that first index will vary most rapidly to be followed by the second index and third index. The natural ordering means:

```
B(1,1,1) = 1
B(2,1,1) = 2
B(1,2,1) = 3
B(2,2,1) = 4
B(1,1,2) = 5
B(2,1,2) = 6
B(1,2,2) = 7
B(2,2,2) = 8
```

The natural order is the default value of ORDER so without the ORDER parameter, RESHAPE will also generate the same B array. However,

```
B=RESHAPE(SOURCE=[1,2,3,4,5,6,7,8],SHAPE=[2,2,2], &
          ORDER=[3,2,1])
```

will force the third index to vary most rapidly to be followed by second and first index. Therefore, the elements of B array would be:

```
B(1,1,1) = 1
B(1,1,2) = 2
B(1,2,1) = 3
B(1,2,2) = 4
B(2,1,1) = 5
B(2,1,2) = 6
B(2,2,1) = 7
B(2,2,2) = 8
```

Similarly,

```
B=RESHAPE(SOURCE=[1,2,3,4,5,6,7,8],SHAPE=[2,2,2], &
          ORDER=[2,1,3])
```

will force the second index to vary most rapidly to be followed by the first and third index.

```
B(1,1,1) = 1
B(1,2,1) = 2
B(2,1,1) = 3
B(2,2,1) = 4
B(1,1,2) = 5
B(1,2,2) = 6
B(2,1,2) = 7
B(2,2,2) = 8
```

Type IV argument: It is possible to use both the PAD and the ORDER arguments simultaneously.

```
B=RESHAPE(SOURCE=[1,2,3,4,5,6],SHAPE=[2,2,2],PAD=[88,99],&
                ORDER=[3,2,1])
```

will set the two unfilled elements to 88 and 99 respectively. So,

```
B(2,2,1) = 88
B(2,2,2) = 99
```

It is perhaps clear that PAD may be absent but ORDER may be present. We close this section with two more examples. The first one uses a two dimensional array, i.e. a matrix with ORDER argument.

```
INTEGER, DIMENSION (2,2):: A
A=RESHAPE([10,20,30,40],[2,2])
```

This will generate a matrix:

$$A = \begin{array}{|c|c|} \hline 10 & 30 \\ \hline 20 & 40 \\ \hline \end{array}$$

Now,

```
A=RESHAPE(SOURCE=[10,20,30,40],SHAPE=[2,2], &
                ORDER=[2,1])
```

will generate A matrix as:

$$A = \begin{array}{|c|c|} \hline 10 & 20 \\ \hline 30 & 40 \\ \hline \end{array}$$

Note that this A array is actually the transpose of the previous A array. Finally, consider the following program:

```
      INTEGER, DIMENSION (2,2,2,2):: W
      INTEGER, DIMENSION (4,4):: X
!     generate W array
      DO I=1, 2
        DO J=1, 2
          DO K=1, 2
            DO L =1, 2
               W(I,J,K,L)=10*I+50*J+70*K+90*L
            ENDDO
          ENDDO
        ENDDO
      ENDDO
      PRINT *, W
      X=RESHAPE(W,[4,4],ORDER=[1,2])
```

```
PRINT *, X
X=RESHAPE(W,[4,4],ORDER=[2,1])
PRINT *, X
END
```

The elements of W array will be:

```
W(1,1,1,1)= 220
W(2,1,1,1)= 230
W(1,2,1,1)= 270
W(2,2,1,1)= 280
W(1,1,2,1)= 290
W(2,1,2,1)= 300
W(1,2,2,1)= 340
W(2,2,2,1)= 350
W(1,1,1,2)= 310
W(2,1,1,2)= 320
W(1,2,1,2)= 360
W(2,2,1,2)= 370
W(1,1,2,2)= 380
W(2,1,2,2)= 390
W(1,2,2,2)= 430
W(2,2,2,2)= 440
```

For natural ordering [1,2], RESHAPE will create a X array having the elements as shown below:

```
X(1,1)= 220
X(2,1)= 230
X(3,1)= 270
X(4,1)= 280
X(1,2)= 290
X(2,2)= 300
X(3,2)= 340
X(4,2)= 350
X(1,3)= 310
X(2,3)= 320
X(3,3)= 360
X(4,3)= 370
X(1,4)= 380
X(2,4)= 390
X(3,4)= 430
X(4,4)= 440
```

When the ORDER parameter is [2,1], RESHAPE will create a X array having the elements as shown below:

```
X(1,1)= 220
X(2,1)= 290
X(3,1)= 310
X(4,1)= 380
X(1,2)= 230
X(2,2)= 300
X(3,2)= 320
X(4,2)= 390
X(1,3)= 270
X(2,3)= 340
X(3,3)= 360
X(4,3)= 430
X(1,4)= 280
X(2,4)= 350
X(3,4)= 370
X(4,4)= 440
```

Readers may verify the result. We close this section by mentioning a rule of RESHAPE, which states that SOURCE cannot be empty.

```
B= RESHAPE(SOURCE =[ ],SHAPE=[3,3],PAD=[99])
```

is not allowed.

11.17 Vector Subscript

Vector subscripts allow the element of an array to be extracted or accessed in any order.

```
INTEGER, DIMENSION(5):: A
        .
A([4,5,1,2,3]) = [10,20,30,40,50]
```

This sets,

```
A[4] = 10
A[5] = 20
A[1] = 30
A[2] = 40
A[3] = 50
```

An index cannot not be repeated. However, most of the compilers do not flag this as error. The last value is taken.

```
INTEGER, DIMENSION(5) :: A=100
        .
A([2,4,3,2,1])=[1,2,3,4,5]
```

Majority of the compilers will generate code so that A(2) will be 4. The present author considers this to be a bug of the compiler.

Now, consider the following program segment.

```
INTEGER,DIMENSION(3,3)::A, B
INTEGER,DIMENSION(3)::C, D
A=RESHAPE([1,2,3,4,5,6,7,8,9],[3,3])
```

The A array is:

$$
A = \begin{array}{|c|c|c|}
\hline
1 & 4 & 7 \\
\hline
2 & 5 & 8 \\
\hline
3 & 6 & 9 \\
\hline
\end{array}
$$

The instruction

```
B=A([3,2,1],[1,3,2])
```

will perform the following assignment:

```
B(1,1) = A(3,1)
B(2,1) = A(2,1)
B(3,1) = A(1,1)
B(1,2) = A(3,3)
B(2,2) = A(2,3)
B(3,2) = A(1,3)
B(1,3) = A(3,2)
B(2,3) = A(2,2)
B(3,3) = A(1,2)
```

So the B matrix will be:

$$
B = \begin{array}{|c|c|c|}
\hline
3 & 9 & 6 \\
\hline
2 & 8 & 5 \\
\hline
1 & 7 & 4 \\
\hline
\end{array}
$$

The result would be same if

```
C = [3, 2, 1]
D = [1, 3, 2]
B = A(C, D)
```

and the B matrix will be as shown above. Note that the indices on the right are obtained from the elements of C and D, rank 1 arrays. For each element of the D array all the elements of C are taken to generate the indices of the right hand side e.g. (3, 1), (2, 1), (1, 1), (3, 3), (2, 3), (1, 3), (3, 2), (2, 2), (1, 2). It is also possible to use the same array both on the right hand side as well as left hand side of the assignment sign.

```
A = A (C,D)
```

will redefine the A array. We shall analyze the instruction A = A (C, D) in details. The above statement is equivalent to:

```
A(1,1) = A(3,1)
A(2,1) = A(2,1)
A(3,1) = A(1,1)
A(1,2) = A(3,3)
A(2,2) = A(2,3)
A(3,2) = A(1,3)
A(1,3) = A(3,2)
A(2,3) = A(2,2)
A(3,3) = A(1,2)
```

but always the existing values (i.e. values before the assignment) of the A array are used on the right hand side of the assignment sign. For example, in the statement:

```
A(3,1) = A(1,1)
```

the existing value of A (1, 1), which is 1, is used though according to the equivalent statement A (1, 1) has already been changed through the statement:

```
A(1,1) = A(3,1)
```

The reader may verify that

```
B = A([3,2,1],[1,2,3])
```

will generate B array as

$$B = \begin{array}{|c|c|c|} \hline 3 & 6 & 9 \\ \hline 2 & 5 & 8 \\ \hline 1 & 4 & 7 \\ \hline \end{array}$$

We conclude this section with an example of a three dimensional array.

```
INTEGER, DIMENSION(2, 2, 2):: X, Y
X= RESHAPE([1,2,3,4,5,6,7,8],[2,2,2])
Y=X([2,1],[1,2],[2,1])
PRINT *, X
PRINT *, Y
END
```

The readers may verify that the output will be:

```
1  2  3  4  5  6  7  8
6  5  8  7  2  1  4  3
```

11.18 WHERE Statement

This statement is used to modify array elements selectively depending upon the values of a logical array (mask). There are three forms of WHERE statements:

Form I:

WHERE (*logical-array-expression*) *array-variable* = expression

Form II:

WHERE (*logical-array-expression*)
   array-variable = *expression*
END WHERE

Form III:

WHERE (*logical-array-expression*)
   array-variable = *expression*
ELSEWHERE
   array-variable=*expression*
END WHERE

The logical array and the array variable must be of same shape. We first illustrate the use of WHERE with a simple example. Suppose a real rank 1 array A of size 10 contains some numbers and we want to take the square root of the elements which are positive.

```
REAL, DIMENSION(10) :: A= &
   [7.0, 39.2, -47.5, 67.25, 100.39, 25.0, -49.0, 0.0, &
   1.0, -32.0]
WHERE (A>0) A=SQRT(A)
PRINT *, A
END
```

Using the Form II type of WHERE statement, the same thing can be achieved.

```
REAL, DIMENSION(10) :: A= &
   [7.0, 39.2, -47.5, 67.25, 100.39, 25.0, -49.0, 0.0, &
   1.0, -32.0]
WHERE (A>=0.0)
 A=SQRT(A)
END WHERE
PRINT *, A
END
```

The logical mask is evaluated. The square root of the elements of the array A corresponding to the true value of the logical mask are taken and stored in the same location. The array elements of A corresponding to the false value of the mask are left untouched. Therefore, the PRINT statement would show that 3rd, 7th and the 10th elements have not been modified; other array elements contain the square root of the original value.

The next program sets the elements of an array of size 50 to 99 if the elements are multiples of the first four prime numbers (2, 3, 5 and 7).

```
INTEGER, DIMENSION(50)::A=[(I,I=1,50)]
PRINT *, A

WHERE (MOD(A,2).EQ.0 .OR. MOD(A,3).EQ.0 .OR. &
  MOD(A,5).EQ.0 .OR. MOD(A,7).EQ.0)
 A=99
END WHERE
PRINT *, A
END
```

If it is desired to set the array elements of A corresponding to false value of the logical array to some value, ELSEWHERE may be used.

```
REAL, DIMENSION(10)  :: A= &
   [7.0, 39.2, -47.5, 67.25, 100.39, 25.0, -49.0, 0.0, &
    1.0, -32.0]
WHERE (A>=0)
 A=SQRT(A)
ELSEWHERE
 A= -999.0
END WHERE
PRINT *, A
END
```

All the array elements of A having negative value are set to -999.0. The space between END and WHERE is optional.

There can be any number of ELSEWHERE with mask; however one of the ELSEWHERE must be without mask. If it is necessary to set all the array elements of A less than -48.0 to -99.0 and other negative elements to -999.0, an ELSEWHERE with mask and another ELSEWHERE without the mask must be added to the above program.

```
REAL, DIMENSION(10)  :: A= &
   [7.0, 39.2, -47.5, 67.25, 100.39, 25.0, -49.0, 0.0, &
    1.0, -32.0]
WHERE (A>=0)
 A=SQRT(A)
ELSEWHERE (A < -48.0)
     A=-99.0
```

```
ELSEWHERE
 A=-999.0
END WHERE
PRINT *, A
END
```

The WHERE statement may be nested, that is, it is possible to have one WHERE inside another WHERE. The rules for nested WHERE are similar to the rules of a nested DO loop.

11.19 FORALL

The "loop statements" discussed in chapter 4 (DO - ENDDO, DO-WHILE-ENDO) are executed cycle by cycle, that is, once the first cycle is over, the second cycle begins. Often the cycles are independent of each other. The simplest example is to set all the elements of an array to zero. In this instant case not only the cycles are independent of each other, but the order in which the cycles are to be executed is arbitrary also. For example, it does matter if the tenth element of the array is initialized before the first element. In such a case parallel execution within a system having more than one processor is possible. The statement FORALL does precisely this job. The syntax of FORALL is:

FORALL $(v1=i1{:}e1{:}s1, v2=i2{:}e2{:}s2, ..., vn=in{:}en{:}sn, mask)$ *array variable*=*expression*

or,

    FORALL $(v1=i1{:}e1{:}s1, v2=i2{:}e2{:}s2, ..., vn=in{:}en{:}sn, mask)$
    array variable=*expression*

    END FORALL

The variables $v1, v2, ... vn$ are integers (scalar). They start with initial values $i1, i2,.....$ in (integer and scalar) and goes up to $e1, e2, ...$ en (integer and scalar) with an increment (stride) $s1, s2,... sn$ (integer and scalar). If the increments are absent, they are assumed to be 1. The optional *mask*, if not present, is assumed to be true always. If it is present, a particular element is processed if the *mask* corresponding to the element is true; otherwise it is not processed.

```
INTEGER, DIMENSION(10)  :: A
!   without mask
INTEGER :: I
FORALL (I=1:10)
 A(I)=0
END FORALL
PRINT *, A
END
```

The next program uses a mask.

```
      INTEGER :: I, J, N=4
      REAL, DIMENSION (4,4) :: B, X=0.0
!      set the B array
       .
      FORALL (I=1:N, J=1:N, B(I,J) /=0)
       X(I,J)=1.0/B(I,J)
      END FORALL
       .
      END
```

This program calculates 1.0/B(I, J) for the non-zero elements of B and stores the value in X

Note the difference of *mask* between WHERE and FORALL. In case of FORALL *mask* can be set for the individual elements.

```
      FORALL (I=1:N, J=1:N, B(I,J) /=0 .AND. I/=J)
       .
      END FORALL
```

In all the assignment statement within FORALL, the original values of the elements are always used – even the value of an element has been modified. The modified value is never used within the FORALL. This is justified as the cycles are executed in any order. So for the sake of consistency of the results always the old values (existing values) are used. This is demonstrated with the help of the following example.

```
      INTEGER,DIMENSION(4,4)::A,B=0
      INTEGER :: I, J, N=4
      A=RESHAPE([(I,I=1,16)],[4,4])
      FORALL (I=2:N-1, J=2:N-1)
       A(I,J)=A(I,J-1)+A(I,J+1)+A(I-1,J)+A(I+1,J)
       B(I,J)=A(I,J)
      END FORALL
      PRINT *, A
      PRINT *, B
      END
```

Each element of A(2:3, 2:3) are redefined by adding the values of its 4 adjacent neighbors. This the A and B matrices are:

1	5	9	13
2	6	10	14
3	7	11	15
4	8	12	16

A–array

0	0	0	0
0	24	40	0
0	28	44	0
0	0	0	0

B–array

Incidentally,

$$B(2,2) = A(2,1) + A(2,3) + A(1,2) + A(3,2)$$

Similar calculations were done for calculating B(2,3), B(3,2) an B(3,3).

11.20 Rules for FORALL

(a) All the indices must be integer and scalar.
(b) The indices are valid only within the FORALL. The FORALL is their scope. The indices do not have any effect on the same named variable outside the FORALL.

```
I=10
FORALL (I=1:100)
.
END FORALL
PRINT *, I
```

will still print I as 10.
(c) The initial value, final value and the stride of any index cannot refer to another index of the FORALL.

```
FORALL (I=1:N, J=I+1:N-1)
.
END FORALL
```

is not a valid FORALL statement.
(d) If the *mask* is absent, it is assumed to be true always.
(e) If the *mask* is present, corresponding to the true value of the *mask*, the assignment statement is executed.
(f) If the mask contains a call to a procedure, it must be PURE (chapter 19).
(g) Scalar assignment statements are not allowed within FORALL, only arrays are allowed.
(h) A FORALL statement may have a label and in that case the END FORALL must have the same label.

```
LAB:    FORALL(...  )
.
        END FORALL LAB
```

(i) Within FORALL, if there is a call to any procedure, the procedure must be PURE.
(j) The FORALL may be nested. Also the FORALL may contain a WHERE statement within it also.
(k) Only an array can be used on the left hand side of the assignment sign within FORALL.
   The structure of FORALL and all its rules ensure cycle-independent, parallel execution of FORALL.

11.21 Programming Example

We conclude this chapter with one complete program. This numerical technique is known as Gauss-Seidel method for solving linear simultaneous equation. We consider three linear simultaneous equations with three unknowns:

$$a_{11}x_1 + a_{12}x_2 + a_{13}x_3 = b_1 \qquad (1)$$
$$a_{21}x_1 + a_{22}x_2 + a_{23}x_3 = b_2 \qquad (2)$$
$$a_{31}x_1 + a_{32}x_2 + a_{33}x_3 = b_3 \qquad (3)$$

Rearranging we get:

$$x_1 = 1/a_{11}(b_1 - a_{12}x_2 - a_{13}x_3) \qquad (4)$$
$$x_2 = 1/a_{22}(b_2 - a_{21}x_1 - a_{23}x_3) \qquad (5)$$
$$x_3 = 1/a_{33}(b_3 - a_{31}x_1 - a_{32}x_2) \qquad (6)$$

a_{11}, a_{22} and a_{33} are not equal to zero.

We choose a guess value, say, $x_1 = x_2 = x_3 = 0$ and substitute x_2 and x_3 in equation (4) and obtain x_1. Using this value of x_1 and guess value of x_3 we obtain x_2 from equation (5). Again using new values of x_1 and x_2 we obtain a new value of x_3. This process is repeated till the difference between the sum of the old absolute values of Xs and the new absolute values of Xs are small compared to some predefined value, say, 1.0E-7.

We shall now solve the equations:

$$4x - y + 2z = 8$$
$$2x + 7y - z = 13$$
$$x + 2y + 5z = 20$$

```
PROGRAM GAUSSSEIDEL
INTEGER, PARAMETER:: SZ=3, ITER=100
INTEGER:: COUNT=0
REAL, DIMENSION (SZ,SZ)::A
REAL, DIMENSION(SZ) :: B, X
REAL:: SUM,RES, EPS=1.0E-7,R
X=[0.0,0.0,0.0]
!        guess value = 0
B=[8.0,13.0,20.0]
A=RESHAPE([4.0,2.0,1.0,-1.0,7.0,2.0, &
       2.0,-1.0,5.0],[3,3])

!        construct A matrix with the coefficients
!        x, y and z (column wise)

DO K=1, ITER
COUNT=COUNT+1
  DO I=1,SZ
  SUM=0.0
  R=0.0
```

```fortran
          DO J=1,SZ
!            Skip when i=j
          IF(I.EQ.J) THEN
           CYCLE
          ENDIF
          SUM=SUM+A(I,J)*X(J)
          ENDDO
         SUM=(B(I)-SUM)/A(I,I)
         RES=ABS(SUM-X(I))
         R=R+RES
!            sum of the residue
         X(I)=SUM
!            redefine X's
       ENDDO
       IF(R .LE. EPS) THEN
        EXIT
       ENDIF
      ENDDO
      IF(COUNT < 100) THEN
       PRINT *, 'Converged after ', COUNT, ' Cycle'
       PRINT *, 'Roots are : ',X
      ELSE
       PRINT *, 'Convergence not achieved ', X
      ENDIF
      END
```

The roots of these equations are 1, 2 and 3.

Chapter 12

ARRAY HANDLING INTRINSICS

Fortran contains several array-handling intrinsics. The intrinsics can be divided into several groups. Though these intrinsics may operate on any array of rank less than or equal to 7, we have chosen arrays of rank less than or equal to two for simplicity. However, just to get a feeling how calculations are performed for array of rank 3 or 4, a separate section has been added and detailed calculations are shown. This can be extended for the higher dimensional arrays.

12.1 Maximum and Minimum

There are four intrinsics under this group – MAXVAL, MINVAL, MAXLOC and MINLOC. MAXVAL and MINVAL, as the names imply, return the maximum and minimum value from an array; similarly, MAXLOC and MINLOC return the locations containing the maximum and minimum elements respectively. Both the MAXVAL and the MINVAL take three arguments – two of them are optional. The first is the name of the array, whose maximum and minimum values are returned.

```
INTEGER, DIMENSION (2):: ML
INTEGER, DIMENSION (3,3):: A
INTEGER :: AMI, AMA
INTEGER, DIMENSION(3)::ARC
!      initialize
A=RESHAPE([17,32,5,11,12,33,2,8,10], [3,3])
AMA=MAXVAL(A)
AMI=MINVAL(A)
PRINT *, AMA, AMI ! AMA=33, AMI=2
END
```

The above program prints 33 and 2 as the highest and the lowest values among the array elements.

17	11	**2**
32	12	8
5	**33**	10

For an array greater than rank 1, say for a two-dimensional array, a second optional argument DIM may be used to find the maximum in the rows or in the columns. For a rank 2 array, DIM=1 corresponds to the columns and DIM=2 corresponds to the rows. When DIM is used, MAXVAL and

MINVAL return an array of rank one less than of the input array and the size same as the shape of the given array in that direction (for a two dimensional array each row or column is a single dimension array). For a 3x3 input array the intrinsic returns a rank 1 array of size 3 both for DIM=1 or DIM=2. However, for an array of shape (3, 4), DIM=1 returns a rank 1 array of size 4 and DIM=2 returns a rank 1 array of size 3. The elements of the return array contain the maximum value of each row or columns depending upon the value of the argument DIM.

```
ARC= MAXVAL(A, DIM=1)
```

will return the maximum value from the respective columns. Obviously, the elements of ARC will be 32, 33 and 10 respectively.

17	11	2
32	12	8
5	**33**	**10**

DIM=1

Similarly,

```
ARC= MAXVAL(A, DIM=2)
```

will return maximum value for the respective rows. In this case the array elements of ARC will be 17, 32 and 33.

17	11	2
32	12	8
5	**33**	10

DIM=2 $\longrightarrow$

The third optional argument is a MASK, which can be used to select an array element that passes through the test.

```
AMA=MAXVAL (A, MASK= A<15)
```

will find maximum value from the array elements which are less than 15. Clearly, AMA in this case will be 12. The array elements 17, 32 and 33 are excluded and not considered while finding the maximum value. The array elements, which are left out because of the MASK, are indicated by striking through its value.

~~17~~	11	2
~~32~~	**12**	8
5	~~33~~	10

The intrinsic MINVAL works in an identical manner.

```
ARC=MINVAL(A, DIM=1)
```

17	11	2
32	12	8
5	33	10

will return 5, 11 and 2 to ARC(1), ARC(2) and ARC(3)respectively.

Similarly,

```
ARC=MINVAL (A, DIM=2)
```

17	11	**2**
32	12	**8**
5	33	10

will return 2, 8 and 5 to ARC(1), ARC(2) and ARC(3) respectively.

```
AMI=MINVAL (A, MASK=A>10)
```

will exclude 2, 5, 8 and 10 as they are less than 10. Naturally, the intrinsic returns 11 to AMI.

17	**11**	2
32	12	8
5	33	10

If the MASK is such that no element could be selected, MAXVAL returns the smallest negative number (in this case integer) available in the system (default kind). Similarly, in case of MINVAL, if the MASK is so chosen such that it excludes all the elements, it returns the highest positive number (in this case integer) available in the system (default kind).

Both DIM and MASK may be present simultaneously:

```
AMA=MAXVAL (A, DIM=1, MASK=A<15)
```

will return 5, 12 and 10 as the array elements of AMA.

17	11	2
32	**12**	8
5	33	**10**

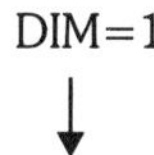

Also,

```
AMI=MINVAL(A, DIM=2, MASK=A<32)
```

will return an array of rank 1 with its elements as 2, 8 and 5.

17	11	**2**
32	12	**8**
5	33	10

DIM=2 ⟶

The intrinsics MAXLOC and MINLOC determine locations that contain the maximum and minimum of an array. It always returns an array of rank 1 and size equal to the rank of the input array. To locate a particular location of a matrix, two subscripts are required. So, to return the position of an element MAXLOC and MINLOC require an array of rank 1 and of size 2.

```
ML=MAXLOC(A)
!  A(3, 2)=33; ML(1)=3, ML(2)=2
ML=MINLOC(A)
!  A(1, 3)=2; ML(1)=1, ML(2)=3
```

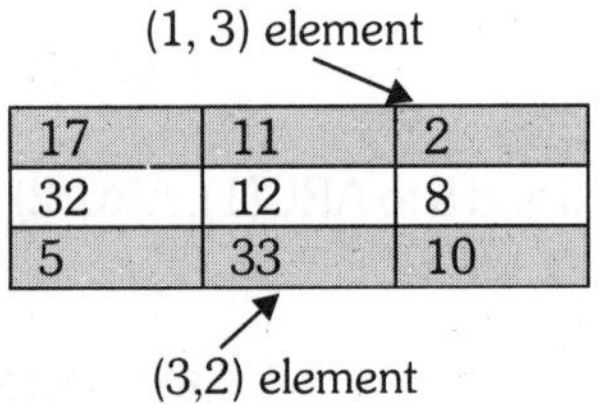

17	11	2
32	12	8
5	33	10

Note that, even when the input to MAXLOC or MINLOC is an array of rank 1, the output from these intrinsics is an rank 1 array of size 1, that is, just one element. The optional parameter DIM may be used with MAXLOC or MINLOC. MAXLOC (A, DIM=1) returns a rank 1 array of sized 3 having elements 2 3 3 (column number). MAXLOC (A, DIM=2) returns similar array having elements 1 1 2 (row number). Similar is the case with MINLOC.

MAXLOC and MINLOC always calculate the location assuming the lower bound of the array in each dimension to be equal to 1, irrespective of its declaration.

```
INTEGER, DIMENSION (0: 4) :: A=[10, -5, 7, 14, 3]
INTEGER, DIMENSION (1) :: LOC
LOC=MAXLOC(A)
```

will return LOC(1) as 4 and not as 3. If it is desired to have the exact location with respect to lower bound, the last expression is to be modified as:

```
LOC = (MAXLOC(A)+LBOUND(A)-1)
```

The same is true for multidimensional arrays also.

It is also possible to use a mask to include (or exclude) certain elements while finding the location.

```
ML=MAXLOC(A, MASK=A<16)
!  A(2, 2)=12; ML(1)=2, ML(2)=2
```

17	11	2
32	12	8
5	33	10

```
ML=MINLOC(A,MASK=A>20)
!  A(2,1)=32; ML(1)=2, ML(2)=1
```

17	11	2
32	12	8
5	33	10

If the maximum or the minimum value occurs more than once within the array, the first one is returned. For multi-dimensional arrays it was mentioned earlier how they are mapped into single dimension. The 'first' is determined after mapping the array into single dimension. MASK can be combined with DIM also.

```
INTEGER, DIMENSION (3, 3):: X
X=RESHAPE([10,9,17,32,65,13,65,19,12], [3, 3])
```

10	32	65
9	65	19
17	13	12

It is seen that when X, a two dimensional array, is mapped into single dimension, the 5th and the 7th locations contain 65. MAXLOC in this case returns 5th location, which is $(2, 2)$.

For zero sized arrays, MAXVAL returns the negative value having the largest available value in the system (same kind type as argument). Similarly, for zero sized arrays, MINVAL returns the largest positive value that the system supports. However, for zero sized arrays both MAXLOC and MINLOC returns zero.

12.2 SUM and PRODUCT

These two intrinsics return the sum and product of array elements respectively. The array may be integer, real or complex. Like MAXVAL and MINVAL, these intrinsics also take 3 arguments. Two of them are optional.

```
INTEGER, DIMENSION (3, 3) :: A
INTEGER :: S, P
INTEGER, DIMENSION (3) :: SA, SP
A=RESHAPE ([2,5,13,8,24,35,12,1,40], [3, 3])
```

2	8	12
5	24	1
13	35	40

Now, S=SUM(A) corresponds the sum of all the elements, that is,

```
S = 2+5+13+8+24+35+12+1+40
```

Similarly, P=PRODUCT (A) corresponds to the product of all the elements,

```
P = 2*5*13*8*24*35*12*1*40
```

Both these intrinsics may take an optional parameter DIM.

```
SA=SUM (A, DIM=1)
```

This returns a rank 1 array of size 3 with,

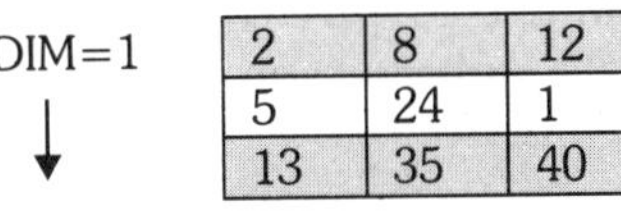


```
SA(1)=2+5+13
SA(2)=8+24+35
SA(3)=12+1+40
```

In an identical manner,

```
SA=SUM (A, DIM=2)
```

returns,

```
SA(1)= 2+8+12
SA(2)= 5+24+1
SA(3)= 13+35+40
```

The following program will sum the series $1+2+3...+100$ without using DO loop.

```
INTEGER :: I
PRINT *, SUM([(I, I=1,100)])
END
```

The implied DO loop will generate an array constant [1, 2, 3, ..., 100] and SUM will add these elements to return the sum of the series.

It is not difficult to guess the result of the PRODUCT intrinsic.

```
PA = PRODUCT (A, DIM=1)
```

returns,

```
PA(1)=2*5*13
PA(2)=8*24*35
PA(3)=12*1*40
```

and,

```
PA=PRODUCT (A, DIM=2)
```

returns,

```
PA(1)=2*8*12
PA(2)=5*24*1
PA(3)=13*35*40
```

Another example of PRODUCT is to evaluate factorial N, for say, N=7.

```
PRINT *, PRODUCT([(I, I=2,7)])
```

Both SUM and PRODUCT may take a second optional argument, MASK. This was discussed in details in the earlier section.

```
SA=SUM(A, DIM=1, MASK=A<20)
```

2	**8**	**12**
5	24	**1**
13	35	40

gives (elements passed through the MASK are shown as bold),

```
SA(1)=2+5+13
SA(2)=8
SA(3)=12+1
```

```
P=PRODUCT(A, MASK=A<10)
```

gives,

$$P=2*5*8*1$$

2	8	12
5	24	1
13	35	40

Finally,

$$PA=PRODUCT(A, DIM=2, MASK=A<10)$$

gives,

```
PA(1)=2*8
PA(2)=5*1
PA(3)=0
```

12.3 Handling of Arrays of More than Two Dimension

All the examples given above used single or two-dimensional arrays. In this section detailed calculations will show how three-dimensional arrays are handled by SUM with the DIM argument. The same logic is applicable for other intrinsics that use DIM as argument. Having understood three-dimensional arrays, it is expected that one should be able to extend the logic for the higher dimensional arrays.

It was already mentioned that when the DIM argument is used, SUM (or similar intrinsics) returns an array of rank one less than that of the input array. The following program will be used throughout this section:

```
INTEGER, DIMENSION (3, 3, 3) :: A
INTEGER, DIMENSION (3, 3) ::B
A=RESHAPE([( I, I=1, 27)], [3, 3, 3])
B=SUM(A,DIM=1)
PRINT *, B
B=SUM(A,DIM=2)
PRINT *, B
B=SUM(A,DIM=3)
PRINT *, B
END
```

The outputs are:

```
6   15  24  33  42  51  60  69  78
12  15  18  39  42  45  66  69  72
30  33  36  39  42  45  48  51  54
```

The contents of A array with the locations are as follows:

1,1,1	1	1,1,2	10	1,1,3	19
2,1,1	2	2,1,2	11	2,1,3	20
3,1,1	3	3,1,2	12	3,1,3	21
1,2,1	4	1,2,2	13	1,2,3	22
2,2,1	5	2,2,2	14	2,2,3	23
3,2,1	6	3,2,2	15	3,2,3	24
1,3,1	7	1,3,2	16	1,3,3	25
2,3,1	8	2,3,2	17	2,3,3	26
3,3,1	9	3,3,2	18	3,3,3	27

When DIM argument is used, the intrinsic returns an array of rank 2 having shape (2 2), one less than the rank of the input array. Consider the case when DIM=1. The (i, j)th of the returned array is,

$$\sum A(:, i, j)$$

where $\sum$ indicates the sum over the first index and ':' stands for all the indices (in this case, 1, 2 and 3). Expanding we get,

```
B(1, 1) = A(1,1,1)+A(2,1,1)+A(3,1,1)
B(2, 1) = A(1,2,1)+A(2,2,1)+A(3,2,1)
B(3, 1) = A(1,3,1)+A(2,3,1)+A(3,3,1)
B(1, 2) = A(1,1,2)+A(2,1,2)+A(3,1,2)
B(2, 2) = A(1,2,2)+A(2,2,2)+A(3,2,2)
B(3, 2) = A(1,3,2)+A(2,3,2)+A(3,3,2)
B(1, 3) = A(1,1,3)+A(2,1,3)+A(3,1,3)
B(2, 3) = A(1,2,3)+A(2,2,3)+A(3,2,3)
B(3, 3) = A(1,3,3)+A(2,3,3)+A(3,3,3)
```

For, DIM=2, the (i,j)th element of the returned array is,

$$\sum A(i, :, j)$$

where $\sum$ indicates the sum over the second index. Expanding we get,

```
B(1, 1) = A(1,1,1)+A(1,2,1)+A(1,3,1)
B(2, 1) = A(2,1,1)+A(2,2,1)+A(2,3,1)
B(3, 1) = A(3,1,1)+A(3,2,1)+A(3,3,1)
B(1, 2) = A(1,1,2)+A(1,2,2)+A(1,3,2)
B(2, 2) = A(2,1,2)+A(2,2,2)+A(2,3,2)
B(3, 2) = A(3,1,2)+A(3,2,2)+A(3,3,2)
B(1, 3) = A(1,1,3)+A(1,2,3)+A(1,3,3)
B(2, 3) = A(2,1,3)+A(2,2,3)+A(2,3,3)
B(3, 3) = A(3,1,3)+A(3,2,3)+A(3,3,3)
```

Finally, for DIM=3, the (i,j)th element of the returned array is,

$$\sum A(i, j, :)$$

where $\sum$ indicates the sum over the third index. Expanding we get,

```
B(1, 1) = A(1,1,1)+A(1,1,2)+A(1,1,3)
B(2, 1) = A(2,1,1)+A(2,1,2)+A(2,1,3)
B(3, 1) = A(3,1,1)+A(3,1,2)+A(3,1,3)
B(1, 2) = A(1,2,1)+A(1,2,2)+A(1,2,3)
B(2, 2) = A(2,2,1)+A(2,2,2)+A(2,2,3)
B(3, 2) = A(3,2,1)+A(3,2,2)+A(3,2,3)
B(1, 3) = A(1,3,1)+A(1,3,2)+A(1,3,3)
B(2, 3) = A(2,3,1)+A(2,3,2)+A(2,3,3)
B(3, 3) = A(3,3,1)+A(3,3,2)+A(3,3,3)
```

Readers may verify that substituting the values of respective array elements of A array, the above mentioned outputs, indeed, agree with the result.

12.4 DOT_PRODUCT

This intrinsic takes two arrays of rank 1 (also same shape) and returns the dot product. The array may be of type integer, real, logical or complex. The dot product is defined as:

$$\sum A_i.B_i \qquad [i =1, n\ (n= \text{size of the array})]$$

```
REAL, DIMENSION(4) :: A=[1.0,2.0,3.0,4.0]
REAL, DIMENSION(4) :: B=[10.0,20.0,30.0,40.0]
REAL :: DP
  .
DP=DOT_PRODUCT(A, B)
```

DP works out as:

```
1.0x10.0+2.0x20.0+3.0x30.0+4.0x40.0 = 300.0
```

For logical arrays, L1 and L2, L1 .AND. L2 is calculated element by element. If one of the results is true, DOT_PRODUCT returns true. If all the results are false, DOT_PRODUCT returns false.

```
LOGICAL, DIMENSION(3) :: L1=[.TRUE., .TRUE., .FALSE.]
LOGICAL, DIMENSION(3) :: L2=[.FALSE., .TRUE., .TRUE.]
PRINT *, DOT_PRODUCT(L1,L2)
END
```

The result is true.

For complex arrays, C1 and C2, DOT_PRODUCT is calculated as:

$$\sum \text{conjugate}(C1)*C2$$

```
COMPLEX, DIMENSION(3) :: C1=[(1,2),(3,4),(5,6)]
COMPLEX, DIMENSION(3) :: C2=[(5,6),(7,8),(25,30)]
COMPLEX :: SUM=(0.0,0.0)
PRINT *, DOT_PRODUCT(C1,C2)         !       direct calculation
C1=CONJG(C1)
DO I= 1, 3
  SUM=SUM+C1(I)*C2(I)
ENDDO
PRINT *, SUM
END
```

Both the PRINT statements would print the same number: (375.0, -8.0).

12.5 MATMUL

Two matrices, when the number of rows of the first matrix is equal to the number of columns of the second matrix, can be multiplied with this intrinsic. The arrays may be integer, real, logical or complex. Actually, the first and the second argument shall be a rank 1 or 2 array. If the first argument is a rank 1 array, the second argument must be a rank 2 array. Similarly if the second argument is a rank 1 array the first argument should be a rank 2 array.

```
REAL, DIMENSION (3, 2) :: A
REAL, DIMENSION (2, 3) :: B
REAL, DIMENSION (3, 3) :: C
!                initialize the matrix
  .

  .

C=MATMUL(A, B)
```

The multiplication is performed (for numeric array) according to the rule of matrix algebra.

$$C_{ij} = \sum A_{ik}*B_{kj} \quad [\text{sum over k}]$$

For logical array the MATMUL 'multiplies' the row of the first matrix by the column of the second matrix element by element by AND operation and if any one of them is true, true value is returned. This is illustrated with the help of two logical matrices:

```
LOGICAL, DIMENSION (3,3):: L1, L2, L3
L1=RESHAPE([.TRUE., .FALSE., .TRUE., .FALSE.,&
  .TRUE., .FALSE., .TRUE., .TRUE., .FALSE.], [3,3])
L2=RESHAPE([.TRUE., .FALSE., .FALSE., .FALSE.,&
  .TRUE., .FALSE., .TRUE., .FALSE., .FALSE.], [3,3])

L3=MATMUL(L1, L2)

PRINT *, L3
END
```

L1=

T	F	T
F	T	T
T	F	F

The output is:
```
T   F   T   F   T   F   T   F   T
```

$$L2 = \begin{array}{|c|c|c|} \hline T & F & T \\ \hline F & T & F \\ \hline F & F & F \\ \hline \end{array}$$

L3(1,1) is obtained as follows:

```
.TRUE.   .AND.   .TRUE.
.FALSE.  .AND.   .FALSE.
.TRUE.   .AND.   .FALSE.
```

This is true because one of the above expressions is true.
Similarly, L3(2, 1) is false as none of the following

```
.FALSE.  .AND.   .TRUE.
.TRUE.   .AND.   .FALSE.
.TRUE.   .AND.   .FALSE.
```

returns true.

If the matrix A is of shape (n, m) and the matrix B is of shape (m, k), the resultant matrix has a shape (n, k). If the matrix A is of shape (n) and the matrix B of shape (n, k), the resultant matrix has a shape (k). If the matrix A is of shape (n, m) and the matrix B of shape (m) the resultant matrix has a shape (n).

12.6 Transpose of a Matrix

The intrinsic TRANSPOSE takes a square matrix (number of rows = number of columns) as its argument and returns the transpose of the original matrix, that is, rows and columns are interchanged.

```
INTEGER, DIMENSION (2, 2) :: A, B
A=RESHAPE ([1, 2, 3, 4], [2, 2])
B=TRANSPOSE (A)
```

The original and the transposed matrix are shown in the adjacent figures.

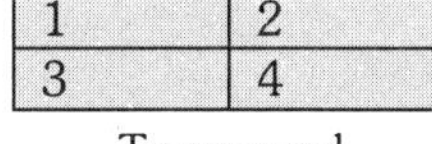

1	3
2	4

Original

1	2
3	4

Transposed

12.7 Array Shift

There are two intrinsics to shift the elements of an array. The first is called EOSHIFT (end of shift) and the second is known as CSHIFT (circular shift).

EOSHIFT: We first illustrate EOSHIFT with an array of rank 1. In the simplest case, this intrinsic takes two arguments – the first is an array of any type (integer, real, complex, logical and character) and the second argument is shift count. The shift count is an integer (scalar). A positive shift count corresponds to left shift and a negative shift count corresponds to right shift. The vacancy created by this operation is filled according to the following table:

Table : 12.1 Characters to Fill the Vacancy in Shift Operation

Type	Value
Integer	0
Real	0.0
Complex	(0.0, 0.0)
Logical	False
Character	Blank

The elements shifted out are lost.

```
INTEGER, DIMENSION(6) :: A=[1, 2, 3, 4, 5, 6]
INTEGER, DIMENSION(6) :: B
.
B=EOSHIFT(A, SHIFT=2)
```

A–array

1	2	3	4	5	6

B–array

3	4	5	6	0	0

As the shift count is 2, elements are shifted 2 places to the left.

Similarly,

```
B=EOSHIFT(A, SHIFT=-3)
```

A–array

1	2	3	4	5	6

B–array

0	0	0	1	2	3

will shift array elements 3 places to the right. One can specify the boundary value by the optional boundary parameter. If the boundary parameter is present, the vacancies created by EOSHIFT are filled with the boundary value instead of the values mentioned in Table 12.1.

```
B=EOSHIFT(A, SHIFT=2, BOUNDARY=999)
```

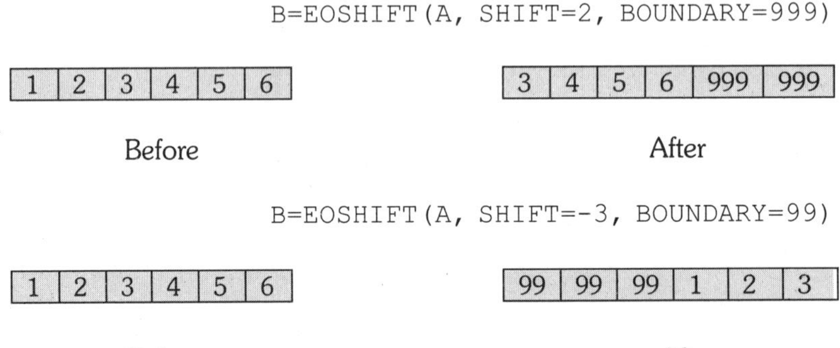

1	2	3	4	5	6

3	4	5	6	999	999

Before   After

```
B=EOSHIFT(A, SHIFT=-3, BOUNDARY=99)
```

1	2	3	4	5	6

99	99	99	1	2	3

Before   After

The array may be of rank greater than one. In that case the shift count may be a scalar or an array of rank one less than the input array. If the shift count is a scalar, all elements are shifted by an equal amount.

```
INTEGER, DIMENSION (3, 3) :: C
INTEGER, DIMENSION (3, 3) :: D
C=RESHAPE([10,20,30,40,50,60,70,80,90], [3, 3])
```

So, the C array becomes:

$$C = \begin{array}{|c|c|c|} \hline 10 & 40 & 70 \\ \hline 20 & 50 & 80 \\ \hline 30 & 60 & 90 \\ \hline \end{array}$$

Now,

```
D=EOSHIFT(C, SHIFT=1)
```

will shift all the columns by one to the left and thus D becomes,

$$D = \begin{array}{|c|c|c|} \hline 20 & 50 & 80 \\ \hline 30 & 60 & 90 \\ \hline 0 & 0 & 0 \\ \hline \end{array}$$

Similarly, when the shift is negative like,

```
D=EOSHIFT(C, SHIFT=-1)
```

all the columns are shifted by one to the right and the matrix becomes,

$$D = \begin{array}{|c|c|c|} \hline 0 & 0 & 0 \\ \hline 10 & 40 & 70 \\ \hline 20 & 50 & 80 \\ \hline \end{array}$$

The shift "left" and "right" for an array may be understood by mapping the two dimensional array into single dimension.

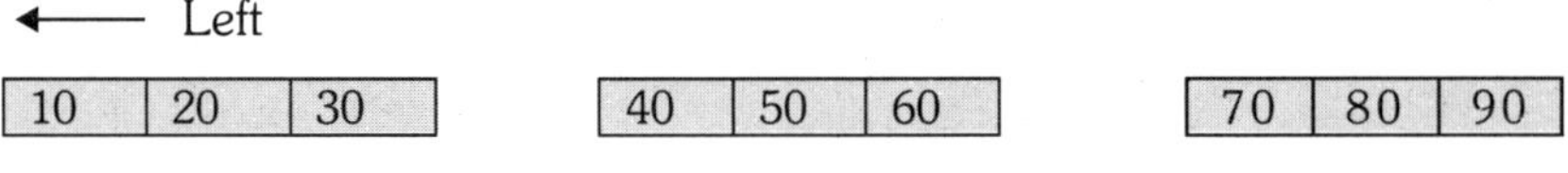

If the optional boundary parameter (as scalar) is specified, the vacancy created is filled in by the boundary value.

```
D=EOSHIFT(C, SHIFT=1, BOUNDARY=999)
```

The above statement will create the matrix D as shown below:

$$D= \begin{array}{|c|c|c|} \hline 20 & 50 & 80 \\ \hline 30 & 60 & 90 \\ \hline 999 & 999 & 999 \\ \hline \end{array}$$

In a similar way, a negative shift count along with the boundary value:

```
D=EOSHIFT(C, SHIFT=-1, BOUNDARY=999)
```

results in D as,

$$D= \begin{array}{|c|c|c|} \hline 999 & 999 & 999 \\ \hline 10 & 40 & 70 \\ \hline 20 & 50 & 89 \\ \hline \end{array}$$

For an array of rank greater than 1, it is possible to apply different shift in different columns and the vacancies created by the shifts may be filled with different values instead of a single value by using the boundary as an array of rank one less than the original array.

```
D=EOSHIFT(C, SHIFT=[1, -1,  2])
```

Now, the SHIFT argument is a rank 1 array and this shifts the first column one to the left, second column one to the right and the third column 2 to the left. The D array thus becomes:

$$D= \begin{array}{|c|c|c|} \hline 20 & 0 & 90 \\ \hline 30 & 40 & 0 \\ \hline 0 & 50 & 0 \\ \hline \end{array}$$

Similarly, with the boundary value of 999, the instruction:

```
D=EOSHIFT(C, SHIFT=[1, -1, 2], BOUNDARY=999)
```

will generate the following D matrix:

$$D= \begin{array}{|c|c|c|} \hline 20 & 999 & 90 \\ \hline 30 & 40 & 999 \\ \hline 999 & 50 & 999 \\ \hline \end{array}$$

It is possible to specify different boundary values for different columns.

```
D=EOSHIFT(C, SHIFT=[1, -1, 2], BOUNDARY=[999, 888, 777])
```

So the D array becomes:

$$D= \begin{array}{|c|c|c|} \hline 20 & 888 & 90 \\ \hline 30 & 40 & 777 \\ \hline 999 & 50 & 777 \\ \hline \end{array}$$

EOSHIFT may take a fourth optional argument, DIM, which is a scalar. If it is absent it is assumed to be 1. It satisfies the inequality:

```
1 <= DIM <=n
```

where n is the rank of the input array.

For the default value of DIM, that is, 1, the shift takes place column wise. The following two statements are thus equivalent:.

```
            D=EOSHIFT(C, SHIFT=1, BOUNDARY=999)
and         D=EOSHIFT(C, SHIFT=1, BOUNDARY=999, DIM=1)
```

In case of the above-mentioned array, if DIM=2, shift will take place row wise.

```
            D=EOSHIFT(C, SHIFT=1, BOUNDARY=888, DIM=2)
```

will generate the D matrix as shown below:

$$
D=
\begin{array}{|c|c|c|}
\hline
40 & 70 & 888 \\
\hline
50 & 80 & 888 \\
\hline
60 & 90 & 888 \\
\hline
\end{array}
$$

Some more examples of EOSHIFT are:

```
D=EOSHIFT(C, SHIFT=[1, -1, 1] , BOUNDARY=[777, 888, 999], &
                DIM=2)
```

$$
D=
\begin{array}{|c|c|c|}
\hline
40 & 70 & 777 \\
\hline
888 & 20 & 50 \\
\hline
60 & 90 & 999 \\
\hline
\end{array}
$$

```
D=EOSHIFT(C, SHIFT=[1, -1, 0], BOUNDARY=[777, 888, 999], &
                DIM=2)
```

$$
D=
\begin{array}{|c|c|c|}
\hline
40 & 70 & 777 \\
\hline
888 & 20 & 50 \\
\hline
30 & 60 & 90 \\
\hline
\end{array}
$$

The third row is not shifted since the shift count is zero.

We conclude this section with an application of EOSHIFT on a three dimensional array of shape (2 2 2).

```
            INTEGER, DIMENSION (2, 2, 2) :: A, B
            A=RESHAPE([ (I, I=1, 8)], [2, 2, 2])
            PRINT *, A
            PRINT *, "++++++++"
```

```
PRINT *, "DIM=1"
B=EOSHIFT(A, 1, DIM=1)
PRINT *, B
B=EOSHIFT(A, -1, DIM=1)
PRINT *, B
PRINT *, "++++++++"
PRINT *, "DIM=2"
B=EOSHIFT(A, 1, DIM=2)
PRINT *, B
B=EOSHIFT(A, -1, DIM=2)
PRINT *, B
PRINT *, "++++++++"
PRINT *, "DIM=3"
B=EOSHIFT(A, 1, DIM=3)
PRINT *, B
B=EOSHIFT(A, -1, DIM=3)
PRINT *, B
END
```

The output will be

```
1  2  3  4  5  6  7  8
++++++++++
DIM=1
2  0  4  0  6  0  8  0
0  1  0  3  0  5  0  7
++++++++++
DIM=2
3  4  0  0  7  8  0  0
0  0  1  2  0  0  5  6
++++++++++
DIM=3
5  6  7  8  0  0  0  0
0  0  0  0  1  2  3  4
```

Let us try to understand the output generated by EOSHIFT. The A array created by RESHAPE will be of the following form:

```
A(1, 1, 1) = 1
A(2, 1, 1) = 2
A(1, 2, 1) = 3
A(2, 2, 1) = 4
A(1, 1, 2) = 5
A(2, 1, 2) = 6
A(1, 2, 2) = 7
A(2, 2, 2) = 8
```

Consider a typical case – DIM=2

The shifting will take place among the elements A(I, :, J), where ':' indicates all possible values. These are shown within brackets:

```
{A(1,1,1),A(1,2,1)}{A(2,1,1),A(2,2,1)}{A(1,1,2),A(1,2,2)}{A(2,1,2),
  A(2,2,2)}
```

Now, A(1,1,1)=1 and A(1,2,1)=3. If one left shift is given by EOSHIFT, A(1,1,1) becomes 3 and A(1,2,1) becomes zero. Similarly one left shift to the pair {A(2,1,1), A(2,2,1)}sets A(2,1,1) to 4 and A(2,2,1) to zero. Proceeding in a similar way it can be shown that the result is finally:

```
3  4  0  0  7  8  0  0.
```

A complex variable contains two elements – a real and an imaginary part.

```
COMPLEX, DIMENSION(4):: C, B
C=[(1.0,2.0), (3.0,4.0),(5.0,6.0),(7.0,8.0)]
B=EOSHIFT(C, SHIFT=1)
PRINT *,B
B=EOSHIFT(C, SHIFT=-1)
PRINT *, B
END
```

The first EOSHIFT, shifts the complex array 1 position to the left (both the real and the imaginary parts) and the second one shifts the complex array 1 position to the right (both the real and the imaginary parts). In the first case the B array becomes:

```
B=[(3,4), (5,6), (7,8), (0,0)]
```

and in the second case the B array becomes:

```
B=[(0,0), (1,2), (3,4), (5,6)]
```

CSHIFT: This intrinsic is used to shift the array elements in a circular fashion, that is, the elements that are shifted out are added at the other end. Like EOSHIFT, positive shift count indicates left shift and the negative shift count indicates right shift.

For an array of rank 1, shift count is a scalar. Following the declaration of the previous section (page 172),

```
B=CSHIFT(A, SHIFT=2)
```

A–array

| 1 | 2 | 3 | 4 | 5 | 6 |

B–array

| 3 | 4 | 5 | 6 | 1 | 2 |

will make the B array as [3, 4, 5, 6, 1, 2].
Similarly,

```
B=CSHIFT(A, SHIFT=-2)
```

A–array

| 1 | 2 | 3 | 4 | 5 | 6 |

B–array

| 5 | 6 | 1 | 2 | 3 | 4 |

will create a B array as [5, 6, 1, 2, 3, 4].

In case of an array of rank 2, it is possible to shift each column or row by the same amount by using the shift count as a scalar or different amounts or directions by using an array of rank one less than the original array. Using the definitions of the C and D arrays of the previous section (page 173),

D=CSHIFT(C, SHIFT=1)

10	40	70
20	50	80
30	60	90

will create a D array of the following form:

D=

20	50	80
30	60	90
10	40	70

On the other hand,

D=CSHIFT(C, SHIFT -1)

will create a D array of the following form:

D=

30	60	90
10	40	70
20	50	80

In a similar way,

D=CSHIFT(C, SHIFT=[1, -1, 1])

will generate the following D array:

D=

20	60	80
30	40	90
10	50	70

The optional parameter DIM, which is, by default 1, as in the previous case, may be specified. DIM=1 affects the column and DIM=2 affects the row. In the following we write the CSHIFT and the corresponding D array.

D=CSHIFT(C, SHIFT=1, DIM=2)

D=

40	70	10
50	80	20
60	90	30

```
D=CSHIFT(C, SHIFT=-1, DIM=2)
```

$$D = \begin{array}{|c|c|c|}\hline 70 & 10 & 40 \\\hline 80 & 20 & 50 \\\hline 90 & 30 & 60 \\\hline \end{array}$$

```
D=CSHIFT(C, SHIFT=[1, -1, 1], DIM=2)
```

$$D = \begin{array}{|c|c|c|}\hline 40 & 70 & 10 \\\hline 80 & 20 & 50 \\\hline 60 & 90 & 30 \\\hline \end{array}$$

The discussions related to the 3-D array of the previous section are equally applicable to this section too and hence will not be repeated here.

12.8 Locating and Counting Array Element

There are three intrinsics in this category. They are ANY, ALL and COUNT. The intrinsics ANY and ALL are used to locate one or more elements, which meet certain condition. The third intrinsic COUNT, counts the number of elements, which satisfies a certain condition. All these instructions are illustrated by means of examples. The program segment uses a two dimensional array containing the marks of three students. Each row indicates the marks of a particular student in different subjects. Each column indicates the marks of a particular subject for all students.

```
LOGICAL :: L1
LOGICAL, DIMENSION(3) :: L2
LOGICAL, DIMENSION(6) :: L3
INTEGER :: N1
INTEGER, DIMENSION(3) :: N2
INTEGER, DIMENSION(6) :: N3
INTEGER, DIMENSION(3,6) :: RESULT
          .
RESULT=RESHAPE(SOURCE = &
       [ 60, 65, 70, 62, 80, 85, &
         75, 68, 88, 77, 92, 90, &
         55, 70, 90, 80, 93, 96], SHAPE=[3, 6], &
              ORDER=[2,1])
```

So the array RESULT will be filled in row wise because of the presence of the ORDER argument.

RESULT =

60	65	70	62	80	85
75	68	88	77	92	90
55	70	90	80	93	96

Subject ↓

Student ⟶

ANY: This intrinsic takes two arguments, MASK and DIM. MASK is of type logical. The optional argument DIM is an integer. In the simplest form MASK could be a condition:

```
MASK = RESULT > 90
```

which tests whether any student has scored more than 90 in any subject. The intrinsic returns a logical value – either true or false.

```
L1 = ANY (RESULT > 90)              ! True
L1 = ANY (RESULT < 50)              ! False
```

The intrinsic ANY will return a logical array if the optional parameter DIM (integer) is used. If DIM=1 is used, ANY returns a logical array of size 6. Similarly, if DIM=2, ANY returns a logical array of size 3.

```
L2 = ANY(RESULT > 90, DIM=2)
```

will return L2(1), L2(2) and L3(3) as false, true and true respectively. The statement examines whether any student scored marks greater than 90 in any subject. In a similar way,

```
L3 = ANY(RESULT < 65, DIM=1)
```

returns L3(1), L3(2), L3(3), L3(4), L3(5) and L3(6) as true, false, false, true, false, false respectively. The statement is equivalent to asking a question "is there any one who scored marks less than 65 in a particular subject". Obviously, the size of the output logical array is the number of subjects. The concept may be extended to arrays of rank greater than 2.

ALL: All tests whether all the elements of an array meet a certain condition. It returns true when the condition is met, otherwise it returns false. Like ANY, it takes two parameters, the first one is logical and the second one, DIM (integer), is optional.

```
L1 = ALL (RESULT > 50)              ! True
L1 = ALL (RESULT > 60)              ! False
```

In the first case ALL tests whether every student has scored more than 50 in all the subjects. The result is true. In the second case since every body has not scored more than 60 in all the subjects, the result is false. ALL accepts a second optional parameter DIM. For DIM=2, it returns an array of size 3 (rows of the matrix). In this case ALL tests whether every student has met a certain condition in each subject.

```
L2 = ALL (RESULT > 65, DIM=2)
```

returns L2(1), L2(2) and L2(3) as false, true and false respectively. Assuming 65% is the pass mark in each subject, the above statement returns that only student number 2 has passed in every subject. Similarly,

```
L3 = ALL (RESULT > 65, DIM=1)
```

returns L3(1), L2(2), L3(3), L3(4), L3(5) and L3(6) as false, false, true, false, true and true respectively. This tells us that all the students have passed in subjects 3, 5 and 6. The input to ALL may be an array of rank more than 2.

COUNT: This intrinsic counts the number of array elements that meet certain conditions. Like the previous two intrinsics, it also takes two arguments of which the second one, DIM, is optional. COUNT returns an integer or integer array depending on the whether optional DIM parameter is present of not.

```
N1 = COUNT (RESULT >= 80)
```

If marks greater than or equal to 80 are considered as "star mark", the above statement returns the total number of array elements that satisfy the condition, which is 9 in this case (bold letter in the fig).

60	65	70	62	**80**	**85**
75	68	**88**	77	**92**	**90**
55	70	**90**	**80**	**93**	**96**

Similarly,

```
N2= COUNT (RESULT >= 80, DIM=2)
```

returns N2(1), N2(2) and N2(3) as 2, 3 and 4 respectively. This indicates that the student 1 obtained star marks in 2 subjects, student 2 in 3 subjects and student 3 in 4 subjects. In a similar manner,

```
N3 = COUNT (RESULT >= 80, DIM=1)
```

returns N3(1), N3(2), N3(3), N3(4), N3(5) and N3(6) as 0, 0, 2, 1, 3 and 3 respectively. The array N3 now contains the number of students who received star marks in each subject. None could obtain star marks in subjects 1 and 2, whereas the number of students received star marks in subjects 3, 4, 5 and 6 are respectively, 2, 1, 3, and 3.

Like ANY and ALL intrinsics, this intrinsic can be applied to arrays of rank greater than 2.

12.9 Packing and Unpacking

In this category there are three intrinsics – PACK, UNPACK and SPREAD.

PACK: This intrinsic is used to generate a single dimension array from a multidimensional array under the control of a mask. It accepts three arguments of which the third argument is optional. The first argument is a multidimensional array and the second argument is a mask. Depending upon the mask, the array elements of the first argument are returned as a single dimension array. The array elements of the multidimensional are taken column wise. The output array is of the same type as that of the input array.

Case I: If the MASK is .TRUE. all the elements of the multidimensional array are selected.

```
INTEGER, DIMENSION (3,3) :: UA
INTEGER, DIMENSION (9) :: PA
LOGICAL, DIMENSION (3, 3) :: M
UA=RESHAPE ([(I, I=1, 9)],[3, 3])
PA=PACK(UA, .TRUE.)
```

UA =

1	4	7
2	5	8
3	6	9

and PA(1), PA(2), ... PA(9) are respectively 1, 2, 3, ... 9. The size of PA is the product of extents of UA. The diagonal elements of a matrix may be extracted very easily using PACK.

```
INTEGER, DIMENSION(16) :: IL
INTEGER, DIMENSION(4,4) :: IB
INTEGER, DIMENSION(4) :: ID
IB=RESHAPE([(I, I=1, 16)], [4, 4])
IL=PACK(IB, .TRUE.)
ID=IL(1 : 16 : 5)
```

The RESHAPE will create a matrix IB

1	5	9	13
2	**6**	10	14
3	7	**11**	15
4	8	12	**16**

The intrinsic PACK will 'linearize' the matrix IB into a rank 1 array IL. The next instruction will pickup only the first, sixth, eleventh and sixteenth elements of IL which are nothing but the diagonal elements of the original array.

Case II: MASK can be a logical array of same shape and size of the input array to PACK. The array elements of the array to PACK corresponding to the true elements of MASK are returned as an array of rank 1. The size of the returned vector is the number of .TRUE. elements of the array. If,

M =

T	F	T
T	F	F
F	F	F

where T and F denote true and false respectively, the returned vector will be [1, 2, 7]. It is perhaps clear that

```
PRINT *, SIZE (PACK(UA, MASK=M))
```

will display 3 as the size of the returned vector. If it is necessary to store the returned vector, it can be assigned to a properly dimensioned variable.

```
PA = PACK(UA, MASK=M)
```

However, better instruction would be:

```
PA(1 : COUNT(M))=PACK(UA, MASK=M)
```

which will count number of true elements (which is 3 in this case) of M and pack the array accordingly.
Case III: PACK can have a third argument VECTOR, which is an array of rank 1 and the same type as the input array. The size of VECTOR must be at least equal to the number of true elements of the MASK. When the VECTOR is present, PACK returns an array of size same as the size of the VECTOR. If the number of true elements, say t, of the MASK is less than the size of the VECTOR, the output is padded with (n-t) elements from the VECTOR starting from the (t+1)th element from the VECTOR.

```
PA = PACK (UA, MASK=M, &
           VECTOR=[10,20,30,40,50,60,70,80,90])
```

will generate PA vector containing $[1, 2, 7, 40, 50, 60, 70, 80, 90]$ as its array elements. Note that, the compiler will flag the following as an error because the size of the VECTOR is less than the size of the PA array and therefore the array that will be generated on the right hand side of the assignment sign will be of size 5. This will not be able to fill in the array PA having a size of 9.

```
PA = PACK (UA, MASK=M, &
           VECTOR=[10,20,30,40,50])          ! error
```

In this case the above statement must be replaced by:

```
PA(1:COUNT(M)) = PACK (UA, MASK=M, &
           VECTOR=[10,20,30,40,50])
```

which generates only the elements of PA corresponding to the true elements of MASK others are ignored. In this case, VECTOR will cause no error. PA(1:COUNT(M)) actually becomes PA(1:3).
 Another way of doing the same thing is as follows:

```
INTEGER, DIMENSION (5) :: VEC=[10, 20, 30, 40, 50]
   .

   .
PA (1 : SIZE(VEC))=PACK(UA, MASK=M, VECTOR=VEC)
```

This will generate the array elements of PA as $[1, 2, 7, 40, 50]$.
UNPACK: This intrinsic is the reverse of the intrinsic PACK. It takes three arguments. The first is a single dimensioned array having size at least t where t is number of true elements in the masked array. UNPACK returns a multidimensional array of the same shape and size of its second argument, which is a logical array. The elements from the first arguments are picked up corresponding to the true value of the elements of the MASK. The elements of the output array are filled in column wise. The third

argument – FIELD – may be a scalar or an array of the same size and shape as the MASK and of the same type as that of the first argument. The elements of the returned array corresponding to the MASK:

F	T	T
T	F	T
T	T	F

are discussed below.

Case I: When the third argument FIELD is a scalar, say 99, and the elements of PA are [1,2,3,4,5,6,7,8,9] consider the following program:

```
INTEGER, DIMENSION (3,3) :: UA
LOGICAL, PARAMETER:: T=.TRUE.
LOGICAL, PARAMETER:: F=.FALSE.
INTEGER, DIMENSION (9) :: PA
LOGICAL, DIMENSION (3,3)::M
PA=[1,2,3,4,5,6,7,8,9]
M=RESHAPE([F,T,T,T,F,T,T,T,F],[3,3])
UA=UNPACK(PA,MASK=M,FIELD=99)
PRINT *, UA
END
```

The elements of matrix UA are:

99	3	5
1	99	6
2	4	99

The third argument FIELD is substituted corresponding to the false elements of the MASK.
Case II: If the FIELD array is of the following form:

100	400	700
200	500	800
300	600	900

the returned array will be:

100	3	5
1	500	6
2	4	900

Note that when FIELD is an array, the elements of FIELD corresponding to the false elements of MASK are transferred to the output array.

SPREAD: This intrinsic is used to replicate a scalar to form a rank 1 array or replicate an array by adding a dimension. It accepts three arguments. The first argument, called the SOURCE, is a scalar or an array of rank less than 7. The second argument DIM is a scalar such that:

```
1 <= DIM <= (n+1)
```

where n is the rank of the first argument. The third argument NCOPIES (scalar) is an integer and the source is replicated NCOPIES times.

Case I: If the source is a scalar, the shape of the resultant array is MAX (NCOPIES, 0). For example,

```
SPREAD (SOURCE=10, DIM=1, NCOPIES=3)
```

results in array [10, 10, 10].

Case II: When the SOURCE is a vector like:

```
INTEGER, DIMENSION(3) :: S=[1, 2, 3]
```

`SPREAD(SOURCE=S, DIM=1, NCOPIES=3)` results in an output array of the form:

1	2	3
1	2	3
1	2	3

On the other hand,

```
SPREAD(SOURCE=S, DIM=2, NCOPIES=3)
```

returns an array of the form:

1	1	1
2	2	2
3	3	3

MERGE: This intrinsic also takes three arguments, TSOURCE, MSOURCE and MASK. TSOURCE may be a scalar or an array. MSOURCE is of same type as TSOURCE. If this is an array, it must be of same shape as TSOURCE. MASK is logical. If MASK is an array it should be of same shape as TSOURCE or MSOURCE.

Case I: When TSOURCE is a scalar like:

```
MERGE(20, 10, M > 15)
```

MERGE returns 20 if M is greater than 15, otherwise it returns 10.

Case II: When TSOURCE, MSOURCE and MASK are:

TSOURCE =

1	4	7
2	5	8
3	6	9

MSOURCE =

10	40	70
20	50	80
30	60	90

MASK =

T	F	F
F	F	T
T	T	F

where T stands for .TRUE. value and F stands for .FALSE. value, MERGE returns:

1	40	70
20	50	8
3	6	90

It may be noted that when a particular array element of MASK is true, the corresponding array element from the SOURCE is taken, and if a particular element of MASK is false, the corresponding element from the MSOURCE is taken.

Chapter 13

INITIALIZATION AND LOCATION SHARING

This chapter deals with the initialization of variables using the DATA statement and sharing of locations by two or more variables through the EQUIVALENCE statement.

A variable may be initialized in two different ways. The first one was discussed in the previous chapters, where the variables are initialized along with their declarations. This initialization ensures that when the execution begins, variables have the values mentioned in the initialization. There is another way of initializing a variable. This is done through the DATA statement.

Sharing of locations among different variables using the EQUIVALENCE statement is not very popular when computer memory has become so cheap. Though the EQUIVALENCE statement is rarely used, it is included for the sake of completeness.

Both DATA and EQUIVALENCE are non-executable statements.

13.1 DATA Statement

The DATA statement can be placed anywhere within the program unit. However it is strongly recommended that this statement be placed at the beginning of the program unit along with other specification statements. Two integer variables I and J may be initialized to 10 and 20 respectively by DATA statement as shown below:

```
        DATA  I /10/
        DATA  J /20/
or,     DATA I /10/, J /20/
or,     DATA I, J /10, 20/
```

All the above declarations are equivalent. Note that either the variables are declared by appropriate declaration or the default I–N rule is followed. Assuming that L, D and C are declared as logical, double precision and complex variables respectively, the following are the DATA statements to initialize these variables.

```
        LOGICAL :: L
        DOUBLE PRECISION :: D
        COMPLEX :: C
        DATA L /.TRUE./
        DATA D /3.1415926589D0/
        DATA C /(2.0, 3.0)/
```

For the complex variable C the first constant corresponds to the real part and the second constant corresponds to the imaginary part. Note that, in the case of a complex variable, the real and the imaginary parts are enclosed with parentheses.

Character variables are also initialized in a similar manner:

```
CHARACTER (LEN=4) :: CH
DATA CH / 'IACS'/
```

If the number of characters is less than the size of the variable, blanks are added at the end. On the other hand, if the number of characters is more than the size, the constant is truncated from the right.

```
CHARACTER (LEN=8) :: CH
DATA CH / 'IACS Calcutta'/
```

The variable CH is initialized to 'IACS Cal' as it can store maximum of 8 characters.

13.2 DATA and Array

An array can be initialized by DATA statement also. A number of options are available.

```
REAL, DIMENSION (4) :: A
DATA A /1.0, 2.0, 3.0, 4.0/
```

The array without any subscripts corresponds to the whole array. Therefore, A(1), A(2), A(3) and A(4) are initialized to 1.0, 2.0, 3.0 and 4.0 respectively. For a two dimensional array, the elements are stored column wise. The next declaration,

```
INTEGER, DIMENSION (2, 2) :: B
DATA B/10, 20, 30, 40/
```

will initialize B(1, 1) to 10, B(2, 1) to 20, B(1, 2) to 30 and B(2, 2) to 40.

A complex dimensioned variable requires two constants for each location, one for the real part and the other for the imaginary part.

```
COMPLEX, DIMENSION (2) :: C
DATA C /(2.0, 3.0), (4.0, 5.0)/
```

C(1) is initialized to (2.0, 3.0) and C(2) is initialized to (4.0, 5.0).

A logical variable can have a value either .TRUE. or .FALSE..

```
LOGICAL, DIMENSION (4) :: L
DATA L /.TRUE., .FALSE., .FALSE., .TRUE./
```

Character arrays are also initialized in a similar way:

```
CHARACTER (LEN=4), DIMENSION (3) :: CH
DATA CH / 'SINP', 'TIFR', 'IACS' /
```

The same concept can be extended to multi-dimensional arrays. It is perhaps redundant to mention that dimensioned quantities may also be initialized element by element.

```
INTEGER, DIMENSION (4) :: A
DATA A (1), A (2), A (3), A (4) / 100, 200, 300, 400/
```

The number of variables present in the DATA statement must be the same as the number of constants given in the data. The compiler will flag an error, if this is violated.

```
INTEGER, DIMENSION (4) :: D
DATA D / 1, 2, 3, 4, 5/              !      Error
```

13.3 Repetition Factor and Initialization

Several consecutive elements of an array can be initialized by a constant through a single instruction.

```
REAL, DIMENSION (10) :: A
DATA A / 10* 100.0/
```

10*100.0 indicates that all the 10 elements of the array A are initialized to 100. Here 10 is the repetition factor. This can be mixed with the usual initialization methods. For example, in the above case, if it is necessary to initialize the first 4 elements to 1.0, 2.0, 3.0 and 4.0, the next 4 elements to 100.0 and the last two to zero, it can be also achieved through the DATA statement.

```
DATA A / 1.0, 2.0, 3.0, 4.0, 4*100.0, 2*0.0/
```

It is possible to initialize only a few contiguous elements:

```
DATA A (1 : 5) /5*10/
```

only A(1) to A(5) are initialized.

13.4 DATA and Implied DO Loop

The DATA statement with the implied DO is a very powerful tool to initialize a dimensioned quantity in a particular order. In the program segment, shown below, A represents a rank 1 array of size 10 and X represents a rank 2 array of shape (2, 2).

```
INTEGER :: I, J
INTEGER, DIMENSION (10) :: A
REAL, DIMENSION (2, 2) :: X
DATA ( A (I), I=1, 10, 2) / 5*100/
```

This statement will initialize A (1), A(3), A(5), A(7) and A (9) to 100. The elements A(2), A(4), A(6) and A(10) are not affected (initialized). Similarly,

```
DATA (( X(I, J), J=1, 2), I=1, 2) / 1.0, 2.0, 3.0, 4.0 /
```

will set X(1, 1), X(1, 2), X(2, 1) and X(2, 2) to 1.0, 2.0, 3.0 and 4.0 respectively.

Note that,

```
DATA X /1.0, 2.0, 3.0, 4.0/
```
or,
```
DATA ((X(I, J), I=1, 2), J=1, 2) / 1.0, 2.0, 3.0, 4.0/
```

are equivalent and will set X (1, 1), X (2, 1), X (1, 2) and X (2, 2) to 1.0, 2.0, 3.0 and 4.0 respectively.

13.5 Comparative Study

In this section we make a comparative study among the different variable "assignment" methods discussed so far. The statements are:

```
INTEGER, PARAMETER :: N=4          !      (1a)
PARAMETER (N=4)                    !      (1b)
DATA N /4/                         !      (2)
N=4                                !      (3)
READ *, N                          !      (4)
```

(1a) and (1b) will associate the constant 4 with the symbolic name N (named constant). This cannot be modified. (2) will initialize the variable N to 4. Since N is a variable (integer) it can be modified and any modification of N will be reflected on the subsequent use of N. The DATA statement merely guarantees the starting value (initial) of N. (3) will set N to a value and every time the program is executed, N will be assigned to 4. Again, N is a variable, so it can be modified. There is one difference between the assignment and initialization. If the variable is initialized, it has the value mentioned in the initialization statement when the execution begins. On the other hand, if the variable is assigned to a value through an assignment statement, the variable, during the execution remains undefined till the assignment is made. However, if the READ statement is used, every time the program is run, the user can supply any value through the input unit (say keyboard). A rule of thumb may be formulated. If a quantity is really constant, say π, the PARAMETER statement/attribute should be used so that it cannot be modified accidentally during the execution of a program. If it is necessary to have a starting value for a variable with the provision that it may be modified during the execution of the program, the DATA statement should be used. The READ statement may be used when a variable assumes different values in different runs. For example, if the program depends on the Atomic Number, the variable corresponding to the Atomic Number can be read during the execution of the program.

13.6 Equivalence (*)

Two or more variables may share the same location within a program unit. It is like a person having a good name and a nickname. The location is same but it can be referred to by two or more names. This is done through EQUIVALENCE statement. Since a variable can store only one value at a time, EQUIVALENCE actually means assigning two names to a single variable. The main reason for using EQUIVALENCE statement is to reuse the locations, which are not required at a given point. However, assigning another name to a variable is convenient because then the new name (but the old location) will have some relation with the actual quantity. We use a hypothetical example to illustrate this point. Suppose we are using a variable AGE to denote the age of a person. In the same program unit suppose it is necessary to use this location to denote the price of a car when operations with the age are over and the value stored in the location AGE is not required. It is desirable to call this location now as PRICE. Of course, no harm is done if the same name AGE is used to denote the price of a car provided one remembers that at that point the variable AGE does not denote the age of a person except that the program loses some amount of readability. It may be noted that the variable can store only one value at a time, so whatever be the name AGE or PRICE the variable contains either the age of a person or the price of the car. So it is the responsibility of the programmer to interpret the variable in the proper manner.

Another possible reason for using the EQUIVALENCE statement is when two persons have developed one program unit and perhaps due to lack of communication between them, they used different name for the same variable. In that case instead of changing the names at several places, the EQUIVALENCE statement can be used. Of course, the above-mentioned situations are hypothetical and now a days as the computer has more memory than it had 30 years ago, the EQUIVALENCE statement is rarely used. In fact, unless there is a very special reason, the use of EQUIVALENCE is discouraged.

13.7 EQUIVALENCE Statement

EQUIVALENCE statement is used to indicate that two or more variables would use the same location in the same program unit.

```
REAL :: A, B
EQUIVALENCE (A,B)
```

Since A and B use the same location, if A is set to 10,

```
PRINT *, B
```

will display 10.

```
REAL, DIMENSION (4) :: A, B
EQUIVALENCE (A(1), B(1))
```

or,

```
EQUIVALENCE (A, B)
```

A(1)	A(2)	A(3)	A(4)
B(1)	B(2)	B(3)	B(4)

will make A and B equivalent. That is, A(1) and B(1), A(2) and B(2), A(3) and B(3), A(4) and B(4) will share same locations.

```
REAL, DIMENSION (2, 2) :: A
REAL, DIMENSION (4) :: B
EQUIVALENCE (A(1, 1), B(1))
```

In this example, A(1, 1) and B(1), A(2, 1) and B(2), A(1, 2) and B(3) and A(2, 2) and B(4) will share location. A two-dimensional array A is mapped into single dimension column wise.

Now, consider the following EQUIVALENCE statement:

```
REAL, DIMENSION (4) :: A, B
EQUIVALENCE (A(1), B(2))
```

Since A(1) and B(2), A(2) and B(3), A(3) and B(4) are sharing same location, B(1) and A(4) are really not sharing locations with any variable. However, B(1) may be referred as A(0) and A(4) as B(5).
   In a similar way,

```
EQUIVALENCE (A(2), B(1))
```

will make A(2) and B(1), A(3) and B(2), A(4) and B(3) equivalent. A(1) and B(4) are not sharing location with any variable but they may be treated as B(0) and A(5).

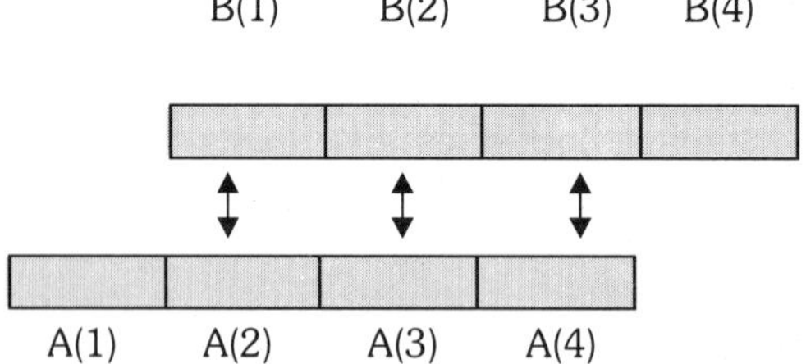

The EQUIVALENCE statement is based on the fact that the locations are assigned sequentially.
   EQUIVALENCE between two different types of variables is not recommended. However, the following is an interesting example.

```
COMPLEX :: C=(1.0, 2.0)
REAL, DIMENSION (2) :: A
EQUIVALENCE (A(1), C)
PRINT *, C
PRINT *, A
END
```

The output will be

```
(1.0, 2.0)
1.0  2.0
```

Complex variable actually consists of two real variables – the real and the imaginary parts. When the array A and the complex variable C are made equivalent, A(1) and the real part of C, A(2) and the imaginary part of C share same location. Therefore, A(1) is essentially the real part of C and A(2) is the imaginary part of C.

A single variable cannot be made equivalent to two different elements of an array.

```
REAL :: A
REAL, DIMENSION (4) :: B
EQUIVALENCE (A, B(1)), (A, B(2))
```

is not allowed.

13.8 EQUIVALENCE and Character Variables

Two character variables of similar or dissimilar length may be made equivalent:

```
CHARACTER (LEN=4) :: A, B
EQUIVALENCE (A, B)
```

This makes A(1:1) equivalent to B(1:1), A(2:2) to B(2:2) and so on.

```
CHARACTER (LEN=4) :: A= 'IACS'
CHARACTER (LEN=3) :: B
EQUIVALENCE (A, B)
```

This will make A(1:1) and B(1:1), A(2:2) and B(2:2), A(3:3) and B(3:3) equivalent. Thus,

```
PRINT *, B
```

will display 'IAC' since the length of the character variable B is 3.

```
EQUIVALENCE (A(2: ), B(1: ))
```

will make second character of A equivalent to the first character of B. Therefore,

```
PRINT *, B
```

will display 'ACS'.

Another interesting property of logical variable can be seen through EQUIVALENCE statement.

```
LOGICAL :: L
INTEGER :: A=2
EQUIVALENCE (A,L)
PRINT *, A
PRINT *, L
END
```

The output is

```
2
T
```

By changing A=2 to A=0, the output becomes

```
0
F
```

This indicates that logical variable stores zero for false value and any other integer value is treated as true value. This can be verified by changing the value of A to any allowed positive or negative integers. Although this is generally the case across all computer languages it should not be used as a short-cut.

Before we conclude this chapter, we advise the readers to avoid these types of "trick". One must not twist the language to extract something, which were not the intention of the designer of the language. For example, extracting the real and the imaginary part of a complex number (section 13.7) by using EQUIVALENCE statement should be avoided; REAL and AIMAG library functions have been provided to perform the same task and such program looks clean, readable and machine independent.

Chapter 14

USER DEFINED TYPES

A user defined type (derived type) is a data structure created by the user consisting of elementary elements of standard types like integer, real, logical, complex, character variables. The structure can be accessed as a whole or the individual elements may be treated separately. This structure is quite flexible and allows mixing various kinds of variables, arrays in any proportion. For example, to prepare employee's company employment record, it is perhaps necessary to create arrays for, say, the serial number, name, address etc and the synchronization among the different elements becomes the responsibility of the programmer. The programmer has to keep track of the relations among the different variables. The variable declared as user data type can be accessed as a whole (all the elementary items together) or the elementary items may be manipulated separately.

14.1 Derived Type

The derived type is illustrated with an example. Consider a record of a person consisting of the following items:

Name:	30 characters
Address:	50 characters
Age:	integer
Blood group:	2 characters
Rh factor:	1 character

The "prototype" of such a derived type is defined as:

```
TYPE PERSON
  CHARACTER (LEN=30) :: NAME
  CHARACTER (LEN=50) :: ADDRESS
  INTEGER :: AGE
  CHARACTER (LEN=2) :: BLOOD_GROUP
  CHARACTER (LEN=1) :: RH_FACTOR
END TYPE PERSON
```

A variable, DONOR, of type PERSON may be defined as:

```
TYPE (PERSON) :: DONOR
```

The variable DONOR contains five elementary items of standard types – character and integer. The variable DONOR as a whole refers to all the elementary items (NAME, ADDRESS, AGE, BLOOD_GROUP and RH_FACTOR) of the DONOR. The individual elements may be referred to as:

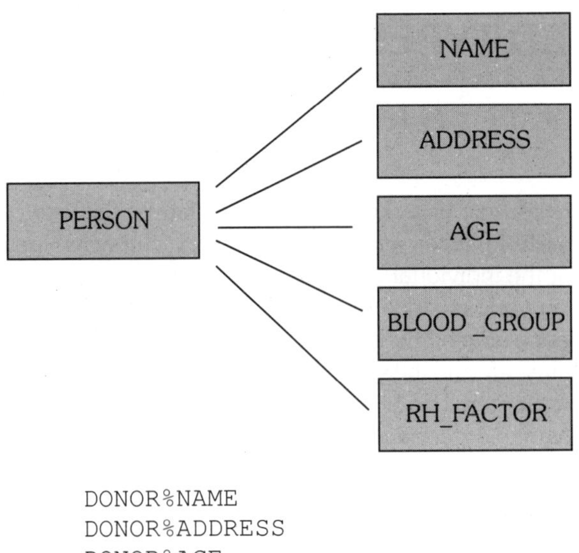


```
DONOR%NAME
DONOR%ADDRESS
DONOR%AGE
DONOR%BLOOD_GROUP
DONOR%RH_FACTOR
```

where the symbol '%' is used to fetch an elementary item from the variable name. Note that NAME, ADDRESS, AGE, BLOOD_GROUP and RH_FACTOR exist with reference to a variable – in this case the variable name is DONOR. We shall see shortly that an element of a derived type may also have a structure.

Another variable of type PERSON can be defined in an identical manner:

```
                    TYPE (PERSON) :: DONOR1
or,                 TYPE (PERSON) :: DONOR, DONOR1
```

In this case DONOR1%NAME refers to the name corresponding to DONOR1, similar to the name corresponding to DONOR (DONOR%NAME).

14.2 Assignment

A derived type variable can be assigned to a value in many ways. Following the definition of the previous section, we can assign values to a variable DONOR:

```
DONOR=PERSON('S RAY', 'CC, IACS', 60, 'O ', '+')
```

The assignment statement needs some explanation. First the type of the variable PERSON must be specified in the assignment. Next the data corresponding to each of its elements are given in the same order as was defined earlier.

An element is just like an ordinary variable and can be assigned in the usual manner.

```
DONOR%NAME= 'S RAY'
DONOR%ADDRESS= "CC, IACS"
DONOR%AGE=60
DONOR%BLOOD_GROUP="O "
DONOR%RH_FACTOR="+"
```

If another variable DONOR1 of type PERSON is equated to DONOR

```
DONOR1=DONOR
```

the elementary items of the variable DONOR1 becomes same as the elementary items of the corresponding variable DONOR.

All the arithmetic, relational and logical operations as permitted by the language can be used with the elementary items. For example, the following statements and the likes

```
DONOR1%AGE=DONOR%AGE+10

IF (DONOR%RH_FACTOR .EQ. '+') THEN
     .
ENDIF
```

are valid.

14.3 Initialization

Initialization of a user type variables can be done in two different ways. One is to initialize at the prototype level and the other at the variable level.

In the prototype level, the prototype is initialized and any variable defined based on the prototype will have the corresponding variable initialized. This can be overridden by explicit initialization.

```
TYPE PERSON
  CHARACTER (LEN=30) :: NAME='S RAY'
  CHARACTER (LEN=50) :: ADDRESS
  INTEGER :: AGE
  CHARACTER (LEN=2) :: BLOOD_GROUP
  CHARACTER (LEN=1) :: RH_FACTOR='+'
END TYPE PERSON

TYPE (PERSON) :: BLOOD_DONOR
```

The variable BLOOD_DONOR will have its NAME and RH_FACTOR initialized by 'S RAY' and '+' respectively. Other elementary items will not be initialized.

When the initialization takes place at the variable level, it can be done in two different ways.

```
                 TYPE (PERSON) :: BLOOD_DONOR=PERSON(&
                     'S RAY', 'CC, IACS', 60, 'O ', '+')
```

or,

```
                 TYPE (PERSON) :: BLOOD_DONOR
                 DATA BLOOD_DONOR/PERSON (& ·
                     'S RAY', 'CC, IACS', 60, 'O ', '+')/
```

The point that must be noted is the presence of the data type – in this case – PERSON in the initialization statement.

14.4 IMPLICIT and Derived Types

Implicit statements can be used to associate a variable that starts with a particular character to be of particular derived type.

```
              IMPLICIT TYPE (DONOR) (D-E)
                 TYPE DONOR
                 CHARACTER(LEN=30) :: NAME
                 CHARACTER (LEN=2) :: BLOOD_GROUP
                 CHARACTER (LEN=1) :: RH_FACTOR
              END TYPE DONOR

              D%NAME= 'Subrata Ray'
              D%BLOOD_GROUP= 'O '
```

The implicit declaration ensures that any variable that starts with either D or E in the program unit is of user defined type DONOR.

14.5 Input-Output

The derived type may be read or displayed as a whole or by individual element. The statement

```
              READ *, BLOOD_DONOR
```

will expect that data for each element is to be supplied sequentially during the execution like:

```
              'SR'     'CC, IACS'   60   'O '  '+'
```

However, individual elements may be read separately also.

```
                 READ *, BLOOD_DONOR%NAME
                 READ *, BLOOD_DONOR%ADDRESS
                 READ *, BLOOD_DONOR%AGE
                 READ *, BLOOD_DONOR%BLOOD_GROUP
                 READ *, BLOOD_DONOR%RH_FACTOR
```

In a similar manner PRINT *, BLOOD_DONOR will display all the elements sequentially on the screen. Individual elements may also be displayed separately.

```
PRINT *, BLOOD_DONOR%NAME
PRINT *, BLOOD_DONOR%ADDRESS
PRINT *, BLOOD_DONOR%AGE
PRINT *, BLOOD_DONOR%BLOOD_GROUP
PRINT *, BLOOD_DONOR%RH_FACTOR
```

We now demonstrate the use of derived type with an example. This program adds two "English Distances" (miles & yards) D1 and D2. Note that this cannot be done through the statement:

```
D3=D1+D2
```

because addition operation is not valid in this particular case as D1, D2 and D3 are not elementary items (real, integer or complex).

```
PROGRAM DISTANCE
!  Add "English" distance

TYPE DIST
  INTEGER :: MILE
  INTEGER :: YDS
END TYPE DIST

TYPE(DIST):: D1,D2,D3

READ *, D1%MILE, D1%YDS, D2%MILE, D2%YDS
!  read elementary items of D1 and D2
!  data validation is not done for simplicity
!  yds must be less than 1760

PRINT *," D1.MILES = ", D1%MILE, " D1.YDS = ",D1%YDS
PRINT *," D2.MILES = ", D2%MILE, " D2.YDS = ",D2%YDS
D3%MILE=0
D3%YDS=D1%YDS+D2%YDS
IF (D3%YDS >=1760) THEN  ! 1760 yds = 1 mile
  D3%MILE=D3%MILE+1
  D3%YDS=D3%YDS-1760
ENDIF
D3%MILE=D3%MILE+D1%MILE+D2%MILE
PRINT *," D3.MILES = ", D3%MILE, " D3.YDS = ",D3%YDS
END
```

14.6 Substrings

A part of the string corresponding to an element (character) can also be accessed:

```
BLOOD_DONOR%NAME(1 : 7)= 'Subrata'
```

This will modify the characters 1 to 7 of the elementary item NAME corresponding to BLOOD_DONOR. It is also possible to read or write a character substring.

```
PRINT *, BLOOD_DONOR%NAME(1 : 7)
```

will print the first seven characters from BLOOD_DONOR%NAME.

14.7 Array and Derived Types

A derived type may be a dimensioned quantity. For example, to store information corresponding to 100 such above mentioned donors, the corresponding declaration would be:

```
TYPE (PERSON), DIMENSION (100) :: BLOOD_DONORS
```

Now BLOOD_DONORS is an array of rank 1 and hence it can be accessed like other arrays through a subscript. BLOOD_DONORS (1) refers to the first donor, BLOOD_DONORS (2) refers to the second donor, BLOOD_DONORS(100) refers to the 100th donor. In general, BLOOD_DONORS (I) refers to the Ith donor.

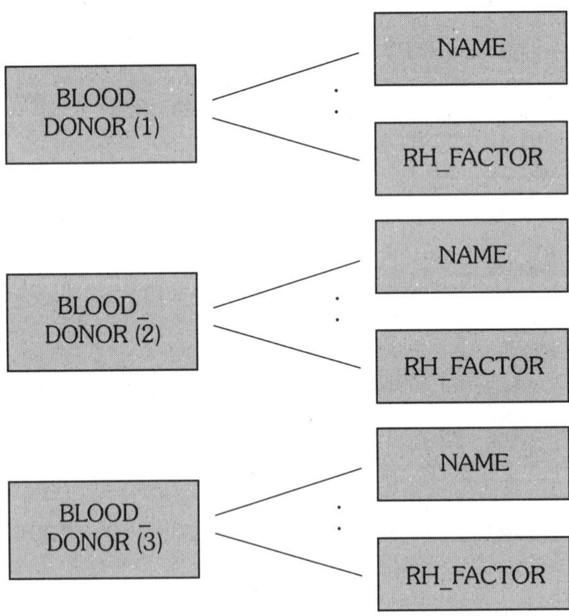

The individual elements of a particular donor can be accessed as:

```
BLOOD_DONORS (1)%NAME='Soumya'
BLOOD_DONORS (2)%BLOOD_GROUP='AB'
BLOOD_DONORS (100)%ADDRESS='20A FORDYCE LANE'
BLOOD_DONORS (10)%AGE=35
AVE =(BLOOD_DONORS(5)%AGE+BLOOD_DONORS(9)%AGE)/2.0
PRINT *, BLOOD_DONORS(3)%NAME(1:10)
```

The last statement prints the first 10 characters from the name of the 3rd BLOOD_DONORS.
    The BLOOD_DONROS array can be initialized, if necessary, like the normal array.

```
TYPE PERSON
  CHARACTER (LEN=30) :: NAME
  CHARACTER (LEN=50) :: ADDRESS
  INTEGER :: AGE
  CHARACTER (LEN=2) :: BLOOD_GROUP
  CHARACTER (LEN=1) :: RH_FACTOR
END TYPE PERSON

TYPE (PERSON), DIMENSION(2) :: BLOOD_DONORS= &
 [PERSON('SR', 'CC, IACS', 60, 'O ', '+'), &
  PERSON('PR', 'TIMES NOW', 24, 'O ', '+')]


PRINT *, BLOOD_DONORS(1)
PRINT *, BLOOD_DONORS(2)

END
```

DATA statement can also be used to initialize the array.

```
TYPE PERSON
  CHARACTER (LEN=30) :: NAME
  CHARACTER (LEN=50) :: ADDRESS
  INTEGER :: AGE
  CHARACTER (LEN=2) :: BLOOD_GROUP
  CHARACTER (LEN=1) :: RH_FACTOR
END TYPE PERSON

TYPE (PERSON), DIMENSION(2) :: BLOOD_DONORS
DATA BLOOD_DONORS/&
 PERSON('SR', 'CC, IACS', 60, 'O ', '+'), &
  PERSON('PR', 'TIMES NOW', 24, 'O ', '+')/


PRINT *, BLOOD_DONORS(1)
PRINT *, BLOOD_DONORS(2)

END
```

This will initialize BLOOD_DONORS (1)%NAME to 'SR' and BLOOD_DONORS(2) TO 'PR'. The other elements are also initialized in identical manner.

14.8 Nested Derived Types

An element of a derived type need not be an elementary item. It may itself be another derived type. If the BIRTHDAY of the donors is to be included, the TYPE declaration can be modified accordingly.

```
TYPE BDAY
   INTEGER:: DD, MM, YY
END TYPE BDAY

TYPE PERSON
   CHARACTER (LEN=30) :: NAME
   CHARACTER (LEN=50) :: ADDRESS
   INTEGER :: AGE
   CHARACTER (LEN=2) :: BLOOD_GROUP
   CHARACTER (LEN=1) :: RH_FACTOR
   TYPE(BDAY) :: BIRTH_DAY
END TYPE PERSON

TYPE (PERSON) :: BLOOD_DONOR
TYPE (PERSON), DIMENSION (10) :: BLOOD_DONORS
```

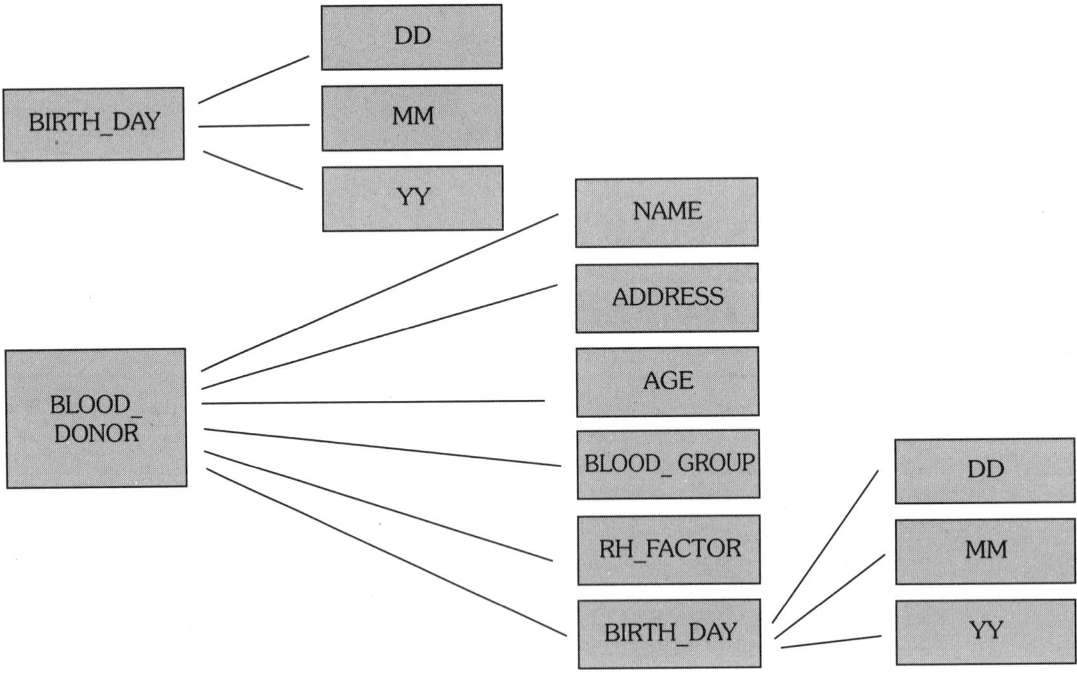

In the above example:

```
BLOOD_DONOR%BIRTH_DAY
```

refers to the birthday of a **BLOOD_DONOR** as a whole. To access the day (DD), month (MM) and year (YY) another level of reference is required.

```
BLOOD_DONOR%BIRTH_DAY%DD
BLOOD_DONOR%BIRTH_DAY%MM
BLOOD_DONOR%BIRTH_DAY%YY
```

Similarly to access an element of the array **BLOOD_DONORS**, explicit reference is necessary:

```
BLOOD_DONORS (1)%BIRTH_DAY%DD
BLOOD_DONORS (1)%BIRTH_DAY%MM
BLOOD_DONORS (1)%BIRTH_DAY%YY
BLOOD_DONORS (2)%BIRTH_DAY%DD
BLOOD_DONORS (2)%BIRTH_DAY%MM
BLOOD_DONORS (2)%BIRTH_DAY%YY
```

A DATA statement to initialize such a variable might be of the form:

```
TYPE BDAY
   INTEGER:: DD, MM, YY
END TYPE BDAY

TYPE PERSON
   CHARACTER (LEN=30) :: NAME
   CHARACTER (LEN=50) :: ADDRESS
   INTEGER :: AGE
   CHARACTER (LEN=2) :: BLOOD_GROUP
   CHARACTER (LEN=1) :: RH_FACTOR
   TYPE(BDAY) :: BIRTH_DAY
END TYPE PERSON

TYPE (PERSON) :: BLOOD_DONOR= &
 PERSON('DR','FORDYCE LANE', 67, 'B ','+',BDAY(20,7,1940))

TYPE (PERSON), DIMENSION (2) :: BLOOD_DONORS
DATA BLOOD_DONORS/&
 PERSON('SR', 'CC, IACS', 60, 'O ', '+',BDAY(19,4,1947)), &
  PERSON('PR', 'TIMES NOW', 24, 'O ', '+',BDAY(15,8,1982))/

PRINT *, BLOOD_DONOR
PRINT *, BLOOD_DONORS(1)
PRINT *, BLOOD_DONORS(2)
END
```

Note that, the data corresponding to BIRTH_DAY, which consists of three elementary items are supplied as DD, MM, YY– the way they appear in the derived type BLOOD_DONOR.

14.9 Arrays as Elementary Items

An elementary item may be a dimensioned quantity. For example, if we want to include telephone numbers (say maximum three) the prototype for the derived type must be modified:

```
TYPE BDAY
   INTEGER:: DD, MM, YY
END TYPE BDAY

TYPE PERSON
   CHARACTER (LEN=30) :: NAME
   CHARACTER (LEN=50) :: ADDRESS
   INTEGER :: AGE
   CHARACTER (LEN=2) :: BLOOD_GROUP
   CHARACTER (LEN=1) :: RH_FACTOR
   TYPE(BDAY) :: BIRTH_DAY
   CHARACTER (LEN=15), DIMENSION(3):: PHONE_NO
END TYPE PERSON

TYPE (PERSON) :: DONOR_LIST
```

The first, second and third telephone numbers may be accessed using appropriate subscripts.

```
DONOR_LIST%PHONE_NO (1)="03324734484"
DONOR_LIST%PHONE_NO (2)="03324166109"
DONOR_LIST%PHONE_NO (3)="03324245028"
```

Like any other variable, telephone number can be read from the keyboard and can be displayed on the screen with READ and PRINT statements.

```
READ *, DONOR_LIST%PHONE_NO (1)
PRINT *, DONOR_LIST%PHONE_NO (3)
```

If the list of donors is a dimensioned variable like:

```
TYPE (PERSON), DIMENSION(100) :: LIST_OF_DONOR
```

the phone number of the individual donor may be accessed as:

```
LIST_OF_DONOR(1)%PHONE_NO(2)="24006625"
!            Second phone number of the first donor
LIST_OF_DONOR(4)%PHONE_NO(3)="22271022"
!            Third phone number of the 4th donor
```

In general,

```
LIST_OF_DONOR(I)%PHONE_NO(J)="24006625"
```

is the Jth phone number of the Ith LIST_OF_DONOR. Of course the integer I and J should have values within the boundaries specified by the declaration. The meaning to the various items associated with the LIST_OF_DONOR is summarized below:

Name	Meaning
LIST_OF_DONOR	List of all the 100 donors
LIST_OF_DONOR (I)	All the elements of the Ith donor
LIST_OF_DONOR(I)%NAME	Name of Ith donor
LIST_OF_DONOR(I)%NAME(1:10)	First 10 characters of the name of the Ith donor
LIST_OF_DONOR(I)%PHONE_NO	All phone number of the Ith donor
LIST_OF_DONOR(I)%PHONE_NO(J)	Jth phone number of the Ith donor

14.10 Inheritance

A derived type may inherit all the components from a previously defined derived type. The derived type may or may not have additional components.

```
TYPE BDAY
   INTEGER:: DD, MM, YY
END TYPE BDAY

TYPE PERSON
   CHARACTER (LEN=30) :: NAME
   CHARACTER (LEN=50) :: ADDRESS
   INTEGER :: AGE
   CHARACTER (LEN=2) :: BLOOD_GROUP
   CHARACTER (LEN=1) :: RH_FACTOR
   TYPE(BDAY) :: BIRTH_DAY
   CHARACTER (LEN=15), DIMENSION(3):: PHONE_NO
END TYPE PERSON

TYPE, EXTENDS (PERSON) :: ACTIVE_DONOR
   INTEGER :: NO_DONATION
END TYPE ACTIVE_DONOR

TYPE (ACTIVE_DONOR) :: DONOR_LIST

DONOR_LIST%NO_DONATION=50
PRINT *, DONOR_LIST%NO_DONATION


END
```

The variable DONOR_LIST inherits the entire components from its parent, that is, the derived type PERSON. In addition, it has its own component. The variable, DONOR_LIST of derived type ACTIVE_DONOR can access all the components of its parent in the usual manner. In addition to this all the components defined in the parent can be accessed through the instruction:

```
DONOR_LIST%PERSON
```

Thus,

```
PRINT *, DONOR_LIST%PERSON
```

will display DONOR_LIST%NAME, DONOR_LIST%ADDRESS, ... , DONOR_LIST%RH_FACTOR.

It has already been mentioned that the "extended type" may not have any additional component. In such a case the "extended type" is merely another name of the "parent type" though it is considered to be of different type.

14.11 SEQUENCE

The computer may not arrange the elements of a derived type in sequence. There may be gaps between elements to increase the efficiency of the program. However, in certain cases it is absolutely essential that the elements are to be arranged in sequence. In such a case, one may force the compiler to arrange the elements in sequence.

```
TYPE PERSON
 SEQUENCE
 CHARACTER (LEN=30) :: NAME
 CHARACTER (LEN=50) :: ADDRESS
 INTEGER :: AGE
 CHARACTER (LEN=2) :: BLOOD_GROUP
 CHARACTER (LEN=1) :: RH_FACTOR
 CHARACTER (LEN=15), DIMENSION(3):: PHONE_NO
END TYPE PERSON
```

If there is a structure within a structure, and if the outer one is sequenced, the inner one must be sequenced also.

14.12 Derived Types and EQUIVALENCE

The EQUIVALENCE statement works on the assumption that storage is arranged in sequence. Naturally, SEQUENCE must be used if EQUIVALENCE between derived types is desired.

14.13 Parameterized Derived Type

Parameterized derived type is a new addition to Fortran. Two types of parameters are available:

- parameter known at the time of compilation (kind type)
- evaluation of the parameter is deferred and becomes available during the run-time (len type)

```
TYPE TWODARRAY(K,L,M)
  INTEGER, KIND :: K=KIND(0.0)
  INTEGER, LEN :: L,M
  REAL(K), DIMENSION(L,M) ::X
END TYPE TWODARRAY
```

One must not confuse the KIND attribute and the KIND intrinsic. Now,

```
TYPE(TWOARRAY(KIND(0.0D0), 20, 20)) ::A
```

defines an object A of derived type TWODARRAY with three parameters – one "KIND" type and two "LEN" TYPE. All parameters are of type integer. For example, the integer parameter K has an attribute KIND and the parameters L and M have attribute LEN. These parameters (L and M) are used to specify the bounds of the an array.

At the time of writing this is not supported by the NAG Fortran compiler.

Chapter 15

LIBRARY FUNCTIONS

Library functions or intrinsics were introduced in the earlier chapters. Some of the library functions will be introduced as and when required in the later chapters also. This chapter is a general introduction to library functions. All the available library functions with their calling sequences are listed in Appendix C.

15.1 Generic Names

A group of library functions may be referred to by their family name and the compiler can substitute the family name by an appropriate particular name depending upon the type of the argument. The family name is called the generic name. This was discussed in earlier chapters.

15.2 Intrinsic Procedures

The Fortran library contains both functions and subroutines. There are five types of intrinsic procedure. User written subprograms (functions and subroutines) will be introduced in chapter 19.

15.3 Pure Procedures

The main property of a PURE procedure is that it has no side effect. This will be discussed in chapter 19.

15.4 Elemental Procedures

The dummy arguments of these procedures contain only scalar argument(s). However, they can be called with array(s) also. Excepting MVBITS, which is a subroutine, all the elemental procedures are functions.

When the elemental procedures are called with scalar(s), the returned value is also scalar. When the elemental procedures are called with array-valued actual argument(s), the procedure acts on every element of the array and returns array having the same shape as the actual argument. In case there is more than one array-value argument, all these arguments must be of same shape.

The library function SIN takes one argument and it returns sine of the argument. The supplied argument must be in radians. The argument can be an array and the library function SIN returns an array of same type and size as the input array containing the sine of the corresponding elements of the input array.

```
REAL, DIMENSION(4) :: A,B
REAL, PARAMETER :: PI=3.1415926
A=[PI/6.0,PI/4.0,PI/3.0,PI/2.0]
B=SIN(A)
PRINT *, B
END
```

This is equivalent to:

```
B(1)=SIN(A(1))
B(2)=SIN(A(2))
B(3)=SIN(A(3))
B(4)=SIN(A(4))
```

The output corresponds to SIN of $\pi/6$, $\pi/4$, $\pi/3$ and $\pi/2$ respectively.

15.5 Inquiry Functions

The enquiry function may or may not have any argument. It makes enquiry about certain things and returns an answer. The result does not depend on the value of the argument, if present. For example, BIT_SIZE(I) returns the number of bits needed to store the variable I.

15.6 Transformational Functions

This type of functions has one or more arrays as argument. It does not act on the array element like the elemental procedure. It may return a scalar or an array created from the input array. MAXVAL is one such function.

15.7 Non-elemental Procedures

These types of procedure are called with scalar arguments and scalars are returned. Except the subroutines MVBITS all the library subroutines are non-elemental.

15.8 Argument Keywords

In the tables of intrinsic procedures (Appendix C), the argument keywords are shown. If the actual arguments are in proper order, keywords may be omitted. However, when the argument keyword is used, the actual keyword may be supplied in any order. For example, the function IBSET (I, POS) may be invoked as:

```
          J = IBSET (J, 3)
or,       J = IBSET (I=J, POS=3)
or,       J = IBSET (POS=3, I=J)
```

If one of the arguments is used with the keyword, the rest must be used with the keyword also.

```
J=IBSET (I=J, 3)
```

is not acceptable as the first argument is used with keyword but the second argument does not contain the keyword POS.

15.9 Variable Number of Arguments

Sometimes the number of essential arguments is not fixed. The library function MAX returns the maximum of its arguments. The number of arguments is at least two, but it can be any number greater than two. MAX (A1, A2) returns the maximum of A1 and A2. However, MAX (A1, A2, A3) returns the maximum of A1, A2 and A3. Note that in the first case MAX takes 2 arguments and in the second case 3 arguments are given to MAX.

15.10 Optional Arguments

Some of the arguments may be optional. They may be omitted, if they are not required. The intrinsic MINVAL contains an optional argument DIM. If the optional argument is not present, the minimum value among the array elements is returned. If the optional argument DIM=1 is used, when the required argument is an array of, say rank 2, the intrinsic returns an array of rank 1 – each element being the minimum value corresponding to each column.

15.11 Available Intrinsics

The intrinsics can be divided into several groups. Appendix C contains short descriptions of each of the intrinsics. The majority of the intrinsics and their usage are discussed in different chapters of this book. The name of the different groups is given below.
- Numeric functions
- Mathematical functions
- Character functions including functions to handle strings with variable length
- Kind functions
- Miscellaneous type conversion functions
- Numeric inquiry functions
- Array inquiry functions
- Other inquiry functions
- Bit manipulation procedures
- Floating-point manipulation functions
- Vector and matrix multiply functions
- Array reduction functions
- Array construction functions
- Array location functions
- Null function
- Allocation transfer procedure
- Random number subroutine
- System environment procedures
- IEEE functions

15.12 INTRINSIC Statement

This statement is used to specify the intrinsic procedure.

INTRINSIC:: *intrinsic-name-list*

where intrinsic-name-list is the name of the intrinsics. The name cannot be repeated in the list.

```
REAL::X= 2.0
INTRINSIC::SQRT
PRINT *, SQRT(X)
END
```

Note that without the INTRINSIC statement the program would work. However it is good programming practice to include this statement to increase the readability of the program.

Chapter 16

FORMAT STATEMENTS

List directed input-output statements were introduced in chapter 1. Though the list directed input-output statements are very convenient, yet users do not have much control over them. Most of the time users prefer to have output in user defined style and design of the output format is one of the important aspects of programming. There is saying, "Input should be user friendly and output should be self explanatory". The FORMAT statement provides adequate facilities to design the input and output and thus programmers are not bogged down by the constraints of the list directed I/O.

The editing specification, associated with the FORMAT statement, during the input operation converts the external form (say ASCII) into the internal form (binary). It is just the reverse for the output operation.

16.1 Editing Specifications

The editing specification may be supplied in three different ways:
- in line form
- in a FORMAT statement
- a character variable containing the editing specification.

Inline form uses the editing specification 'inline' with the list elements.

```
READ '(edit descriptor)', list
PRINT '(edit descriptor)', list
```

It is apparent that if the same editing specification is to be used with another input or output statement, it is to be repeated along with the READ or PRINT statement – it cannot be reused. A FORMAT statement may be used many times and in fact, the same FORMAT statement may be used both for the input and the output statement.

```
        READ   st-no, list
        PRINT st-no, list
st-no   FORMAT (edit descriptor)
```

where *st-no* is an unique statement label. FORMAT is a non-executable statement and can be placed anywhere after the specification (declaration) statement and before the END statement (in case there is any inline procedure [chapter 19] the FORMAT statement should be before the CONTAINS statement). Usually, they are placed immediately after the declarations or just before the END statement. Some programmer prefers to put the FORMAT statement near the corresponding READ or PRINT statement.

The FORMAT statement must have a unique statement number and must contain at least one pair left and right parentheses. In case of nested parentheses the number of left and right parentheses must be the same.

```
        READ 10, A, B, C
10      FORMAT (edit descriptor)
        PRINT 20, P, Q
20      FORMAT (edit descriptor)
```

If the I/O statement does not have any list element, the edit descriptor may be omitted.

```
        PRINT 10
10      FORMAT ( )
```

Another form of I/O statements is:

```
        READ (unit, st-no) list
        WRITE (unit, st-no) list
```

These forms will be discussed in details in chapter 24. The unit number is an integer between 1 and 99. Unit numbers 5 and 6 are usually connected to the keyboard and the screen. For example,

```
        READ (5, 10) A
        WRITE (6, 10) A
10      FORMAT (edit descriptor)
```

will read the variable A from the keyboard and display the result on the screen according to the FORMAT. In this form the 'inline' edit descriptor may also be included:

```
        READ (5, FMT= 'edit descriptor') list
        WRITE (6, FMT= 'edit descriptor') list
```

The third form takes a character variable in place of statement number. This character variable is earlier assigned to a string of characters containing the edit descriptor.

```
        CHARACTER (LEN=20) :: FOR
!           FOR is assigned to some edit descriptor
        READ FOR, A, B, C
        PRINT FOR, A, B, C
```

16.2 I/O Lists

The I/O list is the list of elements to be read or written. For the input, the list must be variable names and for the output the list elements may be variables or expressions. The expression is evaluated before the list elements are displayed.

```
READ(5, 10) A, B, C
WRITE(6, 20) A+I, B-J, C
```

An I/O list may contain a reference to a function provided the function does not contain any I/O instruction.

```
WRITE(6, 100) SQRT(X)
```

The I/O may contain a reference to an array. The array may be used as a whole:

```
INTEGER, DIMENSION (10) :: A
READ(5, 125) A
```

Here, during the execution of the program, data for all the A's must be provided. Array elements may also be referred individually.

```
WRITE(6,100) A(1), A(2), A(3), A(4)
```

Implied DO loop may be used to READ or WRITE array elements:

```
WRITE(6,200) (A(K), K=1,10)
```

Also the array elements may be referred in the following manner:

```
WRITE(6, 25) A(1:3)
```

This is same as A(1), A(2) and A(3).

Similarly,

```
WRITE(6, 26) A(1:10:2)
```

will print A(1), A(3), A(5), A(7) and A(9).

16.3 General Form of FORMAT

The general form of a FORMAT statement is:

```
rfw.d
```

where r, an unsigned integer, is the repetition factor; if is absent it is assumed to be 1 (exception: ' X' edit descriptor); f is the editing specification; w is the width of the field – it may be zero; d is the position of the decimal point. Note that not all editing specifications have all the above-mentioned components (r, w and d). The editing specification or the FORMAT tells the computer how the data is arranged in the input device or how the data will be displayed on the output device. The exact position of the data is dependent on the relative position of the edit descriptor within the FORMAT statement. Consider the following two statements:

```
                READ 100, J1,J2
        100     FORMAT (2I5)
```

and,

```
                READ 200, J1,J3,J2
        200     FORMAT(3I5)
```

In the first case, J2 is available between positions 6 and 10 (first 5 positions are for J1) and in the second case the J2 is available between positions 11 and 15. The edit descriptor just specifies the width of the field but the exact position of the data is governed by the other list elements, if any, and their width.

When a READ statement is executed, data is taken always from a fresh record and similarly when a PRINT (or WRITE) statement is executed, output starts from a new line.

16.4 Carriage Control

When data is transferred from the memory to an external device like the printer, the first character of the output record controls the motion of the carriage. This term has been borrowed from the vocabulary of the typist. The spacing between two lines may be single or double. Sometimes it may be necessary not to move the carriage to the next line after printing the current line or it may be necessary to go to the top of the next page before printing the next line. All these are controlled by the carriage control character of an output record.

As already mentioned the first character of the output record (say for printer) is not printed, it is "eaten" up by the computer. The table below summarizes various carriage control characters.

Character	Carriage Motion
blank	Single space
0 (zero)	Double space
+	No carriage motion
1	Skips to next page

It is the responsibility of the programmer to supply the carriage control character. If it is not supplied, the system will interpret the first character of the record – whatever that may be – as the carriage control character and it is not printed. The carriage control character is not required when the output is taken on the screen (terminal).

16.5 Edit Descriptors

The edit descriptors may be grouped under several categories.

- Integer - I, B, O, Z
- Real - F, E, EN, ES, D
- Complex - F, E, EN, ES, D
- Logical - L
- Character - A
- General - G
- Position - T, TL, TR, X
- Slash - /
- Colon - :
- Sign - S, SP, SS
- Scale - P
- Blank handling - BN, BZ
- String - ' (apostrophe), " (quote), H
- Decimal editing - DC, DP
- Rounding Mode - RU, RD, RZ, RN, RC, RP

16.6 Integer Format

The edit descriptor of integer is 'I'.

```
        READ 10, IND
10      FORMAT(I3)
```

The value of the variable will be read from the external device (keyboard). The edit description I3 indicates the width the field and the data is available between positions 1 and 3 of the input. If the data contains 107, IND will be assigned to 107. By default Fortran ignores leading, trailing and embedded blanks and leading zeros. Unsigned data is assumed to be positive. For negative numbers, minus sign is placed before the number, like -47. A single READ statement may read more than one quantity.

```
        READ 100, J1, J2, J3
10      FORMAT (I3, I4, I6)
```

On the input device J1 is available between positions 1 and 3, J2 is available in the next four positions (4 to 7) and J3 is read between positions 8 and 13. The edit descriptor contains the width of the field and the exact position of the data is relative with respect to the previous field.

```
        READ 10, J1, J2
10      FORMAT(2I5)
```

In this case the repetition factor is 2 and thus it is equivalent to I5, I5. The first five positions contain the value of J1 and the next five positions contain the value of J2.

A PRINT statement with the I descriptor can be used to display integers on the output device.

```
        PRINT 20, J1, J2
20      FORMAT(2I5)
```

will print J1 between positions 1 and 5 and J2 between positions 5 and 10. The numbers are printed right adjusted within the field. Leading zeros are replaced by blanks. If the quantity is positive, '+' sign is not printed. For a negative quantity, a '-' (minus) sign is placed before the number. The integer format may be of the form $w.d$. For input, the 'd' part is ignored. For output, if the 'd' part is present, at least 'd' number of digits is printed – if necessary by adding leading zeros.

```
          PRINT 41, J1
41        FORMAT(I5.5)
```

If the value of J1 is 37, the output will show 00037.

B, O and Z edit descriptors have been discussed in the chapter 17.

16.7 Real Number

There are five edit descriptors under this category. 'F', 'E', 'D', 'EN' and 'ES'. The 'F' descriptor is used for 'normal' real numbers, and the 'E' descriptor is used when the input or the output is desired in scientific notation. The 'D' edit descriptor is used for double precision quantities. 'EN' and 'ES' are both used for the output.

A typical 'F' descriptor may be of the following form:

```
F8.3
```

where 8 is the width of the field and 3 is the position of the decimal point. During input operations if the decimal point is typed explicitly, 'd' has no effect.

```
          READ 105, A
105       FORMAT(F8.3)
```

If the data is supplied as 25.2797, the variable A will be assigned to 25.2797 if the data is available anywhere within the field (position 1 and 8). Leading zeros and blanks are ignored. For positive number, the plus sign is optional. If the number is negative, the minus sign is placed in front of the number. If the data does not contain a decimal point, that is, it is supplied as integer, the actual value of the variable becomes the input number by 10^{-d}, where d is the position of the decimal point. In the above example, if the input data is 12345678, A will be assigned to 12345.678.

A real number may be printed with the 'F' descriptor. The number is printed right adjusted within the field. Leading zeros are replaced by blanks and for positive numbers the plus sign is omitted. For a negative number, the minus sign is placed before the number.

```
          REAL :: A
          A=1.236
          PRINT 200, A
200       FORMAT(F8.3)
```

will display 1.236, but if the format is

```
200       FORMAT (F8.2)
```

the output will be 1.24 (after rounding the last digit).

In scientific notation the editing symbol is 'E' like E16.6, where 16 is the width of the field and 6 is the position of the decimal point. Again during the input operation if the decimal point is typed explicitly, 'd' part is ignored. The data consists of a string of decimal digits followed by 'E' and an integer to specify the exponent. The exponent may be signed. An unsigned exponent is assumed to be positive. For a negative exponent, a minus sign is typed between 'E' and the exponent. The following are valid data:

```
1.2367E4
-37.45E-7
43.2646E-11
-100.37E7
```

If the decimal number is typed explicitly, the data may be typed anywhere within the field. It is recommended that the number be right adjusted within the field as some old compiler may assume trailing blanks as zeros and these zeros become part of the exponent (1 becomes 10, if there is a space after 1). If the decimal point is not typed explicitly, the number becomes:

$$(integer\ part) \times 10^{-d} \times 10^{n}$$

where d is the position of the decimal point and n is the exponent part. If the edit descriptor is E10.3, 0012345E4 will be read as 12.345×10^{4}.

The E descriptor, when used with a PRINT statement, prints the value of the corresponding real variable right adjusted within the field. Usually a zero is printed before the fraction and the exponent is adjusted accordingly.

```
            REAL :: A
            A=12.34
            PRINT 25, A
      25    FORMAT(E10.3)
```

The output will be 0.123E02. The 'D' edit descriptor is similar to the 'E' edit descriptor. It is used for double precision quantities. F, E, and D are interchangeable. For example, the FORMAT statement may contain the edit descriptor F7.3 but the input may be 1.2E04.

There is a second form of E descriptor:

```
            rEw.dEe
```

where e is the number of digits for the exponent field. The following is an example of this edit descriptor

Internal No.	Format	Displayed value
$4.567 * 10^{123}$	E14.3E4	bbb0.457E+0123

There are two other variations of the E format. They are EN and ES. Both are used with the output statement. The EN descriptor prints a variable such that the exponent part is divisible by 3 and the fractional part is between 1 and 999, except when the list element is zero.

Internal value	Edit Descriptor	Output
0.8	EN12.3	800.000E-03
1.256	EN12.3	1.256E+00
1239.672	EN12.3	1.240E+03

The ES edit descriptor ensures that the number before the decimal is between 1 and 9 except when it is zero. The exponent is adjusted accordingly.

Internal value	Edit Descriptor	Output
0.8	ES12.3	8.000E-01
1.256	ES12.3	1.256E+00
37.935	ES12.3	3.794E+01

16.8 Insufficient Width

If the width of the field is not sufficient to display the number, asterisks are printed. A FORMAT with edit descriptor I3 is insufficient to print a variable having a value 9999. A relation exists between the width of the field and the position of the decimal point for E edit descriptor. If the edit descriptor is E$w.d$, we need:

- d places for the digits after the decimal point.
- 1 place for the sign of the exponent.
- 2 places for the exponent (usually).
- 1 place for the letter E.
- 1 place for the decimal itself.
- 1 place for the digit before the decimal point (usually zero)
- 1 place for the sign of the exponent

Therefore, $w >= d+7$. For the D descriptor, where the exponent is usually a 4 digit number, the relation between w and d will be:

$$w >= d+9$$

16.9 FORMAT and List Elements

We have seen that two or more variables may be read or written by a single FORMAT statement.

```
      READ 15, IA, IB, IC
15    FORMAT(I4,I5,I6)
```

It may be noted that in this case there is a one to one correspondence between the list elements and the edit descriptors. Two cases may arise.

Case I: If the edit descriptor contains more items than the list elements like:

```
            READ 35, IA, IB
      35    FORMAT(3I3)
```

the excess edit descriptor is ignored. If the input record contains 123456789, IA will be assigned to 123 and IB to 456. The digits following 6 are ignored and if there is another READ statement following this one, a fresh record will be read.

Case II: If the number of list elements are more than editing specification like:

```
            PRINT 45, IA, IB, IC
      45    FORMAT (I8)
```

the edit descriptor is used repeatedly till the list is exhausted. Each time the format is reused a fresh record is used. To be more precise, when the format is exhausted, the nearest left bracket is traced and between this left bracket and the next right bracket edit descriptors are repeatedly used and each time it comes to the left bracket, a fresh record is generated. In the above example IA, IB and IC will be printed in three separate lines. If the FORMAT is

```
      45    FORMAT (2I8)
```

IA and IB will be printed in one line and IC will be printed in the second line. If the FORMAT contains nested parentheses:

```
            PRINT 55, N, A, B, C
      55    FORMAT(I8,(2F9.2))
```

N, A and B will be printed in the first line using the edit descriptors I8, 2F9.2. As the FORMAT has been exhausted but the list is not exhausted, the edit descriptor 2F9.2 will be used repeatedly till the list is exhausted and since each time this edit descriptor is reused a fresh line will be generated. Therefore, C will be printed in the next line with edit descriptor F9.2. Note that after printing C the additional edit descriptors are ignored as the list has been exhausted. Though all the above examples are based on the PRINT statement, the same is true for READ statement also.

16.10 Complex Numbers

Complex number consists of two parts – real and imaginary. The edit descriptors for these two parts may be same or different.

```
            COMPLEX :: C1
                .

                .
            PRINT 100, C1
      100       FORMAT(2E16.6)
```

Both the real and the imaginary parts are displayed using the E16.6 edit descriptor. If the FORMAT is changed to:

```
100     FORMAT(E16.6, F12.3)
```

the real and the imaginary part will use edit descriptors E16.6 and F12.3, respectively.

16.11 Logical Quantities

The edit descriptor for a logical quantity for the input or the output operation is

```
Lw
```

where w is the width of the field. During input if the first non-blank character of the field is T or t or .T or .t, true value will be assigned to the corresponding list element. Similarly, if the first non-blank character of the field is F or f or .F. or .f., false value is assigned to the corresponding list element. During the output operation, T of F, depending upon the value of the list element, is displayed right adjusted within the field.

```
        LOGICAL :: L1
        READ 200, L1
200     FORMAT(L4)
        PRINT 200, L1
```

If the data supplied is .TRUE., the output will be T preceded by 3 blanks.

16.12 Character Variables

The edit descriptor corresponding to character variable is A. Its form is

```
Aw
```

where w is width of the field. The width may be omitted in which case the width is assumed to be the length of the variable. Three cases may arise.
Case I: The length of the variable is same as the width of the field w.

```
        CHARACTER (LEN=4) :: A
        READ 25, A
25      FORMAT(A4)
        PRINT 25, A
```

The READ statement inputs 4 characters and the PRINT statement prints the same 4 characters.

Case II: The length of the variable is greater than the width of the field.

```
                    CHARACTER (LEN=8) :: A
                    READ 35, A
          35        FORMAT(A4)
                    PRINT 45, A
          45        FORMAT (A6)
```

The first four characters from the input field is read and stored in the leftmost bytes of the variable; trailing blanks are added. If, in the above case, the data contains IACS, the variable A will be set to IACSbbbb, where 'b' stands for blank. The PRINT statement outputs the first six characters of the variable A, which is IACSbb.

Case III: The length of the variable, *l*, is less than the width of the field.

```
                    CHARACTER (LEN=4) :: A
                    READ 55, A
          55        FORMAT(A8)
                    PRINT 56,A
          56        FORMAT(A10)
```

The rightmost *l* characters are stored in the variable. If the data is calcUTTA, the variable A will be set to UTTA. The print statement will display UTTA, right adjusted within the field and naturally will add 6 blanks before UTTTA (bbbbbbUTTA).

The A descriptor without any width reads or writes according to the length of the list element. This is shown in 16.24.

16.13 Scale Factors

The scale factor is used to 'scale' numeric value during input or output operations. At the beginning of each input or output statement, the scale factor, by default, is zero. Once set, it applies to all subsequent F, E, EN, ES, D and G edit descriptor, unless it is changed to some other value. The edit descriptor used for this purpose is:

$$kP$$

If there is no exponent in the edit descriptor, the input is multiplied by 10^{-k} while reading:

```
                    READ 20, A
          20        FORMAT(2PF8.2)
```

If the data is 14.2, it is stored as 0.142. Inputs having exponents are not affected by the scale factor. In the above program segment if the input is 1.24E2, A will be assigned to 124.0.

On output, for the F descriptor, the internal number is multiplied by 10^k. For example, 1.43 under the edit descriptor 2PF8.2 is displayed as 143.00. However, for the E, D and G descriptors, the mantissa is multiplied by 10^k and the exponent is multiplied by 10^{-k}. Therefore, 1.42 (0.142E1) under 2PE12.3 will be displayed as 14.20E-01.

16.14 Leading Signs

These edit descriptor is related to the sign of a number. For a positive number the leading plus sign is replaced by a blank; for a negative number, the negative sign is placed before the number. There are three such edit descriptors related to sign – SP, S and SS.

SP or sign print forces the '+' sign of a positive number to be displayed.

```
              IA=10
              PRINT 10, IA
       10     FORMAT (SP,I4)
```

prints b+10, where b stands for blank. While SP is active, SS or 'sign suppress' suppresses the printing of the positive sign.

```
              IA=10
              JA=20
              KA=30
              PRINT 100, IA, JA, KA
       100    FORMAT (SP,I4,SS,I4,I4)
```

displays b+10bb20bb30.

The third edit descriptor in this category, S, restores the default condition. If the previous FORMAT statement is replaced by:

```
       100    FORMAT (SP, I4,S,I4,I4)
```

the output will be b+10bb20bb30.

16.15 Tab Descriptor

The Tab descriptor specifies the position of the record from which the input may be obtained or the position of the output record where output of the corresponding list element would go.
Case I: The Tab edit descriptor has the form T*n*, where *n* specifies the position of the input or the output record.

```
              READ 111, IA, JA
       110    FORMAT (T2,I2,T6,I2)
```

will set IA to 23 and JA to 67 if the input record is 12345678. Tab edit descriptor always counts the position from the beginning of the record. If the FORMAT statement is replaced by:

```
       110    FORMAT (T6,I2,T2,I2)
```

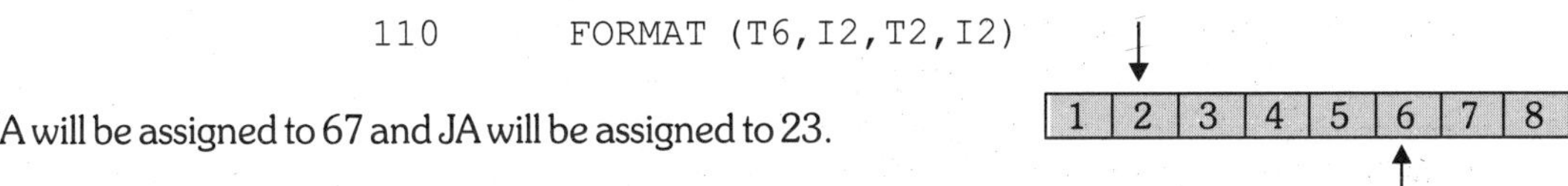

IA will be assigned to 67 and JA will be assigned to 23.

```
          PRINT 30, IA, JA
   30     FORMAT (T2, I4, T10, I4)
```

will print IA from the position 2 (right adjusted in positions 2, 3, 4 and 5) and JA from the position 10 (right adjusted in position 10, 11, 12 and 13). If the FORMAT statement is changed to:

```
   30     FORMAT (T10, I4, T2, I4)
```

IA will be printed from position 10 and JA will be printed from position 2. It may be noted that though in the list, IA appears before JA, JA will be printed before IA (nearer the left margin) because of the T edit descriptor.

Case II: The Tab left edit descriptor has the form TLn, where n is the position relative to the current position to the left.

```
          READ 10, I, J
   10     FORMAT (T6, I1, TL3, I1)
```

| 1 | 2 | 3 | 4 | 5 | 6 | 7 | 8 |

If the data is 12345678, I will be assigned to 6 and J will be assigned to 4. After reading 6 (T6, 6th position), the current position is 7. With respect to this position, 3 positions to the left (TL3) is the 4th position from the left. For output also, position is calculated with respect to the current position to the left. The TL edit descriptor cannot go beyond position 1.

Case III: The Tab right edit descriptor has the form TRn, where n is the position relative to the current position to the right. If the above FORMAT statement is changed to:

```
   10    FORMAT (I1,TR3,I2)
```

| 1 | 2 | 3 | 4 | 5 | 6 | 7 | 8 |

I will be assigned to 1 and J will be assigned to 56. After reading 1 the current position is 2 and 3 places to the right is the position 5.

16.16 The X Descriptor

This edit descriptor is used to skip a few positions of the input field depending upon the repetition factor of 'X' or to insert blanks (horizontally) in an output record. The form of the X edit descriptor is nX, where n is a positive integer greater than zero.

```
          READ 95, IA, IB
   95     FORMAT (2X, I3, 3X, I4)
```

First two positions of the input record are skipped, the contents of the next three locations become the value if IA; next three positions are skipped and IB is read from the next four positions of the input field. If the input is 123456789997, IA will be 345 and IB is set to 9997. When used with an output format, the X edit descriptor inserts blank(s) in the output record. Normally, '1X' is used with an output format to insert a blank at the beginning of a record so that this may be interpreted as carriage control character whenever required.

```
            PRINT 400, A, B, C
400         FORMAT(1X,3F10.3)
```

The peculiarity of X edit descriptor is that it must have a repetition factor, even if it is one.

16.17 The Slash

If a new record is desired at any point, slash (/) is used as edit descriptor. On output, a slash causes the current line to be terminated and subsequent output starts from a new line. On input, the current record is terminated and input begins from the next record.

```
            READ 93, N, (A(I), I=1,N)
93          FORMAT(I5/(5E16.6))
```

N is read from the first record and the A's are read from the subsequent records — 5 from each record. Note the importance of the inner brackets. Because of this pair of brackets, when the format is exhausted, A's are read according to the edit descriptor 5E16.6 till the list is exhausted. Without this pair of brackets, the edit descriptor I5/5E16.6 would have been used resulting in a FORMAT error.

Slash can be repeated or repeat count may be placed before the slash.

```
            PRINT 73, A, B
73          FORMAT(F10.3 /// F8.3)
```

Two blank lines will be inserted between the values of A and B. The above FORMAT may be written as:

```
73          FORMAT(F10.3, 3/, F8.3)
```

In this case the comma after F10.3 is essential. However it is better to use comma both before and after slash (/).

In general, if there are *n* number of slashes between two edit descriptors, (*n-1*) blank lines are skipped, that is, (*n-1*) blank lines are inserted. The slash can be placed at the beginning or at the end of the edit specification also.

```
73          FORMAT (//F10.3///F8.3//)
```

The output will be: two blank lines followed by the value of A according to F10.3 edit descriptor; two more blanks lines followed by the value of B according to F8.3 edit descriptor followed by two blank lines.

16.18 Embedded Blanks

An embedded blank with an input field may be treated in two different ways. By default it is treated as null. However, with an appropriate edit descriptor, it will be interpreted as zero.

```
                READ 100, IA
      100       FORMAT (I3)
```

If the data is 1b2 (b stands for blank), by default, IA will be set to 12. The default can be changed by BZ edit descriptor. If the FORMAT statement is modified as

```
      100       FORMAT (BZ, I3)
```

blanks will be treated as zero and so I will be set to 102. Once set, this will remain effective till the end of the FORMAT statement. This can be forced back to the default value by BN edit descriptor.

```
                READ 400, IA, JA
      400       FORMAT (BZ, I3, BN, I3)
```

If the data is 1b23b4, IA will be set to 102 and J to 34. If the embedded or the trailing blanks are treated as zero, one should be extremely careful while reading data. Trailing blanks after the exponent in scientific notation (E edit descriptor) would make E+01b to E+10.

16.19 General Edit Descriptor

The G edit descriptor, called the General Format, when used, with real number behaves like the F or E edit descriptor depending upon its magnitude. The form of G edit descriptor is either $Gw.d$ or $Gw.dEe$. For integer, character or logical quantities the above edit descriptor follows the rules of Iw, Aw and Lw respectively.

16.20 Strings

Any character string may be displayed by enclosing the string within apostrophes or quotes.

```
                PRINT 100, A
      100       FORMAT ('  The result is =  ', F8.3)
```

The PRINT statement will display the string followed by the value of A according to the edit descriptor F8.3.
   To print an apostrophe, two successive apostrophes must be used.

```
                PRINT 110
      110       FORMAT (' Don''t')
```

The same thing can be done by enclosing the string within quotes.

```
      110       FORMAT (" DON'T")
```

There is another way of printing a string, which is now considered as deleted feature.

```
                PRINT 67
      67        FORMAT (8HIACS Cal)
```

This PRINT statement will display IACS Cal on the screen. The disadvantage of the method (H edit descriptor) is that one has to count the number of characters and that becomes the coefficient of 'H'. Since this is an obsolete feature, it will not be discussed in detail here.

16.21 Colon

Colon editing is useful when it is necessary to terminate the format control because there is no further item in the list. This is illustrated with an example.

```
                    A=32.25
                    PRINT 215, A
          215       FORMAT (' A= ', F5.2,' B= ', F8.3)
```

The PRINT statement of the program will generate an output,

```
          A= 32.25 B=
```

Since the list element does not contain B, it is desirable that the string ' B= ' should not be in the output record. This can be achieved with the help of the colon (:) edit descriptor.

```
          215       FORMAT (' A= ', F5.2 : ' B= ', F8.3)
```

Though the example shows colon editing with the output statement, it can be used to terminate an input statement also. Note that a comma is not required between other edit descriptors and the colon.

16.22 Decimal Editing

This edit descriptor temporarily changes decimal editing mode. The descriptors act on the D, E, F, EN, ES and G edit descriptors.
    The edit descriptor DC changes decimal to comma and DP reinstates comma to decimal.

```
                    F=2.3
                    G=5.3
                    WRITE(6, 10)F, G
          10        FORMAT(DC, F5.2, DP, F5.2)
```

The output will be b2,30b5.30 (b stands for blank)

16.23 Rounding Mode

The rounding mode may be changed during the input or the output statement using the edit descriptors RU, RD, RZ, RN, RC and RP. They are respectively, rounding up, down, zero, nearest, compatible and processor-dependent. The edit descriptors used along with the READ or the WRITE statement overrides the rounding options, if used, with the OPEN statement (chapter 24).

16.24 Variable Format

In place of a FORMAT, a character variable containing the edit descriptor can be used.

```
CHARACTER (LEN=20) :: FORM
FORM='(3I5)'
READ FORM, IA, IB, IC
PRINT FORM, IA, IB, IC
END
```

Three integer variables IA, IB and IC will be read according to the editing specification contained in the character variable FORM, which in this case is 3I5.

The editing specification can be read from the external device and subsequently can be used as a FORMAT for the READ or the PRINT statement.

```
         CHARACTER (LEN=20) :: FORM
         READ 110, FORM              ! read edit descriptor
110      FORMAT(A)                   ! A descriptor without any width
         READ FORM, IA, IB, IC
         PRINT FORM, IA, IB, IC
         END
```

The first READ statement will read the editing specification to be used for the next READ and PRINT statement. If the variable FORM is read as (3I3) (note that the parentheses must be present along with the edit descriptor), the next READ statement, which uses this character variable in place of FORMAT, will use this edit descriptor while reading IA, IB and IC. In the above program the character variable is used to display the number. Note that the length of the character variable must be sufficient to accommodate all the edit descriptors.

16.25 Memory to Memory Input/Output

Usually in any input or output operation, there is a transfer of data between the memory and some external device. However, it is possible to have a situation where one part of the memory may behave as an "external device". Data from one portion of the memory may be transferred to another portion of the memory under the control of a FORMAT. Both "READ", and "WRITE" operations are possible.

```
         CHARACTER (LEN=8) :: CBUF='12345678'
         INTEGER :: IA, IB, IC
         READ (CBUF, 10) IA, IB, IC
10       FORMAT (I1, 1X, I2, 1X, I3)
         PRINT 10, IA, IB, IC
         END
```

The character variable, in this case, behaves as "input device". Data is transferred to IA, IB and IC under the control of the FORMAT statement from the character variable CBUF. Note that in this case also an ASCII character from the location CBUF is converted into binary through the FORMAT statement similar to the conversion of ASCII characters supplied from the keyboard. That is character

"1" becomes integer 1.

In a similar way it is possible to "WRITE" in memory under the control of a FORMAT.

```
        CHARACTER (LEN=12) :: CKUF
        INTEGER :: IA=1, IB=23, IC=567
        WRITE(CKUF, 20) IA, IB, IC
20      FORMAT (3I4)
        PRINT *, CKUF
        END
```

The output from the above program will be bbb1bb23b567, where 'b' denotes blank. It is evident that under the control of the FORMAT, binary numbers are converted into ASCII and stored in the character variable CKUF. As already mentioned the length of the character variable should be sufficient to accommodate the "output". In this case the edit descriptor is 3I4, that is, it will require at least 12 (3x4) characters. The length of the corresponding character variable, in this case CKUF, should be at least 12.

16.26 NAMELIST

Namelist does not require any input or output list; it does not require any FORMAT statement either. Yet it is grouped with the FORMAT statements, as it is very similar to FORMATTED input-output statements. Namelist uses a namelist block, which is declarative statement. However, there is a difference between the list elements of a namelist block and standard list elements associated with the READ/WRITE statement. When the namelist block is used with the READ statement, it is not necessary to specify all the list elements of the namelist block. The elements, which have not been supplied from the input device, retain their current value. A namelist block is defined in the following way:

```
NAMELIST/block-name/ list elements
```

As an example, a namelist block B1 may be defined as:

```
NAMELIST/B1/A, B, C, D
```

where B1 is the name of the block and A, B, C and D are list elements.

The READ statement associated with the namelist block B1 is:

```
        READ (5, B1)
or,     READ (5, NML=B1)
```

The data supplied from the keyboard must have one '&' character in the first position followed by the block name and the *variable name=value* of the variable in any order. For example, if one wants to modify B and D, the data to be supplied as:

```
& B1 B=10.0, D=20.0/
or
& B1 D=20.0, B=10.0 /
```

It is to be noted that the data supplied from the keyboard must start with an ampersand (first non blank character) and ends with a slash as shown above. Note further in this case only the values of B and D have been changed and therefore, A and C would retain their old values. The following program will illustrate this point.

```
INTEGER ::IA, IB, IC, ID
NAMELIST/B1/IA, IB, IC, ID
IA=100
IB=200
IC=300
ID=400
READ(5, B1)
WRITE(6, B1)
END
```

If the data supplied through the keyboard is:

```
&B1 IA=7, ID=27 /
```

The output will be:

```
&B1 IA=7,  IB=200,  IC=300,  ID=27/
```

The output will have the namelist block name attached to it.

The READ statement with namelist is useful when it is necessary to change some and not all the list elements of an input list.

The program unit may have any number of namelist blocks and no two blocks can have same block name. The same namelist block may be used both for the input and the output statement. If the list element is of user type (derived type) or an array, all values must be supplied after the equal sign.

```
INTEGER, DIMENSION(5) :: P=999
NAMELIST /N2/ P
READ (5, N2)
WRITE (6, N2)
END
```

The data may be of the following type:

```
&N2 P=1, 2, 3, 4, 5/           ! all the elements are assigned
&N2 P(1:3)=10, 20, 30/         ! only elements 1, 2 and 3 are assigned
&N2 P(1)=7, P(4)=20/           ! only P(1) and P(4) are assigned.
```

Rules for Namelist: There are some restrictions on the type of the list elements used with namelist:
(a) It cannot be an allocatable array (chapter 21).
(b) It cannot be a pointer (chapter 21).
(c) It cannot be dummy array with non-constant bound (chapter 20).
(d) It cannot be a character array with non-constant character length.
(e) If one of the NAMELIST group-variable is public, all other variable must be public (chapter 19).

Chapter 17

BINARY, OCTAL AND HEX NUMBERS

Strictly speaking, the digits are just symbols – the positions of a digit within a number determines its value. For example, when the base of the number system is 10, the number 123 is actually $1\text{x}10^2+2\text{x}10^1+3\text{x}10^0$. Therefore, if a digit, say 3, appears at the unit position – its value is 3. On the other hand, if the same digit appears at the position of 10, its value is 30. A number may be represented in terms of a base other than 10. The most popular bases are binary (base of 2), octal (base of 8) and hexadecimal (base of 16). However, the numerical value of a particular number is independent of the number system (base) – the value of a particular number is same in all systems. In the next few sections we shall indicate a base other than base 10 by means of a subscript – $(1110)_2$ stands for a binary number.

17.1 Binary Numbers

A "bit" is abbreviation of a BInary digiT. In the binary system, that is, when the base is 2, the available digits are 0 and 1. For example, a number $(1101)_2$ is equal to 13 in the decimal system: $1\text{x}2^3+1\text{x}2^2+0\text{x}2^1+1\text{x}2^0$.

17.2 Octal Numbers

Octal numbers have a base of eight. The available digits are 0 through 7. Three binary digits constitute one octal digit [the highest value is 7, that is, $(111)_2$]. An octal number $(101)_8$ is equal to 65 in the decimal system – $1\text{x}8^2+0\text{x}8^1+1\text{x}8^0$.

17.3 Hexadecimal Numbers

Hexadecimal numbers – popularly known as HEX numbers – have a base of 16. The available digits are 0 through 9, A, B, C, D, E and F. The last six symbols are equivalent to decimal 10, 11, 12, 13, 14 and 15 respectively. Four binary digits constitute one hex digit. The highest value of a hex digit is 'F', that is, 15 in the decimal system. A through F may also be represented by the corresponding lower case letters. The hex number $(101)_{16}$ is equal to 257 in the decimal system – $1\text{x}16^2+0\text{x}16^1+1\text{x}16^0$.

17.4 BOZ Numbers

The binary, octal or hex numbers are represented by the respective digits enclosed within apostrophes or quotes and prefixed by B, O or Z respectively. The following are binary, octal and hex numbers:

```
B'1001' (decimal 9)
B'1111' (decimal 15)
O'127'  (decimal 87)
O'201'  (decimal 129)
Z'12A'  (decimal 298)
Z'1B7'  (decimal 439)
```

The uppercase letters B, O and Z may be substituted by their corresponding lower case counterparts –
b, o and z respectively.

17.5 Integer Variables and BOZ Numbers

An integer variable may be initialized to a binary, octal or hex number through initialization or DATA
statement as hereunder.

```
INTEGER :: A=B'111'
INTEGER :: B=O'171'
INTEGER :: C=Z'1A'
```

Also,

```
INTEGER :: P,Q,R
DATA P/B'1111'/
DATA Q/O'247'/
DATA R/Z'12A'/
```

17.6 Assignment

BOZ numbers cannot be used directly to assign a value to a variable. Integer, real, double precision
and complex variables may be assigned to binary, octal and hex constants through the library
functions INT, REAL, DBLE and CMPLX respectively. This is illustrated through the program
segment shown below. The decimal value corresponding to the binary constants are indicated
through in-line comments.

```
INTEGER :: I,J,K
REAL :: A,B,C
DOUBLE PRECISION :: D1,D2,D3
COMPLEX :: C1,C2,C3,C4

I=INT(B'11')                    ! I=3
J=INT(O'16')                    ! J=14
K=INT(Z'A1')                    ! K=161
A=REAL(B'111')                  ! A=7.0
B=REAL(O'73')                   ! B=59.0
C=REAL(Z'AB')                   ! C=171.0
```

```
      D1=DBLE(B'1111')              ! D1=15.0D0
      D2=DBLE(O'37')                ! D2=31.0D0
      D3=DBLE(Z'3A')                ! D3=58.0D0
      C1=CMPLX(B'101',B'1011')  ! C1=(5.0,11.0)
      C2=CMPLX(O'23',O'56')     ! C2=(19.0,46.0)
      C3=CMPLX(Z'12',Z'11')     ! C3=(18.0,17.0)
      C4=CMPLX(O'53',Z'1A')     ! C4=(43.0,26.0)


      END
```
(* NAG compiler gives compilation error for the DBLE intrinsics)

17.7 Input / Output Operations and BOZ Format

An integer may be assigned to a binary, octal or hex value through a READ statement using B, O or Z format respectively. The next program segment will assign values to the respective variables when the data is supplied through the input device (in this case the keyboard).

```
            INTEGER :: IB, IO, IZ
            .

            .
            READ(*, 10) IB
   10       FORMAT (B4)
```

If the supplied value is 1101, IB will be assigned to 13.

```
            READ (*, 20) IO
   20       FORMAT (O5)
```

If the supplied data is 00472, IO will be assigned to 314.

```
            READ (*, 30) IZ
   30       FORMAT (Z5)
```

If the supplied data is 002C5, IZ will be assigned to 609.
   Similarly, the write statement with B, O and Z format will display the integer as binary, octal and hex number respectively.

```
            WRITE (*, 40) IB
   40       FORMAT (B32)

            WRITE (*, 50) IO
   50       FORMAT (O11)

            WRITE (*, 60) IZ
   60       FORMAT (Z8)
```

17.8 Printing of a Real Number in BOZ Format

B, O and Z format must be used with integer variables only. Sometimes it may be necessary to know the internal representation of a real variable. This can be done in a round about way.

```
          INTEGER :: INUM
          REAL :: ANUM
          EQUIVALENCE (INUM,ANUM)
          ANUM=0.125
          WRITE(*,70) INUM
   70     FORMAT(1X,B32.32)
          END
```

In the above example, INUM and ANUM share the same location. And in our system both the integer and real variable (by default) require 32 bits. The equivalence statement is used to satisfy the grammar of the language that B, O or Z format must be associated with an integer variable. The technique used in this example is machine dependent. The basic assumption is that a normal integer and a real variable both require 32 bits.

In a similar manner, the B format may be substituted by the O or Z format. The problem of printing a double precision quantity in B, O or Z format is left as an exercise.

It may be noted that Fortran provides an intrinsic TRANSFER to do the same job, which is discussed in chapter 23.

Chapter 18

THE FORTRAN NUMERICAL MODEL

This chapter deals with the numeric model of Fortran. A thorough understanding of the numeric model and the intrinsics associated with it is required to write truly machine (hardware) independent computer programs. To understand the numeric model of Fortran, it is necessary to define a few terms, that will be used to define the model.

Bit: Bit stands for binary digit. It can have a value either zero or one.

Byte: Byte is a collection of bits. 8 bits make one byte.

Storage: A variable or constant may occupy one byte or more than one byte depending upon its type. Each byte has a unique address within the system.

Bit Numbering: Bits are numbered from right to left within a byte or combination of bytes. The rightmost bit of a byte or a combination of bytes is numbered as zero. If four contiguous bytes are joined to store a real number, bits are numbered 0 to 31 from right to left.

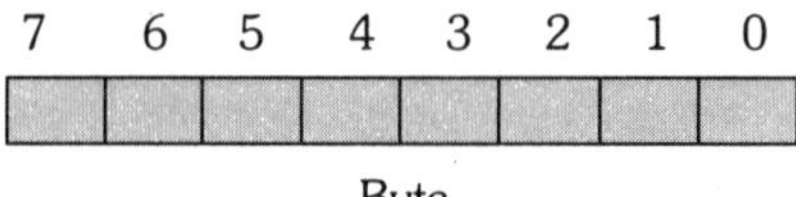

Byte

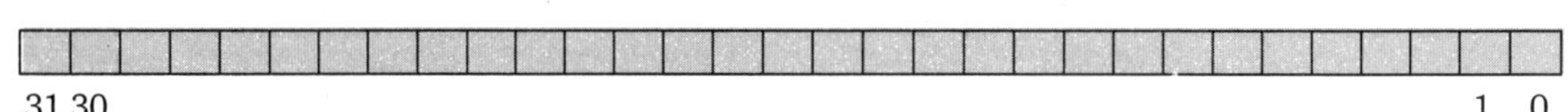

Four bytes

18.1 Numeric Model for Integers

An integer is stored as a binary number. The value of such a binary number is given by:

$$N = s \sum_{k=1}^{n} w_k \cdot b^{(k-1)}$$

where *n* is the total number of bits required to represent the integer, b is the radix or base which is 2 (binary) and w's are integers such that

$$0 <= w < b$$

Naturally, where b is 2, w can be either zero or one; s is either +1 or -1 depending on the sign of the number.

18.2 Base

The base or radix can be determined by the intrinsic RADIX. The argument is either an integer or a real. It may be a scalar or array valued. The base corresponding to an integer is returned by the intrinsic.

```
INTEGER :: I
.
PRINT *, RADIX(I)
```

This prints 2 as the base of the number system.

18.3 Largest Integer

The intrinsic HUGE returns the largest integer available corresponding to the type of the argument. The largest integer for a particular KIND is $2^{(k-1)}$ where k is the total number bits allocated to the integer (without the sign bit; the leftmost bit is sign bit; it is zero if the number is positive and it is one if the number is negative). The following program would print:

```
INTEGER :: I
PRINT *, HUGE(0_1)
PRINT *, HUGE(0_2)
PRINT *, HUGE(0_3)
PRINT *, HUGE(0_4)
END
```

127, 32767, 2147483647 and 922337203685477 corresponding to KIND=1, 2, 3 and 4 for the NAG compiler. These numbers corresponds to $2^7 - 1$, $2^{15} - 1$, $2^{31} - 1$, $2^{63} - 1$. A better way to write this program is to use the integer parameters corresponding to different kinds indirectly.

```
INTEGER, PARAMETER :: VSMALL=SELECTED_INT_KIND(2)
INTEGER, PARAMETER :: SMALL=SELECTED_INT_KIND(3)
INTEGER, PARAMETER :: MEDIUM=SELECTED_INT_KIND(5)
INTEGER, PARAMETER :: BIG=SELECTED_INT_KIND(10)
INTEGER (VSMALL) :: A
INTEGER (SMALL) :: B
INTEGER (MEDIUM) :: C
INTEGER (BIG) :: D

PRINT *, HUGE (A)
PRINT *, HUGE (B)
PRINT *, HUGE (C)
PRINT *, HUGE (D)
```

```
PRINT *, HUGE(0_VSMALL)
PRINT *, HUGE(0_SMALL)
PRINT *, HUGE(0_MEDIUM)
PRINT *, HUGE(0_BIG)
```

18.4 DIGITS for Integer

The intrinsic DIGITS returns the number of bits (without the sign bit) the system allocates to represent an integer. Again, using the variables defined in section 18.3 we find the program segment

```
PRINT *, DIGITS(A)
PRINT *, DIGITS(B)
PRINT *, DIGITS(C)
PRINT *, DIGITS(D)
```

displays 7, 15, 31 and 63 respectively.

18.5 RANGE for Integer

Range returns the exponent range that may be fully represented in this model.

```
PRINT *, RANGE(A)
PRINT *, RANGE(B)
PRINT *, RANGE(C)
PRINT *, RANGE(D)
```

The output from these PRINT statements is 2, 4, 9 and 18 respectively. We have already noted that HUGE returns the largest integer available in the system corresponding to its argument. Now consider HUGE(C). This number is 213748367. Thus,

$$10^x = 214748367$$

or, $$x = \log_{10} 214748367$$

which is 9 when truncated to nearest integer. Similarly, $\log_{10}127$, $\log_{10}32767$, $\log_{10}9223372036854775807$, when integerized by truncation, result in 2, 4 and 18 respectively. In other words RANGE returns $INT(\log_{10}(HUGE(X)))$.

18.6 Representation of Real Numbers

A real number is represented as:

$$X = 0$$

or, $$= s.b^e. \sum (k=1,p) \; f_k.b^{(-k)}$$

or, $$= s.b^e. (1/2 + \sum (k=2,p) \; f_k.b^{(-k)}$$

$$[f_1 \text{ is always 1 which is } 1.2^{(-1)} = 1/2]$$

where, b and p are integers and are greater than 1; f_k is a non-negative integer and is less than b; f1 is non-zero; s is $+1$ for positive number and -1 for negative number; e is an integer such that

$$e_{min} <=e <= e_{max}$$

where e_{min} and e_{max} are system dependent minimum and maximum values of the exponent. This can be achieved by adjusting the exponent such that f_1 is always 1 (except for X=0). For X=0, both e and f_ks are zero. For a real number, bit 31 is the sign bit – which is zero when the number is positive and is 1 when the number is negative. Bits 30 to 23 are used to store the exponent and the bits 22 to 0 contain the fraction. In chapter 20 we shall discuss in detail how a real number is stored within the system according to the IEEE format.

18.7 FRACTION and EXPONENT

The numerical model indicates that the real number consists of two parts – a fraction and an exponent. According to this model when a real number is represented as shown in section 18.6, the intrinsics FRACTION and EXPONENT return the fractional and the exponent parts of a real number respectively.

```
PRINT *, EXPONENT (7.0)
PRINT *, FRACTION (7.0)
```

will display 3 and 0.875 respectively. We shall now try to understand these two number. First we have to express 7.0 according to the prescription given in section 18.6.

$$7.0 = 2^3 \times (0.875)_{10} = 2^3 \times (111)_2$$

We consider a few more examples:

```
0.25 = (.01)₂ = 2⁻¹ (.1)₂ = 2⁻¹ . (0.5)₁₀      !fraction=0.5,  exponent=-1
0.75 = (.11)₂ = 2⁰ (.11)₂ = 2⁰ . (0.75)₁₀      !fraction=0.75, exponent=0
0.0625 = (.0001)₂ = 2⁻³ (.1)₂ = 2⁻³.(0.5)₁₀    !fraction=0.5,  exponent=-3
1.0 = 2¹ (.1)₂ = 2¹.(0.5)₁₀                     !fraction=0.5,  exponent=1
```

18.8 MAXEXPONENT and MINEXPONENT

These two intrinsics return the maximum and the minimum of the exponent values permitted by the numerical model for a particular kind of real number.

```
REAL :: R
PRINT *, MAXEXPONENT (R)
PRINT *, MINEXPONENT (R)
```

will print 128 and -125 (2 to the power) respectively.

18.9 Largest and Smallest Number

The computer is a finite bit machine and obviously it has limit for storing real numbers. The largest and the smallest positive numbers that the machine can store are returned by the intrisics HUGE and TINY.

```
REAL :: R
PRINT *, HUGE (R)
PRINT *, TINY (R)
```

will display the largest and smallest real number (single precision) that the processor can handle. The values that are returned are: 3.4028235E+38 and 1.1754944E-38. If, however, R is declared as DOUBLE PRECISION variable, the corresponding numbers are 1.79769931348623157E+308 and 2.22507385850720014E-308 respectively.

18.10 DIGITS for Real

This intrinsic returns the number of significant digits corresponding to a particular KIND of a real number.

```
PRINT *, DIGITS (0.0)
PRINT *, DIGITS (0.0D0)
```

displays 24 and 53 respectively. The result will be explained in chapter 20.

18.11 RANGE for Real

The RANGE of a real number is defined as the decimal exponent range in a numerical model. For a real number it is given by:

$$\text{MIN(} \log_{10} \text{HUGE}(X), - \log_{10} \text{TINY}(X))$$

So,

```
PRINT *, RANGE (0.0)
```

displays 37 as the range of a the standard real number and

```
PRINT *, RANGE (0.0D0)
```

displays 307 as the range of the double precision number.

18.12 PRECISION

This intrinsic returns the decimal precision of a particular KIND. It is less than or equal to:

$$\text{INT} ((p-1) * \log_{10}(b)) + K$$

where p and b are defined in section 18.6. K is 1 if b is an integral power of 10, otherwise zero.

```
PRINT *, PRECISION (0.0)
```

displays 6. The calculation is shown below:

```
    INT ((23-1)*log₁₀(2))+K
=   INT(22 * 0.3010)
=   INT(6.6)
=   6
```

Similar calculation would show that PRINT *, PRECISION (0.0D0) will display 15.

18.13 SCALE

This intrinsic takes two arguments – real X and integer I. It returns $X.b^I$ (in our system $b=2$). For example SCALE (5.0, 2) returns 20.

18.14 SET_EXPONENT

This exponent takes two arguments, X (real) and I (integer). The intrinsic takes the fractional part of X according to the numerical model (section 18.6) and multiplies by 2^I.

```
PRINT *, SET_EXPONENT(7.0, 2)
```

displays 3.5. Let us try to understand the number. According to section 18.6, the factional and the exponent parts are 0.875 and 3 respectively. Therefore,

```
0.875 * 2² = 3.5
```

18.15 EPSILON

The intrinsic takes one real number, X, as its argument and returns a real number of the same type as X that is almost negligible compared to 1. For real number of standard precision,

```
PRINT *, EPSILON (1.0)
```

will return a real number whose magnitude is 2^{-23} (1.1920929E-07). It is the smallest number that will change the result of computation.

18.16 NEAREST

This intrinsic NEAREST returns the nearest machine representable number of its first argument in a given direction determined by the second argument. Only the sign of the second argument is considered in determining the direction.

If the sign of the second argument is positive, nearest number is just greater than the first argument and if it negative, it is just less than the first argument. consider the following program:

```
REAL :: R
INTEGER:: I
EQUIVALENCE (R,I)
R=1.0
PRINT *, I
R=NEAREST(R,1.0)
PRINT *, I
R=1.0
R=NEAREST(R,-1.0)
PRINT *, I
END
```

The output looks like:

```
1065353216
1065353217
1065353215
```

If the bit pattern corresponding to the real number 1.0 is treated as integer, the value of the corresponding integer is 1065353216. If 1 is added to or subtracted, the number becomes 106535217 and 1065353215 respectively.

18.17 SPACING

The function takes one real argument X. The function returns a real number of the same KIND of its argument, which is the absolute spacing in the numerical model. It is $2^{(e-p)}$ when X is not equal to zero. If X is zero it is TINY(X). Actually, spacing corresponding to a real number X is defined as the difference between X and the next floating point number having the same exponent as that of X. It is, actually, the smallest gap between two numbers of a given type.

$$X=b^e \sum (k=1, p)\ f_k\ b^{-k}$$

Therefore, the next floating point number corresponding to X is:

$$b^e b^{-p} = b^{e-p}$$

18.18 RRSPACING

This intrinsic takes one real argument X and returns the reciprocal of the relative spacing of its argument value. It returns a real number of the same kind as X. The relative spacing near a real number X is $|X.b^{-e}|.b^p$.

18.19 Programming Example

Using one of the intrinsic mentioned above we shall try to find the root of the equation:

$$f(x) = x^2 - 25 = 0$$

The method is Newton-Raphson method discussed in section 5.9. Note that the convergence is tested with the intrinsic SPACING (shown in bold letters within the program). So you cannot get a better result.

```
REAL :: X,XG,FX,FPX,H
INTEGER, PARAMETER::LIMIT=100
INTEGER :: INDEX=1
XG=10.0                    ! guess value
DO WHILE (INDEX <= LIMIT)
   FX=XG**2 -25.0
   FPX=2.0**XG
   H=-FX/FPX
   X=XG+H

   IF(ABS(X-XG) .LE. SPACING(X)) THEN
      EXIT
   ELSE
      INDEX=INDEX+1
      XG=X
   ENDIF
ENDDO
IF(INDEX <= LIMIT ) THEN
     PRINT *, 'Convergence achieved ', XG
ELSE
     PRINT *, 'Convergence no achieved ', XG
ENDIF

END
```

The check for convergence may be replaced by:

```
IF(XG>=NEAREST(X,-1.0) .AND. XG <=NEAREST(X,1.0)) THEN
```

The logic of this program has already been discussed in section 5.9.

It is perhaps apparent that a machine independent program can be developed easily with the help of the above mentioned intrinsic. Often the convergence criterion of a numerical problem is dependent of the machine – the smallest and largest value it can handle, the spacing between two adjacent real numbers etc. Instead of using machine dependent parameters, one can use these intrinsics and make the program more general and portable.

Chapter 19

SUBPROGRAMS

Perhaps the most attractive feature of the Fortran language is the concept of subprogram. A subprogram is just like a main program, which can be compiled independent of main program, debugged and tested by some driver program (the actual main program is not required). Different users can share a subprogram and it can be ported from one program to another. A complicated task is often divided into several 'sub-tasks' having a specific objective for each such 'sub-task'. Program development becomes much easier. For example, a program may require calculation of factorial and Bessel functions. Instead of writing a single program unit, it is always better to design separate subprograms to calculate factorial and Bessel function for a given input. These subprograms can be thoroughly tested. Later on all these subprograms may be combined with the actual main program to form a load module (the module which the computer can execute). Upto now all our examples contained only one program unit − called the main program. Every complete load module must have only one main program and may have one or more subprograms. It is not possible to execute a subprogram directly. A subprogram must be invoked by a main program or another subprogram.

There are basically two types of subprograms − Function Subprogram and Subroutine Subprograms. At the end of this chapter we shall discuss Statement Function, which is really not a subprogram but may be considered somewhat similar to the internal subprogram.

A subprogram may be an external subprogram or an internal subprogram and can be a part of a Module (to be discussed shortly).

An external subprogram (Fig 19.1) is a subprogram that is not contained within a program or another subprogram or a module. An internal subprogram (Fig 19.2, 19.3), on the other hand, is contained within a program or a subprogram or a module. We first discuss Function and Subroutines as external procedure.

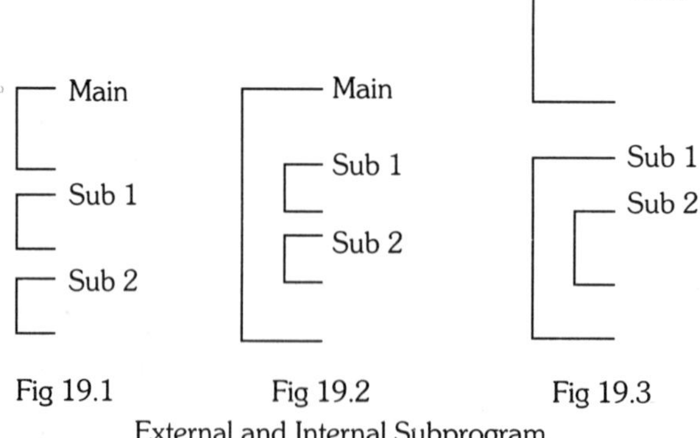

Fig 19.1   Fig 19.2   Fig 19.3

External and Internal Subprogram

19.1 Function

A Function subprogram starts with the keyword FUNCTION followed by the name of the function and the arguments of the function within parentheses. If there is more a one argument, the arguments are separated by a comma. The function returns a value to the calling program in two different ways – through its name or through a RESULT clause. If the RESULT clause is present, the RESULT clause is placed after the right parenthesis. A variable is attached to the RESULT clause and this follows the RESULT and is enclosed within parentheses.

```
FUNCTION function-name(arg1,..,argn) RESULT(res)
```

where *function-name* is the name of the function, *arg1*, *arg2* etc. are the arguments to the function and *res* is the variable through which the function returns a value to the calling program. If the RESULT clause is absent, the function definition is as shown below:

```
type FUNCTION function-name(arg1, arg2,.., argn)
```

where *type* is a type declaration which determines the type of the value (REAL, INTEGER, CHARACTER etc.) the function is supposed to return.

Though in Fortran a function may return one or more values to the calling program, we shall use only functions where one value is transferred from the function to the calling program. Subroutine subprograms will be used to transfer more than one value or no value at all to the calling program.

Usually, the data is exchanged between the calling program and the called program through the arguments of the subprogram (also called dummy parameters). When the subprogram is "called" the actual value of the argument is supplied. For the time being we shall assume that the number and type of the actual and dummy argument are same. This will be relaxed as we proceed.

After the function declaration, usually all the arguments of the functions are declared. Next all the local variables that are required as temporary storage within the function are declared. The body of the function contains Fortran statements. The last statement of the function is the END statement. END may contain FUNCTION and the function name.

```
FUNCTION func-name(arg1,..argn) RESULT(res)
declaration
statement
END FUNCTION func-name
```

We first write a simple function SQR, which takes one argument X – a real number and returns the square of X.

```
FUNCTION SQR(X) RESULT(SQ_X)
REAL :: X, SQ_X
SQ_X = X*X
END FUNCTION SQR
```

It is obvious that the name of the function is SQR and its argument is X. The result is returned through the real variable SQ_X. The argument X is called the dummy parameter or argument. The function does not know what the value of X is. It only knows that it is a scalar and of type real. When the function is invoked, the dummy parameter gets the value to be squared (in this case from the calling program). Note that the function is quite general – for any X it returns the square of X. It may be said that when the function is invoked, the dummy parameter 'points' to the actual parameter. The name X is quite arbitrary. When the function is invoked, the corresponding actual parameter must be a real scalar quantity. As the function returns value through SQ_X, the variable must appear at least once on the left hand side of the assignment sign within the function body.

The function is invoked by writing its name and supplying the actual argument. The above function SQR may be called by the following main program.

```
PROGRAM MAIN
REAL :: Y=40.0,Z,SQR
Z= SQR(Y)
    .

    .
END
```

The function along with its actual argument must appear on the right hand side of an assignment sign in the calling program; it cannot appear on the left hand side of the assignment sign. In this case when the function is invoked the dummy argument X of the function SQR 'points' to the actual variable Y of the calling program. The actual argument Y could be a number or expression. If it is an expression, it is first evaluated.

The function may also be written without the RESULT clause. In this case, the function returns the value through its name and naturally, the function name (without the argument) must appear at least once on the left hand side of the assignment sign within the function body. The function returns value either through the result clause or through the function name.

```
FUNCTION SQR(X)
REAL :: X, SQR
SQR = X*X
END FUNCTION SQR
```

or,

```
REAL FUNCTION SQR(X)
REAL :: X
SQR = X*X
END FUNCTION SQR
```

A function may call another function. Let us define a function CUBE, which using function SQR, calculates cube of its argument.

```
FUNCTION CUBE(X) RESULT(CB)
REAL :: X, CB, SQR
CB = SQR(X) * X
END
```

Note that function CUBE invokes the function SQR. Some more examples of functions are given below.

```
            FUNCTION FACT(N) RESULT(FACTO)
!              Calculates factorial n.
            INTEGER ::N
            REAL :: FACTO
!              Local variable
            REAL :: TEMP
            INTEGER ::I
            IF(N .LT. 0) THEN
               FACTO = -1.0          !ERROR
            ELSE IF(N.EQ.0) THEN
                   FACTO = 1.0   ! factorial zero
                ELSE
                  TEMP = 1.0
                  DO I =1, N
                    TEMP = TEMP *I
                  ENDDO
                  FACTO = TEMP
            ENDIF
            END FUNCTION FACT
```

The function may be invoked as shown below :

```
            X = FACTO(N)
```

where N is defined (say 5) before the function is 'called'.

Though we can write a function without the result clause, it is better to use the RESULT clause always. In fact, it is necessary to use the clause in case of a recursive function (section 19.40).

If the type of the Function name is not explicitly specified (without the result clause), the default I–N rule applies. That is, if the function name starts with I, J, K, L, M or N, it returns an integer value; otherwise it returns a real value. The following is an example of logical function, that is, the function returns a logical quantity (true or false).

Without result clause:

```
            LOGICAL FUNCTION ODD_EVEN(N)
!              Returns Logical value
!              True if N is even otherwise false
            INTEGER :: N
            IF(MOD(N,2).EQ.0) THEN
             ODD_EVEN = .TRUE.
            ELSE
             ODD_EVEN = .FALSE.
            ENDIF
            END FUNCTION ODD_EVEN
```

With result clause:

```
      LOGICAL FUNCTION ODD_EVEN1 (N) RESULT(RES)
!       Same as above with RESULT clause
      INTEGER ::N
      IF(MOD(N,2).EQ.0) THEN
       RES = .TRUE.
      ELSE
       RES = .FALSE.
      ENDIF
      END FUNCTION ODD_EVEN1
```

The above functions may be invoked as:

```
      LOGICAL ODD_EVEN, ODD_EVEN1
      INTEGER ::A=2
      LOGICAL:: RESULT

      RESULT = ODD_EVEN(A)
      PRINT *, RESULT
      RESULT = ODD_EVEN1(A)
      PRINT *, RESULT
      END
```

Some more examples of functions are given below:

```
        INTEGER FUNCTION FACT(N)
        COMPLEX FUNCTION CFUN(A,B,C)
        CHARACTER(LEN=20) FUNCTION CONVERT(CH)
```

The last function declaration tells us that the function CONVERT returns a character of size 20. It may be noted that the type of the arguments and the value returned by the function need not be the same. In the examples shown above, the function CFUN returns a complex number but its arguments, A, B and C need not be complex numbers.

We close this section with one complete program containing a function that takes one character variable as an argument and returns a character variable with the characters in the reversed order. Note that in the function the size of the returned character is specified as assumed size by means of an asterisk.

```
      CHARACTER (LEN=10) :: CH, REVERSE
      READ *, CH
      PRINT *, CH
      CH=REVERSE(CH)
      PRINT *, CH
      END
```

```fortran
FUNCTION REVERSE(CH) RESULT(RES)
CHARACTER(LEN=*) :: CH, RES
INTEGER :: LENGTH, I, IT
LENGTH = LEN(CH)
DO I=1, LENGTH
   IT = LENGTH-I+1
   RES(I:I) = CH(IT:IT)
ENDDO
RES = ADJUSTL(RES)
END
```

19.2 Subroutine

A Subroutine subprogram may return any number of values including zero (no value at all) to the calling program. The subroutine subprogram starts with the keyword SUBROUTINE followed by the name of the subroutine and its arguments within parentheses.

```fortran
SUBROUTINE sub (arg1, arg2,.. argn)
```

where, *sub* is the name of the subroutine and *arg1, arg2, .. argn* are the dummy arguments of the subroutine.

A subroutine may not have any argument at all; in that case the parentheses are omitted.

```fortran
SUBROUTINE sub
```

The subroutine returns the values through its arguments and naturally name of the subroutine does not have any relation with the type of the values the subroutine would return.

After the subroutine declaration, usually the arguments are defined. This is followed by the declarations of the local variables the subroutine may need. These are followed by the Fortran statements. The subroutine is terminated by the END statement.

```fortran
SUBROUTINE SUB(A,B)
INTEGER ::A
REAL :: B
REAL ::T        ! Local variable


fortran statements

.

END SUBROUTINE SUB
```

The portion "SUBROUTINE SUB" after the END statement is optional but can greatly help future maintainers read your program. We illustrate the use of subroutine by means of the following example. This subroutine takes two integer arguments, and interchanges these two arguments.

```
SUBROUTINE EXCHANGE (A, B)
INTEGER :: A, B
INTEGER :: T          ! local variable
T = A
A = B
B = T
END SUBROUTINE EXCHANGE
```

19.3 CALL Statement

The subroutine is invoked from the calling program by a CALL statement. The syntax of the CALL statement is:

CALL *subroutine-name* (*arg1*,.......,*argn*)

where *subroutine-name* is the name of the subroutine and the arguments are actual arguments.

```
CALL EXCHANGE (IA, IB)
```

When the subroutine is invoked the dummy arguments of the subroutine A and B 'points' to the actual arguments IA and IB respectively. Any modifications made to the dummy variables A and B are reflected in the corresponding actual variables IA and IB in the calling program. This will be discussed in details in a subsequent section. Also note that in this case when the subroutine is entered, the dummy variables A and B contain the current value of the actual arguments IA and IB. The main program to call subroutine EXCHANGE is shown below.

```
PROGRAM MAIN
INTEGER :: IA, IB
IA = 10
IB = 20
CALL EXCHANGE (IA, IB)
   .
END PROGRAM MAIN
```

Like in the function, the names of the dummy parameters do not matter – the number and type of the actual and dummy parameters must match. A subroutine may call another subroutine or function. The following subroutine calculates factorial N.

```
SUBROUTINE FACT (F, N)
REAL :: F
INTEGER ::N
INTEGER :: I
IF(N .LT. 0) THEN
   F = -1.0    ! Error
ELSE IF (N.EQ.0) THEN
      F = 1.0
      ELSE
```

```
            F = 1.0
            DO I =1, N
             F = F*I
            ENDDO
        ENDIF
        END SUBROUTINE FACT
```

The subroutine FACT may be called by the following program segment.

```
    REAL :: FACTORIAL
    INTEGER :: N=5
    CALL FACT (FACTORIAL, N)
    .
    .
    END
```

The first argument (actual parameter) FACTORIAL contains the value returned from the subroutine and the second argument is an integer and factorial of this number is returned. The corresponding dummy arguments of FACT are scalars of type real and integer respectively.

The CUBE function discussed in the earlier section may be recast as a subroutine. This subroutine now calls the function SQR.

```
    FUNCTION SQR(N)
    INTEGER :: N,SQR
    SQR = N*N
    END FUNCTION SQR

    SUBROUTINE CUBE(N,C)
    INTEGER :: N,C
    INTEGER :: T,SQR
    T = SQR(N)
    C = T*N
    END SUBROUTINE CUBE
```

A subroutine need not have any argument.

```
    SUBROUTINE MESSG
    PRINT *, "I am Here"
    END
```

When this subroutine is called as

```
    CALL MESSG
```

the message is displayed on the screen. In this case the subroutine neither takes any input from the calling program nor returns anything to the calling program.

A subroutine may take an input from the calling program but it might not return anything to the calling program.

```
SUBROUTINE MESSAGE(N)
INTEGER ::N
INTEGER :: I
DO I=1,N
PRINT *, "I am Here"
ENDDO
END
```

When this subroutine is called with some value greater than zero corresponding to the dummy parameter N, the message is printed N times. The example may seem pointless, but one could envisage cases where some external device like an audible alarm of a power switch is activated.

19.4 INTENT

It is seen that arguments to a subprogram may be of three types.
- Input only
- Output only
- Both input and output

For input only arguments, the subprogram is not supposed to modify the arguments. For an output only argument the subprogram returns the value through it. Similarly, for an argument, which is of the input-output type, the subprogram takes input through the argument from the calling program, modifies and returns the same to the calling program. Fortran provides an additional attribute INTENT for the arguments of the subprogram. As expected, the INTENT may be IN, OUT or INOUT. The purpose of this attribute is to declare the intention of programmer clearly and thereby helping the compiler to perform some additional checks on the arguments. For example, an argument declared with INTENT IN cannot be modified within the subprogram, that is, it cannot appear on the left hand side of the assignment sign within the subprogram. We rewrite subroutine EXCHANGE and subroutine CUBE with INTENT attribute.

```
SUBROUTINE EXCHANGE (A,B)
INTEGER, INTENT(INOUT) :: A, B
.

.

END SUBROUTINE EXCHANGE

SUBROUTINE CUBE(N,C)
INTEGER, INTENT(IN) ::N
INTEGER, INTENT(OUT)::C
.

END
```

19.5 Internal Procedure

The subprograms discussed, so far, are external procedures. An internal procedure is a subprogram that is "contained" within a main program or another subprogram (modules will be discussed later).

The internal procedures are accessible from the unit that contains the internal procedure. We consider again our old example SQR and CUBE to describe the internal subprogram. The internal subprograms are placed immediately before the end statement of their "mother". Before the internal subprogram the keyword CONTAINS must be present. The presence of the CONTAINS statement indicates that the unit contains internal procedure(s). The program does not "fall through" into the internal subprogram. It must be "called" in the usual manner. After executing the statement just before the CONTAINS statement, the control after skipping all the statements belonging to the internal subprogram(s) passes the control to the END statement. The END statement may have a statement number and one can jump on to the END statement from an executable statement to terminate the program. An internal subprogram cannot contain another internal subprogram. It cannot be an argument of a subroutine or a function.

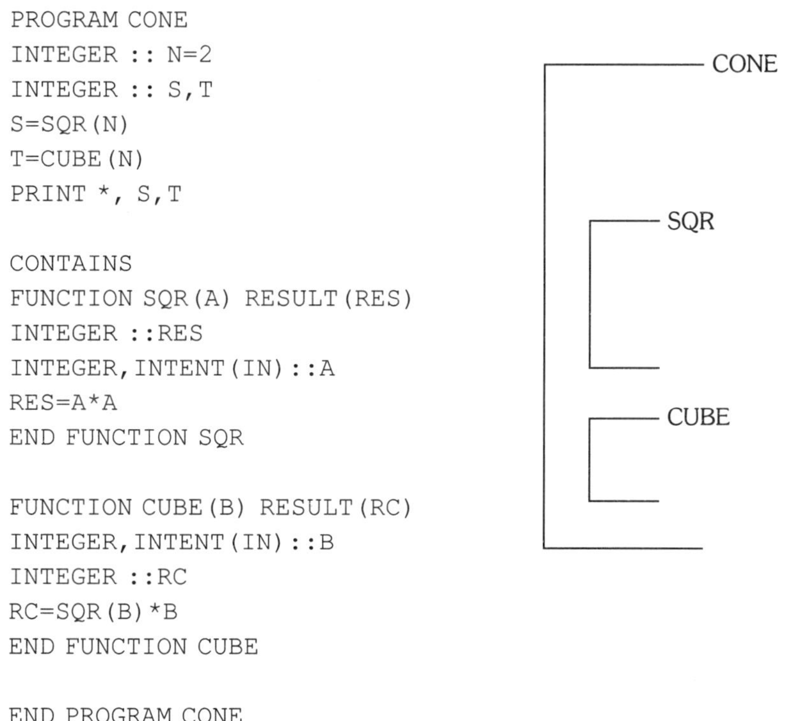


```
PROGRAM CONE
INTEGER :: N=2
INTEGER :: S,T
S=SQR(N)
T=CUBE(N)
PRINT *, S,T

CONTAINS
FUNCTION SQR(A) RESULT(RES)
INTEGER ::RES
INTEGER,INTENT(IN)::A
RES=A*A
END FUNCTION SQR

FUNCTION CUBE(B) RESULT(RC)
INTEGER,INTENT(IN)::B
INTEGER ::RC
RC=SQR(B)*B
END FUNCTION CUBE

END PROGRAM CONE
```

For internal subprograms the type of the function should not be declared within the calling program. For example, compiler will flag an error if

```
INTEGER :: SQR, CUBE
```

statement is introduced before the first executable statement of the program CONE. Internal subprograms can share variables with their "mother". This will be discussed in details in subsequent sections. Note that if an external subprogram SUB is declared, this subprogram cannot call SQR or CUBE. Consider the following program:

```
PROGRAM CONE
INTEGER :: N=4
INTEGER :: T, CUBE
T=CUBE(N)
PRINT *, T
END PROGRAM CONE

FUNCTION CUBE(B) RESULT(RC)
INTEGER,INTENT(IN)::B
INTEGER ::RC
RC=SQR(B)*B

  CONTAINS
  FUNCTION SQR(A) RESULT(RES)
  INTEGER ::RES
  INTEGER,INTENT(IN)::A
  RES=A*A
  END FUNCTION SQR

END FUNCTION CUBE
```

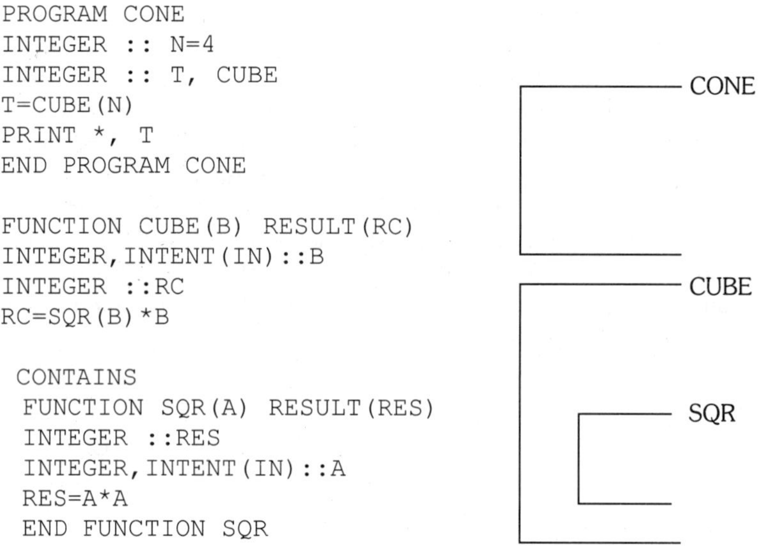

The main program cannot call SQR. Only CUBE can call SQR since SQR is an internal function of CUBE. It is to be noted that CUBE is an external function to CONE and as such it has been declared as an integer within CONE. SQR is an internal function to CUBE and so this has not been declared as an within CUBE. Another example of internal subprogram is given below:

```
PROGRAM MAIN
INTEGER :: SUM, NUM
!           add 1+2+3+...   NUM
READ *, NUM
SUM=MYADD(NUM)
PRINT *, SUM

CONTAINS

FUNCTION MYADD(N) RESULT (RES)
INTEGER, INTENT (IN) :: N
INTEGER :: RES
INTEGER :: TEMP, I
TEMP=0
DO I=1, N
 TEMP=TEMP+I
ENDDO
RES=TEMP
END FUNCTION MYADD

END PROGRAM MAIN
```

19.6 Character Type Argument

The size of a dummy character argument may be declared with an asterisk (*). The length of such a dummy argument is the length of the actual argument. So the length of the dummy character argument becomes "variable". The same subprogram may be called with different actual character arguments having different sizes. The subroutine shown below calculates the number of vowels in the character string.

```
CHARACTER(LEN=10):: C1
CHARACTER(LEN=20):: C2
INTEGER :: NV
READ *, C1              ! read the first string
CALL NVOWEL(NV,C1)
PRINT *, NV             ! no of vowels in C1
READ *, C2             ! read the second string
CALL NVOWEL(NV,C2)
PRINT *, NV             ! no of vowels in C2
END

SUBROUTINE NVOWEL(NUM,STRING)
CHARACTER(LEN=*),INTENT(IN):: STRING
INTEGER, INTENT(OUT)::NUM
INTEGER::L, I
L=LEN(STRING)
NUM=0
DO I=1, L
  SELECT CASE(STRING(I:I))
  CASE('A','E','I','O','U','a','e','i','o','u')
    NUM=NUM+1
  END SELECT
ENDDO
END
```

19.7 Argument Type

We have already mentioned that while calling a subprogram, the number and the type of the argument(s) of actual parameters must match with the corresponding dummy argument(s) of the subprogram. There is, usually, one to one correspondence between the actual arguments and the dummy arguments. This essentially means that the first dummy argument "points" to the first actual argument; the second dummy argument "points" to the second actual argument and so on. There are two ways by which parameters are transferred between the calling program and the called program. They are known as "call by reference" and "call by value".

19.8 Call by Reference

If the actual argument is a variable name, the corresponding argument is said to have been passed by reference. When an argument is passed by reference, any modifications done within the subprogram are reflected in the corresponding actual argument in the calling program. Consider the subroutine EXCHANGE once again.

```
SUBROUTINE EXCHANGE(A,B)
INTEGER :: A,B
INTEGER :: T

END SUBROUTINE EXCHANGE

PROGRAM MAIN
INTEGER ::IA, IB
IA = 3
IB = 4
CALL EXCHANGE(IA,IB)
PRINT *,IA,IB
END PROGRAM MAIN
```

When the subprogram EXCHANGE is called, the dummy argument A and B point to corresponding actual argument IA and IB. Any modifications done on A and B within the subprogram are carried over to the calling program and are reflected in the actual arguments IA and IB. Note that within the subprogram A and B are interchanged and since A and B, respectively, "point to" IA and IB, the changes are also reflected in the calling program. Argument passed in this manner is called "call by reference".

19.9 Call by Value

The actual argument may be a constant or an expression. If it is an expression, it is evaluated and the dummy arguments are "initialized" with these values. The same thing happens if the actual expression is a constant. For example, if the subroutine EXCHANGE is called as

```
CALL EXCHANGE (10,20)
```

the dummy arguments A and B are "initialized" with 10 and 20 respectively. Now the variables A and B are interchanged within the subprogram and after the interchange is done, the value of A is 20 and that of B is 10 as expected. However, when the subprogram returns control to the calling program, the modifications done on A and B within the subprogram are not carried over to the calling program. Arguments transferred in this manner are said to be 'called by value'.

If the actual argument (variable) is enclosed within parenthesis, it is (assumed to have been) passed by value;

```
CALL EXCHANGE ((IA), (IB))
```

will not interchange IA and IB, as the arguments, though not an expression, are passed by value. The situation will be interesting when only one of the actual arguments is passed by value.

```
CALL EXCHANGE ((IA), IB)
```

If IA=3 and IB=4, before the call, IA will remain 3 and IB will 3 after the call. This is due to the fact that the dummy arguments A and B, corresponding to the actual arguments IA and IB are interchanged within the subroutine EXCHANGE. As the first is called by value, the modification done on the corresponding dummy argument within the subroutine is not reflected in the calling program. But as the second argument is called by reference, the modification done on the corresponding dummy argument is reflected in the calling program.

19.10 RETURN Statement

Control from the called program is transferred to the calling program after processing the last executable statement within the subprogram. This is called "normal" return. The subprogram may contain a statement called RETURN which when executed transfers the control back to the calling program. A subprogram may have more than one return statement. In fact, RETURN is always assumed before the END statement of the subprogram. The following function subprogram calculates factorial N and uses the RETURN statement.

```
FUNCTION FACT(N) RESULT(RES)
INTEGER, INTENT(IN) :: N
INTEGER :: RES
IF(N < 0) THEN
  RES = -1             ! Error
RETURN
ENDIF
RES = 1
DO I =1, N
  RES = RES *I
ENDDO
END FUNCTION FACT
```

For N< 0, factorial is not defined, so RES is set to -1. As no further processing is required, control is passed to the calling program by executing RETURN statement.

19.11 Alternate Return (*)

When a RETURN statement is executed within a subprogram either implicitly or explicitly, control is transferred to the statement following the CALL statement of the calling program. A CALL statement may have an alternate return address in the form of a statement number and the subroutine may execute an alternate return to transfer the control back to a statement label mentioned in the CALL statement. Consider the following example:

```
        PROGRAM ALTRET
        INTEGER :: I
        DO I=1, 4
          CALL SUB(I,*10,*20)
          PRINT *,"Normal Return"
          CYCLE
10        PRINT *, "Executed Return 1 in Sub"
          CYCLE
```

```
20          PRINT *,"Executed Return 2 in Sub"
          ENDDO
          END PROGRAM ALTRET

          SUBROUTINE SUB(I,*,*)
          SELECT CASE(I)
          CASE(1)
             RETURN ! Normal Return
          CASE(2)
             RETURN 1
          CASE(3)
             RETURN 2
          CASE(4)
             RETURN 3 ! normal return in this case
          END SELECT

          END SUBROUTINE SUB
```

The CALL statement contains two statement labels 10 and 20 as the second and third arguments. Note that the statement labels are preceded by asterisks. In the subroutine declaration, the corresponding dummy parameters are just asterisks. When the RETURN statement is executed within the subroutine, control is passed to the statement following the CALL statement. This is called the "normal return". If RETURN 1 is executed within the subroutine, control is passed to the statement number 10 of the calling program in this particular case. Similarly, RETURN 2 will transfer the control to the second argument of the CALL statement, that is, statement number 20 of the calling program. In general, RETURN n will transfer the control to the *nth* statement label mentioned in the CALL statement. If n is less than 1 or greater than the number of statements label mentioned in the CALL, standard RETURN is executed, that is, control is passed to the statement following the CALL. For example, in the above example, if RETURN 3 is executed, control is passed to the statement following the CALL statement, as there are only two statement labels in the CALL statement ($n = 2$). As this feature makes a program very unstructured, this feature is rarely used.

19.12 MODULE

We have just seen that data is exchanged between a main program and the subprograms or between subprograms through arguments. There are two other ways of sharing data among different units of programs. They are through the COMMON statement and through the MODULE. The COMMON statement, which is not in much use in Fortran, will be discussed later.

A MODULE is a unit that contains constants, variables and procedures to be shared by different units of a program. A module, like functions or subroutines may be compiled independently of the main program. Later it may be linked with other units by a suitable linker.

A module starts with the keyword MODULE followed by the module name. It ends with the END MODULE statement.

```
          MODULE MYCONS
          INTEGER :: IA,IB
          REAL, PARAMETER :: PI = 3.1415926
          END MODULE MYCONS
```

The MYCONS module may be "called" (used) by a main program or by subprogram through the USE statement.

```
PROGRAM MAIN
USE MYCONS
IA = 10
CALL SUB
PRINT *, IA
END PROGRAM MAIN

SUBROUTINE SUB
USE MYCONS
PRINT *, IA
IA=20
END SUBROUTINE SUB
```

The constants, variables or subprograms defined within a module are available within the units where the module has been used. For example, in program MAIN, IA is set to 10. In the subroutine SUB, the PRINT statement displays 10, because of the USE statement the variable IA of the MAIN and the variable IA of the subroutine SUB are same. Subsequently, IA is set to 20 in the subroutine SUB. Therefore, PRINT statement of MAIN displays 20.

A module may contain internal procedures.

```
MODULE mod-name
declaration

CONTAINS
SUBROUTINE sub
  .
END SUBROUTINE sub

FUNCTION fun
  .
END FUNCTION fun

END MODULE mod-name
```

If the subroutine EXCHANGE is put in a module, it can be accessed by an appropriate USE statement.

```
MODULE SWAP

CONTAINS

SUBROUTINE EXCHANGE(A,B)
INTEGER,INTENT(INOUT)::A,B
INTEGER :: T
```

```
                    T = A
                    A = B
                    B = T
                    END SUBROUTINE EXCHANGE

                    END MODULE SWAP

                    PROGRAM MAIN
                    USE SWAP
                    INTEGER :: IA=10, IB=20
                    CALL EXCHANGE(IA,IB)
                    PRINT *, IA, IB
                    END PROGRAM MAIN
```

It is seen that in this way one can create a program library containing several subprograms and use them as and when needed. A module may use other module but cannot use itself directly or indirectly.

The parameters and variables defined in the module can be selectively "used"; even can be renamed, through USE.

```
        MODULE SELECT
        REAL, PARAMETER :: PI=31415926
        REAL(KIND=KIND(0.0D0)), PARAMETER :: DPI=3.1415926589793D0
        END MODULE SELECT

        PROGRAM MAIN
        USE SELECT, ONLY : DPI
            .

            .
        END PROGRAM MAIN
```

The ONLY clause, placed after the module name, allows the access of a particular item (in this case DPI) or a number of items mentioned with the clause. In the above-mentioned case, only the variable DPI is available in the program the MAIN – the other variable PI, declared in the module SELECT, is not available in the MAIN. Note the comma after the module name and single colon after ONLY. While using a module the variables declared in it may be renamed, if necessary.

```
                    PROGRAM MAIN
                    USE SELECT, MYPI =>DPI


                    END PROGRAM MAIN
```

The variable DPI, declared in the module SELECT is used in MAIN; however in this routine the variable DPI is called as MYPI (renamed). Note the symbol to rename the item. It is the equal sign followed by the greater than sign.

19.13 Module Procedure

A module may contain procedures, which may be used by other units.

```
MODULE MYLIB
   .
CONTAINS

SUBROUTINE sub
   .
END SUBROUTINE sub

FUNCTION func (arg1,.., argn)
   .
END FUNCTION func

END MODULE MYLIB

PROGRAM MAIN
USE MYLIB
   .
   .


END PROGRAM MAIN
```

The unit MAIN may use subprograms *sub* and *func* defined in the module MYLIB. It is apparent that a module may contain both variable declaration as well as subprograms.

The concerned unit may use all the variables and subprograms defined in the module or it may choose selectively variables and subprograms from the module. It is also possible to rename a subprogram within the unit like a variable.

We shall use the following simple module to demonstrate all the features mentioned above.

```
MODULE MYLIB
REAL, PARAMETER :: PI=3.1415926
CONTAINS

SUBROUTINE IEXCHANGE(A,B)
INTEGER, INTENT(INOUT):: A,B
INTEGER :: T
T = A
A = B
B = T
END SUBROUTINE IEXCHANGE
```

```
SUBROUTINE REXCHANGE(P,Q)
REAL, INTENT(INOUT) :: P,Q
REAL :: T
T = P
P = Q
Q = T
END SUBROUTINE REXCHANGE


END MODULE MYLIB
```

Case - I: In this case both the subprograms IEXCHANGE and REXCHANGE are available within MAIN. Also MAIN can access PI.

```
PROGRAM MAIN
USE MYLIB

END
```

Case - II: The unit MAIN can use only the subprogram IEXCHANGE defined in the module IEXCHANGE defined in the module MYLIB

```
PROGRAM MAIN
USE MYLIB, ONLY : IEXCHANGE
.
END
```

Case - III: The unit MAIN can use only the subprogram IEXCHANGE defined in the module. However, this subroutine IEXCHANGE will be called MYEXCHANGE within MAIN.

```
PROGRAM MAIN
USE MYLIB, ONLY : MYEXCHANGE => IEXCHANGE

END
```

Case - IV: The unit MAIN may use both the subprograms IEXCHANGE and REXCHANGE as well as the named constant PI. However, the subprogram IEXCHANGE will be called as MYEXCHANGE within MAIN. Since the subprogram REXCHANGE is not renamed, it is used as REXCHANGE within MAIN.

```
PROGRAM MAIN
USE MYLIB, MYEXCHANGE => IEXCHANGE

END
```

19.14 Public and Private

The variables and procedures defined within a module are by default, PUBLIC. This indicates all the variables and procedures are available to the unit that 'uses' this module.

```
MODULE MYDATA
INTEGER :: N
REAL :: R
 .

 .
CONTAINS

 SUBROUTINE SUB
  .

 END SUBROUTINE SUB
END MODULE MYDATA
```

If this module is 'used' in a unit, the unit has access to all the variables and subprograms. By declaring some variable and subprograms as PRIVATE, the programmer may restrict the usage of a variable or subprogram from outside the module. The statement PUBLIC sets the default to PUBLIC accessibility. Similarly, the statement PRIVATE sets the default to private accessibility.

The access specification, PUBLIC or PRIVATE may be used along with the variable, subprogram, user-defined operator (to be discussed shortly in section 19.25) etc.

```
MODULE MYMOD
PUBLIC              ! Default
PRIVATE :: X,Y,Z, OPERATOR (*)
 .

 .
END MODULE MYMOD
```

The PRIVATE declaration in the above module restricts the use of X, Y, Z and user defined operator (*) outside the module. The creator of the module now has a means of hiding some of the items from units using the module.

Suppose we have a module that is used to diagonalize a matrix. The module may contain more than one subprograms – one of them takes the input from outside and the results of the computation it returns can be made visible outside. Other subprograms which are called by the above mentioned subprogram need not be made available to an user because these subprograms are not to be called from outside and as such they may be made "private" routines. This ensures that even accidentally these private subprograms cannot be called from outside the module. Thus we see that it is possible to restrict the use of a variable or subprogram in two different ways – at the user level by using ONLY or at the developer's level by using PRIVATE.

The function subprogram or subroutine subprogram must not contain PRIVATE or PUBLIC attributes.

19.15 PROTECTED

The public variables of a module can be "protected" from modification using this PROTECTED attribute. These variables may be modified only with the module. This attribute is similar to the attribute INTENT(IN) of a dummy argument of a subprogram. The "protected" variable cannot appear on the left hand side of the assignment sign outside the module.

```
MODULE MYMOD
  INTEGER, PROTECTED::A=30,B=40,C
CONTAINS

  SUBROUTINE MYADD(A,B,C)
  INTEGER:: A,B,C
  C=A+B
  END SUBROUTINE MYADD

END MODULE MYMOD

PROGRAM MAIN
USE MYMOD
CALL MYADD(A,B,C)

!  C=100

PRINT *, A,B,C
END
```

The protected variable "C" is modified inside the subroutine declared within the module. But the protected variable "C" cannot be modified within the program MAIN. For example, the statement, C=100 within the program MAIN (shown as comment and in bold letters) would generate a Fortran error when the comment is removed.

19.16 Scope Rule

The variable defined within a unit is called a local variable for the unit. A variable available in a unit but not defined within the same unit is called a global variable for the unit. At a particular point of time, all the local variables and the global variables are available for manipulation. This fact is illustrated with the help of examples.

Case I: When only main program, but no subprogram, is present, the variables declared within the MAIN program are available within the MAIN program unless they are deallocated (Chapter 21).

```
PROGRAM MAIN
INTEGER :: I
REAL :: R
.
END PROGRAM MAIN
```

The variables I and R are available within the program MAIN. These locations are given back to the system once the job is over. They are available so long as the job runs.

Case II: When a main program and one or more external subprograms are present, the local variables declared within the MAIN program and subprogram are quite independent of each other. For example, in the following program segment

```
PROGRAM MAIN
INTEGER ::I
       .
END PROGRAM MAIN

SUBROUTINE SUB
INTEGER :: I
       .
END SUBROUTINE SUB
```

the variable I of the MAIN program and the variable I of the subroutine SUB are different. They are stored in different locations. Moreover, when the subroutine is exited, the variable I of the subroutine is deallocated and when the subprogram is re-entered, locations are assigned to the variable – the last value does not reappear unless it is a "saved'" variable (will be discussed shortly). Note that, the subprogram can only access the variable declared in the MAIN or other subprogram through arguments or a common block or through the module.

Case III: Internal procedures do have access to all the variables declared within the unit that contains the internal procedure.

```
PROGRAM ABC
INTEGER :: I=10
REAL :: R=20.0
        .
CALL SUB

CONTAINS
   SUBROUTINE SUB
        .

        .
   PRINT *, I, R
   END SUBROUTINE SUB
END PROGRAM ABC
```

The variables I and R are global variables for the internal subroutine SUB. Therefore, PRINT statements within the subroutine prints 10 and 20.0 respectively. Any modifications done on I and R within the subroutine are carried over to the program ABC. However, if the internal subprogram contains a declaration having the same name as that of its "mother", the local variable is only accessible within the subprogram and the corresponding global variable is masked from the subprogram.

```
PROGRAM PQR
INTEGER :: I=10
.
CALL SUB
PRINT *, I                ! I=10

CONTAINS
   SUBROUTINE SUB
   INTEGER :: I=20
   PRINT *, I
   I=30                   ! I=30
   END SUBROUTINE SUB

END PROGRAM PQR
```

Within the subroutine the "global" I, i.e. the variable I declared in the program PQR is unavailable, as there is a name conflict. The subroutine can access only the "local" I declared within it. Note that the modification of I (that is 30) will not disturb the "global" I. When the subroutine is exited, the PRINT statement within the program PQR will display the value of I as 10. The important point is only the name matters – the type of the variable does not. For example, if

```
INTEGER :: I=20
```

within the subroutine is replaced by

```
REAL :: I=20.0
```

the result is the same – namely the local real variable I will mask the global integer variable I.
Case IV: If a module procedure is "used" all the variables and subprograms declared within the module are available to the unit where the module has been used.

```
MODULE MYLIB
INTEGER :: I=10
REAL :: R=20
END MODULE MYLIB

PROGRAM TEST
USE MYLIB
PRINT *, R
.
END PROGRAM TEST
```

This PRINT statement within the program TEST will display 20 because the USE statement will make the variable R available to the unit TEST. It has already been noted that using the attributes ONLY or PRIVATE, variables or subprograms declared may be made unavailable to a unit containing the USE statement.

19.17 Interface Block

An INTERFACE block is a place where information about a subprogram, that is its name, type and number of its arguments are kept for the compiler. The interface block starts with the keyword INTERFACE and ends with the keyword END INTERFACE. Between these two lines the name of the subprogram with the definitions of its arguments are placed.

```
INTERFACE
  SUBROUTINE EXCHANGE(A,B)
   INTEGER, INTENT(INOUT) :: A,B
   END SUBROUTINE EXCHANGE

END INTERFACE
```

The example, given below, does not really require an interface block. Later we shall see that there are situations where an interface is mandatory.

```
PROGRAM MAIN
INTERFACE
  SUBROUTINE EXCHANGE(A,B)
   INTEGER, INTENT(INOUT) :: A,B
   END SUBROUTINE EXCHANGE
END INTERFACE

INTEGER :: IA=10, IB=20
CALL EXCHANGE (IA,IB)
  .
END PROGRAM MAIN

SUBROUTINE EXCHANGE(P,Q)
INTEGER, INTENT(INOUT) :: P,Q
  .

  .
END SUBROUTINE EXCHANGE
```

19.18 Generic Subprograms

We have already encountered generic subprograms in connection with the library functions. For example, SQRT is the generic name of the square root family. If this is used, the compiler from the nature of its argument, can substitute the appropriate routine when the argument is, say, a complex variable by the appropriate function CSQRT. This facility is directly available in Fortran for the user. If a generic subprogram is defined, the compiler by examining the arguments of the "call" statement may substitute the generic name by appropriate names commensurate with the argument. To use generic subprograms, the interface block must be present.

The generic subprogram is illustrated with a very simple example. The EXCHANGE subprogram developed earlier can be used to exchange two integer quantities. Suppose we want to exchange two real numbers. One solution could be to define two subroutines IEXCHANGE and REXCHANGE, one for the integer and the other for the real and call explicitly the appropriate routines depending on the type of the arguments. The other solution is to define a generic subprogram and let the compiler substitute the appropriate subprogram after analyzing the arguments.

```fortran
PROGRAM MAIN
INTERFACE SWAP
  SUBROUTINE IEXCHANGE(A,B)
  INTEGER, INTENT(INOUT) ::A, B
  END SUBROUTINE IEXCHANGE

  SUBROUTINE REXCHANGE(P,Q)
  REAL, INTENT(INOUT) :: P,Q
  END SUBROUTINE REXCHANGE

END INTERFACE

INTEGER :: IA=10, IB=20
REAL :: A=100.0, B=200.0
CALL SWAP(IA,IB)
.

.
CALL SWAP(A,B)
.
END PROGRAM MAIN

SUBROUTINE IEXCHANGE(A,B)
INTEGER, INTENT(INOUT) :: A, B
INTEGER :: T
T=A
A=B
B=T
END SUBROUTINE IEXCHANGE

SUBROUTINE REXCHANGE(P,Q)
REAL,INTENT(INOUT) :: P,Q
REAL :: T
T=P
P=Q
Q=T
END SUBROUTINE REXCHANGE
```

The interface block has a name SWAP and this is the generic name for the subroutine IEXCHANGE and REXCHANGE. When SWAP is called with integer argument, the compiler generates a call to the subroutine IEXCHANGE and similarly when SWAP is called with real arguments, the compiler substitutes the generic name by the appropriate name REXCHANGE. The arguments to the generic name SWAP determine the routine to be used by the program. All the subprograms mentioned within this type of interface block must be of same type, that is, all of them must be either a subroutine subprogram or a function subprogram.

It is possible to include the subprograms within the module. The subprogram becomes local to the module. In this case, the subprograms will be referred to within the interface block as MODULE PROCEDURE. So the above program would look like:

```
MODULE OWNSWAP
  INTERFACE SWAP
  MODULE PROCEDURE SWAPR, SWAPI
  END INTERFACE
CONTAINS
  SUBROUTINE SWAPR (A,B)
  REAL:: A,B
  REAL :: T
  T=A
  A=B
  B=T
  END SUBROUTINE SWAPR

  SUBROUTINE SWAPI(P,Q)
  INTEGER:: P, Q
  INTEGER:: T
  T=P
  P=Q
  Q=T
  END SUBROUTINE SWAPI
END MODULE OWNSWAP

PROGRAM TEST
USE OWNSWAP
REAL ::Y=30.0, Z=40.0
INTEGER:: I=50, J=60
PRINT *, Y,Z
PRINT *, I,J
CALL SWAP(I,J)
PRINT *, I,J
CALL SWAP(Y,Z)
PRINT *, Y,Z
END
```

It is perhaps clear that the interface block does not contain the complete executable code (in fact if the complete executable code is present, it will generate Fortran error). The executable code for the subroutines are either present as external subprograms or as module procedures. The word MODULE may be dropped from MODULE PROCEDURE.

19.19 Abstract Interface

Often an interface block requires a number of declarations of subroutine or function with identical types of argument(s). All such subroutines/functions are to be declared individually within the interface block.

```
INTERFACE
 SUBROUTINE SUB1(A,B)
    INTEGER, INTENT(IN):: A,B
 END SUBROUTINE SUB1

 SUBROUTINE SUB2(A,B)
    INTEGER, INTENT(IN):: A,B
 END SUBROUTINE SUB2

 SUBROUTINE SUB3(A,B)
    INTEGER, INTENT(IN):: A,B
 END SUBROUTINE SUB3
        .
 SUBROUTINE SUBN(A,B)
    INTEGER, INTENT(1N):: A,B
 END SUBROUTINE SUBN

 END INTERFACE
```

This is quite a boring job. This can be avoided by declaring an ABSTRACT interface with a template of the subprogram and associating the subprogram with the template through the PROCEDURE statement.

```
ABSTRACT INTERFACE
   SUBROUTINE SUBTEMP(A, B)
      INTEGER, INTENT(IN) :: A, B
   END SUBROUTINE SUBTEMP
END INTERFACE

PROCEDURE(SUBTEMP):: SUB1, SUB2, SUB3,...., SUBN
```

These subroutines SUB1, SUB2, SUB3, ..., SUBN, in this case do not have to be declared explicitly within the interface block and this saves lot of typing.

```
ABSTRACT INTERFACE
SUBROUTINE XT
END SUBROUTINE XT

SUBROUTINE DUMMY(X)
   INTEGER, INTENT(IN)::X
END SUBROUTINE DUMMY
END INTERFACE
```

```
PROCEDURE(XT)::SUB1
PROCEDURE (DUMMY) :: SUB2
CALL SUB1
CALL SUB2(5)
END

SUBROUTINE SUB1
PRINT *, 'I AM HERE'

END

SUBROUTINE SUB2(N)
INTEGER, INTENT(IN)::N
INTEGER :: I
DO I=1,N
PRINT *, 'XXXXXXXXXXXXXXXXX'
END DO
END
```

This is just a demonstration. It may be noted that in this case the interface block is really not required.

19.20 Arrays as Arguments

An array can be an argument to a subprogram. The dimension of the array (rank) must be specified within the subprogram. It is not necessary to specify the actual size within the subprogram.

```
SUBROUTINE ZERO(A)
INTEGER, DIMENSION(:)::A
A=0
END SUBROUTINE ZERO
```

However, an appropriate interface block must be declared. In the above case, the following interface block in the calling program is required.

```
INTERFACE
  SUBROUTINE ZERO(A)
   INTEGER,DIMENSION(:)::A
  END SUBROUTINE ZERO
END INTERFACE
```

For an array of rank 2, two colons separated by a comma are necessary to specify the dimension within the subprogram. The following subprogram SET_VALUE, stores a particular value in all the locations of a two dimensional array.

```
SUBROUTINE SET_VALUE(X,VALUE)
INTEGER, DIMENSION(:,:)::X
INTEGER, INTENT(IN):: VALUE
X=VALUE
END SUBROUTINE SET_VALUE
```

The corresponding interface block in the calling program will look like

```
INTERFACE
  SUBROUTINE SET_VALUE (X,VALUE)
  INTEGER, DIMENSION(:,:) :: X
  INTEGER, INTENT(IN)::VALUE
  END SUBROUTINE SET_VALUE
END INTERFACE
```

It is obvious that the calling program will have an appropriate declaration for the actual parameter corresponding to X.

```
INTEGER, DIMENSION (3,3) :: Y
```

An internal subprogram, in an identical fashion may use an array as its argument. In this case, an interface block is not required.

The lower bound of the dummy argument of a subprogram may be different from the corresponding actual argument.

```
PROGRAM MAIN
INTEGER, DIMENSION(10)::A
INTERFACE
  SUBROUTINE SUB(A)
  INTEGER, DIMENSION(:) ::A
  END SUBROUTINE SUB
END INTERFACE

A=[1,2,3,4,5,6,7,8,9,10]
CALL SUB(A)
.
END PROGRAM MAIN

SUBROUTINE SUB(B)
INTEGER, DIMENSION(0:)::B
.
END SUBROUTINE SUB
```

As the lower bound of B is zero and the size of the corresponding actual argument is 10, the array B can have subscript between 0 and 9 within the subroutine.

An array within a subprogram may be dimensioned through one of its arguments. This is also called variable dimension.

```
PROGRAM MAIN
INTEGER, DIMENSION(10)::A
.
CALL SUB(A,10)
.
END PROGRAM MAIN

SUBROUTINE SUB(A,N)
INTEGER, DIMENSION(N)::A
.
END SUBROUTINE SUB
```

Following the Fortran-77 style, a rank 1 array may be given a dimension of just one within the subprogram.

```
PROGRAM MAIN
INTEGER,DIMENSION(10)::A
.
CALL SUB(A)
.
END PROGRAM MAIN

SUBROUTINE SUB(A)
INTEGER, DIMENSION(1)::A
.
END SUBROUTINE SUB
```

19.21 User Defined Type as Argument

User defined variables (structures) may be an argument to a subprogram. For an internal procedure, the type declaration in the main unit is sufficient for the subprogram.

```
PROGRAM MAIN
TYPE EMP
  SEQUENCE
  INTEGER ::ID
  CHARACTER(LEN=20) ::NAME
END TYPE EMP

TYPE(EMP) :: P
CALL SET_EMP(P)
.
.
CONTAINS
  SUBROUTINE SET_EMP(Q)
  TYPE(EMP) ::Q
  Q%ID=10
```

```
      Q%NAME="Jaya Chakravarti"
      END SUBROUTINE SET_EMP

  END PROGRAM MAIN
```

For external subprograms, the type declaration must also be present in the subprogram.

```
      PROGRAM MAIN
      TYPE EMP
       SEQUENCE
       INTEGER ::ID
       CHARACTER(LEN=20) ::NAME
      END TYPE EMP

      TYPE(EMP) :: P
      CALL SET_EMP(P)
      .
      END PROGRAM MAIN

      SUBROUTINE SET_EMP(Q)
      TYPE EMP
      SEQUENCE
      INTEGER ::ID
      CHARACTER(LEN=20) ::NAME
      END TYPE EMP

      TYPE(EMP) ::Q
      Q%ID=10
      Q%NAME="Jaya Chakravarti"
      END SUBROUTINE SET_EMP
```

A module containing the type declaration may also be used.

```
      MODULE EMPTYPE
       TYPE EMP
        SEQUENCE
        INTEGER ::ID
        CHARACTER(LEN=20) :: NAME
       END TYPE EMP
      END MODULE EMPTYPE

      PROGRAM MAIN
      USE EMPTYPE
      TYPE(EMP) :: P
      .
      CALL SET_TYPE(P)
      .
      END PROGRAM MAIN
```

```
SUBROUTINE SET_TYPE(Q)
USE EMPTYPE
TYPE(EMP) :: Q
     .
END SUBROUTINE SET_TYPE
```

19.22 Keyword Arguments

It has already been pointed out that there is one to one correspondence between the arguments of the calling program and the called program. Calling by keyword is a very useful facility of Fortran where the arguments are passed through their name defined in the interface block; the ordering of the arguments is not relevant. For example, if the function TRAP is defined as

```
FUNCTION TRAP(A,B)
```

it can be called as

```
        Z = TRAP(A=10,B=20.0)
or,     Z = TRAP(B=20.0,A=10)
```

provided an interface block exists. In the first case, the dummy parameter A gets a value 10 and the second dummy parameter B gets a value 20.0. The example demonstrates the real power of keyword method of argument passing. Note that in the actual "call", the second argument, B appears before A. However, because of the keyword assignment, A gets 10 and B gets 20.0. Note that the following also gives the identical result.

```
Z = TRAP(10.0,B=20.0)
```

The dummy parameter A here gets 10 and the second parameter B gets 20.0. The last example illustrates the use of both the natural method of using actual parameter and keyword usage. It may be noted that once the keyword is used, all the subsequent parameters must be used with keywords. This is illustrated below. Suppose we have defined a function as

```
FUNCTION FUNC(X1,X2,X3,X4)
```

This can be invoked as follows:

```
Z = FUNC(10.0, 20.0, 30.0, 40.0)
Z = FUNC(P1, P2, P3, P4) [P1, P2, P3 and P4 are real]
Z = FUNC(X4=40.0, X1=10.0, X2=20.0, X3=30.0)
Z = FUNC(10.0, 20.0, X4=40.0, X3=30)
Z = FUNC(X1=P1, X2=P2, X3=P3, X4=P4)
Z = FUNC(P1, P2, X4=P4, X3=P3)
```

However, the following is an invalid function call:

```
Z = FUNC(X1=10, X2, X3, X4)
```

The reason is that once the keyword argument is used all the subsequent arguments must be specified in terms of keywords.

If mixed type of arguments is used, the arguments before the keyword argument must have one to one correspondence with the corresponding dummy arguments. The example given below will display the value of TRAP_A as 7.5 in all the three cases.

```
PROGRAM KEY
INTERFACE
  FUNCTION TRAP(P,Q) RESULT(AREA)
  REAL,INTENT(IN)::P,Q
  REAL ::AREA
  END FUNCTION TRAP
END INTERFACE

REAL :: A=10.0, B=20.0, TRAP_A
TRAP_A=TRAP(A,B)
!        Normal Call
PRINT *, TRAP_A
TRAP_A=TRAP(P=10.0,Q=5.0)
!        Through Keyword
PRINT *, TRAP_A
TRAP_A=TRAP(Q=5.0,P=10.0)
PRINT *, TRAP_A
END PROGRAM KEY

FUNCTION TRAP(A,B) RESULT(AREA)
REAL, INTENT(IN) :: A,B
REAL :: AREA
AREA = 0.5*(A+B)
END FUNCTION TRAP
```

In this example, in the interface block the function TRAP is defined in terms of P and Q. If the keyword argument is used, the variable A within the function will be substituted by the value of P irrespective of its position as actual parameter in the calling sequence. This is true for the other parameter also.

19.23 Operator Overloading

In earlier chapters various kind of operators were introduced – namely, arithmetic, relational, logical etc. The operators have a predefined meaning to the compiler. Already we have seen that some of the operators can have different types of arguments. The symbol for unary minus and binary minus are same; from the context, the compiler can determine the meaning of the operator. Also the same binary operator say, addition operator, can be used to add two integers or reals or complex quantities. This process is known as operator overloading. In this case the operators are intrinsically overloaded. A user can overload an operator of his choice. For example, one can overload the multiplication operator (*) in such a way that it performs the multiplication operations between two matrices. Note that when the same multiplication operator gets two integer or real or complex quantities as operands, the normal multiplication operations are performed. While overloading any operator it is illegal to modify the basic characteristics of the concerned operator. The intrinsic meaning of the multiplication operator, in the case integer, real or complex cannot be altered. The multiplication operator is intrinsically binary in nature. It is not possible to overload this binary operator such that it becomes a unary operator. No two overloaded operators can have identical types of arguments. In addition to overloading the intrinsic operator, Fortran allows user defined operators also.

The operators are overloaded through the INTERFACE OPERATOR statement. Suppose we want to overload the unary plus and minus operators such that when the operator operates on a character, it changes the lowercase letter to the corresponding upper case letter and the upper case letter to the corresponding lower case letter respectively.

```
INTERFACE OPERATOR (+)
    .
END INTERFACE

INTERFACE OPERATOR (-)
    .
END INTERFACE
```

The interface block also contains the definition of the subprogram, which the compiler will "call" automatically when the overloaded operator is called into play. The subprogram corresponding to the unary operator has one argument and that for binary operator has two arguments.

```
INTERFACE OPERATOR (+)
  FUNCTION LOW_TO_UP (CH) RESULT (RES)
  CHARACTER, INTENT (IN) ::CH
  CHARACTER :: RES
  END FUNCTION LOW_TO_UP
END INTERFACE

INTERFACE OPERATOR (-)
  FUNCTION UP_TO_LOW (CH) RESULT (RES)
  CHARACTER, INTENT (IN) :: CH
  CHARACTER :: RES
  END FUNCTION UP_TO_LOW
END INTERFACE
```

When these overloaded operators are used, appropriate subprograms are called, which in turn, perform the operations that the operators are supposed to perform.

```fortran
      CHARACTER :: CH1
      READ *, CH1      ! Read a lowercase letter.
      PRINT *, CH1
      CH1 = +CH1
!      Convert to upper case through
!      the overloaded unary + operator
      PRINT *,CH1
      CH1 = -CH1
!      Convert to lowercase through
!      overloaded unary - operator
      PRINT *, CH1
      END
```

Now we have to design the functions LOW_TO_UP and UP_TO_LOW.

```fortran
      FUNCTION LOW_TO_UP(CH) RESULT(RES)
      CHARACTER, INTENT(IN) :: CH
      CHARACTER :: RES
      RES=ACHAR(IACHAR(CH)-IACHAR('a') &
           + IACHAR('A'))
      END FUNCTION LOW_TO_UP

      FUNCTION UP_TO_LOW(CH) RESULT(RES)
      CHARACTER, INTENT(IN) :: CH
      CHARACTER :: RES
      RES=ACHAR(IACHAR(CH)-IACHAR('A') &
           + IACHAR('a'))
      END FUNCTION UP_TO_LOW
```

The next example shows how to overload the addition operator to "add" two strings.

```fortran
      PROGRAM STRINGADD
      INTERFACE OPERATOR(+)
       FUNCTION STR_ADD(S1,S2) RESULT(RES)
       CHARACTER (LEN=*), INTENT (IN) :: S1,S2
       CHARACTER (LEN=LEN(S1)+LEN(S2)) :: RES
       END FUNCTION STR_ADD
      END INTERFACE

      CHARACTER (LEN=9) :: S1
      CHARACTER (LEN=12) :: S2
      CHARACTER (LEN=30) :: S3
      S1 = 'Debasis'
      S2 = 'Sengupta'
      S3 = S1+S2
      PRINT *, S3
      END PROGRAM STRINGADD
```

```
FUNCTION STR_ADD(S1,S2) RESULT(RES)
 CHARACTER(LEN=*), INTENT(IN) ::S1,S2
 CHARACTER(LEN=LEN(S1)+LEN(S2)) ::RES
 RES = TRIM(S1) // " " // TRIM(S2)
END FUNCTION STR_ADD
```

The length of the character variable RES is the sum of the lengths of S1 and S2.

19.24 Overloading Assignment Operator

The Assignment operator can also be overloaded. This is illustrated with an example. In the programming language 'C', anything, that is non-zero, is true and zero is false. We shall now overload the assignment operator such that we will be able to write

logical variable = integer variable

If the integer variable is zero, the logical variable will be set to false, otherwise it will be set to true.
   Overloading the assignment operator is again done through the interface statement.

```
INTERFACE ASSIGNMENT (=)
 .

 .

END INTERFACE
```

Between these two statements, the name and the type of the parameters of the subprogram that the system will call when the overloaded assignment operator is used, are placed.
   In the program given below, when an integer variable INDEX is equated to a logical variable, the system will automatically generate a call to the subroutine FTN_TO_C.

```
PROGRAM FORTTOC
INTERFACE ASSIGNMENT (=)
 SUBROUTINE FTN_TO_C(L,I)
  INTEGER,INTENT(IN) ::I
  LOGICAL, INTENT(OUT)::L
 END SUBROUTINE FTN_TO_C
END INTERFACE

INTEGER :: NUM
LOGICAL :: INDEX
READ *, NUM
INDEX = NUM
PRINT *,INDEX
END PROGRAM FORTTOC
```

```
SUBROUTINE FTN_TO_C(L,I)
INTEGER,INTENT(IN) :: I
LOGICAL, INTENT(OUT) :: L
IF(I .EQ. 0) THEN
 L=.FALSE.
ELSE
 L=.TRUE.
ENDIF
END SUBROUTINE FTN_TO_C
```

19.25 User Defined Operator

A user may define his/her own operator. Such operators are enclosed within periods. Suppose we wish to define an operator MYAND. This will be a binary operator whose operands are integers. If both the operands are non-zero, it will return true otherwise it returns false. Again the user-defined operator requires interface.

```
PROGRAM USEROP
INTERFACE OPERATOR(.MYAND.)
 FUNCTION TESTAND(I1,I2) RESULT(RES)
 INTEGER,INTENT(IN) :: I1,I2
 LOGICAL :: RES
 END FUNCTION TESTAND
END INTERFACE

INTEGER :: NUM1, NUM2
LOGICAL :: LOGI
READ *, NUM1, NUM2
LOGI = NUM1 .MYAND. NUM2
PRINT *, LOGI
END PROGRAM USEROP

FUNCTION TESTAND(I1, I2) RESULT (RES)
INTEGER,INTENT(IN) :: I1,I2
LOGICAL :: RES
IF(I1.NE.0.AND. I2.NE. 0) THEN
 RES=.TRUE.
ELSE
 RES=.FALSE.
ENDIF
END FUNCTION TESTAND
```

19.26 Use Statement and Renaming Operator

A user defined operator defined within a module may be renamed through USE statement.

```
USE MYMOD, OPERATOR (.YOURAND.)=> OPERATOR (.MYAND.)
```

The operator MYAND defined in the module MYMOD can now be accessed as YOURAND in the program shown below. But this is not allowed for intrinsic operators.

```
MODULE MYMOD
INTERFACE OPERATOR(.MYAND.)
 FUNCTION TESTAND(I1,I2) RESULT(RES)
 INTEGER,INTENT(IN) :: I1,I2
 LOGICAL :: RES
 END FUNCTION TESTAND
END INTERFACE
END MODULE MYMOD

PROGRAM USEROP
USE MYMOD, OPERATOR (.YOURAND.)=> OPERATOR(.MYAND.)

INTEGER :: NUM1, NUM2
LOGICAL :: LOGI
READ *, NUM1, NUM2
LOGI = NUM1 .YOURAND. NUM2
PRINT *, LOGI
END PROGRAM USEROP

FUNCTION TESTAND(I1, I2) RESULT (RES)
INTEGER,INTENT(IN) :: I1,I2
LOGICAL :: RES
IF(I1.NE.0.AND. I2.NE. 0) THEN
 RES=.TRUE.
ELSE
 RES=.FALSE.
ENDIF
END FUNCTION TESTAND
```

The present author tested this feature with three Fortran compilers; only the GFORTRAN compiler supports this feature at this moment.

19.27 Priority of Overloaded Operators

The priority of an overloaded operator is same as the corresponding operator defined in Fortran. If the multiplication operator (*) is overloaded, the priority of this overloaded operator will be same as that of the multiplication operator.

19.28 Priority of User Defined Operators

Priority of all user-defined operators is same, and is less than all intrinsic operators.

19.29 Optional Arguments

Arguments to a subprogram may be optional. That is a "call" to the subprogram may or may not contain all the actual parameters if the corresponding dummy parameters have been declared as optional. Obviously, the subprogram must have some way of assigning some value to these optional parameters, if they are not supplied as arguments or the other parameters are such that the optional parameters are not required for this particular call. To use a particular parameter as optional, the keyword OPTIONAL is used.

```
INTERFACE
  FUNCTION OP_DEMO(A1,A2,A3,A4) RESULT (RES)
  INTEGER, INTENT(IN):: A1,A2
  INTEGER, OPTIONAL:: A3,A4
  INTEGER :: RES
  END FUNCTION OP_DEMO
END INTERFACE
```

The interface block above indicates that the first two parameters A1 and A2 must be supplied while calling – the third and the fourth parameter may or may not be present. So the function may be invoked in the following manner. The parameter may appear only once.

```
K = OP_DEMO(10,20,30,40)
!     All the arguments are supplied
!     Call by value
K = OP_DEMO(M1,M2,M3,M4)
!     Call by reference
K = OP_DEMO(M1,M2)

K = OP_DEMO(M1,20,M3)
K = OP_DEMO(M1,20)
```

It is also possible to invoke the function through keyword arguments.

```
K = OP_DEMO(A1=10,A2=20,A3=30,A4=40)
K = OP_DEMO(A2=20,A1=20,A4=40)
K = OP_DEMO(A3=10,A1=20,A2=30)
```

19.30 PRESENT

This intrinsic is used to check the presence of an actual argument within the subprogram body. It was already mentioned that the subprogram must somehow handle the situation when optional argument is not present.

```
IF (PRESENT(A3)) THEN
      .
ELSE
      .
ENDIF
```

The PRESENT intrinsic returns true if the corresponding argument is present in the call to the subprogram – otherwise it returns false. The following program illustrates this feature. The program calls a function with two to four arguments. The first and second arguments must be present and the other two are optional arguments. The function calculates the average of all the arguments present in the call. If any optional argument is absent, it is not considered for calculating the average.

```
PROGRAM CALC_AVERAGE
INTERFACE
  REAL FUNCTION AVERAGE(A1,A2,A3,A4)
  INTEGER, INTENT(IN) :: A1,A2
  INTEGER, OPTIONAL :: A3,A4
  END FUNCTION AVERAGE
END INTERFACE
INTEGER :: A1,A2,A3,A4,AVE

READ *, A1,A2,A3,A4

AVE = AVERAGE(A1,A2,A3,A4)

AVE = AVERAGE(A1,A2,A3)
AVE = AVERAGE(A1,A2)
AVE = AVERAGE(A1=10,A2=20,A4=40)
AVE = AVERAGE(A1=20,A4=40,A2=30)

END PROGRAM CALC_AVERAGE

REAL FUNCTION AVERAGE(A1,A2,A3,A4)
INTEGER, INTENT(IN) :: A1,A2
INTEGER, OPTIONAL :: A3,A4
INTEGER :: NUMBER, TOTAL
NUMBER = 4
TOTAL = A1 + A2
IF(PRESENT(A3)) THEN
  TOTAL = TOTAL+A3
ELSE
  NUMBER = NUMBER-1
ENDIF
IF(PRESENT(A4)) THEN
  TOTAL = TOTAL + A4
ELSE
  NUMBER = NUMBER-1
ENDIF
AVERAGE = REAL(TOTAL)/REAL(NUMBER)
END FUNCTION AVERAGE
```

The logic of the program is easy to follow. If an argument is not present the total number of items is decremented by 1.

19.31 Array Valued Function

A library function like SQRT or SIN etc. may take an array as its argument and return an array of the same size and rank containing the results of the called function. A user-defined function may also return an array.

```
FUNCTION ARR(A1) RESULT(RES)
INTEGER :: A1
INTEGER, DIMENSION(4) ::RES

RES(1)=A1+10
RES(2)=A1+20
RES(3)=A1+30
RES(4)=A1+40
END FUNCTION ARR

PROGRAM MAIN
INTERFACE
  FUNCTION ARR(A1) RESULT(RES)
  INTEGER :: A1
  INTEGER, DIMENSION(4) ::RES
  END FUNCTION ARR
END INTERFACE
INTEGER :: X=100
INTEGER, DIMENSION(4):: Y
Y=ARR(X)
PRINT *, Y                 ! output: 110, 120, 130, 140
END
```

When this function is invoked, it returns an integer array of rank 1 and size 4.

19.32 Save Variable

The local variables of any subprograms are lost on exit from the subprogram and when the subprogram is entered again, it does not remember the last value. If the SAVE declaration is used, the corresponding variable reappears with the last value when the subprogram is entered again. Also if a local variable of a subprogram is initialized either along with its declaration or by a DATA statement, it automatically becomes a SAVE variable.

For example if the following two statements of section 19.30

```
INTEGER :: NUMBER
NUMBER = 4
```

are merged into a single statement

```
INTEGER :: NUMBER=4
```

the variable NUMBER becomes a 'save' variable and we shall see this will invite trouble. Though it is not available outside the subprogram, yet when the function is entered again, the NUMBER reappears with its last value. The initialization is done only once. The program logic expects that the value of the variable NUMBER should be 4 each time the function is entered (total number of arguments). When the function is called for the second time with three arguments, NUMBER becomes 3 and when the function is called again with 4 arguments, the variable NUMBER with the value 3 reappears. Naturally, the calculation of average in this case fails as the wrong value of NUMBER is used to calculate the average.

A variable may be forced to become a save variable through the SAVE declaration.

```
FUNCTION FUNC(A1) RESULT(RES)
        .
INTEGER , SAVE :: NUM
!      Num is now a save variable
INTEGER :: KUNM
```

In this case the variable NUM is a 'saved' variable, but KUNM is not.

However, SAVE without any argument makes all the local variables 'saved' variable.

```
FUNCTION FUNC(A1) RSULT(RES)
        .
SAVE
INTEGER :: NUM
REAL :: R
        .
END FUNCTION FUNC
```

19.33 COMMON Statement

Two or more units may share locations through the COMMON statement. The COMMON statement is hardly used now a days as a better alternative – the module – is now available. The COMMON statement had been a part of almost every program in earlier years.

There are two types of COMMON statements – blank and block. In a blank COMMON no name is given to the COMMON block.

```
PROGRAM MAIN
COMMON A,B,C
        .

END PROGRAM MAIN

SUBROUTINE SUB
COMMON P,Q,R
        .
END SUBROUTINE SUB
```

In the COMMON statement of MAIN, there are three scalars A, B and C. In the subroutine the corresponding items are P, Q and R respectively. The variables P and A, Q and B and R and C share same locations. Therefore, if A is set to 20.0 in the MAIN, this value of is reflected through P in the subroutine SUB. Similarly, if P is set to 100 in the subroutine it is reflected through A in the MAIN unit.

Note that the names do not matter. The relative position of the variables within the COMMON block actually matters. So the names of the variable within the subprogram may be any thing say X, Y and Z. The first variable of the COMMON within the subroutine will share same location with the first variable A of the COMMON block of the main unit. It is, of course, assumed that number and type of the variable in both the COMMON block are same so that the one to one correspondence is maintained.

If the COMMON is of the following form :

```
REAL, DIMENSION(3)::A
COMMON A
     .
END


SUBROUTINE SUB
COMMON P,Q,R
     .
END
```

then A(1) and P, A(2) and Q, and A(3) and R will share same locations. A blank common may be shared between main program and subprograms or between the subprograms. Earlier, we have seen that through arguments, data can be transferred between different units of a program. COMMON is another way of sharing data among different units of a program. Note that, a particular variable appearing in COMMON cannot be passed as an argument to a subprogram. Also the variable cannot appear twice in the common block.

A blank COMMON may also be represented as:

```
COMMON // A, B, C
```

where two successive slash symbols indicate blank COMMON.

There is another type of COMMON, called a block COMMON. In this case a name is attached to a COMMON block and there may be several such COMMON blocks in a unit. In blank COMMON, whether one needs them or not, all the variables must be present in every unit. In block COMMON only the relevant block is required to be present in the unit.

The block name COMMON is placed after the keyword COMMON and is enclosed within two slashes(/).

```
PROGRAM MAIN
COMMON /BLK1/ A,B,C
COMMON /BLK2/ P,Q,R
     .

END
SUBROUTINE SUB1
COMMON /BLK1/A,B,C
     .
END
```

```
SUBROUTINE SUB2
COMMON/BLK2/P,Q,R
.

END
```

Since the subroutine SUB1 contains only block BLK1 it can use and modify the variables A, B and C of the MAIN unit but it cannot access the variables P, Q and R as BLK2 is not present in SUB1. Similarly, through BLK2 subroutine SUB2 may use and modify P, Q and R of the main unit. It cannot touch the variables A, B and C of the main unit.

19.34 BLOCK DATA

A block common may be initialized through a special subprogram called BLOCK DATA. The BLOCK DATA subprogram contains only the declarations and the initialization statements. It cannot contain any executable statements. It is not necessary to call the BLOCK DATA subprogram.

```
PROGRAM MAIN
COMMON /BLK1/ A,B,C
COMMON /BLK2/ P,Q,R
.

END

SUBROUTINE SUB1
COMMON /BLK1/A,B,C
.

END

SUBROUTINE SUB2
COMMON/BLK2/P,Q,R
.

END

BLOCK DATA
COMMON /BLK1/ A,B,C
COMMON /BLK2/ P,Q,R
DATA A,B,C/2.0,3.0,4.0/
DATA P,Q,R/100.0,200.0,300.0/
END
```

A BLOCK DATA subprogram can have a name:

```
BLOCK DATA FB
COMMON /BLK2/ P,Q,R

DATA P,Q,R/100.0,200.0,300.0/
END BLOCK DATA FB
```

There can be any number of named BLOCK DATA subprogram to initialize common blocks; it is not necessary to initialize all the common blocks in a single BLOCK DATA subprogram. But no two BLOCK DATA subprogram can have the same name in a single load module.

```
PROGRAM MAIN
COMMON /BLK1/ A,B,C
COMMON /BLK2/ P,Q,R
PRINT *, A,B,C,P,Q,R
CALL SUB1
CALL SUB2
END

SUBROUTINE SUB1
COMMON /BLK1/A,B,C
PRINT *, A,B,C
END

SUBROUTINE SUB2
COMMON/BLK2/P,Q,R

PRINT *, P,Q,R
END

BLOCK DATA FB

COMMON /BLK2/ P,Q,R
DATA P,Q,R/100.0,200.0,300.0/
END BLOCK DATA FB

BLOCK DATA SB

COMMON /BLK1/ A,B,C
DATA A,B,C/2.0,3.0,4.0/
END BLOCK DATA SB
```

Readers are encouraged to guess the output of this program and verify their observation by executing the program. The final point to be noted is that there can be one blank BLOCK DATA subprogram (BLOCK DATA without a name) in a load module.

The usual rules to initialize variables through DATA statement are applicable also.

19.35 COMMON and DIMENSION

Dimension of a variable may be given along with the COMMON:

```
DIMENSION A(10)
COMMON/BLK1/A
```

and
```
COMMON/BLK1/A(10)
```

are equivalent.

19.36 COMMON and User Type

The COMMON statement works on the assumption that variables are stored sequentially within a block. This may not be true for user defined variables and as such the user defined variables should be forced to occupy consecutive locations.

19.37 COMMON and EQUIVALENCE

When two variables share location within a program unit, the EQUIVALENCE statement is used. When two variables share same locations between two different units, a COMMON is used.

A variable, declared in a common block may be made equivalent to a local variable declared with the same unit. However, there are certain restrictions.

Rule I: Variables declared in a particular common block cannot be made equivalent with one another. Also variables declared in two different common blocks cannot be made equivalent.

```
COMMON /BLK1/A,B,C
EQUIVALENCE (A,B)    !      Not allowed

COMMON/BLK2/P,Q,R
COMMON/BLK3/X,Y,Z
EQUIVALENCE (P,X)    !      Not allowed
```

Rule II: A common block cannot be extended beyond its lower bound through EQUIVALENCE statement.

```
DIMENSION A(10)
COMMON/BLK1/ B(1)
EQUIVALENCE(B(1),A(2))    ! Not allowed
```

Rule III: A common block can be extended in the direction of its upper bound.

```
EQUIVALENCE (B(2),A(1))    !Allowed
```

However, this will increase the size of the common block to 11.

19.38 Entry Point

When a subprogram is called, execution begins from the first executable statement of the subprogram. A subprogram may have more than one entry point. The subprogram name declared along with the subroutine or function statement is called the primary entry point. The other entry points defined through the ENTRY statement are called the secondary entry points. When the subprogram is invoked through the secondary entry point, execution begins from the first executable statements following the secondary entry point. The variables declared after the primary entry point is also available when the subprogram is invoked through secondary entry point.

```
SUBROUTINE SUB(N)
declaration
.
.
ENTRY SUB1(N)
.
.
ENTRY SUB2(N)
.
END
```

An internal subprogram cannot have any ENTRY statement.

19.39 EXTERNAL

We have seen that the name of a subprogram can be anything including the name of an intrinsic function. If the name of an intrinsic is used as the name of an user defined subprogram, it is necessary to pass this information through an EXTERNAL statement. In that case compiler will use correctly the user defined subprogram.

```
PROGRAM MAIN
EXTERNAL SQRT
.
X=SQRT(Y)
.
END

FUNCTION SQRT(X)
.
END
```

Without the EXTERNAL statement, the library function SQRT will be used in the MAIN. The EXTERNAL statement prevents the use of the library function instead the user-defined function SQRT is used.

There is, of course, no harm even if all the external subprograms are declared as EXTERNAL.

```
            PROGRAM MAIN
            EXTERNAL SUB1, SUB2
              .
            END

            SUBROUTINE SUB1
              .
            END

            SUBROUTINE SUB2
              .
            END
```

If a subprogram name is to be used as an argument of a function, it must be declared as EXTERNAL in the calling unit. The following program integrates a function using the trapezoidal rule. One of the arguments to the function TRAP is a function name and so it has been declared as EXTERNAL

```
PROGRAM MAIN
REAL :: A=0.0,B=90,H=0.1,F,RESULT
EXTERNAL F
RESULT = TRAP(F,A,B,H)
PRINT *, RESULT
END PROGRAM MAIN

FUNCTION TRAP(F,A,B,H)
REAL,INTENT(IN)::A,B,H

INTERFACE
  REAL FUNCTION F(X)
  REAL, INTENT (IN)::X
  END FUNCTION F
END INTERFACE

REAL :: RES
INTEGER :: I,NP
NP=NINT((B-A)/H)
RES=0
DO I=1, NP-1
  RES=RES+F(A+I*H)
ENDDO
RES=H/2.0*(F(A)+F(B)+2.0*RES)
TRAP=RES*3.14149265/180.0
END FUNCTION TRAP

FUNCTION F(X)
REAL F
REAL,INTENT(IN)::X
REAL,PARAMETER::PI=3.1416926/180.0
F=SIN(X*PI)
END FUNCTION F
```

19.40 Recursion

A function or a subroutine can call itself. This is called recursion. A recursive procedure (function or subroutine) must have one exit point; otherwise recursion becomes infinite.

A recursive procedure can always be converted into an iterative procedure. For example, calculation of the factorial can be done with a recursive procedure – it can also be performed using iterative method. A recursive procedure consumes more system resources than the corresponding iterative counterpart; it takes more time to perform an identical computation than an iterative procedure. However, as some of the algorithms are intrinsically recursive, it is some times convenient to express such an algorithm as a recursive procedure.

19.41 Recursive Function

A recursive function, say factorial, is declared as:

```
RECURSIVE FUNCTION FACTORIAL(N) RESULT(RES)
```

As the recursive function calls itself, the name of the function cannot be used to return the value calculated from the function – the result clause is required to transfer the value calculated by the function. The complete declaration is given below :

```
RECURSIVE FUNCTION FACTORIAL(N) RESULT(VALUE)
INTEGER, INTENT(IN) :: N
INTEGER :: VALUE
```

In each recursive call new local variables N and VALUE are created. As the recursive function returns value through the result clause, the variable VALUE must appear once on the left hand side of the assignment sign. A complete recursive function to calculate factorial is shown below.

```
RECURSIVE FUNCTION FACTORIAL(N) RESULT(VALUE)
INTEGER,INTENT(IN) :: N
INTEGER :: VALUE
IF(N==1) THEN
  VALUE=1                    !       Exit point
ELSE
  VALUE=N*FACTORIAL(N-1)   !       Calls itself
ENDIF
END FUNCTION FACTORIAL
```

Let us consider a case when the recursive function is called with N=4, that is, the function will return factorial 4.

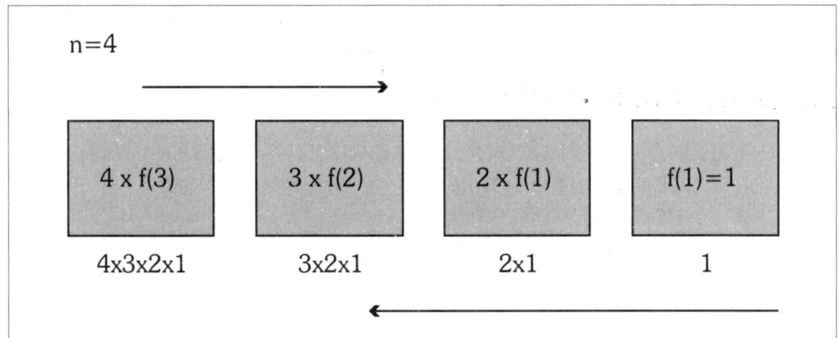

As N is not equal to 1 when the function is called, the "ELSE" part of the IF statement is executed and VALUE can be obtained only when FACTORIAL(N-1), that is, FACTORIAL(3) is known. In fact, FACTORIAL(3) is a call to the recursive factorial function with N=3. This process continues till the FACTORIAL is called with N=1. Now the "THEN" part i.e. the exit part of the recursive function is reached and 1 will be returned, which will, in turn, enable to calculate FACTORIAL(2). Having obtained FACTORIAL(2), now FACTORIAL(3) can be calculated in an identical manner. In a similar manner, ultimately FACTORIAL(4) will be obtained.

The main program to call the recursive FACTORIAL function is shown below:

```
PROGRAM RECUR
INTERFACE
 RECURSIVE FUNCTION FACTORIAL(N) RESULT(VAL)
 INTEGER, INTENT(IN):: N
 INTEGER            :: VAL
 END FUNCTION FACTORIAL
END INTERFACE
INTEGER :: F,N
READ *, N              ! N=4 (say)
F=FACTORIAL(N)
PRINT *, F
END
```

Example of another recursive function is given below.

```
!          Calculation of G.C.D.
           RECURSIVE FUNCTION GCD(N,M) RESULT(GASAGU)
           INTEGER,INTENT(IN) :: N,M
           INTEGER :: GASAGU
           INTEGER :: R     ! Local variable
           R=MOD(N,M)
           IF(R==0) THEN
             GASAGU=M        ! Exit point
           ELSE
             GASAGU=GCD(M,R)
           ENDIF
           END FUNCTION GCD
```

The main program to call the GCD function is shown below:

```
INTEGER :: N=80, M=50
 INTERFACE
  RECURSIVE FUNCTION GCD(N,M) RESULT(GASAGU)
  INTEGER,INTENT(IN) :: N,M
  INTEGER :: GASAGU
  END FUNCTION GCD
 END INTERFACE
PRINT *, GCD(N,M)
END
```

19.42 Recursive Subroutine

A subroutine also can call itself. As subroutine returns the value through its argument, it must not contain any result clause.

The following subroutine calculates the factorial recursively.

```
RECURSIVE SUBROUTINE FACT(N,VALUE)
INTEGER, INTENT(IN) :: N
INTEGER, INTENT(OUT) :: VALUE
IF(N==1) THEN
 VALUE=1        ! Exit point
ELSE
 CALL FACT((N-1),VALUE)
 VALUE=N*VALUE
ENDIF
END SUBROUTINE FACT
```

The main program to call the above subroutine is given below.

```
PROGRAM RECSUB
INTERFACE

 RECURSIVE SUBROUTINE FACT(N,VALUE)
 INTEGER, INTENT(IN) :: N
 INTEGER, INTENT(OUT) :: VALUE
 END SUBROUTINE FACT
END INTERFACE

INTEGER :: NUM, F
READ *, NUM
CALL FACT(NUM,F)
PRINT *, F
END PROGRAM RECSUB
```

The program logic is similar to the recursive function. However, the difference is that the subroutine returns the value through it argument and in this case through the variable VALUE.

The next program sorts an array using the Quick-sort algorithm. The algorithm, based on a technique called "divide and conquer", may be found in any standard textbook on Data Structures.

```
PROGRAM QUICK_SORT
INTERFACE
 RECURSIVE SUBROUTINE QUICK(A,FIRST,LAST)
   INTEGER,DIMENSION(:), INTENT(INOUT)::A
   INTEGER,INTENT(IN)::FIRST, LAST
  END SUBROUTINE QUICK
END INTERFACE
INTEGER, DIMENSION(10)::A=[32,17,31,6,51,-26,19,12,-2,77]
INTEGER::FIRST=1
INTEGER::LAST=10
PRINT *, A
CALL QUICK(A,FIRST,LAST)
PRINT *,A
END
RECURSIVE SUBROUTINE QUICK (A,FIRST,LAST)
INTEGER,DIMENSION(:),INTENT(INOUT)::A
INTEGER,INTENT(IN)::FIRST, LAST
INTEGER::MID,HIGH,LOW,T
MID=A((FIRST+LAST)/2)
HIGH=LAST
LOW=FIRST
DO
   DO WHILE (A(LOW)<MID)
    LOW=LOW+1
   ENDDO
   DO WHILE(A(HIGH)>MID)
    HIGH=HIGH-1
   ENDDO
   IF (LOW<=HIGH) THEN
    T=A(LOW)
    A(LOW)=A(HIGH)
    LOW=LOW+1
    A(HIGH)=T
    HIGH=HIGH-1
   ENDIF
   IF(LOW>HIGH) THEN
    EXIT
   ENDIF
ENDDO
IF(LOW<LAST) THEN
   CALL QUICK(A,LOW,LAST)
ENDIF
IF(FIRST<HIGH) THEN
   CALL QUICK(A,FIRST,HIGH)
ENDIF
END
```

19.43 Recursive Input/Output

Input/output statement can be recursive, that is, when one input/output statement is in operation it can initiate another input/output statement. Till now support from NAG compiler for such I/O is not available.

19.44 Pure Procedure

The main property of a PURE function is that it has no side effect. This implies that its dummy arguments are all defined with INTENT (IN). The definition of PURE subroutine is somewhat similar except the dummy parameters defined with INTENT (OUT) and INTENT (INOUT) may be modified within the subroutine.

A PURE procedure is declared with the suffix PURE:

```
PURE INTEGER FUNCTION FUNC (A, B)
INTEGER, INTENT (IN) :: A, B
    .
    .
END FUNCTION FUNC

PURE SUBROUTINE SUB(A, B, C)
REAL, INTENT (IN) :: A
INTEGER, INTENT(OUT) :: B
INTEGER, INTENT (INOUT) :: C
    .
END SUBROUTINE SUB
```

19.45 Rules for Pure Procedure

(a) All non-pointer (chapter 21) dummy arguments of the PURE function must be of INTENT (IN).
(b) All the non-pointer dummy arguments of the subroutine must have their INTENT specified.
(c) A local variable of a PURE procedure cannot have a SAVE attribute attached to it.
(d) All the internal subprograms of the PURE procedure must be PURE.
(e) The statements: OPEN, CLOSE, INQUIRE, PRINT, ENDFILE, BACKSPACE, REWIND, FLUSH, WAIT, READ, PRINT, WRITE and STOP are not allowed within a pure procedure.
(f) A PURE procedure cannot be a recursive procedure
(g) If the dummy argument of a PURE procedure is the name of another procedure, the corresponding actual procedure (parameter) must be a PURE procedure.
(h) Arguments transferred through the COMMON block cannot be modified inside a PURE procedure. The following program would give compilation error.

```
INTEGER :: A, B
COMMON/BLK1/ C
CALL SUB(A, B)
    .
END
```

```
PURE SUBROUTINE SUB (X, Y)
INTEGER, INTENT (IN) :: X, Y
COMMON/BLK1/ Z
.
Z=20.0                    ! NOT allowed
.
END
```

The PURE procedure has been introduced with an eye to facilitate parallel programming which is beyond the scope of this book.

19.46 Elemental Procedure

An Elemental Procedure is a function or a subroutine whose arguments are all scalars but it can be called with conformable arrays. The result is also scalar. If it is called with arrays, in such a case the procedure acts on every element of the array in identical manner. This is best explained with the help of an example. An Elemental Procedure starts with the keyword ELEMENTAL. All the ELEMENTAL procedures are PURE so the rules stated above are applicable to the ELEMENTAL Procedure.

```
ELEMENTAL SUBROUTINE EXCHANGE (A, B)
REAL, INTENT (INOUT) :: A, B
REAL :: T
T=A
A=B
B=T
END

PROGRAM MAIN
INTERFACE
  ELEMENTAL SUBROUTINE EXCHANGE (A, B)
  REAL, INTENT (INOUT) :: A, B
  END
END INTERFACE

REAL, DIMENSION (3) :: P, Q
P=[10.0, 20.0, 30.0]
Q=[100.0, 200.0, 300.0]

CALL EXCHANGE (P, Q)
PRINT *, P
PRINT *, Q
END
```

The Elemental Subroutine has been declared with scalar arguments A and B. But it is called with the arrays P and Q. The subroutine will interchange P(1) with Q(1), P(2) with Q(2) and P(3) with Q(3).

An Elemental procedure cannot be recursive or vice versa.

19.47 Statement Function

A statement function is similar to a function subprogram containing only one Fortran statement. Moreover, its scope is only within the unit in which it is defined.

The definition of the statement function should be placed before the first executable statement of the unit. Since the value returned from the statement function is through its name, the type of value that the statement function is supposed to return must be specified at the time of declaration. If this is not specified, the statement function name that starts with I, J, K, L, M or N returns an integer value otherwise returns real value. A statement function is defined as follows:

$$st\text{-}funct(arg1,...,argn) = fortran\ statement$$

where *st-funct* is the name of the statement function, arg1 etc. are the dummy arguments and the Fortran statement is a valid Fortran expression.

```
DISCR(A, B, C) = B*B - 4.0*A*C
```

In this case DISCR is the name of the statement function and by default it returns a real value; A, B and C are the dummy parameters which are by default real. The function returns a real value depending on the value of the actual parameter when the function is invoked. The statement function is invoked just like the function subprogram.

```
D = DISCR (3.0, 4.0, 5.0)
```

This sets D to -44. A statement function may use another statement function defined earlier or it may call library functions.

```
DISCR (A, B, C) = SQRT (B*B - 4.0*A*C)
```

The expression on the right hand side may contain a constant. It may also contain (definition of statement function) a variable which is not present in the argument list. In such a case, the current value of such variable is used to evaluate the statement function.

```
MYFUNC (A,B,C) = B*B - 4.0*A*C + D + 2.5
```

Since D is not in the argument list, the current value of D is used when the function is invoked. Note that, since A, B and C are dummy parameters they are substituted by the actual parameters when the statement function is invoked. Statement functions are useful when it is necessary to perform a one-line calculation at different places of a program unit for different variables. As Fortran supports internal subprogram, the statement function is rarely used.

A statement function cannot appear within a BLOCK DATA or a module. The INTENT of the dummy arguments of a statement function is always IN. A statement function cannot be a dummy parameter of any procedure. The dummy arguments and the returned value are always scalar. A statement function can "call" another statement function if it is declared before the calling statement function.

```fortran
INTEGER :: A,B,C,T,ID,JD

ID(A,B)=A*B
JD(A,B,C)=ID(A,B)+C ! JD is 'calling' ID
A=10
B=20
C=30
T=JD(A,B,C)
PRINT *, T
END
```

All the variables, named constants used as arguments must be declared before the definition of the statement function.

Some more definitions of statement functions are given below.

```fortran
LOGICAL INDEX
INDEX (X,Y) = X > Y

COMPLEX CALC, A, B, C
CALC = (A+B)/C
```

19.48 Function Calls and Side Effect

When two logical conditions are connected by logical operators like, AND and OR, evaluation of both the conditions are not always required to arrive at the final result. For example, if two relational expressions are connected by an AND operator and the first relation is false, there is no need to evaluate the second expression. Similarly, if they are connected by OR and the first condition is true there is no need to evaluate the second condition.

```fortran
IF (A>B .AND. F(Q)) THEN
      .
ENDIF
```

Let us suppose F is a logical function (returns true or false) and the program logic demands that it is to be evaluated irrespective of the result of the first condition. If A>B is false it is likely that the function F will not be invoked and this might create logical problem. This is called a side effect. In such a situation the function should be called before the IF statement as shown below.

```fortran
LOGICAL :: L
      .
L=F(Q)
IF(A>B .AND. L) THEN
      .
ENDIF
```

As the function F is called before the IF statement, the logical problem is avoided and at the same time the returned value is used in the IF statement if required.

19.49 EQUIVALENCE and MODULE

If a variable is declared within a module, the same cannot be made equivalent with a local variable.

```
MODULE MYMOD
 INTEGER :: I
END MODULE MYMOD

PROGRAM MAIN
USE MYMOD
INTEGER :: K
EQUIVALENCE (I,K) ! NOT allowed
 .
 .
 .
END
```

The rule is that objects belonging to different scoping unit cannot be made equivalent.

Chapter 20

IEEE ARITHMETIC AND EXCEPTIONS (*)

Most of the modern computers follow IEEE (Institute of Electrical and Electronics Engineers) standards for storing and using floating-point numbers. Based on this standard the present version of Fortran provides a number of functions and subroutines to handle exception conditions. The routines help the programmers to develop efficient numerical software. In this chapter we shall first examine how floating-point numbers are stored according to the IEEE standard.

20.1 Representation of Floating Point Numbers (IEEE Standard)

In section 18.6 it was shown that the floating point numbers are represented as

$$X = 0$$

and,
$$X = s.b^e \times \sum (k=1,p) \; f_k \times b^{-k}$$

where s represents the sign, plus or minus, $b=2$ for binary representation, and f_ks satisfy:

$$0 <= f_k < b$$

For binary $b=2$ and the f_ks are either 0 or 1.

20.2 Single Precision 32 Bit Floating Point Numbers

A single precision 32 bit number is stored in the following way according to the IEEE standard:

Bit 31:   Sign bit, 0 for positive number and 1 for negative number
Bits 30- 23:   Exponent bits (biased, to be discussed shortly)
Bits 22- 0:   Used to store the fraction.

The smallest and the largest numbers that can be stored in the eight bits (30-23) are 0 [$(00000000)_2$] and 255 [$(11111111)_2$] respectively. These two numbers are reserved (to be discussed later). Consequently, the smallest and largest numbers that are stored in these bits are 1 through 254 [$(11111110)_2$]. These are not the actual exponents of a binary number. In order to handle negative exponents efficiently (that is without wasting a bit for the sign of the exponent) the number 127 is added to the exponent that is the exponent is biased with 127. Thus exponent 3 is stored as $127+3=130$ and -3 is stored as $127-3=124$. Thus maximum and minimum value of the exponent bits (after adding 127) is 254 and 1 respectively corresponding to actual exponents 127 and -126 respectively.

The fraction is stored in "normalized" form. The exponent is so adjusted that the number becomes 2^e x 1.yyy... , where yyy etc. are binary digits – either 0 or 1. For example, for the decimal system, 234.56 may be written as 2.3456 x 10^2. Similarly, a binary number 110101.111 may be written as 2^5x1.10101111. A single precision real number having biased exponent between 1 and 254 and the fraction containing 1 before the binary decimal point is termed a "normalized" real number. Therefore, a floating point normalized number looks like:

$$X = s \text{ x } 2^e \text{ x } 1. \text{(normalized binary fraction)}$$

The advantage of storing a fraction in its normalized form is that the most significant bit, which is $2^0=1$ for any fraction, need not be stored – it is implied. So the fraction actually uses 24 bits to store its value, though only 23 bits are allocated for the fraction.

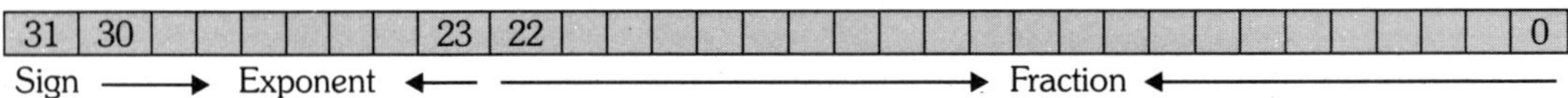

We shall now show the bit pattern of a few real numbers.

(a) $1.25 = 2^0 \text{x} (1.01)_2$
Exponent$= 0+127=127=(01111111)_2$
Fraction $= (1)\ 010\ 0000\ 0000\ 0000\ 0000\ 0000$
$1.25 = 0\ 01111111\ 010\ 0000\ 0000\ 0000\ 0000$ [hidden bit is not shown]

(b) $0.0625=(.0001)_2=2^{-4}\text{x}(1.0)_2$
Exponent $= -4+127=123= (01111011)_2$
Fraction $= (1)\ 000\ 0000\ 0000\ 0000\ 0000\ 0000$
$0.0625 = 0\ 01111011\ 000\ 0000\ 0000\ 0000\ 0000$ [hidden bit not shown]

(c) $-5.0= 2^2 \text{x} (1.01)_2$ (value only)
Sign bit $= 1$
Exponent $= 2+127=129=10000001$
Fraction $= (1)\ 010\ 0000\ 0000\ 0000\ 0000\ 0000$
$-5.0= 1\ 10000001\ 010\ 0000\ 0000\ 0000\ 0000$ [hidden bit not shown]

(d) $-17.625=2^4 \text{x} (1.1015625)_{10} =2^4 \text{x} (1.0001101)_2$ (value only)
Sign bit $=1$
Exponent $= 4+127=131=10000011$
Fraction $= (1)\ 0001101\ 0000\ 0000\ 0000\ 0000$
$-17.625 = 1\ 10000011\ 000\ 1101\ 0000\ 0000\ 0000\ 0000$ [hidden bit not shown]

A double precision number requires 8 bytes (64 bits). For such numbers arrangements are shown below:

Bit 63 :   Sign bit
Bits 62:52   Exponent
Bits 51:0   Fraction

The exponent is biased by 1023. The biased exponent can have a value between 1 and 2046 corresponding to the actual exponent -1022 and 1023. We shall now find out the internal representation of -5.0D0.

Bit 63   Sign bit 1
Bit 62:52   Exponent 10000000001
Bit 51:0   Fraction (1)0100 0000 0000 0000 0000 0000 0000 0000 0000 0000 0000 0000 0000
-5.0D0 = 1 10000000001 0100 0000 0000 0000 0000 0000 0000 0000 0000 0000 0000 0000 0000

20.3 Denormal Numbers

Denormal numbers or denormalized numbers are those, that are less than the smallest normalized floating point number available in the system. They actually fill the gap between zero and the smallest floating point number. As these numbers are smaller than the smallest floating point number, these numbers are also called 'sub-normal' numbers. In IEEE floating point representation, denormal numbers are stored with bias 126 and with all the exponent bits switched off. Also, there is no hidden bit associated with a denormal number. The smallest non zero positive denormal number is represented below:

0000 0000 0000 ....   0001 (total 32 bit, single precision)

Exponent is biased by 126, so the actual exponent is 0-126=-126. Rightmost bit is on and its value is $2^{**}(-23)$. Therefore, the smallest non zero denormal number is:

$$2^{**}(-126) \times 2^{**}(-23) = 2^{**}(-149) = 1.4012985E\text{-}45 \text{ (approximately)}$$

0	0	0	0	0	0	0	0	0	0	0	0	0	0	0	0	0	0	0	0	0	0	0	0	0	0	0	0	0	0	0	1

Smallest Denormal Number

Similarly, the largest denormal positive number is one with all the bits 0 to 23 bits are switched on. It is:

$$2^{**}(-126) \times (1 - 2^{**}(-23)) = 1.1754942E\text{-}38$$

0	0	0	0	0	0	0	0	0	1	1	1	1	1	1	1	1	1	1	1	1	1	1	1	1	1	1	1	1	1	1	1

Largest Denormal Number

Readers are encouraged to find out the smallest and the largest double precision denormal number.

20.4 Zeros

There are two zeros in this representation, positive zero (+0) and negative zero (-0). For positive zero all bits are switched off. For negative zero, sign bit is on and all other bits are zero.

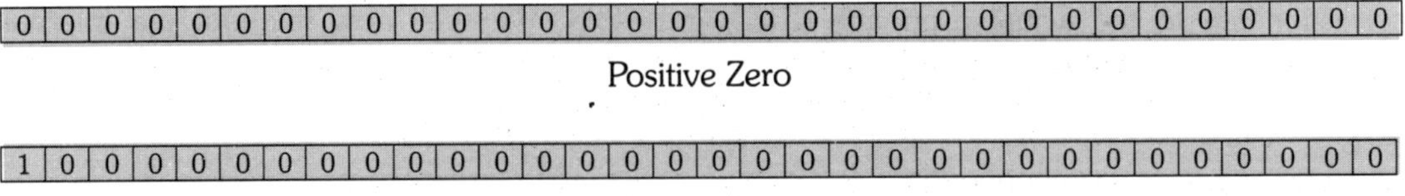

Positive Zero

Negative Zero

Though the bit patterns of the positive and the negative zeros are different, yet the numerical values of -0.0 and 0.0 are the same. For the purpose of comparison, they are treated as equal. However, the PRINT statement displays the negative sign of the negative zero. The library function SIGN (which takes two arguments and the sign of the second argument is transferred to the first argument) respects the sign of the negative zero. The following program illustrates these points.

```
      REAL :: R1,R2,R3=5.0, R4=5.0
      R1=-0.0
      R2=0.0
      R3=SIGN(R3,R1)          ! R1 = -0.0, R3 = -5.0
      R4=SIGN(R4,R2)          ! R2 = 0.0, R4 = 5.0
      PRINT 10, R1,R2,R3,R4
  10  FORMAT(4F8.1)

      END
```

The output of the program is:

```
-0.0   0.0 -5.0   5.0
```

20.5 Infinity

There are two infinities positive (+∞) and negative (-∞). Positive infinity is represented by the following bit combinations: sign bit off, all exponent bits on and all other bits zero. Negative infinity is same as positive infinity except the sign bit is on. The infinite values are created by division by zero or by arithmetic overflow.

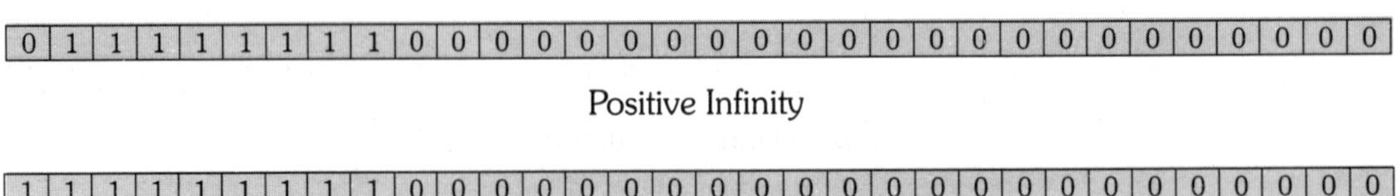

Positive Infinity

Negative Infinity

20.6 NaN (not a number)

Not a number is created by invalid operation like 0/0 or 0x∞. NaN is represented with all bits of the exponent as 1 and the fractional parts as non-zero. There are two types of NaN, signaling and quiet. If an operand contains signaling NaN, the invalid exception signal is generated and result becomes a quiet NaN. Quiet NaN as operand does not raise any exception. For a quiet NaN the most significant bit of the fractional part is 1 and for a signaling NaN the most significant bit of the fractional part is zero.

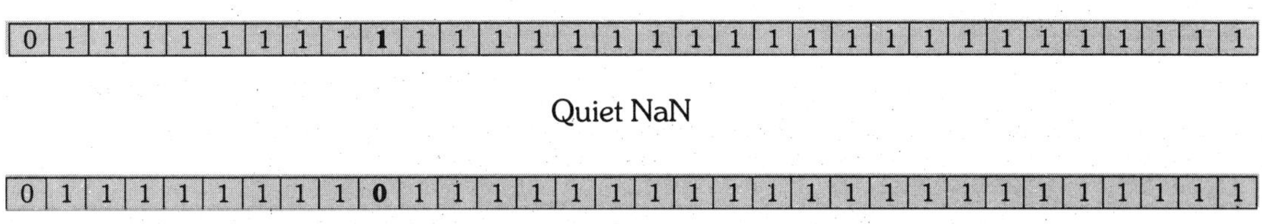

Quiet NaN

Signaling NaN

20.7 Summary of IEEE "Numbers"

Table 20.1 summarizes single precision IEEE "numbers".

Table 20.1 IEEE Numbers

Type	Sign	Exponent	Mantissa
Positive zero	0	0	0
Negative zero	1	0	0
Denormalized number	0 or 1	0	Non zero
Positive infinity	0	255	0
Negative infinity	1	255	0
NaN (quiet)	0	255	Non zero, bit 23 is on
NaN (signaling)	0	255	Non zero, bit 23 is off
Normalized number	0 or 1	1 to 254	any

IEEE has defined operations of these so-called "special numbers". If one of the operand is NaN the result is NaN. Table 20.2 summarizes the result of operations of other "special numbers".

Table 20.2 Operations Involving "Special" Numbers

0 + 0 = 0	∞ + ∞ = ∞
0 - 0 = 0	∞ - ∞ = NaN
0 * 0 = 0	∞ * ∞ = ∞
0 / 0 = NaN	∞ / ∞ = NaN
0 ** 0 = NaN	∞ ** ∞ = ∞
0 + (-0) = 0	∞ + (-∞) = NaN
0 - (-0) = 0	∞ - (-∞) = ∞
0 * (-0) = -0	∞ * (-∞) = -∞
0 / (-0) = NaN	∞ / (-∞) = NaN
0 ** (-0) = NaN	∞ ** (-∞) = 0
-0 + 0 = 0	-∞ + ∞ = NaN
-0 - 0 = -0	-∞ - ∞ = -∞
-0 * 0 = -0	-∞ * ∞ = -∞
-0 / 0 = NaN	-∞ / ∞ = NaN
-0 ** 0 = NaN	-∞ ** ∞ = NaN
-0 + (-0) = -0	-∞ + (-∞) = -∞
-0 - (-0) = 0	-∞ - (-∞) = NaN
-0 * (-0) = 0	-∞ * (-∞) = ∞
-0 / (-0) = NaN	-∞ / ∞ = NaN
-0 ** (-0) = NaN	-∞ ** (-∞) = NaN
0 + ∞ = ∞	-0 + ∞ = ∞
0 - ∞ = -∞	-0 - ∞ = -∞
0 * ∞ = NaN	-0 * ∞ = NaN
0 / ∞ = 0	-0 / ∞ = -0
0 ** ∞ = 0	-0 ** ∞ = 0
0 + (-∞) = -∞	-0 + (-∞) = -∞
0 - (-∞) = ∞	-0 - (-∞) = ∞
0 * (-∞) = NaN	-0 * (-∞) = NaN
0 / (-∞) = -0	-0 / (-∞) = 0
0 ** (-∞) = ∞	-0 ** (-∞) = ∞

20.8 IEEE Modules

IEEE exception handling in Fortran is performed through three modules IEEE_EXCEPTIONS, IEEE_ARITHMETIC and IEEE_FEATURES. The module IEEE_EXCEPTIONS is used for exceptions, the module IEEE_ARITHMETIC is used for IEEE arithmetic and the module IEEE_FEATURES is used to control the features supported by the compiler. The modules are included in the program by USE statements:

```
USE IEEE_ARITHMETIC
USE IEEE_EXCEPTIONS
USE IEEE_FEATURES
```

Chapter 19 contains detailed discussions on MODULE and USE statements. The IEEE_ARITHMETIC contains an USE statement for IEEE_EXCEPTIONS, that is, IEEE_ARITHMETIC modules appear to contain an USE IEEE_EXCEPTIONS statement. All the functions of IEEE modules are pure (chapter 19) and procedure names are generic. An exception may or may not cause program termination. For example, exception condition like division by zero may or may not terminate a program. Normally, the job is aborted when division by zero occurs. However, by suitable instructions, the programmer may allow the program to continue.

20.9 IEEE_FEATURES

This module defines IEEE features. The module defines a data type IEEE_FEATURE_TYPE. The following named constants are defined in this module:

```
IEEE_DATATYPE
IEEE_DENORMAL
IEEE_DIVIDE
IEEE_HALTING
IEEE_INEXACT_FLAG
IEEE_INF
IEEE_INVALID_FLAG
IEEE_NAN
IEEE_ROUNDING
IEEE_SQRT
IEEE_UNDERFLOW_FLAG
```

For a particular processor, some of the IEEE features are available by default; some others, being inefficient and perhaps slow, are not available by default and support for some may not be available at all. When the IEEE features are not included by USE, the processor will support only the default features. When IEEE features are used, support for all the available IEEE features will be provided. It is possible to use an ONLY clause with the USE statement to provide support for a particular feature. For example, suppose the default feature does not support denormalized numbers. In such a case, all the underflowed values are treated as zero. There is no "smooth" transition from the "TINY" (smallest normalized floating point number) number to zero. However, if the compiler is forced to compile program with denormalized support (assuming such support exists, not as default) the transition from "TINY" number to zero becomes smooth through the denormalized numbers. The is achieved with appropriate USE statement:

```
USE IEEE_FEATURES ! all the features are available
USE IEEE_FEATURES, ONLY : IEEE_DENORMAL
```

20.10 IEEE Flags

There are five IEEE flags – IEEE_OVERFLOW, IEEE_DIVIDE_BY_ZERO, IEEE_INVALID, IEEE_UNDERFLOW and IEEE_INEXACT.

IEEE_OVERFLOW: Overflow is a condition when the number is too large to be represented in a given machine. The flag is set when overflow occurs.

IEEE_DIVIDE_BY_ZERO: When division by zero is attempted this flag is set.

IEEE_INVALID: This flag is set when the arithmetic operation is invalid.

IEEE_UNDERFLOW: This happens when the value of a real number is too small and it cannot be represented with its full precision (there is loss of precision).

IEEE_INEXACT: This occurs when the result of computation is not exact.

20.11 Derived Types and Constants Defined in the Modules

The module IEEE_EXCEPTIONS defines following derived data type:
(a) IEEE_FLAG_TYPE: The named constants defined in this module are IEEE_INVALID, IEEE_OVERFLOW, IEEE_DIVIDE_BY_ZERO, IEEE_UNDERFLOW and IEEE_INEXACT. Also this module defines array constants IEEE_USUAL and IEEE_ALL with

```
IEEE_USUAL=[IEEE_OVERFLOW,IEEE_DIVIDE_BY_ZERO,IEEE_INVALID]
!   dimension 3
```

and

```
IEEE_ALL = [IEEE_USUAL, IEEE_UNDERFLOW, IEEE_INEXACT]
!   dimension 5
```

(b) IEEE_STATUS_TYPE: This is used to save the current floating point status.

The module IEEE_ARITHMETIC defines the following derived data types:
(a) IEEE_CLASSTYPE: This is used to identify the class of a floating point number. The named constants defined in this module are:

```
IEEE_SIGNALING_NAN
IEEE_QUIET_NAN
IEEE_NEGATIVE_INF
IEEE_POSITIVE_INF
IEEE_NEGATIVE_NORMAL
IEEE_NEGATIVE_DENORMAL
IEEE_NEGATIVE_ZERO
IEEE_POSITIVE_ZERO
IEEE_POSITIVE_DENORMAL
IEEE_POSITIVE_NORMAL
IEEE_OTHER_VALUE
```

(b) IEEE_ROUND_TYPE: This is used to define a rounding mode. The named constants defined in the modules are:

```
IEEE_NEAREST
IEEE_TO_ZERO
IEEE_UP
IEEE_DOWN
IEEE_OTHER (for other mode)
```

There are four types of rounding mode for formatted input/output – IEEE_NEAREST, IEEE_TO_ZERO, IEEE_UP and IEEE_DOWN.

IEEE_NEAREST: The result is rounded to the exact result to the nearest representable value.

IEEE_TO_ZERO: The result is rounded to the exact result towards zero to next representable value.

IEEE_UP: The result is rounded to the exact result towards +infinity to the next representable value.

IEEE_DOWN: The result is rounded to the exact result towards -infinity to the next representable value.

20.12 IEEE Operators

Only the relational operators equal (.EQ., ==) and not equal (.NE., /=) can be used to compare class and round type. The result is either true or false.

20.13 Inquiry Functions (Arithmetic Module)

In all subsequent discussions of this section, if the argument X of the function is absent, the argument is assumed to be any kind of real number. Also all these program segments contain two statements:

```
USE IEEE_ARITHMETIC
REAL :: X
```

IEEE_SUPPORT_DATATYPE([X]): This function returns true if the processor supports the variable of type (kind) X, otherwise if returns false:

```
USE IEEE_ARITHMETIC
REAL :: X
IF (IEEE_SUPPORT_DATATYPE(X)) THEN
  PRINT *, 'X is supported datatype'
ELSE
  PRINT *, 'X is not supported datatype'
ENDIF
END
```

IEEE_SUPPORT_DENORMAL([X]): This function returns true if the processor supports IEEE denormalized numbers. It returns false, otherwise. The optional argument X is real of any kind. It may be scalar or array valued.

```
IF (IEEE_SUPPORT_DENORMAL(X)) THEN
  PRINT *, 'DENORMAL is supported '
ELSE
  PRINT *, 'DENORMAL is not supported '
ENDIF
```

IEEE_SUPPORT_DIVIDE([X]): This function returns true if the processor supports divide with the accuracy specified in the IEEE standard for real variable of same kind type parameter as X. Otherwise it returns false.

```
IF (IEEE_SUPPORT_DIVIDE(X)) THEN
  .
ELSE
  .
ENDIF
```

IEEE_SUPPORT_INF([X]): This function returns true if the processor supports IEEE infinity for same kind type as X. It returns false otherwise.

```
IF (IEEE_SUPPORT_INF(X)) THEN
  .
ELSE
  .
ENDIF
```

IEEE_SUPPORT_NAN([X]): This function returns true if not-a-number is supported by the processor for the same kind type variable X. It returns false otherwise.

```
IF (IEEE_SUPPORT_NAN(X)) THEN
  .
ELSE
  .
ENDIF
```

IEEE_SUPPORT_HALTING(*flag*): This function returns true if the processor has the ability to control program termination for the following exception condition:

```
IEEE_INVALID
IEEE_OVERFLOW
IEEE_DIVIDE_BY_ZERO
IEEE_UNDERFLOW
IEEE_INEXACT
```

It returns false otherwise.

```
IF (IEEE_SUPPORT_HALTING(IEEE_DIVIDE_BY_ZERO)) THEN
 PRINT *, &
  'Program termination can be controlled for Divide by Zero exception'
ELSE
 PRINT *, &
  'Program termination can NOT be controlled for Divide by Zero exception'
ENDIF
```

IEEE_SUPPORT_ROUNDING (*roundvalue*, [X]): This function returns true if the round value of type TYPE(IEEE_ROUND_TYPE) is supported for the same kind type parameter X. The round value must be one of the following type:

```
                    IEEE_NEAREST
                    IEEE_TO_ZERO
                    IEEE_UP
                    IEEE_DOWN
                    IEEE_OTHER (for other mode)
```

```
IF (IEEE_SUPPORT_ROUNDING (IEEE_NEAREST, X)) THEN
 PRINT *, 'Rounding according to IEEE nearest mode is supported'
ELSE
 PRINT *, 'Rounding according to IEEE nearest mode is NOT supported'
ENDIF
```

IEEE_SUPPORT_FLAG(*flag*, [X]): It returns true if a flag mentioned below is supported for the same kind type as X. It returns false otherwise. The flags may be one of the following:

```
                    IEEE_OVERFLOW
                    IEEE_DIVIDE_BY_ZERO
                    IEEE_INVALID
                    IEEE_UNDERFLOW
                    IEEE_INEXACT
```

```
IF (IEEE_SUPPORT_FLAG (IEEE_DIVIDE_BY_ZERO, X)) THEN
 PRINT *, 'Divide by Zero flag is supported for the variable X'
ELSE
 PRINT *, 'Divide by Zero flag is NOT supported for the variable X'
ENDIF
```

IEEE_SUPPORT_SQRT([X]): This function returns true if the SQRT function has been implemented according to the IEEE standard for same type kind variable X, it is false otherwise.

```
IF (IEEE_SUPPORT_SQRT (X))THEN
 PRINT *, 'SQRT has been implemented according to IEEE standard'
ELSE
 PRINT *, 'SQRT has been NOT implemented according to IEEE standard'
ENDIF
```

IEEE_SUPPORT_STANDARD([X]): This function returns true if all inquiry functions mentioned earlier, namely,

```
IEEE_SUPPORT_DATATYPE
IEEE_SUPPORT_DENORMAL
IEEE_SUPPORT_DIVIDE
IEEE_SUPPORT_FLAG (for every valid flag)
IEEE_SUPPORT_HALTING (for every valid flag)
IEEE_SUPPORT_INF
IEEE_SUPPORT_NAN
IEEE_SUPPORT_ROUNDING(for every round value)
IEEE_SUPPORT_SQRT
```

return true. It returns false otherwise.

```
IF (IEEE_SUPPORT_STANDARD (X)) THEN
  PRINT *, 'Follows IEEE standard fully'
ELSE
  PRINT *, 'Does not fully support IEEE standard'
ENDIF
```

IEEE_SUPPORT_UNDERFLOW_CONTROL([X]): This is available only in Fortran 2003. It returns true if the processor supports underflow control mode for variables of same kind type as X. It returns false otherwise. At the time of writing no compiler supports this feature.

IEEE_SUPPORT_IO([X]): This function returns true if the processor supports base conversion (described as IEEE_UP, IEEE_DOWN, IEEE_ZERO and IEEE_NEAREST) during formatted input/output. IBM XL Fortran compiler supports this feature.

```
IF (IEEE_SUPPORT_IO(X)) THEN
  PRINT *, 'Supports base conversion'
ELSE
  PRINT *, 'Does not support base conversion'
ENDIF
```

20.14 IEEE_CLASS

This function returns the class of the variable used as its argument. The result is of derived type IEEE_CLASS_TYPE defined in the IEEE_ARITHMETIC module. The result is of one of the following:

```
IEEE_SIGNALING_NAN
IEEE_QUIET_NAN
IEEE_NEGATIVE_INF
IEEE_POSITIVE_INF
IEEE_NEGATIVE_NORMAL
IEEE_NEGATIVE_DENORMAL
IEEE_NEGATIVE_ZERO
```

```
            IEEE_POSITIVE_ZERO
            IEEE_POSITIVE_DENORMAL
            IEEE_POSITIVE_NORMAL
            IEEE_OTHER_VALUE

   USE IEEE_ARITHMETIC
   TYPE (IEEE_CLASS_TYPE) :: RES
   REAL :: R=20.0
   RES=IEEE_CLASS(R)
   IF (RES == IEEE_POSITIVE_NORMAL) THEN
     PRINT *, 'Positive normal'
   ELSE
     PRINT *, 'Not Positive normal'
   ENDIF
   END
```

Since R is a positive number, the "THEN" path will be followed and the PRINT statement with 'Positive normal' will be executed. If R is changed to -20.0, the RES will not be equal to IEEE_POSITIVE_NORMAL and as such the "ELSE" path will be followed.

20.15 IEEE_COPY_SIGN

This function takes two arguments, X and Y (both real). It returns the absolute value of X with the sign of Y.

```
   USE IEEE_ARITHMETIC
   REAL :: A=5.0, B=-10.0
   IF (IEEE_SUPPORT_DATATYPE(A).AND.&
       IEEE_SUPPORT_DATATYPE(B)) THEN
     A=IEEE_COPY_SIGN(A,B)
   ENDIF
   PRINT *, 'A = ', A, 'B = ', B
   END
```

The value of A will be absolute value of A with the sign of B, that is, -5.0

20.16 IEEE_VALUE

This intrinsic takes two arguments – the first one X is a real variable and the second one is of type IEEE_CLASS_TYPE. It returns a real of the same kind type as X with the value set by the second argument.

```
   USE IEEE_ARITHMETIC
   REAL :: R
   R=IEEE_VALUE(R, IEEE_POSITIVE_INF)
   PRINT *, R
   END
```

The variable R is set to IEEE positive infinity. The PRINT statement will display Infinity.

20.17 IEEE_IS_FINITE

This function takes a real argument. If returns true if the value of the argument is finite, that is, it is neither IEEE infinity nor IEEE NaN. If the argument is not finite it returns false.

```
USE IEEE_ARITHMETIC
REAL :: X=-27
IF (IEEE_SUPPORT_DATATYPE(X)) THEN
 IF(IEEE_IS_FINITE(X)) THEN
   PRINT *, 'X is a finite number'
 ELSE
   PRINT *, 'X is not a finite number'
 ENDIF
ENDIF
END
```

In this case X is a finite number.

20.18 IEEE_IS_NAN

This function takes one real argument and tests whether the value of the argument is NaN. It returns true if the argument is a NaN and returns false otherwise.

```
USE IEEE_ARITHMETIC
REAL :: R
R=IEEE_VALUE(R, IEEE_QUIET_NAN)
IF (IEEE_IS_NAN(R)) THEN
   PRINT *, 'It is a NaN'
ELSE
   PRINT *, 'It is NOT a NaN'
ENDIF
PRINT *, R
END
```

Note that PRINT *, R displays - It is a NaN.

20.19 IEEE_IS_NEGATIVE

This function takes one real argument. It returns true if the argument is a negative number, otherwise it returns false.

```
USE IEEE_ARITHMETIC
REAL :: R=-10
IF (IEEE_IS_NEGATIVE(R)) THEN
   PRINT *, 'It is a negative number'
ELSE
   PRINT *, 'It is NOT a negative number'
ENDIF
END
```

If the value of R is set to negative infinity, still the number is considered to be a negative number.

```
USE IEEE_ARITHMETIC
REAL :: R
R=IEEE_VALUE(R, IEEE_NEGATIVE_INF)
IF (IEEE_IS_NEGATIVE(R)) THEN
   PRINT *, 'It is a negative number'
ELSE
   PRINT *, 'It is NOT a negative number'
ENDIF
END
```

In the above case the "THEN" path of the IF statement will be followed, as the processor considers minus Infinity as negative number. Also if R is set to IEEE_NEGATIVE_ZERO, IEEE_IS_NEGATIVE treats the number as negative number.

20.20 IEEE_IS_NORMAL

A real variable is considered to be normal if it belongs to one of the following categories:

```
IEEE_POSITIVE_NORMAL
IEEE_NEGATIVE_NORMAL
IEEE_POSITIVE_ZERO
IEEE_NEGATIVE_ZERO

USE IEEE_ARITHMETIC
REAL :: R
R=IEEE_VALUE(R, IEEE_POSITIVE_INF)
IF (IEEE_IS_NORMAL(R)) THEN
   PRINT *, 'R is a normal number'
ELSE
   PRINT *, 'R is NOT a normal number'
ENDIF
END
```

Since the value of R is IEEE_POSITIVE_INF, the "ELSE" path of the IF statement will be chosen.

20.21 IEEE_LOGB

This function takes one real number as argument and returns the unbiased exponent.
Case I: If the value is neither infinity nor NaN, the returned value is unbiased exponent.
Case II: If X=0, the result is negative infinity and the flag IEEE_DIVIDE_BY_ZERO is set.
Case III: If X=NaN, the result is also NaN.
Case IV: If X is either +infinity or -infinity, the result is +infinity.

Assuming one instruction (which will be discussed shortly) that allows the program to continue even if divide by zero occurs, the following program allows us to test all the cases mentioned above.

```
USE IEEE_ARITHMETIC
REAL :: R, E
CALL IEEE_SET_HALTING_MODE(IEEE_ALL, .FALSE.)! assume NOW
READ *,R
E=IEEE_LOGB(R)
PRINT *, E
END
```

20.22 IEEE_NEXT_AFTER

This function takes two arguments X and Y (both real) and returns the next representable neighbor of X according to the direction of Y. A positive Y indicates the neighbor to the right (greater than X) and a negative Y indicates the neighbor to the left (less than X).
Case I: If X is equal to Y, the result is same as X and no exception flags are signaled.
Case II: When X is not equal to Y, the intrinsic returns the next representable neighbor of X, the direction being determined by the sign of Y. IEEE_OVERFLOW and IEEE_INEXACT flags are signaled when X is finite but IEEE_NEXT_AFTER(X,Y) is infinite. The flags IEEE_UNDERFLOW and IEEE_INEXACT are signaled when IEEE_NEXT_AFTER(X,Y) is either zero or denormalized.
Case III: If X or Y is quiet NaN, the result is one of the input NaN values.

20.23 IEEE_REM

This is a remainder function independent of rounding mode. It takes two real arguments, X and Y. The function returns X–Y*N where the integer N is the nearest to the exact value of X/Y satisfying the condition:

$$ABS(N - X/Y) = 1/2, N \text{ is even.}$$

```
USE IEEE_ARITHMETIC
PRINT *, IEEE_REM(5.0, 3.0)    ! prints -1
PRINT *, IEEE_REM(4.0, 3.0)    ! prints 1
PRINT *, IEEE_REM(3.0, 2.0)    ! prints 1
PRINT *, IEEE_REM(4.0, 2.0)    ! prints 0
END
```

20.24 IEEE_SCALB

This intrinsic takes two arguments, real X and integer I. It returns a real of the same kind type as X whose value is (2**I)*X. If X is finite but X*(2**I) exceeds the capacity of the machine, the overflow flag is signaled and result is infinity with the sign of X. If X*(2**I) is too small, underflow flag is set and the result is nearest representable number with the sign of X. If X is infinite, the result is X, but no exception flags are set.

```
USE IEEE_ARITHMETIC
PRINT *, IEEE_SCALB(2.0,2)        ! 8.0
PRINT *, IEEE_SCALB(5.0,3)        ! 40.0
PRINT *, IEEE_SCALB(-2.0,2)       ! -8.0
PRINT *, IEEE_SCALB(-5.0,2)       ! -20.0
END
```

20.25 IEEE_GET_ROUNDING_MODE

This subroutine takes a variable of type IEEE_ROUND_TYPE as its argument. It returns the current rounding mode. The rounding mode can be of one of the following type:

```
IEEE_NEAREST
IEEE_TO_ZERO
IEEE_UP
IEEE_DOWN
IEEE_OTHER (for other mode)

USE IEEE_ARITHMETIC
TYPE (IEEE_ROUND_TYPE) :: ROUND
CALL IEEE_GET_ROUNDING_MODE(ROUND)
IF (ROUND==IEEE_NEAREST) THEN
  PRINT *, 'Nearest'
ELSE IF (ROUND==IEEE_TO_ZERO) THEN
  PRINT *, 'To zero'
ELSE IF (ROUND==IEEE_UP) THEN
  PRINT*, 'Up'
ELSE IF (ROUND==IEEE_DOWN) THEN
  PRINT *, 'Down'
ELSE IF (ROUND==IEEE_OTHER) THEN
  PRINT *, 'Other'
ENDIF
END
```

In this case the PRINT statement displays 'Nearest' because this is the default-rounding mode.

20.26 IEEE_SET_ROUNDING_MODE

This subroutine also takes one argument of type IEEE_ROUND_TYPE and sets the rounding mode to one of the permitted values, that is, IEEE_NEAREST, IEEE_TO_ZERO, IEEE_UP or IEEE_DOWN.

```
USE IEEE_ARITHMETIC
TYPE (IEEE_ROUND_TYPE) :: ROUND
CALL IEEE_SET_ROUNDING_MODE(IEEE_UP)

CALL IEEE_GET_ROUNDING_MODE(ROUND)
IF (ROUND == IEEE_UP) THEN
  PRINT *, 'IEEE_UP'
ELSE
  PRINT *, 'IEEE_UP not set'
ENDIF

END
```

In this case the program segment displays 'IEEE_UP' because the rounding mode is set to IEEE_UP.

20.27 IEEE_RINT

This function takes one real variable X as its argument and rounds according to the current mode of rounding. The returned value is of same kind type as X. If X is either infinity or NaN, it returns infinity or NaN.

```
USE IEEE_ARITHMETIC
CALL IEEE_SET_ROUNDING_MODE(IEEE_NEAREST)
PRINT *, IEEE_RINT(2.3)

CALL IEEE_SET_ROUNDING_MODE(IEEE_UP)
PRINT *, IEEE_RINT(2.3)

CALL IEEE_SET_ROUNDING_MODE(IEEE_TO_ZERO)
PRINT *, IEEE_RINT(5.99)

CALL IEEE_SET_ROUNDING_MODE(IEEE_DOWN)
PRINT *, IEEE_RINT(8.93)

PRINT *, IEEE_RINT(-0.1)

END
```

The outputs are 2.0, 3.0, 5.0, 8.0 and -1.0 respectively.

20.28 IEEE_UNORDERED

This function takes two real arguments, X and Y. It returns true if X or Y or both are NaN, otherwise it is false.

```
USE IEEE_ARITHMETIC
REAL :: X, Y=0.0
X=IEEE_VALUE(X,IEEE_QUIET_NAN)
PRINT *, IEEE_UNORDERED(X,Y)

END
```

The result returned is true as X is NaN.

20.29 IEEE_GET_HALTING_MODE

This subroutine takes two arguments, the first one is of type IEEE_FLAG_TYPE and the second one is logical. The logical is true if the exception specified by the first argument would cause halting, otherwise it is false.

```
LOGICAL ::L
     .
CALL IEEE_GET_HALTING_MODE(IEEE_OVERFLOW, L)
```

If L is true, arithmetic overflow would halt the program, if it is false, the program would not terminate in case of arithmetic overflow. The default values of these flags for the NAG compiler are:

```
IEEE_OVERFLOW             = .TRUE.
IEEE_DIVIDE_BY_ZERO       = .TRUE.
IEEE_INVALID              = .TRUE.
IEEE_UNDERFLOW            = .FALSE.
IEEE_INEXACT              = .FALSE.
```

For IBM XL compiler the default values are all false.

20.30 IEEE_SET_HALTING_MODE

This subroutine can set or reset the halting mode. It takes two parameters, the first one is of type IEEE_FLAG_TYPE and the second one is logical. If the logical halting parameter is true, the program will halt when the exception corresponding to the flag occurs. If the logical parameter is false, the program does not stop when the exception corresponding to the flag occurs.

Program will not terminate when the divide by zero takes place if the following instruction is executed before the flag is set.

```
CALL IEEE_SET_HALTING_MODE(IEEE_DIVIDE_BY_ZERO, .FALSE.)
```

All halting modes can also be set or reset by a single instruction:

```
CALL IEEE_SET_HALTING_MODE(IEEE_ALL, .FALSE.) ! Reset
CALL IEEE_SET_HALTING_MODE(IEEE_ALL, .TRUE.)  ! set
```

20.31 IEEE_GET_STATUS and IEEE_SET_STATUS

These two subroutines take a single argument of type IEEE_STATUS_TYPE.

The IEEE_GET_STATUS gets the current value of the floating point status and the IEEE_SET_STATUS restores the floating point status. An example will make this point clear.

```
      USE IEEE_ARITHMETIC
      TYPE (IEEE_STATUS_TYPE) :: STAT
      CALL IEEE_GET_STATUS(STAT)
!       floating status is stored in STAT

      CALL IEEE_SET_FLAG(IEEE_ALL, .FALSE.) ! flags are changed
      .

      CALL IEEE_SET_STATUS(STAT) ! flags are restored

      END
```

The call to the subroutine IEEE_GET_STATUS stores the floating point status in the variable STAT. IEEE_SET_FLAG changes the floating point status. After the calculations are over, the original status is restored through the call to the subroutine IEEE_SET_STATUS.

20.32 IEEE_GET_FLAG and IEEE_SET_FLAG

Both these subroutines take two arguments – the first one is FLAG of type IEEE_FLAG_TYPE (intent IN). The second argument FLAGVALUE is a logical variable having intent OUT.

The subroutine IEEE_GET_FLAG returns the status of FLAG – true if it is set, false if it is not set.

```
      CALL IEEE_GET_FLAG(IEEE_OVERFLOW, FLAGVALUE)
```

If overflow flag is signaling, FLAGVALUE is true, if it is not signaling FLAGVALUE is false.

The subroutine IEEE_SET_FLAG can be called if IEEE_SUPPORT_HALTING(FLAG) is true. The FLAGVALUE, true, sets the corresponding flag to signaling mode and false sets the corresponding flag to non-signaling mode.

```
      CALL IEEE_SET_FLAG(IEEE_DIVIDE_BY_ZERO, .FALSE.)
```

This call will make the DIVIDE_BY_ZERO flag non-signaling.

The following example shows the use of IEEE_GET_FLAG, IEEE_SET_FLAG.

```
      PROGRAM FLAG
      USE IEEE_ARITHMETIC
      LOGICAL, DIMENSION(5):: FV

      CALL IEEE_GET_FLAG(IEEE_ALL,FV)
      PRINT *, 'Initial status : ', FV
```

```
CALL IEEE_SET_FLAG(IEEE_DIVIDE_BY_ZERO,.TRUE.)
CALL IEEE_GET_FLAG(IEEE_ALL,FV)
PRINT *, 'Status after modification : ',FV
END
```

The outputs of the program are:

```
Initial status : F F F F F
Status after modification : F T F F F
```

20.33 IEEE_GET_UNDERFLOW_MODE and IEEE_SET_UNDERFLOW_MODE

Both these subroutines take a logical variable as its argument. For the first one, that is, IEEE_GET_UNDERFLOW_MODE, if the returned value is true, the present underflow mode is gradual. If it is false, the present underflow mode is abrupt. For IEEE_SET_UNDERFLOW_MODE if the argument is true, gradual underflow is set; if it is false gradual underflow is removed. At the time of writing, no Fortran compiler supports these features.

20.34 IEEE_SELECTED_REAL_KIND

This function takes two integers, P and R as its argument. At least one argument must be specified. The result is a kind parameter (integer) for the IEEE real data type having decimal precision at least P digits and an exponent R.

If no kind parameter corresponding to 'P' is available, it returns -1; if kind corresponding to 'R' is not available it returns -2; if kind corresponding to both 'P' and 'R' are not available, it returns -3. If more than one kind parameter is supported the kind parameter corresponding to smallest decimal precision is returned.

```
USE IEEE_ARITHMETIC
INTEGER :: S
S=IEEE_SELECTED_REAL_KIND(6,35)
PRINT *, S

S=IEEE_SELECTED_REAL_KIND(12)
PRINT *, S

S=IEEE_SELECTED_REAL_KIND(12,400)
PRINT *, S

S=IEEE_SELECTED_REAL_KIND(50,300)
PRINT *,S

S=IEEE_SELECTED_REAL_KIND(12,300)
PRINT *,S

S=IEEE_SELECTED_REAL_KIND(50,400)
PRINT *,S
```

```
S=IEEE_SELECTED_REAL_KIND(P=6)
PRINT *, S

END
```

The output are: 1, 2, -2, -1, 2, -3, 1 respectively.

20.35 Programming Examples

The following program shows transition of a number from "normal" to a "denormal" when the number is repeatedly divided by 10.0; it ultimately becomes zero.

```
USE IEEE_ARITHMETIC

REAL :: X=10.0
DO
IF (X.EQ.0.0) THEN
  STOP 'ZERO REACHED'
ENDIF

IF(IEEE_IS_NORMAL(X)) THEN
  PRINT *, X, ' NORMAL'
ELSE
  PRINT *, X, ' DENORMAL'
ENDIF
X=X/10.0
ENDDO
END
```

The last line of the output is "1.4012985E-45 Denormal". Readers are advised to run this program to have a feeling for the denormal number.

The second program demonstrates the use of Floating Overflow. It calculates factorial and after the calculation, check is made for overflow. The program is exited when overflow occurs. However, at the beginning of the program halting due to overflow is disabled and the "control" is given to the programmer.

```
USE IEEE_ARITHMETIC
!        Calculation of factorial 1,2,3,4 .....
REAL :: F1, F2
INTEGER :: N=2
LOGICAL::FLAG
IF(.NOT. (IEEE_SUPPORT_HALTING(IEEE_OVERFLOW))) THEN
  PRINT *, &
    'Program termination cannot be controlled&
    & by overflow condition'
  STOP
ENDIF
```

```
     CALL IEEE_SET_HALTING_MODE(IEEE_OVERFLOW, .FALSE.)
!       Job will not be aborted when overflow occurs
     F1=1.0
     F2=F1
     DO
      F1=N*F1   ! 1x2x3x4.....

      CALL IEEE_GET_FLAG(IEEE_OVERFLOW, FLAG)
       IF(FLAG)THEN
         EXIT ! exit when there is overflow, last valid factorial
              ! is printed
       ENDIF
      F2=F1   ! F2 contains the last valid result
      N=N+1
     ENDDO
     PRINT *, 'Factorial upto ', N-1, ' is possible, Value ... ', F2

     END
```

The output of the program is:

```
Factorial upto 34 is possible, Value ... 2.95232328E+38
```

The output tells that this particular processor can calculate upto factorial 34 (normal precision). The processor flags overflow (if it is signaling) if an attempt is made to calculate factorial 35.

The next program shows a method to prevent program termination due to an invalid arithmetic operation. The example calls the library function square root (SQRT) with a negative real number as its argument.

```
     USE IEEE_ARITHMETIC
     REAL:: X,Y
     X=-4.0
     CALL IEEE_SET_HALTING_MODE(IEEE_INVALID, .FALSE.)
     Y=SQRT(X)
     PRINT *, Y
     END
```

Square root of a real negative number is an invalid arithmetic operation. If the call to the subroutine IEEE_SET_HALTING_MODE(IEEE_INVALID, .FALSE.) is initiated with the first parameter as IEEE_INVALID and the second parameter as .FALSE. the job will not be aborted when the statement Y=SQRT(X) is executed with negative real number as argument. It is, of course, the responsibility of the programmer to handle such a situation. The PRINT statement will display NaN. Note that the program will be aborted with "Arithmetic Exception" if the call to the subroutine is removed because the default action is "abort".

Chapter 21

DYNAMIC MEMORY MANAGEMENT

Dynamic Memory Management, i.e., managing the memory during the execution of a program, is one of the new features of the Fortran language. It was mentioned in chapter 11 that the size of the array is to be declared at compilation time and, therefore, if the array-size changes from one run to another, it is necessary to re-compile the program with this changed value of the array-size; the alternative is to define an array of sufficiently large size so that the program can handle all kinds of problems. The first one is clearly not convenient and the second one sometimes may block a large amount of memory even when the requirement is small. Fortran allows an array to be 'allocatable' and thus its size may be specified during the execution of the program. This enables it to grab memory dynamically and release the same to the system when it is no longer required.

The second important addition to Fortran is the use of Pointer. A Pointer is a variable, which during execution can 'point' to another variable. The pointer becomes the 'alias' of such a variable. The pointer may change this association dynamically and thereby a pointer may 'point' to different variables during the execution of a program.

21.1 Allocatable Array

An array can be declared 'allocatable' by specifying only the rank. The size of the array is specified during the execution.

```
INTEGER, ALLOCATABLE, DIMENSION(:) :: A
```

This declares A as an allocatable array of rank 1. The size of the array is specified later through ALLOCATE statement.

```
ALLOCATE(A(1000))
```

Memory locations sufficient to store 1000 such A are obtained from the system through this ALLOCATE statement. The array is then accessed in the usual manner. The argument of ALLOCATE need not be constant. It may be a variable or even an expression.

```
READ *, N
  .
ALLOCATE (A(N))
ALLOCATE (A(2*N+1000))
```

While allocating an array, both the lower and upper bounds can be specified. Of course, the lower bound is 1, if it is not specified.

```
ALLOCATE (A(0:1999))
```

The subscript of A may vary between 0 and 1999.

The following are examples of allocatable arrays of rank more than 1. The ranks are specified by colons separated by a comma.

```
        REAL, ALLOCATABLE, DIMENSION(:,:) :: B
!         2-D allocatable array
        REAL, ALLOCATABLE, DIMENSION(:,:,:) :: C
!         3-D allocatable array
```

These allocatable arrays are given memory locations with the ALLOCATE statement.

```
        ALLOCATE (B(100,100))
        ALLOCATE (B(0:99,0:99))
        ALLOCATE (B(-10:10,10:20))
        ALLOCATE (C(5,5,5))
        ALLOCATE (C(0:5,-1:10,10:20))
        ALLOCATE (C(0:5,10,20))
```

As the maximum rank of an array is seven, there can be no more than seven colons in the allocatable statement shown above.

Two or more allocatable variables may be allocated locations by a single ALLOCATE statement.

```
        ALLOCATE (A(1000),B(10,10))
```

Some compilers do not allow the following statements:

```
        ALLOCATE (A(1000), B(SIZE(A),SIZE(A)))
```

This is possible, if the ALLOCATE statement is broken into two ALLOCATE statements.

```
        ALLOCATE (A(1000))
        ALLOCATE (B(SIZE(A),SIZE(A)))
```

If, for some reason, the ALLOCATE statement fails to allocate locations, the job is aborted. This can be prevented, if a 'status variable'

$$STAT = integer\text{-}variable$$

is used with the ALLOCATE statement, where *integer-variable* is set to zero if the system could assign the requisite number of locations mentioned in the ALLOCATE statement; it returns non-zero if the requisite number of locations cannot be made available to the program. If STAT is used, the program continues even if the system fails to allocate the requisite number of locations. It is the responsibility of the programmer to take necessary action, should such a situation arise.

```
ALLOCATE (A(10000), STAT=ISTAT)
.
IF(ISTAT .EQ. 0) THEN
!              locations allocated
ELSE
!              locations not allocated
ENDIF
```

If more than one variable is assigned locations through a single allocate statement, the status indicates the results of all allocations together.

```
ALLOCATE (A(10000), B(10), STAT=ISTAT)
```

Successful execution of allocate statement sets ISTAT to zero. Unsuccessful execution of ALLOCATE statement sets ISTAT to a processor dependent positive integer. The status variable cannot be allocated in the same ALLOCATE statement.

Allocated array may be of size zero. Also once an array is allocated, it cannot be allocated again without first deallocating the array.

ALLOCATE with the SOURCE attribute is used to produce a 'clone'. In the example given below the allocated array A gets the values of the elements from the array B.

```
INTEGER, ALLOCATABLE,  DIMENSION(:)::A
INTEGER, DIMENSION(5)::B=[1,2,3,4,5]
ALLOCATE(A(5), SOURCE=B)
PRINT *,A
END
```

The PRINT statement will display 1 2 3 4 5.

The extents of the array A and B must be same. For example the following statements

```
ALLOCATE(A(3), SOURCE=B)
ALLOCATE(A(10), SOURCE=B)
```

are not acceptable.

21.2 DEALLOCATE

The allocated arrays may return locations back to the system by the DEALLOCATE statement.

```
DEALLOCATE(A)
DEALLOCATE(A,B)
```

Once an array is deallocated, the array is no longer available and if the variable is allocated again, old values do not reappear.

Like the ALLOCATE statement, unsuccessful deallocation causes the job to be terminated. Again, the STAT = *integer-variable* may be used to monitor the status of the deallocation process. Successful deallocation causes the integer variable to be returned with zero; unsuccessful deallocation sets the integer variable to be returned with a processor dependent positive value. Note that, if STAT is present, the job is not aborted even if system fails to deallocate an array. The integer variable associated with STAT cannot be deallocated in the same DEALLOCATE statement.

21.3 ALLOCATED Intrinsic

This intrinsic is used to test whether an allocatable array has been allocated by ALLOCATE statement. This intrinsic returns true if the array has been allocated, otherwise it returns false.

```
        IF (ALLOCATED(A)) THEN
!               A has been allocated
        ELSE
!               A has not been allocated
        ENDIF

        IF(ALLOCATED(A)) THEN
          DEALLOCATE(A)
        ENDIF
```

21.4 Derived Type and Allocate

Like the standard variables a user defined type variable may be an allocated array.

```
    TYPE MYTYPE
      INTEGER::A
      REAL::B
    END TYPE MYTYPE

    TYPE(MYTYPE),ALLOCATABLE,DIMENSION(:)::C
    ALLOCATE(C(2)) ! note this statement
    C(1)%A=2
    C(1)%B=2.5
    C(2)%A=10
    C(2)%B=10.5
    PRINT *,C(1)%A,C(1)%B
    PRINT *,C(2)%A,C(2)%B
    DEALLOCATE(C)
    END
```

The elementary items of a user defined variable may also be an allocated array:

```
TYPE MYTYPE
 INTEGER::A
 REAL::B
 INTEGER,ALLOCATABLE,DIMENSION(:)::E
END TYPE MYTYPE

TYPE(MYTYPE),ALLOCATABLE,DIMENSION(:)::C
ALLOCATE(C(2))
ALLOCATE(C(1)%E(2))
ALLOCATE(C(2)%E(3))
C(1)%A=2
C(1)%B=2.5
C(2)%A=10
C(2)%B=10.5
C(1)%E(1)=27
C(1)%E(2)=37
C(2)%E(3)=100
PRINT *,C(1)%A,C(1)%B
PRINT *,C(2)%A,C(2)%B
PRINT *,C(1)%E(1),C(1)%E(2)
PRINT *,C(2)%E(3)
END
```

The variable C is an allocatable array of rank 1. It has been allocated and its size has become 2. It contains an integer allocatable elementary item. This has been allocated individually for C(1) and C(2). The elementary items corresponding to C(1) are C(1)%E(1) and C(1)%E(2) and corresponding to C(2) are C(2)%E(1), C(2)%E(2) and C2%E(3).

21.5 Allocated Array and Subprogram

The local variable of a subprogram may be an allocated array. On exit from the subprogram, the locations are lost. Moreover, when the subprogram is entered again, the locations allocated earlier are not available to the program. This is illustrated with an example.

```
PROGRAM ALLOC_DEMO
INTEGER :: I
DO I=1,2
CALL SUB(I)
 .
ENDDO
END PROGRAM ALLOC_DEMO

SUBROUTINE SUB(I)
INTEGER :: I
INTEGER, ALLOCATABLE, DIMENSION(:) :: A
IF(I.EQ.1) THEN
 ALLOCATE(A(5))
```

```
      A=[1,2,3,4,5]
      ENDIF
      PRINT *, A
      END SUBROUTINE SUB
```

When the subprogram is entered for the first time, locations are allocated – the PRINT statement works correctly. When the subroutine is entered for the second time with I=2 the PRINT statement tries to access an array which is not available and therefore, it is not legal. In the earlier version of Fortran (Fortran 90), if the local array is not deallocated explicitly, it used to create problems. Let us see what happens when the IF statement of the subprogram is removed and the number of times the DO loop to be executed is increased in the main program (assume that the earlier version of Fortran compiler is being used).

```
      DO I=1,10000
      CALL SUB(I)
      ENDDO
      END

      SUBROUTINE SUB(I)
      INTEGER :: I
!        I is not used
      INTEGER, ALLOCATABLE, DIMENSION(:) :: B
      ALLOCATE(B(10000))
      B(1)=100
      END SUBROUTINE SUB
```

Each time the subroutine is entered, B array is allocated. Since the B array is not deallocated in the subprogram, the locations, though unavailable on exit from the subroutine, are not released to the system – the locations remain attached somehow to the program without any facility of being accessed by the program. Each time the subroutine is called, fresh locations are assigned to B and unavailable locations allocated during the earlier call remain attached to the program. This goes on and the subroutine grabs memory locations in each call and does not release the same on exit from the subroutine and so more and more memory locations continue to get attached to the program. Ultimately, after several such calls, when no more locations can be allocated, the ALLOCATE statement within the subroutine fails and the job is aborted.

The present version of Fortran (Fortran 2003) automatically deallocates the allocated array on exit from the subprogram.

If the allocatable array is declared with SAVE attribute and allocated only once, the locations reappear with the last value on subsequent entry to the subroutine. The second method is to declare the allocatable array within a module and USE the module within the subroutine. Allocatable arrays declared within a module are not released when the subroutine is exited. Both these methods are illustrated below.

Method I: Allocatable array is declared with SAVE attribute

```
INTEGER :: I
DO I=1,100
CALL SUB(I)
ENDDO
END

SUBROUTINE SUB(I)
INTEGER::I
INTEGER, ALLOCATABLE, SAVE, DIMENSION(:) :: C
IF (I .EQ. 1) THEN
  ALLOCATE(C(5))
  C=[10,20,30,40,50]
ENDIF
PRINT *, C
END
```

The PRINT statement will not fail when the value of I is greater then 1 (it is assumed that the first call to the subroutine is executed with I = 1). This is due to the fact that because of the SAVE attribute the C array will reappear with its last value when the subroutine is entered again (I greater than 1). However, it is a fact that the C array is unavailable when the subroutine is exited.

Method II: The allocatable array is declared within a module so that the same array is available when the subroutine is entered again.

```
MODULE MYALLOC
INTEGER, ALLOCATABLE, DIMENSION(:) :: D
END MODULE MYALLOC

PROGRAM MAIN
INTEGER :: I
DO I=1, 100
CALL SUB(I)
ENDDO
END

SUBROUTINE SUB(I)
USE MYALLOC
INTEGER :: I
IF(I.EQ.1) THEN
  ALLOCATE(D(5))
  D=[100,200,300,400,500]
ENDIF
  .
END
```

21.6 Allocate and Dummy Parameter

An allocatable array may be a dummy argument of a subprogram. In such a case both the actual and the dummy parameter must be declared as an allocatable array with identical rank. The array is allocated either in the calling program or in the called program depending on the INTENT. Interface block must be present.

Case I: The INTENT is OUT. In this case, array is allocated within the subprogram.

```
PROGRAM CASEI
INTEGER, ALLOCATABLE, DIMENSION(:) ::A
INTERFACE
   SUBROUTINE SUB(A)
   INTEGER, INTENT (OUT), ALLOCATABLE, DIMENSION(:)::A
   END
END INTERFACE

CALL SUB(A)
PRINT *,A
DEALLOCATE (A)
END

SUBROUTINE SUB(B)
INTEGER, INTENT(OUT), ALLOCATABLE, DIMENSION(:) ::B
ALLOCATE (B(5))
B=[1,2,3,4,5]
END
```

The output is 1 2 3 4 5.

Case II: The INTENT is IN. In this case the array is allocated within the calling program.

```
PROGRAM CASEII
INTEGER, ALLOCATABLE, DIMENSION(:) :: A
INTERFACE
  SUBROUTINE SUB(A)
  INTEGER, INTENT(IN), ALLOCATABLE, DIMENSION(:) ::A
  END
END INTERFACE

ALLOCATE (A(5))
A=100
CALL SUB(A)
PRINT *, A
DEALLOCATE (A)
END

SUBROUTINE SUB(B)
INTEGER, INTENT(IN), ALLOCATABLE, DIMENSION(:) ::B
PRINT *, B
END
```

The outputs are:

```
100    100  100  100   100
100    100  100  100   100
```

Case III: The INTENT is INOUT. The array is allocated either in the calling or within the called program. Since the INTENT is INOUT, the array is supposed to carry some value from the calling program. This implies the array is allocated in the calling program. However, inspite of the fact that the INTENT is INOUT, if the array does not carry any input from the calling program, the array may be allocated within the called program. This is not proper; improper use of INTENT seems to be a bad programming practice.

```
PROGRAM CASEIII
INTEGER, ALLOCATABLE, DIMENSION(:) :: A
INTERFACE
  SUBROUTINE SUB(A)
  INTEGER, INTENT(INOUT), ALLOCATABLE, DIMENSION(:) ::A
  END
END INTERFACE

ALLOCATE (A(5))
A=100
CALL SUB(A)
PRINT *, A
DEALLOCATE (A)
END

SUBROUTINE SUB(B)
INTEGER, INTENT(INOUT), ALLOCATABLE, DIMENSION(:) ::B
PRINT *, B
B=[1,2,3,4,5]
END
```

The output is:

```
100  100   100   100   100
1     2     3     4     5
```

21.7 Character and Allocatable Arrays

Since the size of a character variable can be specified in the character declaration, allocatable character arrays need to be mentioned separately.

```
CHARACTER(LEN=30),ALLOCATABLE,DIMENSION(:)::CH
     .
ALLOCATE(CH(100))
```

The above ALLOCATE statement will allocate sufficient memory locations to accommodate a character array of size 100 with each element of size 30 characters.

Fortran 2003 allows specification of length of a character variable to be deferred and it can be allocated by ALLOCATE statement.

```
CHARACTER(:), ALLOCATABLE:: CH(:)
        .
        .
ALLOCATE(CHARACTER(10)::CH(20))
```

The array CH will have 20 elements, each having size of 10 characters. Similarly, the allocatable attribute may also be used with scalars.

```
CHARACTER(:), ALLOCATABLE ::C
        .
        .
ALLOCATE(CHARACTER(15)::C)
```

The variable C will have size of 15 characters.

These last two features are not supported by the present NAG compiler.

21.8 Allocatable Function

A function returns value through its name or through the RESULT clause. The result of the function may have an allocatable attribute. The following program demonstrates this feature.

```
PROGRAM MAIN
INTERFACE
  FUNCTION AC(X,N)
  REAL,ALLOCATABLE,DIMENSION(:)::AC ! note this declaration
  REAL,DIMENSION(:),INTENT(IN)::X
  INTEGER,INTENT(IN)::N
  END
END INTERFACE

REAL,ALLOCATABLE,DIMENSION(:)::Y,Z
REAL , PARAMETER::FAC=3.1415926/180.0 ! degree to radian
INTEGER::I,N
PRINT *,'Enter the value of N'
READ *,N
ALLOCATE(Y(N),Z(N))
DO I=1,N
   Y(I)=30.0*FAC*I    ! 30, 60, 90 degree etc.
ENDDO
PRINT *,SIN(Y)+COS(Y)
Z=AC(Y,N)
PRINT *,Z
END
```

```
FUNCTION AC(X,N)
REAL,ALLOCATABLE,DIMENSION(:)::AC
REAL,DIMENSION(:),INTENT(IN)::X
INTEGER,INTENT(IN)::N
ALLOCATE(AC(N))                     ! note this statement
AC=SIN(X)+COS(X)
END
```

The two PRINT statements should give identical result.

If the function returns the value through the RESULT clause, the above program is to be modified to take into account of this fact.

```
PROGRAM MAIN
INTERFACE
 FUNCTION AC(X,N) RESULT(RES)
 REAL,ALLOCATABLE,DIMENSION(:)::RES
 REAL,DIMENSION(:),INTENT(IN)::X
 INTEGER,INTENT(IN)::N
 END
END INTERFACE

REAL,ALLOCATABLE,DIMENSION(:)::Y,Z
REAL , PARAMETER::FAC=3.1415926/180.0
INTEGER::I,N
PRINT *,'Enter the value of N'
READ *,N
ALLOCATE(Y(N),Z(N))
DO I=1,N
   Y(I)=30.0*FAC*I
ENDDO
PRINT *,SIN(Y)+COS(Y)
Z=AC(Y,N)
PRINT *,Z
END

FUNCTION AC(X,N) RESULT (RES)
REAL,ALLOCATABLE,DIMENSION(:)::RES
REAL,DIMENSION(:),INTENT(IN)::X
INTEGER,INTENT(IN)::N
ALLOCATE (RES(N))
RES=SIN(X)+COS(X)
END
```

No explanation is, perhaps, needed for this program. This also calculates $SIN(X)+COS(X)$ for N values and returns the values through the RESULT clause. The present version of Fortran is capable of allocating automatically the correct size of variable Z depending upon the size of the returned array and would deliver the correct result if the statement ALLOCATE(Y(N),Z(N)) is replaced by ALLOCATE (Y(N)). The present author tested this with three different Fortran compilers and none seems to support this feature.

21.9 Allocation Transfer

The subroutine MOVE_ALLOC is used to 'move' allocation including the values of different locations from one array (FROM) to another array (TO). The syntax of MOVE_ALLOC is as shown below:

```
CALL MOVE_ALLOC(FROM, TO)
```

After the subroutine is called the 'FROM' array is deallocated; the 'TO' array is allocated obtaining all values from the corresponding locations of 'FROM' array.

```
REAL, ALLOCATABLE:: A(:), B(:)
ALLOCATE(A(10))
A(4)=100
CALL MOVE_ALLOC(A,B)
PRINT *, B(4)
END
```

The PRINT statement will display 100 because while moving the allocation, the subroutine has set B(4)=A(4). The GFORTRAN compiler supports this feature.

21.10 Restriction on Allocatable Arrays

The COMMON statement (chapter 19) works on the assumption that the storage is assigned in a sequential fashion and moreover the size of the COMMON block must be available during compilation. An allocatable array whose size will be available only during execution, therefore, cannot appear in a common block. However, this is not a serious limitation as different units may share locations through a module.

21.11 Solution of Linear Equation by Gauss Method

In this programming example a 3x3 linear simultaneous equation will be solved by the Gauss method. This method solves linear simultaneous equation by setting elements below the diagonal to zero by arithmetic manipulation. If the equations are:

$$a_{11}x_1 + a_{12}x_2 + a_{13}x_3 = b_1 \tag{1}$$
$$a_{21}x_1 + a_{22}x_2 + a_{23}x_3 = b_2 \tag{2}$$
$$a_{31}x_1 + a_{32}x_2 + a_{33}x_3 = b_3 \tag{3}$$

By arithmetic manipulation this can be changed to:

$$a_{11}x_1 + a_{12}x_2 + a_{13}x_3 = c_1 \tag{4}$$
$$d_{22}x_2 + d_{23}x_3 = c_2 \tag{5}$$
$$d_{33}x_3 = c_3 \tag{6}$$

From equation (6) one can get x_3 and substituting this value in (5) the value of x_2 is obtained from (5). Having obtained the value of x_2 and x_3, it is easy to find the value of x_1 from (4).

The program below uses ALLOCATE, DEALLOCATE, MAXLOC and MAXVAL. Any standard text book on Numerical Method may be consulted for the Gauss' algorithm.

```fortran
PROGRAM GAUSSTEST
REAL, DIMENSION(3,4)::A
REAL, DIMENSION(3)::X
INTERFACE
  SUBROUTINE GAUSS(A,X,N,NP1)
  REAL,INTENT(INOUT), DIMENSION(:,:)::A
  REAL,INTENT(OUT), DIMENSION(:)::X

  INTEGER, INTENT(IN):: N, NP1
  END SUBROUTINE GAUSS
END INTERFACE

! the equation is AX=B
! in the program the array A contains the actual array A plus
! the rightmost column contains B.
! the roots of the equation are returned through the array X


  A=RESHAPE([1,3,-1,1,2,1,1,7,1,5,32,1],[3,4])
  CALL GAUSS(A,X,3,4)
  PRINT *, X
END

SUBROUTINE GAUSS(A,X,N,NP1)
IMPLICIT NONE
INTEGER, INTENT(IN):: N, NP1

REAL,INTENT(INOUT), DIMENSION(:,:)::A
REAL,INTENT(OUT), DIMENSION(:)::X
REAL, DIMENSION(:), ALLOCATABLE:: T
REAL:: F,SUM
INTEGER::L, KP1,NM1,I,J,K, IP1
ALLOCATE(T(NP1))
NM1=N-1
DO K=1, NM1

! by arithmetic manipulation set the triangle below the diagonal
! to zero

  KP1=K+1

! largest element in each column
```

```fortran
      L=MAXVAL (MAXLOC (ABS (A (K:N,K))))+K-1
      IF(L.NE.K)  THEN

!   interchange the row if necessary

       T(K:NP1)=A(K,K:NP1)
       A(K,K:NP1)=A(L,K:NP1)
       A(L,K:NP1)=T(K:NP1)
      ENDIF
       DO I=KP1,N
       F=A(I,K)/A(K,K)
        DO J=KP1, NP1
        A(I,J)=A(I,J)-F*A(K,J)
         ENDDO
       ENDDO
      ENDDO

!  back substitution

       X(N)=A(N,NP1)/A(N,N)
       DO I = NM1,1,-1
        IP1=I+1
        SUM=0.0
         DO J=IP1,N
          SUM=SUM+A(I,J)*X(J)
         ENDDO
        X(I)=(A(I,NP1)-SUM)/A(I,I)
       ENDDO

      DEALLOCATE (T)
      RETURN
      END
```

The program is used to solve the following equations:

$$X+Y+Z=5$$
$$3X+2Y+7Z=32$$
$$-X+Y+Z=1$$

The roots of the equations are 2.0, -1.0, 4.0.

21.12 Pointer

A pointer is an object that is set to point to another object (variable, array, derived type etc.); it can dynamically associate itself with another object. When a variable is declared, the declaration informs the compiler about the variable and, if it is initialized, the initial value. For an array, its type, rank and size are specified. The compiler accordingly allocates enough memory for the object. The information about the object is called the descriptor which describes the object and memory locations that contain the value of the object. For a pointer variable only the descriptor without the memory location is specified and during the execution of the program it is made to point to a memory location. Also a pointer can dynamically change its association during the execution of the program.

A pointer must point to the right kind of object. For example, an integer pointer can point to an integer quantity and a real pointer must point to a real quantity. An integer pointer cannot point to a real quantity.

21.13 POINTER Declaration

A pointer is declared as shown below.

```
            INTEGER, POINTER :: IP
!              IP can point to an integer
            REAL, POINTER :: RP
!              RP can point to an real quantity
            CHARACTER(LEN=30), POINTER :: CP
!              CP is a character pointer
```

The pointer IP can point to an integer. Similarly, the pointer RP can point to a real quantity. The pointer CP can point to a character variable of length 30. It can, however, made to point 30 characters from a character variable having length greater than 30 characters.

21.14 TARGET

A pointer can point to a variable which has been declared with TARGET attribute.

```
            INTEGER, TARGET :: A, B
            REAL, TARGET :: R, S
            CHARACTER(LEN=30), TARGET :: C
```

If the variable has not been declared with TARGET attribute, a pointer cannot point to such a variable. A pointer can, however, point to another pointer.

21.15 Pointer Status

Pointer may exist in three different states:
- Undefined
- Null
- Associated

At the beginning of the program, pointers are all in the undefined state. In the null state, a pointer does not point to anything but it is not in an undefined state. In the associated state, the pointer points to some object.

21.16 Pointer Initialization

A pointer can be initialized to NULL along with its declaration.

```
REAL, POINTER :: RP=>NULL()
```

Pointers can be initialized through DATA statements also.

```
DATA RP/NULL()/
```

21.17 Pointer Assignment

The pointer IP, for instance, may be made to point to an integer variable through the pointer assignment. There is a special symbol for this purpose. It is equal sign followed by the greater than sign (=>).

```
IP => A
```

Now IP points to A. Thus now IP is an alias to A.

```
A = 2
```

and

```
IP =2
```

are same. Subsequently, IP may point to say B.

```
IP => B
```

At this moment IP becomes alias to B – it no longer points to A. However, this dissociation of the pointer with A does not disturb the value of A. Consider the following program segment:

```
INTEGER, POINTER :: IP, IQ
INTEGER, TARGET :: A=10, B=20
IP => A
IQ => B

IP = IQ
IQ => IP
```

After the first two statements are executed, IP points to A and IQ points to B. The statement

```
IP = IQ
```

is equivalent to

```
A = B
```

and both IP and IQ still point to A and B respectively. The final statement,

```
IQ => IP
```

forces the pointer IQ to point to A. Now both the Pointers point to A. Now consider the following program segment:

```
CHARACTER(LEN=5), POINTER :: CP
CHARACTER(LEN=18), TARGET :: CH = &
 &"Indian Association"

CP => CH            ! Not allowed
CP => CH(1:5)       ! Allowed
CP => CH(14:18)     ! Allowed
```

The first statement will give compilation error, as the size of the pointer and the Target are different. The second statement will make the pointer to point to the string "India". Finally, the last statement will make the pointer to point to the sting "ation". Following the same logic the following program segment will give compilation error.

```
INTEGER, PARAMETER :: S1=SELECTED_REAL_KIND(4,307)
INTEGER, PARAMETER :: S2=SELECTED_REAL_KIND(6,37)
INTEGER (KIND=S1), TARGET :: A=10.0
INTEGER (KIND=S2), POINTER :: IA
IA=>A               ! not same type
```

21.18 NULLIFY

This intrinsic is used to dissociate a pointer from a target.

```
NULLIFY(PA)
```

where PA is a pointer which was pointing to a target. After NULLIFY is executed, the pointer is not pointing to anything. It is in null state.

21.19 Pointer as Alias

A section of an array may be referred to with the help of a pointer. The pointer acts as an alias. Consider a 4x4 (rank 2) array.

1,1	1,2	1,3	1,4
2,1	**2,2**	**2,3**	2,4
3,1	**3,2**	**3,3**	3,4
4,1	4,2	4,3	4,3

Suppose it is necessary to access a section of the array marked with bold digits with a pointer.

```
INTEGER,TARGET,DIMENSION(4,4)::A
INTEGER,POINTER,DIMENSION(:,:)::PA
INTEGER::I,J
DO I=1,4
   DO J=1,4
     A(I,J)=10*I+J
   ENDDO
ENDDO
PRINT *,A

PA=>A(2:3,2:3)
PRINT *,PA
END
```

11	12	13	14
21	**22**	**23**	24
31	**32**	**33**	34
41	42	43	43

A-array

The outputs will be

```
11  21  31  41  12  22  32  42  13  23  33  43  14  24  34  44
22  32  23  33
```

The statement PA=>A(2:3, 2:3) makes the pointers to point to the array section such that,

```
PA (1,1) points to A (2,2)
PA (2,1) points to A (3,2)
PA (1,2) points to A (2,3)
PA (2,2) points to A (3,3)
```

As a result PRINT statement displays the content of the location A(2,2), A(3,2), A(2,3) and A(3,3).

21.20 ALLOCATE and POINTER

A pointer can be made to point to an object without the pointer assignment. This is done through ALLOCATE statement.

```
INTEGER, POINTER :: IP
        .
ALLOCATE (IP)
```

Now the system will allocate some memory location which can store only integers and which can be accessed through the pointer IP. There is no name attached to the location.

21.21 Pointers and Arrays

A pointer can point to an array of the right type. The pointer declaration must contain the rank of the target array.

```
INTEGER, POINTER, DIMENSION(:) :: PT
INTEGER, TARGET, DIMENSION(10) :: A
.
A = [1,2,3,4,5,6,7,8,9,10]
PT => A
```

The array elements may be accessed through PT(1), PT(2) .. etc.

21.22 Pointers and Allocatable Arrays

A pointer may point to an allocatable array.

```
INTEGER, ALLOCATABLE, TARGET, DIMENSION(:) :: A
INTEGER, POINTER, DIMENSION(:) :: AP
.
ALLOCATE(A(100))
AP => A
```

One hundred locations have been allocated to A and the pointer AP is made to point to A.
   A Pointer may be made to point to an unnamed array created by ALLOCATE statement.

```
INTEGER, POINTER, DIMENSION (:) :: IP
.
ALLOCATE(IP(100))
IP=200
.
```

The ALLOCATE statement creates an unnamed array of size 100 and the pointer points to that array. These locations are accessed through the pointer IP in the usual manner, that is, IP(1) will point to the first integer and so on.
   In array pointer assignment the lower bound may be set to any value. Consider the following program:

```
REAL, DIMENSION(-5:5), TARGET::A=100.0
REAL,POINTER:: P1(:),P2(:), P3(:)

P1=>A
P2=>A(-5:5)

PRINT *,LBOUND(P1), UBOUND(P1)
PRINT *,LBOUND(P2), UBOUND(P2)

END
```

The outputs of the program are:

```
-5 5
1 11
```

This indicates that the statement PA=>A set the lower and upper bound of P1 to -5 and 5 respectively. On the other hand, P2=>A(-5:5) sets the lower and upper bound of P2 to 1 and 11.

The statement:

$$P3(10:)=>A(-5:5)$$

should set the lower and upper bound of P3 to 10 and 20 respectively. However, the NAG compiler does not support this feature.

The target of a multidimensional array pointer could be a single dimensional array pointer.

```fortran
REAL, POINTER:: A(:), B(:,:), C(:)
INTEGER :: N=5, I

ALLOCATE(A(N*N)) ! n*n=25
A=[(I, I=1,25)]
B(1:N, 1:N)=> A        ! array elements are 1 to 25 columnwise
C=>A(1:N*N:N+1)
PRINT *, C
END
```

Readers may verify that the C array will contain the diagonal elements of B. Another way of writing the same statement is:

$$C=>A(::N+1)$$

where both the lower and the upper bound of A is replaced by colons (:).

21.23 DEALLOCATE – Pointer

Like an allocatable array, a pointer, IP, may be deallocated by DEALLOCATE statement.

```fortran
DEALLOCATE (IP)
```

21.24 Unreferenced Storage

Again consider the following program segment.

```fortran
INTEGER, POINTER, DIMENSION(:) :: PTR
        .
ALLOCATE(PTR(100))
```

If the pointer PTR is made to point to some other location or nullified, the memory locations created by the above ALLOCATE statement are not available afterwards; moreover these locations are not given back to the system – they remain 'hanging' within the program. The correct strategy would be to deallocate the pointer PTR first and subsequently modify its association with the target, set to null.

21.25 ASSOCIATED Intrinsic

This intrinsic tests for the association of a pointer with some target or some particular target. It returns TRUE if it is associated with a target or with a particular target, otherwise returns FALSE.

```
INTEGER, POINTER :: PA
INTEGER, TARGET :: A,B
PA=>A
```

Now,

```
ASSOCIATED (PA)
```

or,

```
ASSOCIATED(POINTER=PA, TARGET=A)
```

returns true. However,

```
ASSOCIATED(POINTER=PA, TARGET=B)
```

returns false as the pointer PA is not associated with the target B.

21.26 Dangling Pointer

Consider the following program segment :

```
INTEGER, POINTER :: PTR1, PTR2
       .
ALLOCATE(PTR1)
       .
PTR2 => PTR1
       .
```

The ALLOCATE statement allocates locations in memory which can be accessed through PTR1. The pointer assignment statement makes both PTR2 and PTR1 as alias of the same location. It PTR1 is deallocated and the location is returned to the system, the pointer PTR2 is still pointing to some non-existent location. So if PTR2 is used the result may be unpredictable. This is called 'dangling pointer'. One should set PT2 to null before deallocating the pointer PT1.

21.27 Pointer within Subprogram

Pointers declared within a subprogram become undefined on exit from the subprogram. This can be prevented if the pointer is declared with SAVE attribute.

```
REAL, POINTER, SAVE :: PTR
```

The SAVE attribute ensures that when the subprogram is entered for the second time, the pointer does not become undefined.

```
SUBROUTINE SUB(I)
INTEGER :: I
INTEGER, POINTER, SAVE :: PTR
     .
IF(I.EQ.1) THEN
  ALLOCATE(PTR)
  PTR=10
ENDIF
     .
PRINT *, PTR
     .
END
```

The pointer is allocated when the subroutine is entered for the first time (I=1). Subsequently, the subroutine is entered with the value of I not equal to one. This ensures that the condition for the IF statement is false. However, because of the SAVE attribute, the pointer allocated earlier reappears with its last value.

21.28 Pointer and Derived Type

A pointer may point to a derived type variable also.

```
TYPE EMP
  INTEGER :: ID
  CHARACTER(LEN=30) :: NAME
END TYPE EMP

TYPE(EMP), POINTER :: DTYPE
TYPE(EMP), TARGET :: EMPLOYEE
     .
DTYPE => EMPLOYEE
DTYPE%ID=100
DTYPE%NAME="Soumya Chakravarti"
```

Memory space may be created for a derived object through a pointer.

```
ALLOCATE(DTYPE)

DTYPE%ID=200
```

The ALLOCATE statement with a pointer DTYPE of type EMP will create space for one such object.

21.29 Self Referencing Pointer

A derived type may have an elementary item which can point to a variable of similar type (derived type).

```
TYPE EMP
  INTEGER :: ID
  CHARACTER(LEN=30) :: NAME
  TYPE(EMP), POINTER :: NEXT
END TYPE EMP
```

The elementary item NEXT is a pointer which can point to record of type EMP.

```
TYPE (EMP), TARGET :: E1, E2
E1%ID=10
E1%NAME="Some Name"
E2%ID=20
    .
E1%NEXT=>E2
```

The elementary item ID of E2 can be accessed as

```
E2%ID
```

or, with reference to E1, it is

```
E1%NEXT%ID
```

With this kind of facility one can easily build up a linked list.

21.30 Linked List (*)

We now give an example of doubly linked list. The logic of this program is slightly difficult. This section may be skipped during the first reading.

In a doubly linked list, each record has two referencing pointers. In our case they are PRIOR and NEXT. The PRIOR pointer points to the previous record and the next pointer points to the next record in the list. The PRIOR pointer corresponding to the first record is 'nullified' as there is no record before the first record. The NEXT pointer corresponding to the last record is also 'nullified' as there is no record after the last record. Two more pointers, START and LAST always point to the first and the last record respectively.

Records can be added to the list; also they can be deleted from the list. When a record is added, space is created in the memory for it and similarly, when a record is deleted, space is returned to the system. The adjustments of various pointers are taken care of by the program logic.

The module LINK_LIST contains the description of the record and the definition of the pointers START and LAST. The module is used by various subprograms.

```
MODULE LINK_LIST
TYPE ADDR
  CHARACTER(LEN=30)  ::  NAME
  CHARACTER(LEN=40)  ::  ADDRESS
  INTEGER :: PIN
  TYPE(ADDR), POINTER :: NEXT
  TYPE(ADDR), POINTER :: PRIOR
 END TYPE ADDR
TYPE(ADDR), POINTER :: START
TYPE(ADDR), POINTER :: LAST
END MODULE

!     The main program is L_LIST. Depending upon the input
!     it performs various operation, like - insertion, deletion,
!     listing and searching

      PROGRAM L_LIST
      USE LINK_LIST
      LOGICAL :: BOOL=.TRUE.
      INTEGER :: CHOICE
      NULLIFY(START)
      DO WHILE(BOOL)

!         Make a selection

      CALL MENU(CHOICE)
      SELECT CASE (CHOICE)
       CASE(1)

!         Insert record

      CALL ENTER
      CASE(2)

!         Delete record

      CALL DELREC
      CASE(3)

!         List records
```

```fortran
        CALL LIST
        CASE(4)

!          Search a name

        CALL SEARCH
        CASE(5)

!          Exit from the program

         BOOL=.FALSE.
         CASE DEFAULT
         PRINT *, "The input should be between 1 & 5"
        END SELECT
        ENDDO
        END PROGRAM L_LIST

!      This subprogram MENU displays a menu and reads an integer
!      from the keyboard

         SUBROUTINE MENU(CHOICE)
         INTEGER, INTENT(OUT) :: CHOICE
         PRINT *
         PRINT *, "********* MENU *********"
         PRINT *, "1. Enter a name"
         PRINT *, "2. Delete a name"
         PRINT *, "3. List the names"
         PRINT *, "4. Search a name"
         PRINT *, "5. Quit"
         PRINT *, "********* MENU *********"

         READ *, CHOICE
         END SUBROUTINE MENU

!      This Subroutine ENTER adds a record to the list and
!      '@' is typed as name the routine is exited.

         SUBROUTINE ENTER
         USE LINK_LIST
         TYPE(ADDR), POINTER :: INFO
         DO

!          Create a space for a record

         ALLOCATE(INFO)
         PRINT *
         PRINT *, "Enter Name"
         READ *, INFO%NAME
```

```fortran
       IF(INFO%NAME(1:1) .EQ. "@") THEN
        EXIT
       ENDIF
       PRINT *, "Enter Address"
       READ *, INFO%ADDRESS
       PRINT *, "Enter Pin"
       READ *, INFO%PIN
!         List not empty
       IF(ASSOCIATED(START)) THEN
        LAST%NEXT => INFO
        INFO%PRIOR => LAST
        LAST => INFO
        NULLIFY(LAST%NEXT)
       ELSE
!         List empty
        START => INFO
        NULLIFY(START%NEXT)
        LAST => START
        NULLIFY(START%PRIOR)
       ENDIF
       ENDDO
       END SUBROUTINE ENTER

!     This Subroutine is used to display the list on the screen.

       SUBROUTINE LIST
       USE LINK_LIST
       INTERFACE
        SUBROUTINE SHOW(INFO)
        USE LINK_LIST
        TYPE(ADDR), POINTER :: INFO
        END SUBROUTINE SHOW
       END INTERFACE
       TYPE(ADDR), POINTER :: INFO
!         Start from the beginning
       INFO => START
       DO WHILE (ASSOCIATED(INFO))
        CALL SHOW(INFO)
!         Fetch the next item from the list
        INFO => INFO%NEXT
       ENDDO
       END SUBROUTINE LIST

!     This subroutine actually displays the list on the screen
!     after getting the record from the Subroutine LIST.

       SUBROUTINE SHOW(INFO)
       USE LINK_LIST
```

```fortran
        TYPE(ADDR), POINTER :: INFO
        PRINT *
        PRINT *, INFO%NAME
        PRINT *, INFO%ADDRESS
        PRINT *, INFO%PIN
        PRINT *, "-------------------------"
        PRINT *
        END SUBROUTINE SHOW

!       This Subroutine is used to delete a record. The routine
!       can delete any record from the list. Note that the first
!       and other records are handled in a different ways.
!       After the deletion the record pointers are modified
!       accordingly.

        SUBROUTINE DELREC
        USE LINK_LIST
        TYPE(ADDR), POINTER :: INFO
        CHARACTER(LEN=30) :: NAM
        LOGICAL :: INDEX
        INTERFACE
         SUBROUTINE FIND(INFO,NAM,INDEX)
         USE LINK_LIST
         TYPE(ADDR), POINTER :: INFO
         CHARACTER(LEN=30), INTENT(IN) :: NAM
         LOGICAL :: INDEX
         END SUBROUTINE FIND
        END INTERFACE
        INDEX=.FALSE.
        PRINT *
        PRINT *, "Type the name to be deleted"
        PRINT *
        READ *, NAM
        CALL FIND(INFO,NAM,INDEX)
        IF(INDEX) THEN
         IF(ASSOCIATED(INFO,START)) THEN
!           First record
            IF (.NOT.(ASSOCIATED(INFO%NEXT))) THEN
!           FIRST RECORD AND ONLY RECORD
              NULLIFY(START)
            ELSE
!           First record but  not only record
            START=>INFO%NEXT
            NULLIFY(START%PRIOR)
           ENDIF
         ELSE
!           Other than first record
          INFO%PRIOR%NEXT => INFO%NEXT
```

```fortran
      IF(ASSOCIATED(INFO,LAST)) THEN
!       Last record
        LAST =>INFO%PRIOR
       ELSE
        INFO%NEXT%PRIOR=INFO%PRIOR
       ENDIF
      ENDIF
!       Release the location
      DEALLOCATE(INFO)
      PRINT *
        PRINT *, TRIM(NAM), " deleted from the list"
      PRINT *
     ELSE
      PRINT *, "Name not present in the list"
     ENDIF
     END
!       The Subroutine SEARCH is used to display a
!       particular name
SUBROUTINE SEARCH
USE LINK_LIST
TYPE(ADDR), POINTER :: INFO
CHARACTER(LEN=30) :: NAM
LOGICAL :: INDEX
INTERFACE
 SUBROUTINE SHOW(INFO)
 USE LINK_LIST
 TYPE(ADDR), POINTER :: INFO
 END SUBROUTINE SHOW
 SUBROUTINE FIND(INFO,NAM,INDEX)
 USE LINK_LIST
 TYPE(ADDR), POINTER :: INFO
 CHARACTER(LEN=30), INTENT(IN) :: NAM
 LOGICAL :: INDEX
 END SUBROUTINE FIND
END INTERFACE

INDEX=.FALSE.
PRINT *, "Type the name to be Searched"
READ *, NAM
CALL FIND(INFO,NAM,INDEX)
IF(INDEX) THEN
!    Record found
 CALL SHOW(INFO)
ELSE
 PRINT *, "Name not found"
ENDIF
END SUBROUTINE SEARCH
```

```
SUBROUTINE FIND(INFO,NAM,INDEX)
USE LINK_LIST
TYPE(ADDR), POINTER :: INFO
CHARACTER(LEN=30), INTENT(IN) :: NAM
LOGICAL :: INDEX
INFO => START
DO WHILE(ASSOCIATED(INFO))
 IF(NAM .EQ. INFO%NAME) THEN
  INDEX = .TRUE.
  EXIT
 ELSE
  INFO => INFO%NEXT
 ENDIF
ENDDO
END SUBROUTINE FIND
```

21.31 Function and Pointer

The program given below sorts an array using a function and returns the array through the RESULT clause.

```
PROGRAM SORTX
INTERFACE
 FUNCTION SORT(A) RESULT(RES)
  INTEGER, DIMENSION(:) :: A
  INTEGER, POINTER, DIMENSION(:) :: RES
 END FUNCTION SORT

END INTERFACE

INTEGER,TARGET, DIMENSION(10)::A=[10,-5,2,23,-10,6,100,0,-1,1]
 PRINT *, SORT(A)
END PROGRAM SORTX

FUNCTION SORT(A) RESULT(RES)
INTEGER,TARGET, DIMENSION(:):: A
INTEGER, POINTER, DIMENSION(:) ::RES
INTEGER :: I,J,LENGTH, TEMP
ALLOCATE (RES(SIZE(A)))
RES=>A
LENGTH=SIZE(A)
!    Not an efficient sort
DO I=1, LENGTH-1
  DO J=I+1,LENGTH
    IF(RES(I) .GT. RES(J))THEN
!      interchange
      TEMP=RES(I)
      RES(I)=RES(J)
```

```
        RES(J)=TEMP
      ENDIF
    ENDDO
  ENDDO
END FUNCTION SORT
```

21.32 Pointers and Subprograms

The argument of a subprogram may be a Pointer. Two cases may arise.
Case I: The actual argument is a pointer but the dummy argument is not a pointer. In this case, the actual argument must point to a target.

```
PROGRAM MAIN
INTEGER, TARGET::A=10
INTEGER, POINTER::PA
PA=>A
CALL SUB(PA)
PRINT *, PA            ! A is now 100
END
SUBROUTINE SUB(B)
INTEGER ::B
B=100
END
```

Case II: The dummy argument is pointer. In this case the actual argument must be a pointer and an explicit interface must be used.

```
PROGRAM MAIN
 INTERFACE

  SUBROUTINE SUB(A)
  INTEGER, POINTER ::A
  END SUBROUTINE SUB

 END INTERFACE

INTEGER, TARGET :: B=100
INTEGER, POINTER :: PB
PB=>B
CALL SUB(PB)
PRINT *, PB            ! PB is now 200
END

SUBROUTINE SUB(B)
INTEGER, POINTER :: B
B=200
END SUBROUTINE SUB
```

21.33 Pointer Intent

The dummy pointer argument of a subprogram may have an INTENT attribute attached to it. The intent used in this context refers to its association and not to the target variable. If the INTENT is IN, the pointer cannot be modified, that is, cannot be "re-associated" with another target. It cannot be set to NULL either. If the INTENT is OUT, the association is not defined when the subprogram is entered. It has an association on exit from the subprogram.

```
INTEGER, TARGET::X=10
INTEGER, POINTER::PTR
INTERFACE
  SUBROUTINE TESTPTR(P)
  INTEGER, POINTER, INTENT(IN)::P
  END SUBROUTINE TESTPTR
END INTERFACE

PTR=>X
PRINT *, PTR
CALL TESTPTR(PTR)
PRINT *, X
END
SUBROUTINE TESTPTR(P)
INTEGER, POINTER, INTENT(IN)::P
P=27

END SUBROUTINE TESTPTR
```

We reiterate that INTENT(IN) refers to the "association" of pointer with the target. This pointer P cannot point to any other target inside the subroutine TESTPTR. Nor it can be set to null by P=>NULL(). However, INTENT(IN) has no connection with the target that P is pointing to. The target can be modified, X was 10 when the subroutine is called, it is 27 on exit from the subroutine. If the INTENT is set to INOUT, the pointer P may be made to associate itself with another target within the subprogram, if necessary. Also it can be set to NULL().

```
SUBROUTINE TESTPTR(P)
INTEGER, POINTER, INTENT(INOUT)::P
P=27
P=>NULL()
END SUBROUTINE TESTPTR
```

It is needless to mention that the corresponding interface block in the main program must be modified – INTENT(IN) is to be changed to INTENT(INOUT).

21.34 Procedures and Pointers

The procedure pointer is associated with a procedure. The interface may be either explicit or implicit.

```
PROCEDURE(PROC), POINTER::P=>NULL()
```

This defines a procedure pointer P with an interface PROC. The pointer is initialized to NULL. The procedure pointer P is made to point to a procedure PROC through the statement P=>PROC and the subsequent call uses this P in place of the procedure name. Here the interface is explicit.

```
PROCEDURE(PROC), POINTER::P=>NULL()
INTERFACE
  SUBROUTINE PROC(A,B)
  INTEGER, INTENT(IN)::A
  INTEGER, INTENT(OUT)::B
  END SUBROUTINE PROC
END INTERFACE

INTEGER :: X=10, Y
P=>PROC
CALL P(X,Y)
PRINT *, X,Y
END

SUBROUTINE PROC(A,B)
  INTEGER, INTENT(IN)::A
  INTEGER, INTENT(OUT)::B
  B=A+10
END SUBROUTINE PROC
```

The next example shows an implicit interface. Pointers with implicit interface are defined as:

```
PROCEDURE(), POINTER::P=>NULL()
```

Note that for implicit interface, the interface name is absent, however the left and right brackets are present as shown.

```
!    IMPLICIT INTERFACE
PROCEDURE(), POINTER::P=>NULL()

INTEGER :: X=10, Y
P=>PROC
CALL P(X,Y)
PRINT *, X,Y
```

```
CONTAINS
SUBROUTINE PROC(A,B)
 INTEGER, INTENT(IN)::A
 INTEGER, INTENT(OUT)::B
 B=A+100
 END SUBROUTINE PROC
END
```

The component of a derived type may be a procedure pointer.

```
TYPE PROCTEST
 INTEGER :: I,J
 PROCEDURE(PROC), POINTER::P
END TYPE PROCTEST
ABSTRACT INTERFACE
 SUBROUTINE PROC(A,B)
 INTEGER, INTENT(IN)::A
 INTEGER, INTENT(OUT)::B
 END SUBROUTINE PROC
END INTERFACE

PROCEDURE(PROC)::SUB1
TYPE(PROCTEST)::X
X%I=10
X%P=>SUB1
CALL X%P(X%I, X%J)
PRINT *, X%I, X%J
END

SUBROUTINE SUB1(A,B)
 INTEGER, INTENT(IN)::A
 INTEGER, INTENT(OUT)::B
 B=A+50
END SUBROUTINE SUB1
```

Another way of writing the above program is shown below. Here a local procedure pointer (P1) is defined and the call to the procedure is made through P1.

```
TYPE PROCTEST
 INTEGER :: I,J
 PROCEDURE(PROC), POINTER::P
END TYPE PROCTEST
ABSTRACT INTERFACE
 SUBROUTINE PROC(A,B)
 INTEGER, INTENT(IN)::A
 INTEGER, INTENT(OUT)::B
 END SUBROUTINE PROC
END INTERFACE
```

```
PROCEDURE(PROC)::SUB1
PROCEDURE(PROC), POINTER:: P1

TYPE(PROCTEST)::X
X%I=10

P1=>SUB1

CALL P1(x%i, x%j)
PRINT *, X%I, X%J
END

SUBROUTINE SUB1(A,B)
 INTEGER, INTENT(IN)::A
 INTEGER, INTENT(OUT)::B
 B=A+50
END SUBROUTINE SUB1
```

The procedure pointer is not yet supported by the NAG Fortran compiler. Section 21.34 was tested with the g95 Fortran compiler.

21.35 Allocate with Source

Allocate statement with SOURCE attribute may use pointer in place of array.

```
INTEGER, POINTER, DIMENSION(:)::A
INTEGER, DIMENSION(5)::B=[1,2,3,4,5]
ALLOCATE(A(5), SOURCE=B)
PRINT *,A
END
```

The PRINT statement will display:

1 2 3 4 5

The array B is copied on to the pointer array A.

Chapter 22

STRING WITH VARIABLE LENGTH

The character variable (string) was introduced in chapter 8. It was pointed out there that the length of the character variable needs to be specified at compilation time. The present version of Fortran supports character strings of variable length by using a module called ISO_VARYING_STRING. The character variable that will have this property (variable length) must be of type VARYING_STRING defined in the module ISO_VARYING_TYPE. Strictly speaking, it is not a feature of the language as it is introduced through a module written in Fortran/95.

```
PROGRAM VARINGSTR
USE ISO_VARYING_STRING
TYPE (VARYING_STRING) :: NAME, SURNAME
TYPE (VARYING_STRING), DIMENSION (10):: FNAME
         .
```

The variables NAME and SURNAME are of the type VARYING_STRING and the variable FNAME is an array of rank 1 of size 10 of the type VARYING_STRING. These variables may have their length changed dynamically during the execution of the program. The length must be non-negative and there is no restriction on the size as such; there may be some processor dependent upper bound. The characters are numbered 1, 2, 3, ... n when n is the length of the string. Note, that the declarations of the VARYING_STRING type variables do not contain any reference to their size. In all subsequent discussions v refers to a variable string and c refers to a standard character string. This chapter is based on a report ISO/IEC 1539-2: 2000. An implementation of the module ISO_VARYING_STRING is available from ftp.nag.co.uk/sc22wg5/ISO_VARYING_STRING.

22.1 Assignment

The assignment sign can be used to assign a constant or a variable of the usual character type or a VARYING_STRING type to a VARYING_STRING type variable. The following operations are allowed:

$$v = constant$$
$$c = constant$$
$$v = c$$
$$v = v$$
$$c = v$$

As indicated above, v and c stand for VARYING_STRING type and standard character type variables.

```
USE ISO_VARYING_STRING
TYPE(VARYING_STRING)::V, V1
CHARACTER(LEN=10) :: C
V="KOLKATA"
C=V
V1=V
PRINT *, C
END
```

Case I: When the two sides of the assignment sign contain variables of type VARYING_STRING, the length of the variable on the left hand side of the assignment sign becomes equal to the length of the variable on the right hand side of the assignment sign.

In the above example, the length of V is 7 and when the variable V1 is equated to V, the length of V1 becomes also 7. Again, if the statement

```
V1 ="IACS"
```

is executed the length of V1 becomes 4.

Case II: When a VARYING_STRING type is equated to a character variable, the length of the VARYING_STRING type variable becomes the length of the character variable. Thus if one writes,

```
V1 = C
```

the length of V1 becomes 10 as the length of C is 10.

Case III: When an ordinary character variable is equated to a VARYING_STRING type variable, three cases may arise:

(a) If the length of the variables on both sides of the assignment sign is same, it is a simple assignment

```
TYPE(VARYING_STRING)::V="IACS"
CHARACTER(LEN=4) :: C
C=V
```

(b) If the length of the ordinary character variable is more than the VARYING_STRING type variable, blanks are added at the end.

```
TYPE(VARYING_STRING)::V="IACS"
CHARACTER(LEN=10) :: C
C=V
```

C becomes "IACSbbbbbb", where 'b' indicates blank.

(c) If the length of the ordinary character variable is less than the VARYING_STRING type variable, truncation from the right takes place.

```
TYPE(VARYING_STRING)::V="IACS, Kolkata"
CHARACTER(LEN=10) :: C
C=V
```

As the length of C is 10 and the length V is 13, due to truncation from the right, C will be set to "IACS, Kolk". The next program illustrates all the above mentioned points:

```
USE ISO_VARYING_STRING
TYPE (VARYING_STRING) :: V
CHARACTER (LEN=4) :: C1
CHARACTER (LEN=8) :: C2
CHARACTER (LEN=2) :: C3

V="IACS"
C1=V
C2=V
C3=V
PRINT *, C1, LEN(C1)
PRINT *, C2, LEN(C2)
PRINT *, C3, LEN(C3)
END
```

The outputs are:

```
IACS  4
IACSbbbb  8
IA  2
```

22.2 Concatenation

Concatenation may be performed between constants and variables of the standard character type and variables of VARYING_STRING type. The resultant string has a length equal to the sum of the length of each string.

```
USE ISO_VARYING_STRING
TYPE (VARYING_STRING) :: V, V1, V2
CHARACTER (LEN=4) :: C="IACS"
V= "KOLKATA "
V2=" INDIA"
V1= V // "700032"          ! "KOLKATA 700032"
V1= C //','// V            ! "IACS,KOLKATA "
V1= V // V2                ! "KOLKATA INDIA"
END
```

All the above-mentioned concatenation operations are valid.

22.3 Comparison

Two strings may be compared in the usual manner. Relational operators are:

Less than	<	or .LT.
Less than or equal to	<=	or .LE.
Greater than	>	or .GT.
Greater than or equal to	>=	or .GE.
Equal to	==	or .EQ.
Not equal to	/=	or .NE.

The result of comparison is either true or false. The first non-matched character decides the issue. This was discussed in details in chapter 8. If the strings are of unequal length, blanks are added to the smaller string to make the length same as the bigger one. The comparison may be performed between v and v, c and v, v and c and also between c and c.

```
USE ISO_VARYING_STRING
TYPE (VARYING_STRING) :: V, V1
CHARACTER (LEN=4) :: C="IACS"
LOGICAL :: L
V="ABCD"
V1="EFGH"
L= V <= V1
L= V == V1
L= V > C

IF (V .EQ. V1) THEN
  .
ELSE
  .
ENDIF
```

22.4 Extended Meaning of Intrinsics

The intrinsics ADJUSTL, ADJUSTR, CHAR, IACHAR, ICHAR, INDEX, LEN, LEN_TRIM, LGE, LGT, LLT, LLE, REPEAT, SCAN, TRIM and VERIFY were discussed in chapter 8. With the introduction of the module ISO_VARYING_STRING, these intrinsics can accept VARYING_STRING variables as argument also. In other words, the capabilities of the intrinsics have been extended to include variables of type VARYING_STRING. There is no point in repeating the old story again. We give one or two examples of the intrinsics with a VARYING_STRING variable as its argument. Using the declaration of the section 22.3 we may use:

```
I=LEN (V)
V1=REPEAT (V,4)
```

It is thus seen that all the discussions of chapter 8 are equally applicable for string with variable length except that appropriate VARYING_STRING variable argument is to be used.

22.5 PUT

The subroutine PUT is used to write a record to an external file.

```
CALL PUT (unit, string)
```

where *string* is a VARYING_STRING type variable. If no *unit* is mentioned, the default unit is 6 − the screen. The *unit* is an integer (scalar).

```
CALL PUT (string)
```

PUT can have one optional argument *iostat*. It is a scalar and an integer. It returns zero when the PUT operation is successful; it returns some positive number in case of any error. If *iostat* is absent, in case of any error, the job is terminated. The PUT subroutine writes the string at the current position of the record. For example,

```
CALL PUT(V)
CALL PUT(V1)
```

will write the value of V followed by the value of V1 as one record.

22.6 PUT_LINE

PUT_LINE takes identical arguments to PUT. The only difference is that after execution it terminates the current record and a new record (new line) begins.

```
CALL PUT_LINE(6,V)
CALL PUT_LINE(V1)
CALL PUT_LINE(V1, iostat)
CALL PUT_LINE(6, V1, iostat)
```

22.7 GET

The subroutine GET can be used to input a VARYING_STRING variable. In its simplest form it is

```
CALL GET(V)
```

where V is variable of the type VARYING_STRING.

```
USE ISO_VARYING_STRING
TYPE (VARYING_STRING) :: V
CALL GET(V)
```

This reads V from the keyboard. There are other forms of GET.

```
CALL GET (unit, string)
```

If *unit* (scalar) is omitted if is assumed to be the keyboard (unit 5).

```
CALL GET (string, maxlen)
```

maxlen is an integer (scalar), if used, specifies maximum number of characters to be read from the input device. It is optional.

```
CALL GET (V, 4)
```

will read only 4 characters from the keyboard and store in the location V. If *maxlen* is zero or negative nothing will be read and the string will be a null string. If *maxlen* is omitted, it is assumed to be HUGE(1).

```
CALL GET (string, set)
```

Here *set* is a scalar of either of the type standard character or of the type VARYING_STRING. This variable contains a set of characters that may be used as the terminator. The reading is terminated when the input matches any member from the set of characters. The terminal character is not stored in the string.

```
CALL GET (string, set, separator)
```

where separator is a scalar and of type VARYING_STRING type. It is also optional. When *separator* is used, the actual character that separated (terminated) the record, is stored in the location *separator*.

```
CALL GET (string, set, separator, maxlen, iostat)
```

where *iostat*, an optional parameter, is a scalar and integer. After the "read" operation is performed, it is zero if read operation is valid and end of record is not encountered; a positive value indicates an error condition and a negative value indicates that either an end of file or an end of record is reached. If *iostat* is absent, when end of file or end of record is reached the job is terminated.

```
USE ISO_VARYING_STRING
TYPE (VARYING_STRING) :: V,SEPARATOR,SET
INTEGER :: MAXLEN=20, IOSTAT
SET="#"
CALL GET(V,SET,SEPARATOR,MAXLEN,IOSTAT)
PRINT *, LEN(V)
CALL PUT_LINE(SEPARATOR)
CALL PUT_LINE(V)
PRINT *, IOSTAT
END
```

The outputs form the program are when the input is "ASSOCIATION#OF" :

```
11
#
ASSOCIATION
0
```

The output tells us that 11 characters have been stored in the location V. The character "#" acted as separator which was taken from the variable SET and it was stored in the location SEPARATOR; as the GET operation is successful, the value of IOSTAT is zero.

22.8 EXTRACT

This function extracts a string from a VARYING_STRING or a character string. It can have optional *start* and *finish* parameters; both are integers. It returns a VARYING_STRING from the position *start* to *finish*. If *start* is omitted or less than 1, it is taken to be 1; if *finish* is not present or more than the length of the string, it is assumed to be LEN(*string*). If *finish* is less than *start*, a null string is returned. If *finish* is less than *start*, no character is removed.

```
USE ISO_VARYING_STRING
TYPE (VARYING_STRING) :: V, V1
V="INDIAN ASSOCIATION"
V1=EXTRACT(V,3,6)
CALL PUT_LINE(V1)
END
```

The output is "DIAN" (character positions 3-6)

22.9 REMOVE

The arguments are same as EXTRACT. It removes the string from *start* to *finish*.

```
USE ISO_VARYING_STRING
TYPE (VARYING_STRING) :: V, V1
V="INDIAN ASSOCIATION FOR THE CULTIVATION OF SCIENCE"
V1=REMOVE(V,19,38)
CALL PUT_LINE(V1)
END
```

The output is "INDIAN ASSOCIATION OF SCIENCE" after removing characters 19 to 38 from the string. Note that the blank character before 'FOR' is also included.

22.10 REPLACE

This function replaces a string by a substring between positions *start* and *finish*. If *start* is not supplied or it is less than one, it is assumed to be one. If *finish* is not supplied or is greater than the length of the string, *finish* is assumed to be LEN(*string*).

```
USE ISO_VARYING_STRING
TYPE (VARYING_STRING) :: V, V1
V="INDIAN ASSOCIATION FOR THE CULTIVATION OF SCIENCE"
V1=REPLACE(V,8,38,"INSTITUTE")
CALL PUT_LINE(V1)
END
```

The output is "INDIAN INSTITUTE OF SCIENCE". The function replaces the substring "ASSOCIATION FOR THE CULTIVATION" by "INSTITUTE".

There is another form of REPLACE.

REPLACE(*string, target, substring, every, back*)

The *string* is searched for the occurrence of the string present in the *target*. When a match is found, it is replaced by *substring*. If *every* is true all such occurrences are replaced, otherwise only the first occurrence is replaced; the default value of *every* is false. If *back* is true the search takes place in the backward direction. If it is false the search takes place in the forward direction. The default is false.

```
USE ISO_VARYING_STRING
TYPE (VARYING_STRING) :: V, V1, V2
V="INDIAN ASSOCIATION FOR THE CULTIVATION OF SCIENCE"
V1="TI"
V2=REPLACE (V,V1, "xx",.TRUE.,.FALSE.)
CALL PUT_LINE(V2)
END
```

The output is "INDIAN ASSOCIAxxON FOR THE CULxxVAxxON OF SCIENCE". As *every* is true all occurrence of "TI" is replaced by "xx".

22.11 SPLIT

This subroutine splits a string into two substrings. The splitting is done through a set of "splitting characters".

CALL SPLIT (*string, word, set*)

where *string* and *word* are of type VARYING_STRING, *set* is of type CHARACTER or VARYING_STRING. The subroutine divides the *string* into two when a character from the set of characters matches with any character of string. The characters that are passed over are transferred to the variable *word* and removed from the string. If a fourth optional argument *separator* is present the matched character is stored in that location, otherwise it is dropped. There is a fifth optional argument *back*, the default value of *back* is false. If it is true, searching starts from the end of the string. Obviously, *back* is logical variable; *set* and *separator* are either of type CHARACTER or VARYING_STRING.

```
USE ISO_VARYING_STRING
TYPE (VARYING_STRING) :: V, WORD, SET, SEPARATOR
SET="FC"
V="INDIAN ASSOCIATION FOR THE CULTIVATION OF SCIENCE"
CALL SPLIT(V,WORD,SET,SEPARATOR)
CALL PUT_LINE(WORD)
CALL PUT_LINE(V)
CALL PUT_LINE(SEPARATOR)
END
```

The outputs are:

```
INDIAN ASSO
IATION FOR THE CULTIVATION OF SCIENCE
C
```

It is not difficult to interpret the output. The string V is scanned. When it hits the character 'C' – one of the character from the variable SET, all characters from the first character of V up to character just before the character 'C' are transferred to the variable WORD and all these characters including the matched character 'C' are deleted from the variable V. However because of the presence of the variable SEPARATOR, the matched character is transferred to the variable SEPARATOR.

Chapter 23

HANDLING OF BITS

Fortran contains a number of intrinsics to manipulate a single bit or a group of bits. These include bit-testing, bit setting, shifting of bits, logical operations like "and", "or" etc., and transferring bits from one location to another. In our subsequent discussion whenever the type of any array is not mentioned, it is assumed as an integer array. Also to keep the diagrams simple, only the rightmost 8 bits are shown — leftmost 24 bits (which are zero because of choice of value for the variable or constant) are not shown in the diagram.

23.1 BIT_SIZE

This library function takes an integer as argument and returns the "size" of the variable, that is, the number of bits used to store the integer. The returned integer is the same type as the argument.

```
INTEGER, PARAMETER :: S1=SELECTED_INT_KIND(2)
INTEGER, PARAMETER :: S2=SELECTED_INT_KIND(4)
INTEGER, PARAMETER :: S3=SELECTED_INT_KIND(9)
INTEGER, PARAMETER :: S4=SELECTED_INT_KIND(12)
INTEGER (KIND=S1) :: K1
INTEGER (KIND=S2) :: K2
INTEGER (KIND=S3) :: K3
INTEGER (KIND=S4) :: K4
INTEGER :: L1, L2, L3, L4
L1=BIT_SIZE(K1)              ! L1=8
L2=BIT_SIZE(K2)              ! L2=16
L3=BIT_SIZE(K3)              ! L3=32
L4=BIT_SIZE(K4)              ! L4=64
PRINT *, L1, L2, L3, L4
END
```

This program shows the number of bits required to represent integers of various kinds in the system. These are processor dependent.

23.2 BTEST

Case I: This intrinsic takes two integers as arguments, first one is an integer variable and the second one is an integer or integer expression. The function tests the bit of the first argument whose position is specified by the second argument POS (if the second argument is an expression, it is first evaluated). It returns true if the bit in question is on and returns false if the bit is off.

```
INTEGER :: A=10
LOGICAL :: L1, L2

L1=BTEST(A,3)    ! true
L2=BTEST(A,4)    ! false

PRINT *, L1, L2
END
```

(only rightmost eight bits are shown)

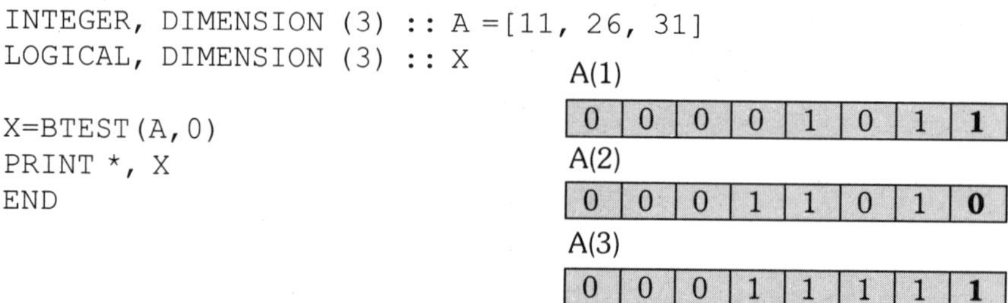

The value of A is 10. It is internally stored as $(1010)_2$ with 28 leading zeros. Bits 1 and 3 are on and the rest are zero. Therefore, BTEST (A, 3) is true and BTEST (A, 4) is false The second argument POS satisfies this inequality:

$$0 <= POS < BIT\_SIZE (A)$$

If the above condition is not satisfied, the result is false. Note that BIT_SIZE returns the number of bits in A, which is 32 in this case. Bits are numbered 0 to 31 and hence POS has to be less than BIT_SIZE (A).

Case II: The first argument to the intrinsic is an array. The second argument is a scalar. The intrinsic tests the bit of the elements of the first argument whose position is specified by the second argument (POS). The intrinsic returns a logical array of the same shape and size as the first argument.

```
INTEGER, DIMENSION (3) :: A =[11, 26, 31]
LOGICAL, DIMENSION (3) :: X

X=BTEST(A,0)
PRINT *, X
END
```

A(1)

A(2)

A(3)

X(1) will be true as bit 0 of A(1) is on. Similarly, X(2) is false and X(3) is true.

Case III: Both the first and the second arguments may be array of same shape. In this case the intrinsic tests the bit of all the elements of the first array whose position is stored in the second array.

```
INTEGER, DIMENSION (3) :: A=[21, 36, 53]
INTEGER, DIMENSION (3) :: POS=[0, 5, 7]
LOGICAL, DIMENSION (3) :: X

X=BTEST(A, POS)

PRINT *, X
END
```

A(1)

A(2)

A(3)

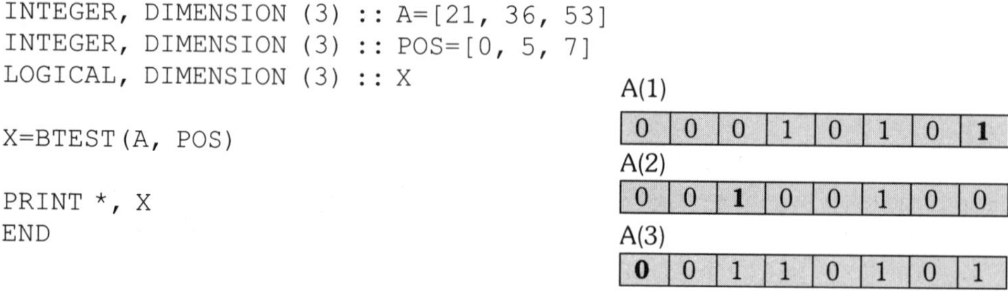

X(1) will be true as the bit 0 of A(1) is on. Similarly, X(2) is true and X(3) is false.

23.3 IBSET

Case I: This intrinsic also takes two arguments – first one is an integer variable and second one (POS) is an integer or integer expression. The function returns an integer of the same kind as the first argument with the bit whose position is specified by the second argument set to one.

```
INTEGER :: K1=13
INTEGER :: K2
K2=IBSET(K1,1)

PRINT *, K2
END
```

Before

0	0	0	0	1	1	**0**	1

After

0	0	0	0	1	1	**1**	1

when bit 1 of K1 is set, the number becomes 15. The second argument POS satisfies the following inequality:

```
0 <= POS <BIT_SIZE(K1)
```

Case II: The first argument to the intrinsic is an array. The second argument is a scalar. The intrinsic sets the bit of the elements of the first argument whose position is specified by the second argument. The intrinsic returns an array of the same type as the first argument.

```
INTEGER, DIMENSION (3) :: A=[22, 36, 53]
INTEGER, DIMENSION (3) :: B
B=IBSET(A,3)
PRINT *, B

END
```

A(1)

0	0	0	1	**0**	1	1	0

A(2)

0	0	1	0	**0**	1	0	0

A(3)

0	0	1	1	**0**	1	0	1

Thus B(1), B(2) and B(3) become 30, 44 and 61 respectively as bit 3 of each element is switched on and it adds $2^3=8$ to all the elements of A.

Case III: Both the first and the second arguments may be arrays of the same shape. In this case the intrinsic sets a bit of each element of the array A by the corresponding elements of the second array whose position is stored in the second array.

```
INTEGER, DIMENSION (3) :: A=[20,36,53]
INTEGER, DIMENSION (3) :: POS=[1,0,3]
INTEGER, DIMENSION (3) :: B

B=IBSET(A, POS)

PRINT *, B
END
```

A(1)

0	0	0	1	0	1	**0**	0

A(2)

0	0	1	0	0	1	0	**0**

A(3)

0	0	1	1	**0**	1	0	1

Thus B(1), B(2) and B(3) become 22, 37 and 61 respectively. The bits that will be switched on are indicated by bold letter.

```
B(1) = A(1)+2 [bit 1 is switched on]
B(2) = A(2)+1 [bit 0 is switched on]
B(3) = A(3)+8 [bit 3 is switched on]
```

23.4 IBCLR

Case I: This intrinsic also takes two arguments — first one is an integer variable and second one (POS) is an integer or integer expression. The function returns an integer of same kind as first argument with bit position as specified by the second argument set to zero, keeping all other bits unchanged.

```
INTEGER :: A=14
INTEGER :: B

B=IBCLR(A,1)
PRINT *, B
END
```

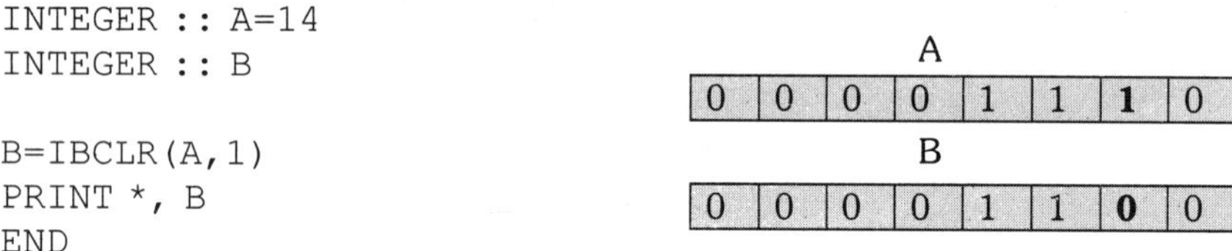

As bit 1 of A is set to zero, the number becomes 12 and thus B becomes 12. The second argument POS satisfies the inequality:

```
0 <= POS < BIT_SIZE (A)
```

Case II: The first argument is an array and the second argument is a scalar. The intrinsic clears the bit of all the elements of the first argument whose position is specified by the second argument (POS). The intrinsic returns an array of the same type as the first argument.

```
INTEGER, DIMENSION (3) :: A=[22,36,53]
INTEGER, DIMENSION (3) :: B
B=IBCLR(A,2)

PRINT *, B
END
```

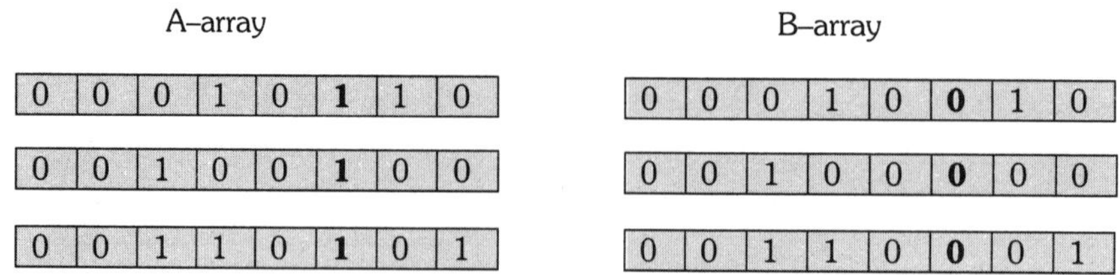

Thus B(1), B(2) and B(3) will become 18, 32 and 49 respectively.

Case III: Both first and second argument may be an array of same shape. It returns an array of the same type as the input array. The intrinsic clears a bit of each element of the input array by the value stored in the corresponding elements of the second array.

```
INTEGER, DIMENSION (3) :: A=[22,36,53]
INTEGER, DIMENSION (3) :: POS=[1,2,0]
INTEGER, DIMENSION (3) :: B

B=IBCLR(A, POS)
PRINT *, B
END
```

A–array   B–array

| 0 | 0 | 0 | 1 | 0 | 1 | **1** | 0 |

| 0 | 0 | 0 | 1 | 0 | 1 | **0** | 0 |

| 0 | 0 | 1 | 0 | 0 | 1 | 0 | 0 |

| 0 | 0 | 1 | 0 | 0 | **0** | 0 | 0 |

| 0 | 0 | 1 | 1 | 0 | 1 | 0 | **1** |

| 0 | 0 | 1 | 1 | 0 | 1 | 0 | **0** |

The elements of the B array become 20, 32 and 52 respectively.

23.5 IBITS

Case I: This intrinsic takes three integer arguments. The first one is an integer variable, second (POS) and third (LEN) are integer constants or expressions. This function returns an integer after extracting LEN number of bits starting from the position POS of the integer variable. The extracted bits are stored right adjusted within the destination field.

```
INTEGER :: I, J
DATA I / B"10110010"/
J=IBITS(I,4,3)

PRINT *, J
END
```

I   J

| 1 | **0** | 1 | 1 | 0 | 0 | 1 | 0 |

| 0 | 0 | 0 | 0 | 0 | **0** | 1 | 1 |

The second argument POS satisfies the following inequality:

```
LEN+POS <= BIT_SIZE(I)
```

Case II: The first argument can be an array. In this case, the intrinsic returns an array of the same type and shape as the first argument. The intrinsic performs same operations mentioned under Case I on every element of the array.

```
INTEGER, DIMENSION (3) :: A
INTEGER, DIMENSION (3) :: B
DATA A / B"10110010", B"10011010", B"01111001"/

B=IBITS(A,4,3)
PRINT *, B
END
```

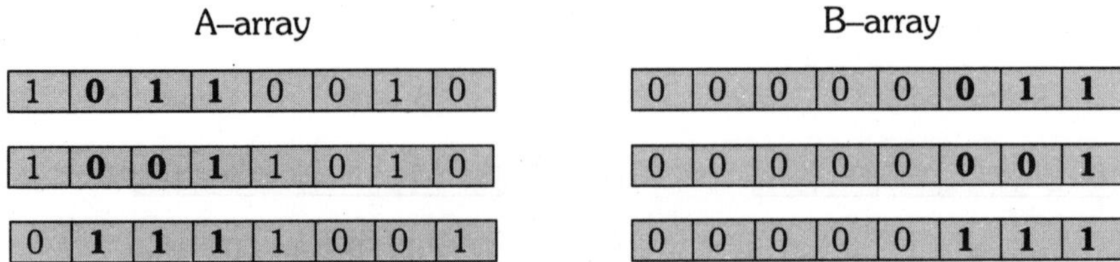

The elements of the B array become 3, 1 and 7 respectively.

Case III: When the first argument is an array, the second argument can also be an array of the same shape. In this case, the bits are extracted from each element of the array taking the starting position from the corresponding element of the POS array.

```
INTEGER, DIMENSION (3) :: A, B
INTEGER, DIMENSION (3) :: POS
DATA A / B"10110010", B"10011010", B"01111001"/
DATA POS/ 4,1,3/

B=IBITS(A,POS,3)
PRINT *, B
END
```

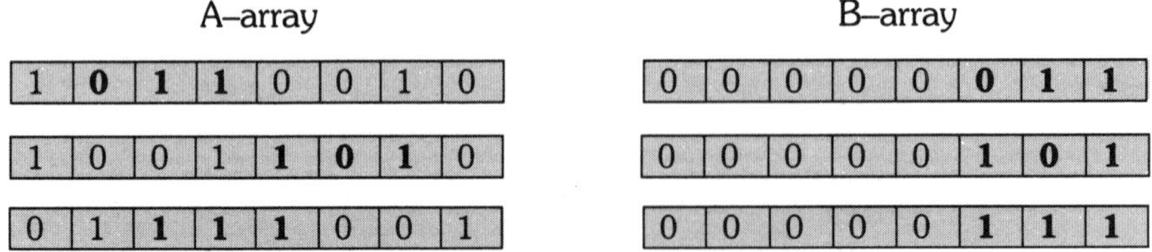

It may be observed from the above diagram that the elements of B-array become 3, 5 and 7 respectively.

Case IV: Like the second argument POS, the third argument LEN may also be an array of shape similar to the first argument. In this case, the number of bits extracted depends upon the content of the corresponding elements of the LEN array.

```
INTEGER, DIMENSION (3) :: A, B
INTEGER, DIMENSION (3) :: POS, LEN
DATA A / B"10110010", B"10011010", B"01111001"/
DATA POS/ 4,2,3/
DATA LEN /2,1,3/
```

```
B=IBITS(A,POS,LEN)
PRINT *, B
END
```

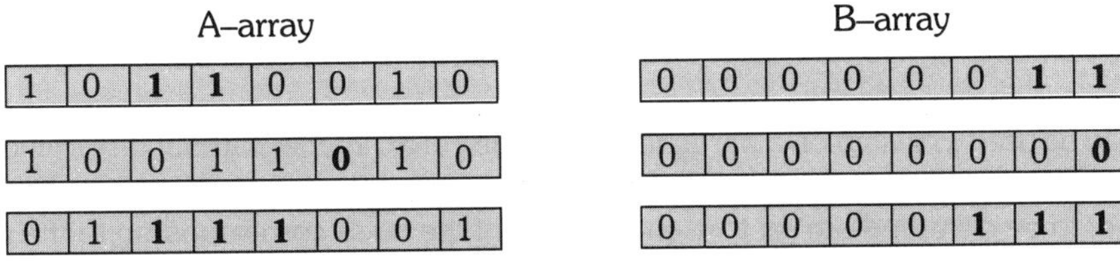

A–array

B–array

The elements of B array become 3, 0 and 7 respectively.

Case V: It is perhaps apparent that POS may be a scalar and LEN may be an array of same shape as the first argument.

```
INTEGER, DIMENSION (3) :: A, B
INTEGER, DIMENSION (3) :: LEN
INTEGER :: POS=2
DATA A / B"10110010", B"10011010", B"01111001"/
DATA LEN /2,1,3/

B=IBITS(A,POS,LEN)
PRINT *, B
END
```

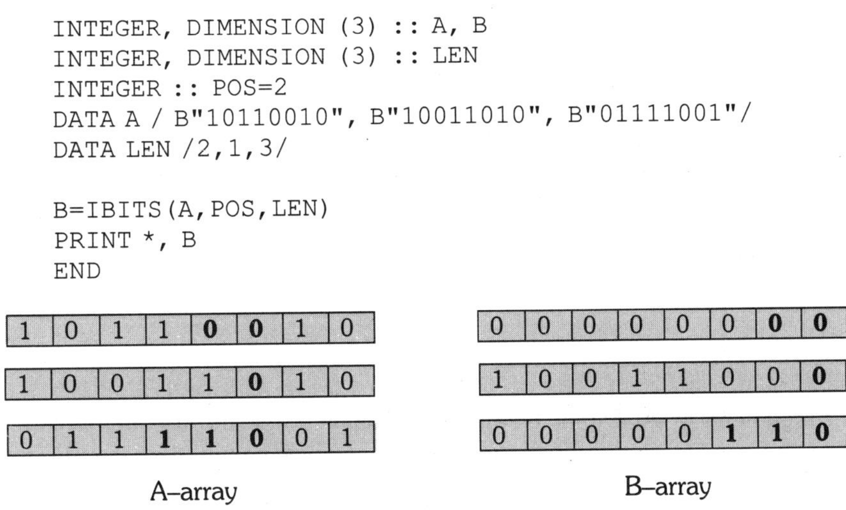

A–array

B–array

The elements of B array are respectively 0, 0 and 6.

23.6 IAND

Case I: This function takes two integers as arguments — the arguments must be of same kind. It returns an integer of the same kind as its arguments after logical "anding" of the bits of the first argument with the corresponding bits of the second argument. The truth table for IAND is shown below:

I	0	0	1	1
J	0	1	0	1
IAND (I, J)	0	0	0	1

Truth Table - IAND

```
INTEGER :: I, J, K
I=13
J=25
K=IAND(I,J)
PRINT *, K
END
```

I

| 0 | 0 | 0 | 0 | 1 | 1 | 0 | 1 |

J

| 0 | 0 | 0 | 1 | 1 | 0 | 0 | 1 |

K

| 0 | 0 | 0 | 0 | 1 | 0 | 0 | 1 |

IAND intrinsic may be used to switch off a particular bit (or bits) of an integer without disturbing other bits by using a suitable mask (second argument). The bits of the mask corresponding to the bits of the source that are not to be disturbed are set to 1 and the bits of the mask corresponding to the source that are to be switched off are set to zero.

```
INTEGER, PARAMETER :: S=SELECTED_INT_KIND(2)
INTEGER (KIND=S) :: I, MASK, K
DATA I/B"10110110"/
DATA MASK /B"11111001"/

K=IAND (I, MASK)          ! bits 1 and 2 are switched off.
```

Case II: The first argument is an array and the second argument is a scalar. All the elements of the array are "anded" with the second argument and the function returns an array of the same shape as of the first argument.

```
INTEGER, DIMENSION(4) :: A, C
 .
 .
C=IAND (A,2)
```

Case III: Both the arguments of IAND may be an array of same shape and size. In this case, each element of the first argument is "anded" with the corresponding element of the second array. The function returns an array of the same type as the first argument.

```
INTEGER, DIMENSION(4) :: A, B, C
 .
 .
C=IAND (A,B)
```

A(1) is "anded" with B(1) and the result is stored in C(1), A(2) is "anded" with B(2) and so on.

23.7 IOR

Case I: This intrinsic is same as IAND in every respect, but the truth table is different. First, we consider a case where the both the first and second argument are scalar.

I	0	0	1	1
J	0	1	0	1
IOR (I, J)	0	1	1	1

Truth Table - IOR

```
INTEGER :: I, J, K
I=12
J=3
K=IOR(I,J) ! K=15
PRINT *, K
END
```

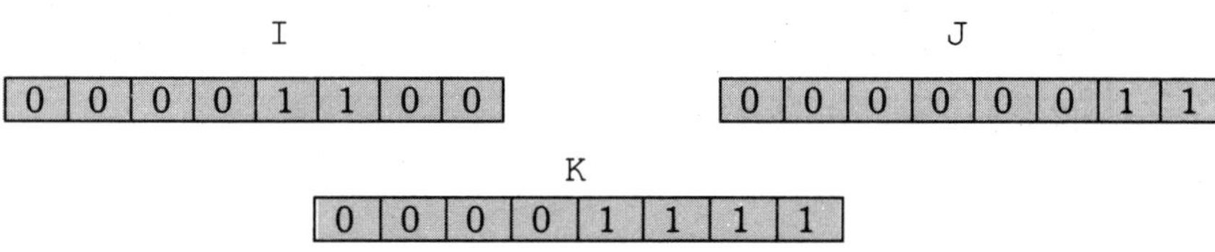

Inclusive or (IOR) may be used to switch on a particular bit (bits) of an integer keeping the other bits untouched under the influence of a mask. In this case, the bits of the "mask" corresponding to the bits of the source that would remain unaffected are set to zero and the bits of the mask corresponding to the bits of the source that are to be switched on are set to one.

```
INTEGER :: I, MASK, K
DATA I/B"10101001"/
DATA MASK /B"00010010"/
K=IOR(I, MASK) ! bits 1 and 4 are switched on.
```

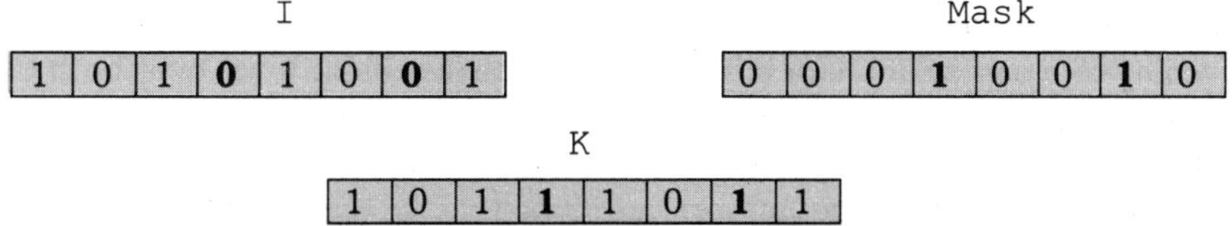

Case II: Like IAND, first argument is an array and the second argument is a scalar. All the elements of the array are "ored" with the second argument and the function returns an array of the same shape as the first argument.

```
INTEGER, DIMENSION(4) :: A, C
 .
 .
C=IOR (A,2)
```

Case III: Both the argument of IOR may be arrays of the same shape and size. In this case, each element of the first argument is "ored" with the corresponding element of the second array.

```
INTEGER, DIMENSION(4) :: A, B, C
    .
    .
C=IOR(A,B)
```

A(1) is "ored" with B(1) and the result is stored in C(1), A(2) is "ored" with B(2) and so on.

23.8 IEOR

Case I: IEOR also takes two integers of the same kind as its arguments and returns an integer of the same kind after *exclusive* "oring" the first argument with the second argument according to the following table.

I	0	0	1	1
J	0	1	0	1
IEOR (I, J)	0	1	1	0

Truth Table - IEOR

```
INTEGER :: I, J, K
DATA I /B"10101011"/
DATA J /B"10110000"/
K=IEOR(I,J)
```

I

1	0	1	0	1	0	1	1

J

1	0	1	1	0	0	0	0

K

0	0	0	1	1	0	1	1

The exclusive or (IEOR) is often used for bit "flipping" − that is, switching on a particular bit (or bits) if it is off or switching off a particular bit (or bits) if it is on. Again a suitable mask must be chosen − the bits of the mask corresponding to the bits of the source that would remain unaffected are set to zero and the bits of the mask corresponding to the bits of the source that are to be flipped are set to one. In the above example bits 4, 5 and 7 of the variable I are flipped.

Case II: Like IAND, first argument is an array and the second argument is a scalar. All the elements of the array are exclusive "ored" with the second argument and the function returns an array of the same shape as the first argument.

```
INTEGER, DIMENSION(4) :: A, C
    .
    .
C=IEOR (A,3)
```

Case III: Both the argument of IEOR may be arrays of same shape. In this case, each element of the first argument is exclusive "ored" with the corresponding element of the second array. The function returns an array of the same type as the first argument.

```
INTEGER, DIMENSION(4) :: A, B, C
.
.
C=IEOR(A,B)
```

A(1) is exclusive "ored" with B(1) and the result is stored in C(1), A(2) is exclusive "ored" with B(2) and so on.

23.9 NOT

Case I: NOT takes one integer as its argument and returns an integer of the same kind as the argument after changing zero bits to one and the one bits to zero (logical complement). The truth table for NOT is:

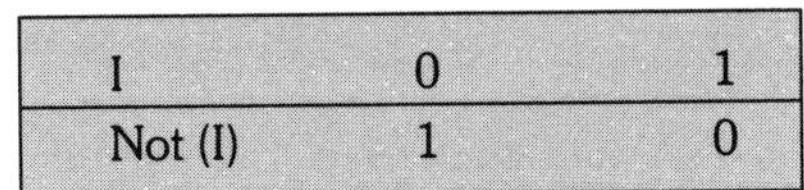

I	0	1
Not (I)	1	0

Truth Table - NOT

```
INTEGER, PARAMETER:: S1=SELECTED_INT_KIND(2)
INTEGER (KIND=S1) :: I, J
DATA I/B"10101010"/
J=NOT(I)
```

I

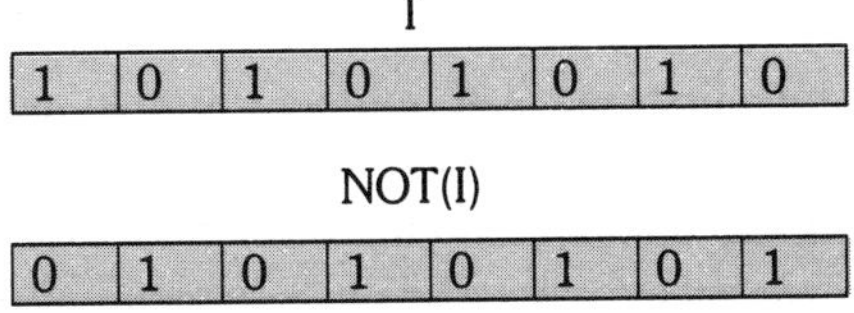

1	0	1	0	1	0	1	0

NOT(I)

0	1	0	1	0	1	0	1

Case II: The arguments of NOT may be an integer array. In that case, the returned array is of same type and size as the input array.

```
INTEGER, DIMENSION (3) :: A, B
.
.
B=NOT(A)
```

NOT operates on every element of the array A and the result is stored in the corresponding element of B array, that is, the above statement is equivalent to:

```
B(1) = NOT (A(1))
B(2) = NOT (A(2))
B(3) = NOT (A(3))
```

23.10 Programming Example

This program prints an integer in binary format without using 'B' edit descriptor. The logic of the program is to check each bit of the integer; if it is on, (one) 1 is displayed and if it is off, 0 is displayed. To print the zeros and ones in one line, an option of the WRITE statement is used — ADVANCE= 'NO'. This will be discussed in chapter 24. At this stage it is sufficient to mention that this particular option will prevent carriage movement, that is, the zeros and ones will be displayed in one line. Without this option the bits would be displayed in different lines (one character per line).

```
      INTEGER :: NUM, SZ, J, K
      READ *, NUM                         ! Read the integer
      SZ=BIT_SIZE(NUM)
      DO J=1, SZ                          ! no of bits
      IF(BTEST(NUM,SZ-J)) THEN            ! tests from the left (bit 31)
         K=1
      ELSE
         K=0
      ENDIF
      WRITE (6, 20, ADVANCE='NO') K
20    FORMAT(I1)
      ENDDO

      END
```

23.11 ISHFT

Case I: This function takes two arguments, first one is an integer variable and the second one is an integer expression (constant, variable, arithmetic expression) called shift count. The function returns an integer of same kind as the first argument after shifting the bits either to left or to right depending upon the sign of the shift count. A positive shift count indicates a left shift and a negative shift count indicates a right shift. In either case, the vacancy created by the shift at either end is filled with zeros.

```
      INTEGER, PARAMETER :: S=SELECTED_INT_KIND(2)
      INTEGER(KIND=S) :: S1, S2
      S1=15
      PRINT *, S1        ! 15
      S2=ISHFT(S1,1)
      PRINT *, S2        ! 30
      S2=ISHFT(S1,2)
      PRINT *, S2        ! 60
      S2=ISHFT(S1,-1)
      PRINT *, S2        ! 7
      S2=ISHFT(S1,-2)
      PRINT *, S2        ! 3
      END
```

S1=15

0	0	0	0	1	1	1	1

One left shift: 30

0	0	0	1	1	1	1	0

Two left shift: 60

0	0	1	1	1	1	0	0

One right shift: 7

0	0	0	0	0	1	1	1

Two right shift: 3

0	0	0	0	0	0	1	1

Case II: The first argument is an array and the shift count is a scalar. The shift count acts on each element of the array. The intrinsic returns an array of the same type as the first argument.

```
INTEGER, PARAMETER :: S=SELECTED_INT_KIND(2)
INTEGER(KIND=S), DIMENSION (3) :: S1=[15,30,50]
INTEGER(KIND=S), DIMENSION (3) :: S2, S3

S2=ISHFT(S1,1)          ! S2 : 30, 60, 100
PRINT *, S2
S3=ISHFT(S1,-1)         ! S3 : 7, 15, 25
PRINT *, S3
```

Positive shift count

0	0	0	0	1	1	1	1
0	0	0	1	1	1	1	0
0	0	1	1	0	0	1	0

S1

0	0	0	1	1	1	1	0
0	0	1	1	1	1	0	0
0	1	1	0	0	1	0	0

S2

Negative shift count

0	0	0	0	1	1	1	1
0	0	0	1	1	1	1	0
0	0	1	1	0	0	1	0

S1

0	0	0	0	0	1	1	1
0	0	0	0	1	1	1	1
0	0	0	1	1	0	0	1

S3

Case III: The shift count may be an array of the same type as the first argument. Each element of the first argument is shifted by an amount specified in the corresponding element of the shift count array. The function returns an array of the same type as the first argument.

```
INTEGER, PARAMETER :: S=SELECTED_INT_KIND(2)
INTEGER(KIND=S), DIMENSION (3) :: S1=[15,30,22]
INTEGER(KIND=S), DIMENSION (3) :: SH=[1, -1, 2]
INTEGER(KIND=S), DIMENSION (3) :: S2
```

```
S2=ISHFT(S1,SH)   ! S2: 30, 15, 88

PRINT *, S2
END
```

0	0	0	0	1	1	1	1
0	0	0	1	1	1	1	0
0	0	0	1	0	1	1	0

0	0	0	1	1	1	1	0
0	0	0	0	1	1	1	1
0	1	0	1	1	0	0	0

      S1   S2

It may be noted that in this case, shift count for the array elements are different − one left shift for S(1), one right shift for S(2) and 2 left shift for S(3).

23.12 ISHFTC

There are two forms of ISHFTC. First one takes two arguments like ISHFT and works almost similar to ISHFT − only difference is that the bits shifted out are added to the other end. This shift is also known as circular shift.

Case I: Both arguments are scalar.

```
INTEGER, PARAMETER :: S=SELECTED_INT_KIND(2)
INTEGER (KIND=S) :: I,SH,J
DATA I/ B"10011101"/
SH=1
J=ISHFTC(I,SH)
PRINT 10, I
PRINT 10, J
10      FORMAT (B8.8)
END
```

I

1	0	0	1	1	1	0	1

J

0	0	1	1	1	0	1	1

Case II: The first argument is an array (say rank 1) and the second argument is scalar. All the elements of the array are circularly shifted by same amount (second argument). The function returns an array of the same type as the first argument. The bits are shown in bold letters.

```
INTEGER, PARAMETER :: S=SELECTED_INT_KIND(2)
INTEGER (KIND=S),DIMENSION(3) :: I,J
INTEGER :: SH
DATA I/ B"10011101", B"01010101", B"10101010" /
SH=-1
J=ISHFTC(I,SH)
PRINT 10, I
PRINT 10
PRINT 10, J
10      FORMAT (B8.8)
END
```

I

1	0	0	1	1	1	0	1
0	1	0	1	0	1	0	1
1	0	1	0	1	0	1	0

J

1	1	0	0	1	1	1	0
1	0	1	0	1	0	1	0
0	1	0	1	0	1	0	1

Case III: Both first and second arguments are arrays of same shape. All elements of the first array are shifted according to the values of the corresponding elements of the second array. The function returns an array of the same type as the first argument.

```
INTEGER, PARAMETER :: S=SELECTED_INT_KIND(2)
INTEGER (KIND=S),DIMENSION(3) :: I,J
INTEGER (KIND=S), DIMENSION(3) :: SH= [1, -1, 2]
DATA I/ B"10011101", B"01010101", B"10101010" /

J=ISHFTC(I,SH)
PRINT 10, I
PRINT 10
PRINT 10, J
10      FORMAT (B8.8)
        END
```

I

1	0	0	1	1	1	0	1
0	1	0	1	0	1	0	1
1	0	1	0	1	0	1	0

J

0	0	1	1	1	0	1	1
1	0	1	0	1	0	1	0
1	0	1	0	1	0	1	0

Discussions related to the shifting with ISHFT are all valid in these cases also. Only difference is that the bits shifted out in ISHFT are lost and zeros are added at the other end. In case of ISHFTC the bits that are shifted out are added at the other end in the same order as they are shifted causing a circular shift.

Case IV: The second form of ISHFTC takes three arguments. The third argument (SIZE) determines the "operational zones" of the shift operation. When this argument is absent, that is, first form of ISHFTC, all the bits participate in the shift operation as shown above. If the third argument SIZE is present only the rightmost number of bits as specified in SIZE, participate in the shift − other bits are not affected.

```
INTEGER, PARAMETER :: S=SELECTED_INT_KIND(2)
INTEGER (KIND=S) :: I,SH,J
DATA I/ B"10011101"/
SH=1
J=ISHFTC(I,SH,4)
PRINT 10, I
PRINT 10, J
10      FORMAT (B8.8)
        END
```

The PRINT statements display 10011101 and 10011011 respectively. Let us try to understand the second number from the diagram:

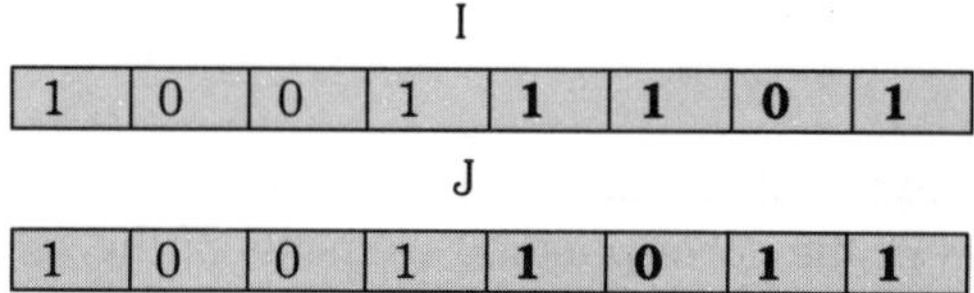

As the third argument SIZE is 4, only 4 rightmost bits participate in the shift operation and other bits remain unaffected. Thus 1101, after a circular left shift, becomes 1011.

Note, that several combination of the arguments are possible. For example, the various forms of ISHFTC discussed under Case I, II and III may also have this SIZE parameter. In addition to this, the SIZE parameter may itself be an array of the same shape as the first argument. We illustrate two such cases.

```
INTEGER, PARAMETER :: S=SELECTED_INT_KIND(2)
INTEGER (KIND=S),DIMENSION(3) :: I,J
INTEGER (KIND=S), DIMENSION(3) :: SH= [1, -1, 2]
DATA I/ B"10011101", B"01010101", B"10101000" /

J=ISHFTC(I,SH,4)
PRINT 10, I
PRINT 10
PRINT 10, J
10      FORMAT (B8.8)
        END
```

Here the first and second arguments are rank 1 arrays. The shift operations are restricted to the rightmost 4 bits of all the elements of the array. We shall mention the results from the program – 10011101, 01010101, 10101000 from the PRINT *, I and 10011011, 01011010, 10100010 from the PRINT *, J. The readers are advised to verify the results.

The next example is a modification of the last example with the third argument as a rank 1 array as well. Depending upon the value of the different elements of this array, the number of participating bits in the shift operation of the first argument will come into play.

```
INTEGER, PARAMETER :: S=SELECTED_INT_KIND(2)
INTEGER (KIND=S),DIMENSION(3) :: I,J, SIZ(3)
INTEGER (KIND=S),DIMENSION(3) :: SH= [1, -1, 2]
DATA I/ B"10011101", B"01010101", B"10101000" /
DATA SIZ /4,3,5/
```

```
        J=ISHFTC(I,SH,SIZ)
        PRINT 10, I
        PRINT 10
        PRINT 10, J
10      FORMAT (B8.8)
        END
```

Again we mention the output from this program: PRINT *, I will display 10011101, 01010101, 10101000 and PRINT *, J will display 10011011, 01010110, 10100001. It may be verified that 1 left shift, 1 right shift and 2 left shifts are performed on I(1), I(2) and I(3), where 4, 3 and 5 rightmost bits have participated in the shift operations for the three array elements respectively produce these results.

23.13 MVBITS

Case I: This intrinsic (subroutine) takes five integers as argument.

```
        CALL MVBITS (SOURCE, SPOS, LEN, DEST, DPOS)
```

SOURCE and DEST are integer variables of the same kind other arguments are integers or integer expressions. SOURCE, SPOS, LEN and DPOS are input to the subroutine and DEST is both an input and an output parameter to the subroutine. Bits from the SOURCE starting from SPOS of length LEN are transferred to DEST starting from bit position DPOS of the destination.

```
        CALL MVBITS (S,1,4,D,4)
```

will transfer 4 bits starting from the bit position 1 of S (bits 4, 3, 2 and 1). The bits are transferred to D starting from bit position 4.

S   D

The table below shows how bits are moved.

Source	Destination
Bit 1	Bit 4
Bit 2	Bit 5
Bit 3	Bit 6
Bit 4	Bit 7

Other bits of the destination are not affected. The example below shows how four 8-bit integers are packed into a 32-bit integer.

```fortran
      INTEGER, PARAMETER :: S1=SELECTED_INT_KIND(2)
      INTEGER, PARAMETER :: S2=SELECTED_INT_KIND(9)
      INTEGER (KIND=S1) :: I, J, K, L, SZ, DZ        ! 8 bit
      INTEGER (KIND=S2) :: T, IPACK                  ! 32 bit

      I=10
      J=64
      K=31
      L=11
      SZ=BIT_SIZE(I)              ! SZ=8
      DZ=BIT_SIZE(IPACK)          ! DZ=32
      IPACK=0
      T=I
!                       Pack
!      source and destination of MVBITS must be same kind
      CALL MVBITS (T,0,SZ,IPACK,DZ-SZ)
!      I goes to bits 31:24 of IPACK
      T=J
      CALL MVBITS(T,0,SZ,IPACK,DZ-2*SZ)
!      J goes to bits 23:16 of IPACK
      T=K
      CALL MVBITS(T,0,SZ,IPACK,DZ-3*SZ)
!      K goes to bits 15:8 of IPACK
      T=L
      CALL MVBITS(T,0,SZ,IPACK,DZ-4*SZ)
!      L goes to bits 7:0 of IPACK

!      Now unpack
      I=0
      J=0
      K=0
      L=0

      L=IBITS(IPACK,0,SZ)
!      rightmost 8 bits
      IPACK=ISHFT(IPACK, -SZ)              !right shift
      K=IBITS(IPACK,0,SZ)
!      rightmost 8 bits
      IPACK=ISHFT(IPACK, -SZ)              !right shift
      J=IBITS(IPACK,0,SZ)
!      rightmost 8 bits
      IPACK=ISHFT(IPACK, -SZ)              !right shift
      I=IBITS(IPACK,0,SZ)
      PRINT *, I,J,K,L
      END
```

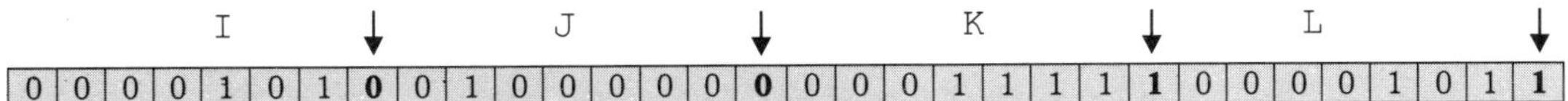

The following inequalities hold good for MVBITS.

```
LEN >= 0
SPOS >= 0
DPOS >= 0
SPOS+LEN <= BIT_SIZE (SOURCE)
DPOS+LEN <= BIT_SIZE (DEST)
```

The SOURCE and DEST may point to the same variable.

Case II: The arguments SOURCE and DEST of MVBITS may be arrays of the same shape and size. Other parameters may be integers or integer arrays. If they are integers, bits from SOURCE(1) to DEST(1), SOURCE(2) to DEST(2) etc. are transferred as discussed above. However, if SPOS, LEN, DPOS are integer arrays, the corresponding array elements are used, that is, while transferring bits from SOURCE(1) to DEST(1), the corresponding parameters SPOS(1), LEN(1) and DPOS(1) are used. Readers may convince themselves that the outputs of the following program:

```
INTEGER, DIMENSION (2) :: SO, SP, LEN, DEST, DPOS
SP=[1,2]
DEST=0
DPOS=[3,4]
SO=63
LEN=[2,3]
CALL MVBITS(SO,SP,LEN,DEST,DPOS)
PRINT *, DEST
END
```

are 24 and 112.

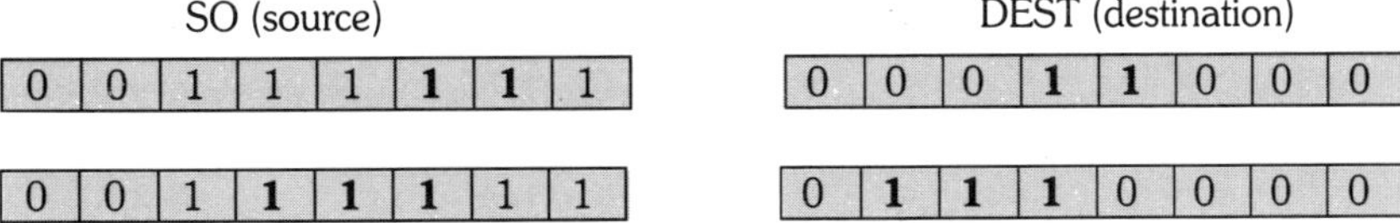

23.14 TRANSFER

This intrinsic takes three arguments, the third one, SIZE, is optional. The function interprets the bit pattern of the first argument as the type of second argument. The bit pattern of 0.5 (*see* chapter 18 & 20) is:

```
0 01111110  000 0000 0000 0000 0000 0000
```

Now,

```
INTEGER :: I
I=TRANSFER(0.5,0)
```

interprets the bit pattern of 0.5 as integer and this bit pattern corresponds to the integer value 1056964608. This 'trick' may be used to print the bit pattern of a real number with 'B' format. It may be noted that 'B' format can be used with integers only and TRANSFER is used to copy the bit pattern to an integer variable, so that the same may be displayed in 'B' format.

Both the first and the second argument may be array valued. If the second argument is of rank 1 array, the function returns an array of size just sufficient to accommodate the source.

```
COMPLEX, DIMENSION(2) :: C1
C1=TRANSFER([1.0,2.0,3.0,4.0], [(0.0, 0.0)])
```

Thus the complex number C1(1) becomes $1+2i$ and C(2) becomes $3+4i$. It may be noted that the second argument (0.0, 0.0) indicates that the first numbers are to be treated as complex numbers. The optional argument SIZE must be a scalar and integer. If this is present, the result is an array of rank 1 of size equal to SIZE.

```
PRINT *, TRANSFER([1.0,2.0,3.0,4.0],[(0.0, 0.0)],1)
```

will print (1.0, 2.0) because the TRANSFER function will create a rank 1 complex array of size 1. Replacing the last parameter by 2, the PRINT state will print (1.0, 2.0) (3.0, 4.0) because now the function will create a rank 1 array of size 2.

Chapter 24

EXTERNAL FILES

The output of a program may be the input of another program. In such cases it is convenient to store the output of the first program to some external device so that it is available even after the end of the job. Subsequently the same can be read by the second program from the same external device knowing the structure of the data on the output device. Sometimes it is not convenient to supply the input to a program from the keyboard during the execution. In such cases the data may be supplied from some external device. The creation of such data on the external device may be accomplished by some other software not necessarily by Fortran.

In the following we first describe a few terms that are required for handling external files.

24.1 Record

A record is collection of related objects. For example, an employee record may consist of a name of a person, his address, age, sex, salary, date of joining, date of retirement etc. There are three types of records:

- Formatted
- Unformatted
- End File

24.2 File

A file is collection of records. For example, a collection of employees' record containing information about all the employees of an institution makes an "employee" file. Three types of files are available in Fortran.

- Sequential
- Direct
- Stream

24.3 Formatted Records

A formatted record consists of string of characters as permitted by the system (usually ASCII characters). The record length of such a record is the total number of characters present in the record. Within a Fortran program, formatted records are generated through formatted output (WRITE/PRINT) statement. It is read by a formatted input (READ) statement. A formatted record may be created by a program other than a Fortran program. A record having length equal to zero is permitted.

24.4 Unformatted Records

Unformatted records are processor dependent; they are read or written by unformatted READ or WRITE Fortran statement. The length of the unformatted record is usually calculated as the total number of bytes required to store the record. Record having length equal to zero is permitted.

24.5 Endfile Record

This is special type of record that signals end of a file of a sequential file. The end of file record is the last record of a file. There is no length property associated with the Endfile record.

24.6 Sequential Files

A sequential file can be read sequentially. It is not possible to read 10th record without reading the first 9 records. It is also necessary to create the file sequentially.

24.7 Direct Files

A direct file can be read in any order, that is, one can read directly the 10th record without having to read the first 9 records. Similarly, it is possible to create 10th record without creating the first 9 records. The record size of all records of a direct file is same.

24.8 Stream Files

In a steam oriented input output operation a record is read or written in term of bytes or some integer multiples of bytes. This is discussed at the appropriate place.

24.9 Unit Numbers

A file is accessed within a Fortran program through a unit number. The unit number can be any positive integer between 1 and 99.

24.10 Scratch and Saved Files

A file created within a program may be temporary or permanent. A temporary file, normally called a scratch file, is deleted from the system when the job ends. A scratch file does not require any name. A permanent file, on the other hand, remains available on the external device after the job ends. This file must have a name — either supplied by the programmer or the default supplied by the system.

24.11 OPEN, CLOSE and INQUIRE Statements

In this section we shall discuss three statements, OPEN, CLOSE and INQUIRE.

The OPEN statement makes a connection between the unit number and the external file. Some files like keyboard (input), screen (output), and error file are usually pre-connected to some fixed unit number. These files are not to be opened explicitly. Usually, unit 5 is connected to the keyboard and unit 6 is connected to the screen during interactive mode.

A CLOSE statement is used to terminate in a tidy manner the connection between the unit number and the external file.

An INQUIRE statement is used to make an inquiry about a file. The syntax of all the three statements are similar:

```
OPEN(UNIT=unit no, olist=value)
CLOSE(UNIT=unit no, olist=value)
INQUIRE(UNIT=unit no, olist=value)
```

where *olist* is an optional specifier. The optional specifiers are discussed below. All the optional specifiers are not available to all the three statements. Again some specifiers are dependent on other specifiers.

24.12 Optional Specifiers

UNIT=*unit-number* (open, inquire, close)

As already mentioned, UNIT establishes a connection between the Fortran program and the file. All transactions take place through the unit-number. UNIT=*unit-number* may be replaced by just the *unit-number*. Normally the unit-number is the first item of *olist*.

```
OPEN(UNIT=10, .....)
CLOSE(UNIT=20)
INQUIRE (30, ....)
```

FILE=*char-variable* (open, inquire)

The character string is the name of the file to be connected with the unit. If the STATUS= 'SCRATCH', this specifier is not required — the system uses a processor dependent file name.

```
OPEN(UNIT=10,FILE='A.DAT')
```

For a successful execution of the OPEN statement, unit 10 will be connected with the file 'A.DAT'. For an INQUIRE statement, FILE= , is used to make an inquiry about a file. It is not necessary to connect the file; it is not necessary to open the file either.

```
INQUIRE (FILE='T37.F95', ...)
```

STATUS=*char-variable* (open)

The character string can be 'OLD', 'NEW', 'SCRATCH', 'REPLACE' or 'UNKNOWN'. If 'NEW' is specified, the file must not be present. If 'OLD' is specified, file must be present. If 'SCRATCH' is specified, the file is created and subsequently deleted at the end of the job. In this case, FILE= , must not be present. If 'REPLACE' is specified and the file is present, the existing file is deleted and a new file is created; if the file is not present, a new file is created like 'NEW'. If 'UNKNOWN' is specified, the STATUS becomes processor dependent.

```
OPEN(UNIT=10, file='A.DAT', STATUS='REPLACE')
```

ACCESS= *char-variable* (open, inquire)

The character string can be 'SEQUENTIAL', 'DIRECT' or 'STREAM' depending upon the access. The default is 'SEQUENTIAL'. For an existing file, the access must be an allowed value. For an INQUIRE statement if no file is connected it returns 'UNDEFINED'.

```
CHARACTER (LEN=10) :: ACC
OPEN (20, ACCESS='SEQUENTIAL')
INQUIRE (20, ACCESS=ACC)
```

If the unit 20 is opened in SEQUENTIAL mode, the INQUIRE statement will set the character variable ACC to 'SEQUENTIAL'

ACTION= *char-variable* (open, inquire)

The character string can be 'READ, 'WRITE' or 'READWRITE'. If the ACTION is 'READ', the file is opened in read only mode and as such WRITE/PRINT and ENDFILE statements cannot be used on that file. If the ACTION is 'WRITE', a READ operation is not permitted for such connection. If 'READWRITE' is the value of the ACTION, there is no restriction. If ACTION is omitted, the default is processor dependent. The default is usually 'READWRITE'.

```
CHARACTER (LEN=10):: ACC
OPEN(10,ACTION='WRITE')
INQUIRE (10, ACTION=ACC)
PRINT *, ACC
END
```

FORM= *char-variable* (open, inquire)

The character string can be 'FORMATTED' or 'UNFORMATTED'. If this is omitted, it is 'FORMATTED' for a sequential file and 'UNFORMATTED' for the direct or stream access.

```
CHARACTER (LEN=10) :: ACC
OPEN(10, ACCESS='SEQUENTIAL',FORM='FORMATTED', &
      FILE='FORM.DAT', STATUS='NEW')
INQUIRE(10, FORM=ACC)
PRINT *, ACC

END
```

The INQUIRE statement returns 'FORMATTED' and stores this value in ACC.

ASYNCHRONOUS= *char-variable* (open, inquire)

The character string can be 'YES' or 'NO'. If it is 'YES', asynchronous input/output is allowed in the corresponding unit. The default is 'NO' (*see* section 24.19).

BLANK= *char-variable* (open, inquire)

The character string is either 'NULL' or 'ZERO'. The default is 'NULL'. This specifier, BLANK, can be used only for formatted input. It determines how blanks during the numeric input are to be interpreted. When the value is 'NULL', blanks are ignored. However, if the field is completely blank, it is taken as zero. When the value is 'ZERO' blanks will be treated as zeros. This has no effect on output.

```
CHARACTER (LEN=10) :: ACC
OPEN(10,BLANK='ZERO')
INQUIRE (10, BLANK=ACC)
PRINT *, ACC
END
```

DECIMAL=*char-variable* (open, inquire)

The character string is either 'COMMA' or 'POINT'. This specifier can be used only with formatted input or output. The default value is 'POINT'. If the file is opened with DECIMAL='COMMA', the decimal points are replaced by a comma. If the unit 10 is opened with DECIMAL='COMMA', the file created by the program:

```
REAL :: R=10.2

OPEN (10, FILE='A.DAT',STATUS='NEW', DECIMAL='COMMA')
WRITE(10, 20)R
20      FORMAT(F8.3)
END
```

will be

```
bb10,200.
```

However, if DECIMAL= 'POINT' is absent or it is omitted, the file will contain: bb10.200.

In the above program if an inquiry is made about the specifier DECIMAL, COMMA will be returned.

```
REAL :: R=10.2
CHARACTER (LEN=15) :: ACC=" "
OPEN (10, FILE='A.DAT',STATUS='NEW', DECIMAL='COMMA')
WRITE(10, 20)R
20      FORMAT(F8.3)
INQUIRE(10, DECIMAL=ACC)
PRINT *, ACC
END
```

If there is no connection between the unit number and the file or the file is not opened for formatted input or output, INQUIRE will return the value of the specifier as 'UNDEFINED'.

DELIM= *char-variable* (open, inquire)
The character string may be 'APOSTROPHE', 'QUOTE' or 'NONE'. The specifier is permitted for formatted output statements. This specifier is the current value of the delimiter that will be used to delimit character constants for list directed or namelist output operation. If 'NONE is specified, the characters will not be delimited by any character (apostrophe or quote). The default value is 'NONE'

```
CHARACTER (LEN=10) :: C='AVBDWB'
CHARACTER (LEN=10) :: ACC
OPEN(10, ACCESS='SEQUENTIAL',FORM='FORMATTED', &
        DELIM='QUOTE',FILE='DELIM.DAT', STATUS='NEW')
WRITE(10,*)C
INQUIRE(10, DELIM=ACC)
PRINT *, ACC
END
```

The output file DELIM.DAT will have a record "AVBDWBbbbb", where b represents blank.
The INQUIRE statement with DELIM=*char-variable* returns the value of the DELIM specifer. If there is no connection between the unit and the file or FORM is not 'FORMATTED', 'UNDEFINED' is returned. In the above program the value of ACC will be 'QUOTE' as the file has been opened with DELIM= 'QUOTE'.

PAD=*char-variable* (open)
The character string can be 'YES' or 'NO'. This is available only for formatted I/O. The default value is 'YES'. If the value is 'YES', blank characters are used for padding if the list and format specification combination require more characters than the number of characters available in the record. If the value is 'NO', the number of characters in the record must not be less than the number of character required for the list and format specification (The exception is when ADVANCE= 'NO' is specified or EOR= , or IOSTAT= specification is present).

POSITION=*char-variable* (open, inquire)
The character string can be 'ASIS', 'REWIND' or 'APPEND'. This is available for sequential or stream access. When a file is created, it is positioned at the beginning. 'REWIND' positions the file at the beginning of the file. 'APPEND' positions the existing file just before the end of file mark. If there is no end of file mark, the file is positioned at the end of the last record. If POSITION= 'ASIS' and the file exists and is connected, the position remains unaltered. However, if the file exists and is not connected, 'ASIS' leaves the file position unspecified.
INQUIRE returns POSITION= 'UNDEFINED' if the file is not connected.

RECL= *integer* (open, inquire)
The positive integer indicates the size of each record of a direct I/O. This should not be specified for stream access. For sequential access, if this is not specified, the default value is dependent on the processor.

ROUND=*char-variable* (open, inquire)

The character string can be 'UP', 'DOWN', 'ZERO', 'NEAREST', 'COMPATIBLE' or 'PROCESSOR_DEFINED'. This specifier is applicable for formatted I/O (just for I/O). This specifies the I/O rounding mode. At this moment no compiler supports this feature.

SIGN=*char-variable* (open, inquire)

The character string can be 'PLUS', 'SUPPRESS' or 'PROCESSOR_DEFINED'. This is available for formatted I/O. If it is 'PLUS', '+' sign is included for positive numbers. The default is 'PROCESSOR_DEFINED' which is usually 'SUPPRESSED', that is, '+' sign is suppressed when the number is positive.

For INQUIRE, if the unit is not connected the *char-string* is set to 'UNDEFINED'

ERR= *label* (open, inquire)

If any error condition occurs during the execution of an OPEN or INQUIRE statement, control is passed to the statement label mentioned along with ERR.

```
OPEN (10, ERR=100, ....)
```

Control will be passed to the statement label 100, if an error is detected while opening the file. If ERR=*label* (or IOSTAT=) is not present, the job is terminated.

IOSTAT= *integer variable* (open, inquire)

During the opening of a file, zero is returned if no error condition occurs. The specifier becomes a processor dependent positive number if an error occurs. In case of an error, if neither IOSTAT nor ERR is present, the job is terminated. For successful execution of an INQUIRE statement, IOSTAT returns 0.

IOMESG= *char-variable*

In the case of any error or end of file or end of record occurring during the execution of an I/O statement or with an OPEN or INQUIRE statement, the processor sets some explanatory message to this variable; it remains unaltered if there is no error (EOF or EOR). Consider the following program:

```
CHARACTER (LEN=40) :: IM='XXXXX'
INTEGER:: IS
OPEN(10, &
FILE='FORM.DAT', STATUS='NEW',IOSTAT=IS, IOMSG=IM)
PRINT *, IM
END
```

Let us assume that a file FORM.DAT already exists in the disk. The OPEN statement would then be unsuccessful because STATUS= 'NEW' is expected to create a new file. If the file exists, an error condition results. Now IM is set to 'XXXXX'. When there is an error condition, processor will change this string of character by some explanatory message, which is in this case "NEW file already exists". Note that in this case the IOSTAT= *specifier* must be present.

END=*label*

    If an end of file is detected during the input, the control is passed to the statement *label* mentioned along with END. If end of file occurs and the END=*label* is omitted, the job is terminated.

DIRECT= *char-variable*, STREAM=*char-variable* (inquire)

    The *char-string* can have the value 'YES' or 'NO' depending upon whether direct access mode or stream access mode respectively is allowed for the file or not. It returns 'UNKNOWN' if the processor cannot determine the exact status.

EXIST=*logical variable* (inquire)

    This checks if the file specified by the specifier FILE is available on disk. It returns true if the file exists, false otherwise.

FORMATTED= *char-variable*, UNFORMATTED=*char-variable* (inquire)

    On inquiry *char-string* would contain 'YES' or 'NO' depending upon FORM specifier and 'UNKNOWN' if the processor is unable to determine the status.

NAME= *char-variable* (inquire)

    On inquiry the char-string would contain the name of the file or 'UNKNOWN'.

```
CHARACTER(LEN=15) ::CH
OPEN(25,FILE='SEQF.DAT',STATUS='REPLACE',FORM='FORMATTED')
INQUIRE (25,NAME=CH)
```

NAMED=*logical variable* (inquire)

    On inquiry the logical variable is true if the file has a name. It is false otherwise.

NEXTREC= *integer variable* (inquire)

    This is used for direct I/O. Its value is last record +1. If the file does not contain any record, it is 1. If the is not a direct file it is undefined.

NUMBER= integer variable (inquire)

    The unit number assigned to a file (FILE=) is returned to the integer variable. If no unit is connected to the file, -1 is returned (though it is not mentioned in the Fortran Report, the file name is case sensitive) for the NAG compiler (even under Windows). The file name written in the OPEN statement must be exactly same as the file name given in the INQUIRE statement.

```
INTEGER:: N
OPEN(25,FILE='SEQF.DAT',STATUS='REPLACE',FORM='FORMATTED')
INQUIRE(FILE='SEQF.DAT', NUMBER=N)
```

Here N will be 25. However if FILE= 'sEQF.DAT', N will be -1 (note that in this case 'sEQF.DAT' would not be considered same as 'SEQF.DAT' even under Windows).

OPENED= *logical variable* (inquire)

    On inquiry the logical variable is true if the corresponding file is open, false otherwise.

```
LOGICAL :: L
OPEN(25,FILE='SEQF.DAT',STATUS='REPLACE',FORM='FORMATTED')
INQUIRE(25, OPENED=L)
PRINT *, L
```

Here L is true. The INQUIRE statement may of the form

```
        INQUIRE(FILE='SEQF.DAT', OPENED=L)
```

POS=*integer* (inquire)

This is used with stream I/O. It returns the number of file storage unit immediately following the current position. If the file is not connected it is undefined.

READ=*char-variable*, WRITE=*char-variable*, READWRITE=*char-variable* (inquire)

All these three specifiers are similar in nature. If the ACCESS matches with the specifier, the value of the character string is 'YES', if does not match the value is 'NO' and the value is 'UNKNOWN' if the processor is unable to determine.

```
        CHARACTER(LEN=15)  ::CH
        OPEN(25,FILE='SEQF.DAT',STATUS='REPLACE',FORM='FORMATTED', &
            ACTION='WRITE')
        INQUIRE(25, WRITE=CH)
        PRINT *, CH
```

Since ACTION= 'WRITE', the value of CH will be 'YES'.

SEQUENTIAL=*char-variable* (inquire)

The char-variable is set to 'YES' if the file is opened with ACCESS= 'SEQUENTIAL', 'NO' otherwise, 'UNKNOWN' if the processor is unable to determine.

SIZE= *integer* (inquire)

On inquiry the integer contains the size of an existing disk file. If the processor cannot determine the size of the file, -1 is returned.

```
        INTEGER :: N
        INQUIRE (FILE='XXA.DAT', SIZE=N)
        PRINT *, N
```

Before we end this section, here is complete list of specifiers for OPEN and INQUIRE statements.

OPEN:

- UNIT
- ACCESS
- ACTION
- ASYNCHRONOUS
- BLANK
- DELIM
- ENCODING
- ERR
- FILE
- FORM
- ISMSG
- IOSTAT
- PAD
- POSITION

- RECL
- ROUND
- SIGN
- STATUS

INQUIRE:

- UNIT
- FILE
- ACCESS
- ACTION
- ASYNCHRONOUS
- BLANK
- DECIMAL
- DELIM
- DIRECT
- ENCODING
- ERR
- EXIST
- FORM
- FORMATTED
- ID
- IOMSG
- IOSTAT
- NAME
- NAMED
- NEXTREC
- NUMBER
- OPENED
- PAD
- PENDING
- POS
- POSITION
- READ
- READWRITE
- RECL
- ROUND
- SEQUENTIAL
- SIGN
- SIZE
- STREAM
- UNFORMATTED

24.13 Kind Type Parameters of Integer Specifiers

The present version of Fortran allows integer specifiers like NEXTREC, NUMBER etc to be of any type (kind) of integer. Earlier versions of Fortran allowed these integer specifiers to be of default kind only.

24.14 ENDFILE Statement

The syntax of an ENDFILE statement is:

                       ENDFILE *unit-no*
like   ENDFILE 10

This statement writes a special record called 'end-of-file' on a file opened for sequential access. The file is positioned after the end of file record.

24.15 REWIND Statement

REWIND statement brings the record pointer to the beginning of a file. If the record pointer is at the beginning, the statement has no effect. The syntax of REWIND is

                       REWIND *unit-no*
like   REWIND 25

24.16 BACKSPACE Statement

The BACKSPACE statement backspaces one record of the specified unit. If the file pointer is at the beginning of the file, no action is taken. If the file pointer is just after the end of file mark, it is positioned before the end of file mark. Sometimes the BACKSPACE statement writes an end of file record before backspacing. In that case the record pointer is positioned before the record that precedes the end of file record. Example of BACKSPACE statement:

                       BACKSPACE 10

where 10 is unit number. It is prohibited to backspace a file that is connected but does not exist. BACKSPACE is not allowed for a unit which is being written through NAMELIST or list-directed formatting.

24.17 Data Transfer Statement

The READ statement is used to read data from a file and PRINT or WRITE statement is used to write data on a file. The syntax of the READ statement is

                       READ(*unit-no, io-control-list*) *list*
or,   READ *format, list*

        The syntax of PRINT and WRITE statements are:

                       PRINT *format, list*
                       WRITE(*unit-no, io-control-list*) *list*

24.18 READ / WRITE Statement

The "READ format, list" and "PRINT format, list" have already been discussed in chapter 16 and as such it will not be repeated here. The *io-control-list* of READ and WRITE statements are:

- UNIT= *unit-no*
- FMT= *format*
- NML= *namelist-group-name*
- ADVANCE= *char-sting*
- BLANK= *char-string* [READ]
- DECIMAL= *char-string*
- DELIM= *char-string* [WRITE only]
- END= *label* [READ]
- EOR= *label* [READ]
- ERR= *label*
- IOMSG= *character variable*
- IOSTAT= *integer variable*
- PAD= char-string
- POS= *integer*
- REC= *integer*
- ROUND= *char-string*
- SIGN= *char-string* [WRITE]
- SIZE= *integer variable* [READ].

24.19 Asynchronous Input/Output

In synchronous input/output operation, the system waits till the operation is completed. Asynchronous input/output, on the other hand, continues to execute following instructions and input/output operations proceed asynchronously. It is the responsibility of the programmer not to use the data before the transfer is over and the programmer is supposed to check the status of the I/O operation before using the data.

The file must be opened with ASYNCHRONOUS= 'YES' in the OPEN statement.

24.20 FLUSH

The FLUSH statement acts on an external file and causes all data to be written on the external file so as to make it available to other processes; data thus placed in the external file even by a non-Fortran program may thus be made available to a READ statement. Essentially, FLUSH "flushes input/output buffer".

```
FLUSH unit-number
FLUSH 10
FLUSH(10)
```

The FLUSH statement may have usual specifications like IOSTAT, IOMESG, ERR. Once the FLUSH statement is executed, the most recent data is available from the external file.

24.21 Rules of the Input-Output Control List

(a) A particular I/O control specifier may appear only once.

(b) UNIT= unit number may be written without UNIT=. If UNIT= is omitted, the corresponding unit number must be the first item in the I/O control specification list.

(c) DELIM and SIGN can be used only with READ statement.

(d) BLANK, PAD, ERR, EOR, SIZE can be used only with READ statement.

(e) The label (statement number) associated with ERR, EOR, and END must be in same scoping unit as the READ statement.

(f) If NML= *namelist-group-name* is replaced by just the *namelist-group-name*, it should be the second item in the I/O control list.

(g) If the unit number is other than a file number, REC and POS, I/O control must not be present.

(h) If REC is present, END and *namelist-group-name* must not be present and Format must not be list directed (asterisk).

(i) If ADVANCE is used for sequential or stream with Format statement, the unit must be an integer (not internal I/O).

(j) If EOR or SIZE is used, ADVANCE must appear in the control list.

(k) If ASYNCHRONOUS='YES', the unit number must be an integer.

(l) If ID appears, ASYNCHRONOUS must be 'YES'.

(m) If POS is present, *io-control-list* should not contain REC.

(n) DECIMAL, BLANK, PAD, SIGN and ROUND specifier can only be used with Format or *namelist-group-name.*

(o) SIZE and EOR can be used only with ADVANCE= 'NO'.

(p) For ADVANCE, ASYNCHRONOUS, DECIMAL, BLANK, DELIM, PAD, SIGN and ROUND trailing blanks in the list of I/O control are ignored. Also the list elements are case independent.

24.22 IS_IOSTAT_END

If the variable I is used as IOSTAT=I, this function [IS_IOSTAT_END(I)] returns true if the end of file condition is reached; if returns false otherwise.

24.23 IS_IOSTAT_EOR

If the variable I is used as IOSTAT=I this function [IS_IOSTAT_EOR(I)] returns true if the end of record is reached; it returns false otherwise.

24.24 Examples of File Operations

(a) Creation of a Formatted Sequential File.

```
          INTEGER::A=2
          REAL::B=20.5
          CHARACTER(LEN=5)::C='INDIA'
          DOUBLE PRECISION::D= 3.1415926589D0
          COMPLEX::E=(2.0,3.0)
          OPEN(25,FILE='SEQF.DAT',STATUS='REPLACE',FORM='FORMATTED')
          WRITE(25,100)A,B,C,D,E
100       FORMAT(I5,F8.3,A5,D20.10,2F8.3)
          CLOSE(25)
          END
```

(b) Reading a Formatted Sequential File.

```
          INTEGER::A
          REAL::B
          CHARACTER(LEN=5)::C
          DOUBLE PRECISION::D
          COMPLEX::E
          OPEN(25,FILE='SEQF.DAT',STATUS='OLD',FORM='FORMATTED')
          READ(25,100)A,B,C,D,E
100       FORMAT(I5,F8.3,A5,D20.10,2F8.3)
          PRINT *,A,B,C,D,E
          CLOSE(25)
          END
```

(c) Creation of Unformatted Sequential File.

```
          INTEGER::A=2
          REAL::B=20.5
          CHARACTER(LEN=5)::C='INDIA'
          DOUBLE PRECISION::D= 3.1415926589D0
          COMPLEX::E=(2.0,3.0)
          OPEN(25,FILE='SEQF.DAT',STATUS='REPLACE',FORM='UNFORMATTED')
          WRITE(25)A,B,C,D,E
          CLOSE(25)
          END
```

(d) Reading Unformatted Sequential File

```
          INTEGER::A
          REAL::B
          CHARACTER(LEN=5)::C
```

```
      DOUBLE PRECISION::D
      COMPLEX::E
      OPEN(25,FILE='SEQF.DAT',STATUS='OLD',FORM='UNFORMATTED')
      READ(25)A,B,C,D,E
      PRINT *,A,B,C,D,E
      CLOSE(25)
      END
```

(e) Creation and Reading of Formatted Direct File.

```
      INTEGER::A=2,P
      INTEGER::I,IREC=1
      REAL::B=20.5,Q
      CHARACTER(LEN=5)::C='INDIA',R
      DOUBLE PRECISION::D=3.1415926589D0,S
      COMPLEX::E=(2.0,3.0),T
      OPEN(25,ACCESS='DIRECT',FILE='SEQF.DAT',STATUS='REPLACE',&
        FORM='FORMATTED',RECL=54)
      DO I=1,10
      WRITE(25,100,REC=IREC)A+I,B,C,D,E
      IREC=IREC+1
      ENDDO
100   FORMAT(I5,F8.3,A5,D20.10,2F8.3)
      IREC=7
      READ(25,100,REC=IREC)P,Q,R,S,T

      PRINT *,P,Q,R,S,T
      CLOSE(25)
      END
```

(f) Creation and Reading of Unformatted Random File.

```
      INTEGER::A=2,P,N
      INTEGER::I,IREC=1
      LOGICAL::L1
      REAL::B=20.5,Q
      CHARACTER(LEN=5)::C='INDIA',R
      CHARACTER(LEN=30)::CH1
      DOUBLE PRECISION::D= 3.1415926589D0,S
      COMPLEX::E=(2.0,3.0),T
      OPEN(25,ACCESS='DIRECT',FILE='SEQF.DAT',STATUS='REPLACE',&
        FORM='UNFORMATTED',RECL=29)
      INQUIRE(25,NAME=CH1)
      INQUIRE(25,NAMED=L1)
      INQUIRE(FILE='SEQF.DAT',NUMBER=N)
      PRINT *,N
      PRINT *,L1
      PRINT *,CH1
```

```
DO I=1,10
WRITE(25,REC=IREC)A+I,B,C,D,E
IREC=IREC+1
ENDDO
INQUIRE(25,NEXTREC=N)

PRINT *,N
INQUIRE(25,FORMATTED=CH1)
PRINT *,"==========",CH1

INQUIRE(25,SIZE=N)
PRINT *,N
IREC=3
READ(25,REC=IREC)P,Q,R,S,T

PRINT *,P,Q,R,S,T
CLOSE(25)
END
```

No explanations are given for these programs. Readers are requested to read these program; they can type and run these programs and try to explain the results.

24.25 Stream Input-Output

Input-output operations of standard Fortran are basically record oriented. Though for the direct I/O the records can be accessed randomly, yet record size for this type of I/O is fixed.

Often the situation is quite different. If the file is generated by a non-Fortran program or by some package or by some measuring instrument, the structure of records may not be similar to standard Fortran. In such a case the input-output statements discussed in the previous sections are not suitable for data transfer. Fortunately, Fortran provides an alternative way, called stream I/O, for accessing these types of records.

24.26 Storage Unit of Stream I/O

In case of stream I/O the basic storage unit is a byte. The system keeps track of the number of bytes required for a particular type of variable — four for standard integer and real, eight for complex variable and so on. An internal counter is maintained containing the byte position of the next item to be read/written on/from the file. This is incremented automatically when a variable is written to the file and the increment takes place according to the type of the variable. The next item is written at the current position of the record pointer. Similarly, by setting a value to the counter, the corresponding item may be fetched randomly from the file. When the file is opened, the counter is set to 1. The concept of 'record' ceases to exist for files created by stream I/O.

24.27 Stream I/O Type

Stream I/O can be of two types – formatted and unformatted. Unformatted stream I/O is more convenient than formatted stream I/O. We shall first discuss unformatted stream I/O.

24.28 File Opening

The file to be created for stream I/O is opened in the following manner.

```
OPEN(10,FILE="STREAM.DAT",ACCESS="STREAM",STATUS="NEW",&
     FORM="UNFORMATTED")
```

If an existing file created earlier is to be opened, the corresponding OPEN statement is:

```
OPEN(10,FILE="STREAM.DAT",ACCESS="STREAM",STATUS="OLD",&
     FORM="UNFORMATTED")
```

Access is specified as "STREAM" meaning thereby that the file will be accessed in stream mode. The default FORM of stream I/O is UNFORMATTED, so in the above case FORM= "UNFORMATTED" is redundant.

24.29 Unformatted Stream File

This is illustrated with an example shown below:

```
      PROGRAM STREAMIO
      REAL::R=2.0,R1
      INTEGER::A=10,PPOS
      CHARACTER(LEN=7)::CH="SUBRATA"
      CHARACTER(LEN=4)::CH1
      DOUBLE PRECISION::D=3.141592658D0
      COMPLEX::C=(2.0,3.0)
      OPEN(10,FILE="STREAM.DAT",ACCESS="STREAM",STATUS="REPLACE")
      WRITE(10)R,A,CH
      WRITE(10)D,C
      INQUIRE(10,POS=PPOS)
      INQUIRE(10,ACCESS=CH)
      PRINT *,CH
      PRINT 20, PPOS-1
20    FORMAT('TOTAL NO OF BYTES WRITTEN  ',I3)

      READ(10,POS=11)CH1
      PRINT *,CH1
      READ(10,POS=28)R1
      PRINT *,R1
      CLOSE(10)
      END
```

The outputs from the program are:

```
STREAM
TOTAL NO OF BYTES WRITTEN   31
BRAT
```

Let us try to understand the output. The WRITE statement will create a file containing 4 bytes each for R and A, 7 bytes for CH, 8 bytes of for D and 8 bytes for C. This is depicted below:

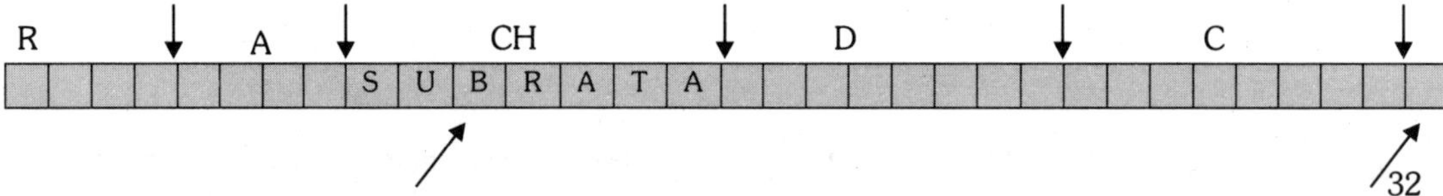

The INQUIRE statement will return 32 as the that is the next position where writing can take place. Having set POS to 11, the READ statement reads 'BRAT' and stores it in the location CH1 (the length of the CH1 being 4).

24.30 Formatted Stream I/O

In formatted stream I/O, the file must be opened with FORM= "FORMATTED" and I/O operations are performed with the Format statement. The difficulty in formatted stream I/O is that each WRITE statement adds a record terminator, which is machine dependent. It may be a carriage return or line feed or both or some other character. Therefore, the so-called random reading/writing is difficult to perform as counting of bytes may not be easy because of the presence of additional record terminating character(s). However, POS=1 when the file is opened and the value of POS may be determined by an INQUIRE statement. Formatted stream file I/O is rarely used. However, the following program shows creation of formatted stream file.

```
          REAL::R=2.0
          INTEGER::A=10,PPOS
          CHARACTER(LEN=7)::CH="SUBRATA"
          DOUBLE PRECISION::D=3.141592658D0
          COMPLEX::C=(2.0,3.0)
          OPEN(10,FILE="STREAM.DAT",ACCESS="STREAM", FORM="FORMATTED", &
            STATUS="NEW")
          WRITE(10,40)R,A,CH
40        FORMAT(F8.3,I3,A7)
          WRITE(10,21)D,C
21        FORMAT(D20.10,2E16.6)
          INQUIRE(10,POS=PPOS)
          PRINT 20, PPOS-1
20        FORMAT('TOTAL NO OF BYTES WRITTEN  ',I3)
          CLOSE(10)
          END
```

The output shows 74, that is, 4 additional characters have been added (8+3+7+20+2*16=70). We now read the same file byte by byte and print the record in A Format. We add a few lines to the above program but we display the complete program below:

```
        REAL::R=2.0
        INTEGER::A=10,PPOS
        INTEGER*1 Y
        CHARACTER(LEN=7)::CH="SUBRATA"
        CHARACTER (LEN=1)::X
        DOUBLE PRECISION::D=3.141592658D0
        COMPLEX::C=(2.0,3.0)
        OPEN(10,FILE="STREAM.DAT",ACCESS="STREAM", FORM="FORMATTED", &
         STATUS="REPLACE")
        WRITE(10,40)R,A,CH
40      FORMAT(F8.3,I3,A7)
        WRITE(10,21)D,C
21      FORMAT(D20.10,2E16.6)
        INQUIRE(10,POS=PPOS)
        PRINT 20, PPOS-1
20      FORMAT('TOTAL NO OF BYTES WRITTEN  ',I3)
        PPOS=1                     ! start from the beginning
        DO I=1,74
        READ(10,23,POS=PPOS)X    ! Read one character at a time in A format
        PPOS=PPOS+1                ! increment the record pointer
23      FORMAT(A1)

        WRITE (6,24,ADVANCE='NO')X ! print the character in A format
24      FORMAT(A1)
        ENDDO
        CLOSE(10)
        END
```

The outputs are:

```
TOTAL NO OF BYTES WRITTEN  74
   2.000 10SUBRATA        0.3141592658D+01      0.200000E+01      0.300000E+01
```

24.31 Rule of Thumb – File Structure

The choice of file structure obviously lies with the programmer. However, a rule of thumb may be formulated. The formatted I/O requires conversion (binary to ASCII and ASCII to binary). On the other hand, unformatted I/O does not require any conversion because the data as it is laid out in the computer memory is written directly to disk.

If the output of a program becomes the input to another program and that too in a different machine, formatted I/O should be used. It is difficult to read the binary file if it is created in a machine of different type, for example the representation of a number may be laid out in a different arrangement of bits. Unformatted I/O is recommended so long as I/O operations are performed within the same machine. It is faster because no conversion takes place. All scratch files normally use unformatted I/O.

The choice of sequential or direct (random) I/O is governed by the nature of the problem. If the data is to be read sequentially, a sequential file is used. When the records are accessed in random, direct file is preferred.

The choice between sequential, direct and stream I/O is dictated by the nature of the file. If the file is created by a Fortran program, sequential or direct I/O is preferred. If the file is created by non-Fortran program / package / some instrument having record structure different from Fortran, most of the time such file cannot be properly read by standard Fortran READ statement. In such a case stream I/O may be an alternative and should be tried though you need to understand the structure of the data to make use of it later.

Chapter 25

INTEROPERABILITY BETWEEN FORTRAN AND C

A Fortran program can call a C function; similarly a C program can 'call' a Fortran subprogram. Fortran provides a mechanism by which Fortran variables may be "interoperable" with C. This is achieved by declaring Fortran entries as interoperable with C by appropriate declaration. We shall demonstrate this feature by writing short programs in Fortran and C. It will be assumed that the readers have working knowledge in the programming language C. No attempt will be made to "teach" C programming language.

For some historical reason, C programmers normally use lower case letters to write C programs. It was mentioned in chapter 1 that normally Fortran is case insensitive – programmers as well may use lower case letters to write a Fortran program. To maintain symmetry all the examples in this chapter will be written in lower case letters.

All these examples have been tested with the NAG Fortran compiler running under Linux. The C compiler that came along with the Linux was used to compile C programs.

25.1 Interoperability of Intrinsic Types

To make the entries of Fortran and C interoperable, the Fortran program must use a module called *iso_c_binding*. This module contains several named constants, which are used as kind parameters for the entries of Fortran. Table 25.1 contains a list of such named constants. The numerical values of the named constants are compiler dependent as shown in Table 25.1. A compiler may not support every item mentioned in Table 25.1. A negative value indicates that the support for that particular item is not available.

Character type interoperability deserves special mention – either the length parameter is omitted or it is initialized by a single character. The reason is that a C character variable can accommodate only one character.

Table 25.1. Interoperability between Fortran and C

Type	Named Constant	Value (NAG)	Value (g95)	C type or types
Integer	c_int	3	4	int
	c_short	2	2	short int
	c_long	3	4	long int
	c_long_long	4	8	long long int
	c_signed_char	1	1	signed char, unsigned char
	c_short_t	3	4	size_t
	c_int8_t	1	1	int8_t
	c_int16_t	2	2	int16_t
	c_int32_t	3	4	int_32_t
	c_int64_t	4	8	int64_t
	c_int_least8_t	1	1	int_least8_t
	c_int_least16_t	2	2	int_least16_t
	c_int_least32_t	3	4	int_least32_t
	c_int_least64_t	4	8	int_least64_t
	c_int_fast8_t	3	1	int_fast8_t
	c_int_fast16_t	3	4	int_fast16_t
	c_int_fast32_t	3	4	int_fast32_t
	c_int_fast64_t	4	8	int_fast64_t
	c_intmax_t	4	4	intmax_t
	c_intptr_t	3	4	intptr_t
Real	c_float	1	4	float
	c_double	2	8	double
	c_long_double	-4	-1	long double
Complex	c_float_complex	1	4	float_complex
	c_double_complex	2	8	double_complex
	c_long_double_complex	-4	-1	long_double_complex
Logical	c_bool	1	-1	_Bool
Character	c_char	1	1	char

Some other named constants, which are the unprintable characters of C language, are also available. The meaning of these named constants is obvious from their names. Table 25.2 contains a list of these named constants together with their internal values.

Table 25.2 Unprintable Named Constant

Named constant	Internal value
c_null_char	0
c_alert	7
c_backspace	8
c_form_feed	12
c_new_line	10
c_carriage_return	13
c_horizontal_tab	9
c_vertical_tab	11

The table 25.2 was generated using the following program.

```fortran
use iso_c_binding
integer(c_int)::a

a=iachar(c_null_char); print *, a
a=iachar(c_alert); print *, a
a=iachar(c_backspace); print *, a
a=iachar(c_form_feed); print *, a
a=iachar(c_new_line); print *, a
a=iachar(c_carriage_return); print *, a
a=iachar(c_horizontal_tab); print *, a
a=iachar(c_vertical_tab); print *, a

end
```

25.2 Interoperability with a C Pointer

C pointers are addresses. To make it interoperable with Fortran two derived types are available in the module. They are *c_ptr* and *c_funptr*. These are interoperable with the C object and function pointer types respectively. The module also provides two more named constants, *c_null_ptr* and *c_null_funptr*. The module also contains two procedures:

c_loc(x) returns the C address of *x* and *c_funloc(x)* returns the C address of the procedure *x*.

25.3 Compilation and Linking

The compilation and linking are done in the following manner:
  Compilation:

```
f95 -c myfort.f95
cc -c myc.c
```

  Linking:

```
f95 -o myout myfort.o myc.o
```

The name of the executable file is *myout*, which is executed in normal way.

25.4 Fortran and C Interoperability - Examples

Case I: Dummy parameters of C functions are integers (scalars)

```
!        Fortran program
use iso_c_binding
interface
 integer(c_int) function func(a,b,c) bind (c)
 use iso_c_binding
 integer(c_int), value :: a,b,c
 end function func
end interface

integer(c_int) :: a=10, b=20, c=30
print *, func(a,b,c)
end
```

```
/* c program */

int func (int a, int b, int c)
{return (a+b+c);
}
```

In the above program two new items are introduced. To make a procedure interoperable, it must have an explicit interface and a *bind* attribute as shown above. The *value* attribute is used with the dummy parameter (scalar). It ensures that a copy of the content of the actual parameters is passed to the procedure. The function returns a value 60, which is displayed by the PRINT statement of the Fortran program.

Case II: Dummy arguments are floating point variables

  This example is same as the above example, except that the dummy arguments are floating point variables.

```fortran
! Fortran program
use iso_c_binding
interface
 real(c_float) function func(a,b,c) bind (c)
 use iso_c_binding
 real(c_float), value :: a,b,c
 end function func
end interface

real(c_float) :: a=10.0, b=20.0, c=30.0
print *, func(a,b,c)
end
```

```c
/* c program */
float func (float a, float b, float c)
{return (a+b+c);
}
```

Case III: Dummy arguments are pointers

Fortran and C pointers are not same. The former is an alias to a variable and the later contains an address of a variable. The Fortran function *c_loc(x)* returns the address of an object (*c* address) where x must be of interoperable type with *target* attribute. The next program swaps the values of two variables a and b using a C function swap.

```fortran
! Fortran program
use iso_c_binding
interface
 subroutine  swap(a,b) bind(c)
 use iso_c_binding
 type(c_ptr), value :: a,b
 end subroutine swap
end interface

integer(c_int), target:: a=10,b=20
print *, a, b
call swap(c_loc(a), c_loc(b))
print *,a, b
end
```

```c
/* c program */

swap (int *a, int *b)
{ int t;
  t=*a;
  *a=*b;
  *b=t;
}
```

Note that when the C function swap is called from the Fortran routine, the address of the variable obtained through the function c_loc is passed to the swap routine.

Case IV: Dummy argument is a dimensioned quantity (Rank 1)

In this example the C function will set every element of a single dimension array to some value.

```fortran
! Fortran program
use iso_c_binding
interface
 subroutine init(a,n) bind(c)
 use iso_c_binding
 integer(c_int),dimension(10) ::a
 integer(c_int),value :: n
 end subroutine init
end interface

integer (c_int), dimension(10):: a=10
integer(c_int):: n=10
print *, a
call init (a,n)
print *, a
end
```

```c
/* c program */
void init (int a[], int n)
{int i;
 for (i=0; i<n; ++i)
  a[i]=200+i;
}
```

Case V: Accessing the array through pointer

```fortran
! Fortran program
use iso_c_binding
interface
  subroutine sub(a,n) bind(c)
  use iso_c_binding
  type(c_ptr), value :: a
  integer(c_int), value ::n
  end subroutine sub
end interface

integer(c_int), target, dimension(10)::x=100
integer(c_int):: n=10
print *, x
call sub(c_loc(x(1)),n)
print *, x
end
```

```c
/* c program */
int sub(int *x, int n)
{int i;
 for (i=0; i<n; ++i)
  *(x+i)=200+i;
}
```

Case VI: Dummy argument is an array of rank greater than 1

There is a major difference between Fortran and C in storing multi-dimensional arrays. Fortran stores a multidimensional array column-wise while C stores the array row-wise. Therefore, to access a Fortran array having shape (2 3 4), that is, dimension (2, 3, 4), it must be dimensioned as (4, 3, 2) in C program. Also the Fortran dimension normally specifies the upper bound with lower bound equal to 1. On the other hand, the C-array statement specifies the 'size' with lower bound equal to zero. Therefore, the upper bound is equal to (size-1). Thus, a Fortran array with dimension (2, 3, 4) when accessed within a C program should be dimensioned as (4, 3, 2), with lower bounds equal to zero and upper bounds are 3, 2 and 1 respectively. The following program illustrates these points. For example, a(1, 2, 3) must be accessed as a[2][1][0] within C program. The rule of thumb is: invert the Fortran indices and subtract 1 from each dimension. This argument is valid when the lower bound of the Fortran array in each dimension is 1.

Note that if the Fortran array is declared as a(2:3, 3:5, 4:7) the corresponding C array must be declared as a[4][3][2].

```fortran
! Fortran program
use iso_c_binding
  interface
    subroutine sub(a) bind(c)
    use iso_c_binding
    integer(c_int), dimension(2,3,4)::a
    end subroutine sub
  end interface

integer(c_int), dimension(2,3,4)::a
integer:: i,j,k
a=reshape([[(i, i=1,24)], [2,3,4]])
do k=1,4
 do j=1,3
  do i=1,2
    print *,'a(',i,',',j,',',k,') = ',a(i,j,k)
  enddo
 enddo
enddo
print *,'---------- '
call sub(a)
do k=1,4
 do j=1,3
  do i=1,2
    print *,'a(',i,',',j,',',k,') = ',a(i,j,k)
  enddo
 enddo
enddo
end
```

```c
/* c program */
void sub(int a[4][3][2])
{int i,j,k;
  for(i=0; i<4; ++i)
   for(j=0; j<3; ++j)
    for(k=0; k<2; ++k)
     a[i][j][k]=100*i+10*j+k;
}
```

The output from the program is shown below:

```
a( 1 , 1 , 1 ) =   1
a( 2 , 1 , 1 ) =   2
a( 1 , 2 , 1 ) =   3
a( 2 , 2 , 1 ) =   4
a( 1 , 3 , 1 ) =   5
a( 2 , 3 , 1 ) =   6
a( 1 , 1 , 2 ) =   7
a( 2 , 1 , 2 ) =   8
a( 1 , 2 , 2 ) =   9
a( 2 , 2 , 2 ) =   10
a( 1 , 3 , 2 ) =   11
a( 2 , 3 , 2 ) =   12
a( 1 , 1 , 3 ) =   13
a( 2 , 1 , 3 ) =   14
a( 1 , 2 , 3 ) =   15
a( 2 , 2 , 3 ) =   16
a( 1 , 3 , 3 ) =   17
a( 2 , 3 , 3 ) =   18
a( 1 , 1 , 4 ) =   19
a( 2 , 1 , 4 ) =   20
a( 1 , 2 , 4 ) =   21
a( 2 , 2 , 4 ) =   22
a( 1 , 3 , 4 ) =   23
a( 2 , 3 , 4 ) =   24
----------
a( 1 , 1 , 1 ) =   0
a( 2 , 1 , 1 ) =   1
a( 1 , 2 , 1 ) =   10
a( 2 , 2 , 1 ) =   11
a( 1 , 3 , 1 ) =   20
a( 2 , 3 , 1 ) =   21
a( 1 , 1 , 2 ) =   100
a( 2 , 1 , 2 ) =   101
a( 1 , 2 , 2 ) =   110
a( 2 , 2 , 2 ) =   111
a( 1 , 3 , 2 ) =   120
a( 2 , 3 , 2 ) =   121
```

```
a ( 1 , 1 , 3 ) =  200
a ( 2 , 1 , 3 ) =  201
a ( 1 , 2 , 3 ) =  210
a ( 2 , 2 , 3 ) =  211
a ( 1 , 3 , 3 ) =  220
a ( 2 , 3 , 3 ) =  221
a ( 1 , 1 , 4 ) =  300
a ( 2 , 1 , 4 ) =  301
a ( 1 , 2 , 4 ) =  310
a ( 2 , 2 , 4 ) =  311
a ( 1 , 3 , 4 ) =  320
a ( 2 , 3 , 4 ) =  321
```

It may be noted from the above output that inside the C function a[2][1][0] is set to
2*100+1*10+0=210 which is shown as a(1, 2, 3) within the Fortran program following the
prescription given above.

Case VII: Dummy argument is a user derived type variable

In this program we introduce a new statement *import*. This statement allows us to access the
named entries from the host scoping unit within the interface block. The components must be of "C
type". Pointers and allocatables are not allowed and it must not be a sequenced type or type-bound
procedure. This "type" cannot be extended. It is obvious that items to be imported are declared in the
host-scoping unit before the interface block. The bind attribute must be used explicitly to make the
user defined type (derived type) interoperable.

```
! Fortran program
use iso_c_binding
type, bind(c):: mytype
 integer(c_int) :: a,b
 real(c_float) :: s
end type mytype
interface
 subroutine sub(y) bind(c)
import
type(c_ptr),value::y
 end subroutine sub
end interface

type(mytype), target:: y
y%a=20
y%b=30
y%s=40.0
print *, y%a, y%b, y%s

call sub(c_loc(y))

print *, y%a, y%b, y%s
end
```

```c
/* c program */
  typedef struct{
    int a, b;
    float c;
    }mytype;
  int sub ( mytype *x)
  {x->a=130;
   x->b=240;
   x->c=99.0;
   }
```

Note that, in this case, the address of the variable (pointer) is passed to the C function and through the pointer the elementary items of the derived data type are accessed.

Case VIII: One of the elementary item of the derived type is a rank 1 array

```fortran
!    Fortran program
use iso_c_binding
type, bind(c):: mytype
 integer(c_int) :: a,b
 real(c_float) :: s
 integer(c_int), dimension(5)::d
end type mytype
interface
 subroutine sub(y) bind(c)
import
type(c_ptr),value::y
 end subroutine sub
end interface

type(mytype), target:: y
y%a=20
y%b=30
y%s=40.0
y%d=450
print *, y%a, y%b, y%s, y%d
call sub(c_loc(y))
print *, y%a, y%b, y%s, y%d
end
```

```c
/* c program */
  typedef struct{
    int a, b;
    float c;
    int d[];
    }mytype;
```

```c
int sub(mytype *x)
{int i;
  for (i=0; i<5;++i) ! size of the array could be an argument
    x->d[i]=i*3;

  x->a=130;
  x->b=240;
  x->c=99.0;
}
```

The C function changes all the elementary items of the derived type and the changes are reflected in the calling program.

Case IX: Function name as argument

In the following example the dummy argument is the address of a function. The Fortran program calls a C function which, in turn, calls Fortran function *fun1* and *fun2* depending on the address that is passed through the first argument of *cfunc*.

```fortran
!   Fortran program
program main
use iso_c_binding
interface

  integer(c_int) function fun1(a,b) bind(c)
  use iso_c_binding
    integer(c_int),value:: a,b
  end function fun1

  integer(c_int) function fun2(a,b) bind(c)
   use iso_c_binding
    integer(c_int),value:: a,b
  end function fun2

  integer(c_int) function cfunc(f,a,b) bind(c)
   use iso_c_binding
   type(c_funptr), value:: f
   integer(c_int), value :: a,b
   end function cfunc

  end interface

  integer(c_int):: x=120, y=150, z
  z=cfunc(c_funloc(fun1),x,y) ! cfunc will call function fun1
  print *, z                  ! z=x+y

  z=cfunc(c_funloc(fun2),x,y) ! cfunc will call function fun2
  print *, z                  ! z=x-y
  end program main
```

```fortran
!                           Functions begins
          integer(c_int) function fun1(a,b) bind(c)
           use iso_c_binding
           integer(c_int),value:: a,b
           fun1=a+b
          end function fun1

          integer(c_int) function fun2(a,b) bind(c)
           use iso_c_binding
           integer(c_int),value:: a,b
           fun2=a-b
          end function fun2
```

```c
/* c program */
int cfunc(int (*f)(int, int), int a, int b)
{return((*f)(a,b));
}
```

25.5 Interoperation with Global Variable

Fortran and C program units can share location. Two cases may arise:
Case I: In this case the C global variable is accessed by Fortran using the bind(c) attribute. It can only be declared within a module. It cannot be a part of common block.

```fortran
!    Fortran program
module mymod
 use iso_c_binding
 integer (c_int), bind(c):: ftnc
end module mymod
program main
use mymod
interface
   subroutine sub() bind(c)
   end subroutine sub
end interface
ftnc=350
print *, ftnc
call sub
print *, ftnc
end
```

```c
  /* c program */
int ftnc;
void sub()
{ftnc=587;
}
```

Case II: The variable is part of a common block. If the common block contains only one variable, the C program unit declares the variable through the name of the common block. The common block is also declared with the bind attribute.

```fortran
!    Fortran program
use iso_c_binding
common /blk/a
integer(c_int)::a
bind (c):: /blk/
interface
 subroutine sub() bind(c)
 end subroutine sub
end interface
a=2
print *, a
call sub()
print *, a
end
```

```c
/* c program */
int blk;
void sub()
{blk=30;
}
```

If the common block contains more than one variable, the corresponding 'C' variable is declared as a structure with the name of the common block as the variable name. The elementary items of the structure correspond to the variables of the Fortran program which belong to a common block.

```fortran
!    Fortran program

use iso_c_binding
interface
   subroutine sub() bind(c)
   end subroutine sub
end interface

common /blk/r, s
real (c_float) :: r,s
bind(c) :: /blk/
r=10.0
s=20.0
print *, r,s
call sub
print *, r,s
end
```

```c
/* c program */
struct {float r,s;}blk;
void sub()
{ blk.r=300.56;
  blk.s=400.45;
}
```

The above programs show how a 'Fortran' variable is modified within a C function and the modified values are carried over to the calling program.

Case III: Fortran variable (a) is used in the C procedure with different name (myowna).

```fortran
!    Fortran program
module mymod
 use iso_c_binding
 integer(c_int) ::a
 bind(c,name='myowna') ::a
end module mymod

program main
use mymod
interface
 subroutine sub() bind(c)
 end subroutine sub
end interface
a=27
print *, a
call sub
print *, a
end
```

```c
/* c program */
int myowna;
void sub()
{myowna=37;
}
```

In the above example the Fortran variable 'a' will be called as 'myowna' within the C function. The bind statement contains *name='myowna'* which does this job.

Case IV: Function name within Fortran is *sub* – the name of the C function is *mysub*.

```fortran
!    Fortran program
module mymod
 use iso_c_binding
 integer(c_int) ::a
 bind(c,name='myowna') ::a
end module mymod
```

```fortran
program main
use mymod
interface
 subroutine sub() bind(c,name='mysub')
 end subroutine sub
end interface
a=27
print *, a
call sub
print *, a
end
```

```c
/* c program */
int myowna;
void mysub()
{myowna=37;
}
```

In the above example, Fortran variable 'a' is known as 'myowna' within the C program. Also a call to subroutine 'sub' generates a call to C routines 'mysub'. All these are accomplished though the *name parameter* of bind. If the C name and the Fortran name are same, the Fortran name is converted into lower case. It is possible to choose a different name with the name clause. However, the C-routine uses the C-name and Fortran uses the Fortran-name.

25.6 C–Fortran Interoperation

In this section we shall show how a C main program can call a Fortran subprogram.

```c
/* c program */

#include <stdio.h>
int  main()
{int a=10, b=20, c=30, d;
  int func(int, int, int);

  d=func(a,b,c);
  printf("%d  %d %d %d \n", a,b,c,d);
}
```

```fortran
!   Fortran program
function func(a,b,c) result (res) bind(c)
use iso_c_binding
integer(c_int), value::a,b,c
integer(c_int) :: res

res = a+b+c
end
```

The Fortran function calculates a+b+c and returns the result to the calling C program. The dummy parameters must be of "c-type". The arguments cannot be of assumed shape, allocatable, optional or pointer.

The next program calls a Fortran subroutine and gets back the result through one of the argument of the subroutine.

```
/* c program */
#include <stdio.h>
int  main()
{int a=10, b=20, c=30, d;
  void func(int, int, int, int *); /* 4th argument is a pointer */
  func(a,b,c,&d);
  printf("%d %d %d %d  \n", a,b,c,d);
}


                           !    Fortran program
                           subroutine func(a,b,c,d) bind(c)
                           use iso_c_binding
                           integer(c_int),value::a,b,c
                           integer(c_int), intent(out)::d
                           d=a+b+c
                           end
```

The point to be noted here is that the fourth actual parameter of the "call" statement is a C pointer and the corresponding Fortran dummy argument has been declared with intent (out). This is necessary because C parameters are passed by value and the Fortran parameters are passed by reference. That is why first three dummy arguments of the Fortran routine have the value attribute associated with them.

The next program swaps two 'C' variables using a Fortran subroutine.

```
/* c program */
#include <stdio.h>
int main()
{int a=10, b=20;
  void swap (int *, int *);
  printf("%d %d\n", a, b);
  swap (&a, &b);
  printf("%d %d\n", a, b);
}


                           !    Fortran program
                           subroutine swap (a,b) bind(c)
                           use iso_c_binding
                           integer(c_int), intent(inout)::a,b
                           integer :: t
                           t=a
                           a=b
                           b=t
                           end subroutine swap
```

The statements that require special attention are shown in bold. The subroutine swap is called with the address of a and b (pointers). The corresponding dummy parameters have been declared as intent (inout).

In this chapters a few examples of Fortran – C interoperation are shown. Readers are encouraged to do experiments with different kind of variables.

Chapter 26

MISCELLANEOUS INSTRUCTIONS

This chapter contains some Fortran instructions, that could not be accommodated in the earlier chapters. The reason being either they do not fit in to any chapter or a thorough knowledge of more than one chapter is required for understanding the topic. That is why they are placed at the end of the book.

26.1 Intrinsic Modules

Fortran provides five intrinsic modules. These are IEEE_ARITHMETIC, IEEE_EXCEPTIONS, IEEE_FEATURES, ISO_C_BINDING and ISO_FORTRAN_ENV. Future versions of the compiler may provide some more. It is possible to define a user-defined module having the same name and one of them (supplied or user defined) can be used in a particular scoping unit. To use the system intrinsic module the following is the prescription:

```
PROGRAM MAIN
USE, INTRINSIC :: IEEE_ARITHMETIC
 .
END
```

However, to use the user defined intrinsic module having the same name the following procedure is adopted:

```
MODULE IEEE_ARITHMETIC
  CONTAINS
    SUBROUTINE SUB
    PRINT *, 'I AM HERE'
    END SUBROUTINE SUB
END MODULE IEEE_ARITHMETIC

PROGRAM MAIN
  USE, NON_INTRINSIC :: IEEE_ARITHMETIC
  CALL SUB
  END
```

The USE statement with the attribute ensures that the system's module IEEE_ARITHMETIC is not loaded and in its place the user defined module IEEE_ARITHMETIC is accessed. If the statement

USE, NON_INTRINSIC :: IEEE_ARITHMETIC is replaced by USE IEEE_ARITHMETIC without INTRINSIC or NON_INTRINSIC, the user defined module gets preference over the intrinsic (system) module. However, if the compiler fails to locate the user defined module it uses the intrinsic module.

26.2 Computing Environment

A new module called ISO_FORTRAN_ENV has now been made available in Fortran. Table 26.1 shows the named constants available in the module and their values for the NAG Fortran compiler.

Table 26.1 Named Constant in ISO_FORTRAN_ENV

Named constant	Value
INPUT_UNIT	5
OUTPUT_UNIT	6
ERROR_UNIT	0
IOSTAT_END	-1
IOSTAT_EOR	-2
NUMERIC_STORGAE_SIZE	32
CHARACTER_STORAGE_SIZE	8
FILE_STORAGE_SIZE	8

INPUT_UNIT, OUTPUT_UNIT and ERROR_UNIT are the unit numbers associated with READ * and PRINT * statements. IOSTAT_END and IOSTAT_EOR are the values assigned to IOSTAT=*variable* when end of file or end of record is encountered. NUMERIC_STORAGE_SIZE, CHARACTER_STORAGE_SIZE and FILE_STORAGE_SIZE are, respectively, the number of bits required for numeric, character and file storage units. The program shown below may be used to find out the values of the above-mentioned named constants. However, use the constant names and not the current numerical values.

```
USE ISO_FORTRAN_ENV
PRINT *, INPUT_UNIT
PRINT *, OUTPUT_UNIT
PRINT *, ERROR_UNIT
PRINT *, IOSTAT_END
PRINT *, IOSTAT_EOR
PRINT *, NUMERIC_STORAGE_SIZE
PRINT *, CHARACTER_STORAGE_SIZE
PRINT *, FILE_STORAGE_SIZE

END
```

26.3 Type Parameter Inquiry

This is used to inquire about the value of type parameter of a data object; inquiry may be made for both intrinsic and derived types. It always returns a scalar.

```
INTEGER, PARAMETER:: S=SELECTED_REAL_KIND(6, 37)
REAL(KIND=S)::A
        .
        .
PRINT *, A%KIND
```

This returns KIND(A). Similarly, if CH is character variable CH%LEN returns the length of the string, same as LEN(CH). The NAG compiler does not support this feature.

26.4 Changes in the Intrinsic Functions

The intrinsic functions MAX, MIN, MAXLOC, MINLOC now accept character type. The intrinsic functions IACHAR, ICHAR, COUNT, INDEX, LBOUND, LEN, LEN_TRIM, MAXLOC, SCAN, SHAPE, SIZE, UBOUND and VERIFY accept an additional optional argument KIND.

26.5 Array Constructors

In the following program as the lengths of the different elements are not same, it is supposed to give a Fortran error (GFORTRAN does not give any error).

```
CHARACTER(LEN=20),DIMENSION(4)::C
C=["ABC", "ABCDEF", "P", "ASDFGHJ"]
PRINT *,C
END
```

To circumvent this programming error, the present version of Fortran allows type specification with an array constructor:

[*type spec :: array-construction-list*]

The above program may be modified as shown below:

```
C=[CHARACTER(LEN=20):: "ABC", "ABCDEF", "P", "ASDFGHJ"]
```

This declaration ensures that the length of each element will be 20; the compiler will add the required number of blanks. The NAG compiler does not support this feature. However the g95 compiler supports this feature.

26.6 ASSOCIATE

This statement is used to associate name entries with expressions within the ASSOCIATE block. The so-called 'associate name' exists only within the ASSOCIATE block. The statement is very suitable especially when the derived type variable contains embedded derived type objects like: a%b%c. A name can be associated with this object to avoid repeating this again and again. The ASSOCIATE statement is demonstrated with the help of an example.

```
REAL ::  X,   THETA,   YM
REAL :: R=1.5

X = 10.0
THETA = 0.9
YM = 0.7

ASSOCIATE ( Z => R * COS(THETA)+R*SIN(THETA), T => YM)
   PRINT *, T,   X+Z,   X-Z, Z
   T = 2.5*T
END ASSOCIATE

PRINT *, YM

END
```

Within the ASSOCIATE block X+Z and X-Z are respectively X+(R*COS(THETA)+R*SIN(THETA)) and X-(R*COS(THETA)+R*SIN(THETA)). T is set to 2.5*T. This will be reflected in the PRINT statement outside the ASSOCIATE block (PRINT *, YM). Note Z and T do not exist outside the ASSOCIATE block. The NAG compiler does not support this feature. The program was compiled using IBM XL Fortran compiler. The readers may verify that the outputs of this program are:

```
0.70  12.107  7.892  2.107
1.750
```

26.7 Enumeration

A set of named integer constants (also called enumerators) is called an enumeration. The system chooses the kind is such a way that these are interoperable with the corresponding C type enumeration.

```
USE ISO_C_BINDING

ENUM, BIND(C)
   ENUMERATOR :: RED=1, GREEN=3
   ENUMERATOR :: BLUE=5
END ENUM
INTEGER (C_INT) :: A
```

```
A=RED
PRINT *, A
A=GREEN
PRINT *,A
END
```

The outputs are 1 and 3.

If the value is not specified it taken as one more than previous one.

```
ENUM, BIND(C)
 ENUMERATOR :: RED=1, GREEN=3
 ENUMERATOR :: BLUE
END ENUM
```

The value of BLUE, in this case, is 4, one greater than 3 (GREEN). If the first item is not given any value, it is taken as zero.

```
ENUM, BIND(C)
 ENUMERATOR :: RED, GREEN
 ENUMERATOR :: BLUE
END ENUM
```

The values of RED, GREEN and BLUE are respectively 0, 1 and 2 respectively. However, for the following declaration:

```
ENUM, BIND(C)
 ENUMERATOR :: RED, GREEN=5
 ENUMERATOR :: BLUE
END ENUM
```

RED, GREEN and BLUE are respectively 0, 5 and 6 respectively.

26.8 Polymorphic Variables

A variable is called "polymorphic" if its data type may vary during the execution of the program. It is either a pointer or an allocated variable or a dummy data object. A polymorphic variable is defined by the CLASS keyword. The rules for TYPE and CLASS are similar. However, there are several additional rules for CLASS.

a) It is used to declared a polymorphic object,

b) CLASS (*) refers to an unlimited polymorphic object (to be discussed shortly),

c) The CLASS keyword is used to declare an entity, which must be either a dummy argument or have the pointer/allocatable attribute. The derived type must not be a sequenced type, bind type or intrinsic type.

```
TYPE TWOD
  REAL:: X,Y
END TYPE TWOD
CLASS(TWOD), POINTER:: PTR
```

The pointer PTR may point to any object of TYPE(TWOD) or its extensions. This pointer can access the components of the declared elements in the TYPE declaration directly. It cannot access the components of the extensions directly though it can point to the extension during the execution of the program. During the compilation time, compiler knows the declaration of the pointer and the type of the object the pointer is supposed to point. Therefore, during execution this pointer PTR can point to an object of type:

```
TYPE, EXTENDS(TWOD)::THREED
  REAL::Z
END TYPE THREED
```

but it cannot access the component Z directly though it can access the components X and Y.

Unlimited polymorphic entities are defined using (*) in place of CLASS specifier.

```
CLASS (*), POINTER ::P
```

This allows a pointer to refer to any object. This type of object can be used as actual argument of a subprogram or as a selector of a SELECT TYPE statement. This object cannot appear on the left hand side of the assignment sign.

26.9 SELECT TYPE Construct

This construct allows the execution of one of its constituent blocks depending upon the dynamic type of a variable or expression. It is possible to access the components of the extensions. The syntax of the SELECT TYPE construct is:

```
SELECT TYPE (associate-name=>selector)
type-guard-block
         .
         .
END SELECT
```

The associate-name is similar to the ASSOCIATE construct discussed in section 26.6.

The type-guard-block may be one of the following:

```
TYPE IS (derive-type-spec)
CLASS IS (derive-type-spec)
CLASS DEFAULT
```

The block attached to a *type-guard-block* is executed if the dynamic type selector matches exactly with the derived type. The block is selected according to the following prescription:

(a) if the TYPE IS block matches, it is executed, otherwise

(b) if a single CLASS IS matches, it is executed, otherwise

(c) if there is a match with several CLASS IS blocks, the one which is the extension of all the others is taken.

(d) There may be a CLASS DEFAULT block. If there is no match with any of the block, this is executed.

All these are explained with the help of examples:

```fortran
TYPE TWOD
 REAL:: X,Y
END TYPE TWOD

TYPE, EXTENDS(TWOD)::THREED
 REAL::Z
END TYPE THREED

TYPE(THREED), TARGET::DIM3=THREED(10.0, 20.0, 30.0)
TYPE(TWOD), TARGET:: DIM2=TWOD(100.0, 200.0)

CLASS(TWOD), POINTER::P

P=>DIM3
 SELECT TYPE (V=>P)
 TYPE IS(TWOD)
  PRINT *, V
 TYPE IS(THREED)
  PRINT *, V

 END SELECT
END
```

As the pointer P is assigned to DIM3 the block TYPE IS(THREED) will be selected and the output will be 10.0, 20.0 and 30.0.

```fortran
TYPE TWOD
 REAL:: X,Y
END TYPE TWOD

TYPE, EXTENDS(TWOD)::THREED
 REAL::Z
END TYPE THREED

TYPE(THREED), TARGET::DIM3=THREED(10.0, 20.0, 30.0)
TYPE(TWOD), TARGET:: DIM2=TWOD(130.0, 240.0)

CLASS(TWOD), POINTER::P
```

```
   P=>DIM3
    SELECT TYPE (V=>P)
    TYPE IS (TWOD)
     PRINT *, V
    CLASS IS(THREED)
     PRINT *, V%X, V%Y, V%Z
    END SELECT
 END
```

In this case the block "CLASS IS" is selected and V%X, V%Y and V%Z are printed (CLASS IS block cannot use V with the I/O statement). Now, consider the following:

```
 TYPE TWOD
  REAL:: X,Y
 END TYPE TWOD

 TYPE, EXTENDS(TWOD)::THREED
  REAL::Z
 END TYPE THREED

 TYPE(THREED), TARGET::DIM3=THREED(10.0, 20.0, 30.0)
 TYPE(TWOD), TARGET:: DIM2=TWOD(100.0, 200.0)

 CLASS(TWOD), POINTER::P

 P=>DIM3
    SELECT TYPE (V=>P)
    TYPE IS(TWOD)
     PRINT *, V
    CLASS DEFAULT
     PRINT *, "No match"

    END SELECT
 END
```

The selector does not match with TYPE IS. Therefore the default path is chosen. If the CLASS DEFAULT were absent, no block would be selected.

26.10 Type Bound Procedure

A type bound procedure is required when it is necessary to "call" a procedure depending upon the nature of a polymorphic object. In other wards, the procedure is chosen (selected) according to the type of the dynamic object.

26.11 Type Bound Procedure with Specific Binding

A procedure may be bound to a type. This is illustrated with several examples. In the following example, DIST is a type bound procedure with specific binding for the type POINT. The name of the module procedure is P2D. Several attributes are available for binding. They are PASS, NOPASS, PUBLIC, PRIVATE, NON_OVERRIDABLE and DEFERRED. We first discuss PASS and NOPASS.

The type bound procedure DIST and P2D1 are Public. Note that the module procedures P2D and P2D1 are Private. Also observe that in the type bound procedure declaration (shown in bold letters) the explicit binding is shown (DIST=>P2D). This is not necessary if the name of the actual procedure is same as the type bound procedure (P2D1), that is, the name of the type bound procedure and the actual procedure are the same (the PUBLIC declaration is applicable to the actual procedure not to the type bound procedure).

If PASS or NOPASS is not specified or PASS without argument is specified, the scalar through which the type bound procedure is accessed becomes the first argument of the procedure. For example, P%DIST(Q) essentially means calling the type bound procedure DIST with two arguments P and Q.

```
MODULE MYMOD

TYPE :: POINT
   REAL :: X, Y
   CONTAINS
     PROCEDURE, PASS :: DIST => P2D
     PROCEDURE, PASS :: P2D1
END TYPE POINT

PRIVATE P2D, P2D1

CONTAINS
REAL FUNCTION P2D(A, B)

   CLASS (POINT), INTENT (IN) :: A, B
   P2D = SQRT ( (A%X - B%X)**2 + (A%Y - B%Y)**2 )

END FUNCTION P2D
REAL FUNCTION P2D1(A)
   CLASS(POINT), INTENT(IN)::A
   P2D1=SQRT((A%X+A%Y))
END FUNCTION P2D1

END MODULE

PROGRAM MAIN
USE MYMOD
TYPE (POINT):: P=POINT(7.0,4.0), Q=POINT(2.0,5.0)
REAL:: L
L=P%DIST(Q)
```

```
PRINT *, L
L=P%P2D1()
PRINT *, L
END
```

Notice the statements L=P%DIST(Q) and L=P%P2D1(). The procedures are invoked by a scalar variable of type POINT. Because of the presence of PASS, these are passed as the first argument to the procedures and for the first call Q is passed as the second argument to the procedure.

However, if in the procedure declaration the PASS of P2D1 is replaced by NOPASS as below:

```
MODULE MYMOD
TYPE :: POINT
   REAL :: X, Y
   CONTAINS
    PROCEDURE, PASS :: DIST => P2D
    PROCEDURE, NOPASS :: P2D1
END TYPE POINT

PRIVATE P2D, P2D1

CONTAINS
REAL FUNCTION P2D(A, B)

    CLASS (POINT), INTENT (IN) :: A, B
    P2D = SQRT ( (A%X - B%X)**2 + (A%Y - B%Y)**2 )

END FUNCTION P2D
REAL FUNCTION P2D1(A)
    CLASS(POINT), INTENT(IN)::A
    P2D1=SQRT((A%X+A%Y))
END FUNCTION P2D1

END MODULE

PROGRAM MAIN
USE MYMOD
TYPE (POINT):: P=POINT(7.0,4.0), Q=POINT(2.0,5.0)
REAL:: L
L=P%DIST(Q)
PRINT *, L
L=P%P2D1(P)
PRINT *, L
END
```

the corresponding call to P2D1 would be P%P2D1(P) and not P%P2D1() because of the presence of NOPASS.

If PASS(*arg-name*) is specified for a type bound procedure, the type bound procedure has a dummy argument with the same name. These are shown in bold letter in the following program.

```
MODULE MYMOD

TYPE :: POINT
   REAL :: X, Y
   CONTAINS
       PROCEDURE, PASS(A) :: DIST => P2D

END TYPE POINT


CONTAINS
REAL FUNCTION P2D(A, B)

   CLASS (POINT), INTENT (IN) :: A, B
   P2D = SQRT ( (A%X - B%X)**2 + (A%Y - B%Y)**2 )

END FUNCTION P2D
END MODULE

PROGRAM MAIN
USE MYMOD
TYPE (POINT):: A=POINT(3.0,4.0), B=POINT(4.0,5.0)
REAL:: L
L=A%DIST(B)
PRINT *, L
END
```

Another is example of NOPASS is shown below.

```
MODULE MYMOD

TYPE :: POINT
   REAL :: X, Y
   CONTAINS
       PROCEDURE, NOPASS :: DIST => P2D

END TYPE POINT

CONTAINS
REAL FUNCTION P2D(A, B)

   CLASS (POINT), INTENT (IN) :: A, B
   P2D = SQRT ( (A%X - B%X)**2 + (A%Y - B%Y)**2 )

END FUNCTION P2D
END MODULE
```

```
PROGRAM MAIN
USE MYMOD
TYPE (POINT):: P=POINT(3.0,4.0), Q=POINT(4.0,5.0), N
REAL:: L
L=N%DIST(P,Q)
PRINT *, L
END
```

Without the attribute NOPASS the statement L=N%DIST(P,Q) will pass N as the first argument and P and Q as the second and third arguments respectively (which is not desired). The NOPASS attribute ensures that N is not passed as the first argument; P and Q are passed as the first and second arguments respectively.

26.12 Generic Binding

This section contains discussion on type bound generic procedures. Two or more type bound procedures may have a generic name and depending upon the type of the argument(s) the appropriate procedure is invoked. The program that follows calls the generic name twice once with real argument and the next time with complex argument. Depending upon the argument either P1 or P2 is invoked.

```
MODULE GENMOD
  PRIVATE
  TYPE, PUBLIC :: GENT
   REAL :: X,Y
  CONTAINS
   PRIVATE
   PROCEDURE :: P1
   PROCEDURE :: P2
   GENERIC, PUBLIC ::GPROC=>P1,P2
  END TYPE
  CONTAINS
   SUBROUTINE P1(A,B)
   CLASS(GENT), INTENT(IN)::A
   REAL, INTENT(OUT):: B
   PRINT *, 'Entering .... P1'
   B=SQRT(A%X**2+A%Y**2)
   END SUBROUTINE P1

   SUBROUTINE P2(A,B)
   CLASS(GENT), INTENT(IN)::A
   COMPLEX,INTENT(OUT)::B
   PRINT *, 'Entering .... P2'
   B=CMPLX(A%X,A%Y)
   END SUBROUTINE P2
END MODULE GENMOD
```

```
      USE GENMOD
      TYPE(GENT)::X=GENT(2.0,3.0)
      COMPLEX :: C
      REAL :: D
      CALL X%GPROC(D)
      PRINT *, D
      CALL X%GPROC(C)
      PRINT *,C
      END
```

Note that the GENERIC name is PUBLIC, but the individual procedure names P1 and P2 are PRIVATE. Therefore, the procedures P1 and P2 cannot be called (like CALL X%P1(D)) from main program directly. They must be called through the generic name shown.

A generic type bound procedure may be an operator or an assignment as shown below:

```
      MODULE MYMOD
       TYPE POINT
        REAL :: X,Y
       END TYPE POINT
       TYPE, EXTENDS(POINT) :: POINT3D
        REAL:: Z
       CONTAINS
        PROCEDURE, NOPASS :: P1=>DIST1
        PROCEDURE, NOPASS :: P2=>DIST2
        GENERIC:: ASSIGNMENT(=) => P1,P2
       END TYPE POINT3D

      CONTAINS
       SUBROUTINE DIST1(A,B)
       CLASS(POINT), INTENT(OUT)::A
       TYPE(POINT3D), INTENT(IN)::B
       PRINT *, 'Enter routine ... P1'
       A%X=SQRT(B%X**2+B%Y**2+B%Z**2)
       A%Y=B%Y
       END SUBROUTINE DIST1

       SUBROUTINE DIST2(A,B)
       CLASS(POINT3D), INTENT(OUT)::A
       TYPE(POINT), INTENT(IN)::B
       PRINT *, 'Enter routine .........p2'
       A%X=B%X
       A%Y=B%Y
       A%Z=SQRT(B%X**2+B%Y**2)
        END SUBROUTINE DIST2
      END MODULE MYMOD
```

```
PROGRAM MAIN
USE MYMOD
TYPE(POINT)::X=POINT(3.0,4.0)
TYPE(POINT3D)::Y=POINT3D(1.0,1.0,1.0)
PRINT *, X
X=Y
PRINT *, X

END
```

When X=Y is executed, a call is made to the type bound procedure P1. However if the three statements before END are replaced by the following three statements:

```
PRINT *, Y
Y=X
PRINT *, Y
```

a call is made to the procedure P2 because now the statement is Y=X.

26.13 Overriding Type Bound Procedures

If the binding name specified in the type definition is identical to the binding name inherited from the parent, the binding obtained from the type definition overrides the binding inherited from the parent.

```
MODULE MYMOD

TYPE :: P2D
   REAL :: X, Y
   CONTAINS
   PROCEDURE, PASS:: DIST => DIST2D
END TYPE P2D
TYPE, EXTENDS (P2D) :: P3D
   REAL :: Z
   CONTAINS
   PROCEDURE, PASS :: DIST => DIST3D
END TYPE P3D
CONTAINS


REAL FUNCTION DIST2D (A, B)
   CLASS (P2D), INTENT (IN) :: A, B
   DIST2D = SQRT ((A%X - B%X)**2 + (A%Y - B%Y)**2)

END FUNCTION DIST2D
```

```
REAL FUNCTION DIST3D ( A, B )
   CLASS (P3D), INTENT (IN) :: A
   CLASS (P2D), INTENT (IN) :: B
   SELECT TYPE(B)
      CLASS IS (P3D)
      DIST3D = SQRT((A%X-B%X)**2 + (A%Y-B%Y)**2 + (A%Z-B%Z)**2)
      PRINT *, 'RETURN'
      RETURN
   END SELECT
   PRINT *, " P3D, dynamic type: incorrect ARGUMENT"
   STOP
END FUNCTION DIST3D

END MODULE MYMOD

PROGRAM MAIN
USE MYMOD

TYPE (P3D)::X=P3D(4.0,5.0,6.0)
TYPE (P3D):: Y=P3D(5.0,6.0,8.0)
REAL:: R
R=X%DIST(Y)
PRINT *, R
END
```

In this case DIST3D will be called as type definition (DIST3D) overrides the inherited binding (DIST2D).

This overriding may be prevented by the following declaration in the parent type:

```
TYPE :: P2D
 REAL :: X, Y
CONTAINS
 PROCEDURE, PASS, NON_OVERRIDABLE:: DIST => DIST2D
END TYPE P2D
```

26.14 Deferred Binding

Sometimes a 'template' of a type is created which is used to create an extension. The 'base type' is not used to create any object. In such a case the type bound procedures have a DEFERRED attribute and the definition of the type contains an ABSTRACT keyword. The following program demonstrates these features.

```
MODULE MYMOD
 TYPE, ABSTRACT :: ABSTYPE
 CONTAINS
   PROCEDURE(ABSINT), DEFERRED :: P1
   PROCEDURE(ABSINT), DEFERRED :: P2
 END TYPE ABSTYPE
```

```
ABSTRACT INTERFACE
  SUBROUTINE ABSINT(A)
  IMPORT :: ABSTYPE
  CLASS (ABSTYPE), INTENT(INOUT):: A
  END SUBROUTINE ABSINT
END INTERFACE

TYPE, EXTENDS(ABSTYPE):: NEWABSTYPE
  REAL, PRIVATE :: I,J
CONTAINS

  PROCEDURE :: P1=>NEWP1
  PROCEDURE :: P2=>NEWP2
  PROCEDURE :: SETVALUE
  PROCEDURE :: GETVALUE
ENDTYPE NEWABSTYPE

CONTAINS
SUBROUTINE NEWP1(A)
CLASS(NEWABSTYPE), INTENT(INOUT)::A
A%I=A%I+A%J
END SUBROUTINE NEWP1

SUBROUTINE NEWP2(A)
CLASS(NEWABSTYPE), INTENT(INOUT)::A
A%I=A%I-A%J
END SUBROUTINE NEWP2

SUBROUTINE SETVALUE(A,L,M)
CLASS(NEWABSTYPE),INTENT(OUT)::A
REAL, INTENT(IN)::L,M
A%I=L
A%J=M
END SUBROUTINE SETVALUE

SUBROUTINE GETVALUE(A)
CLASS(NEWABSTYPE),INTENT(IN)::A
PRINT *, A%I, A%J
END SUBROUTINE GETVALUE

END MODULE MYMOD

PROGRAM MAIN
USE MYMOD
TYPE(NEWABSTYPE):: A, B

CALL SETVALUE(A,4.0, 5.0)
CALL SETVALUE(B,6.0, 7.0)
```

```
CALL GETVALUE(A)
CALL NEWP1(A)
CALL GETVALUE(A)

CALL GETVALUE(B)
CALL NEWP2(B)
CALL GETVALUE(B)
END
```

The output is

```
4.0                    5.0
9.0                    5.0
6.0                    7.0
-1.0                   7.0
```

26.15 Finalization

A derived type may be made 'finalizable' through the FINAL statement. The FINAL statement specifies the name of the subroutine to be called automatically by the compiler when the local variables are destroyed at the end of procedure call. Essentially the finalization procedure is used for the 'cleaning operation'. This facility is available only for derived types. The conditions are: there are no SEQUENCE or BIND attributes.

The FINAL subroutine name, a module procedure, is defined with exactly one dummy argument. The argument must not be a pointer or allocatable variable or polymorphic variable. The dummy argument must not have INTENT(OUT). Moreover, two final subroutines must not have same type of dummy argument. The following is an example of final binding.

```
MODULE MYMOD
 TYPE :: FIRST
   REAL A,B
 END TYPE FIRST
   TYPE, EXTENDS(FIRST) :: SECOND
   REAL,POINTER :: C(:),D(:)
CONTAINS
   FINAL :: FSECOND
   END TYPE SECOND
   TYPE, EXTENDS(SECOND) :: THIRD
   REAL,POINTER :: E
CONTAINS
   FINAL :: FTHIRD
   END TYPE THIRD
```

```fortran
      CONTAINS
        SUBROUTINE FSECOND(X) ! Type (second) finilizer
          TYPE(SECOND) :: X

          PRINT *, 'ENTER FSECOND'
          IF (ASSOCIATED(X%C)) THEN
            PRINT *, ' C was allocated and is now being deallocated'
            DEALLOCATE(X%C)
          END IF
          IF (ASSOCIATED(X%D)) THEN
            PRINT *, ' D was allocated and is now being deallocated'
            DEALLOCATE(X%D)
          END IF
        END SUBROUTINE FSECOND
        SUBROUTINE FTHIRD(Y) ! Type(third) finalizer
          TYPE(THIRD) :: Y

          PRINT *, 'ENTER FTHIRD'
          IF (ASSOCIATED(Y%E)) THEN
            PRINT *, ' E was allocated and is now being deallocated'
            DEALLOCATE(Y%E)
          END IF
        END SUBROUTINE FTHIRD
      END MODULE MYMOD

      PROGRAM MAIN
        CALL SUB
      END PROGRAM

      SUBROUTINE SUB
        USE MYMOD
        TYPE(FIRST):: X1
        TYPE(SECOND):: X2
        TYPE(THIRD):: X3

        ALLOCATE(X2%C(5))
        X2%C=[1.0, 2.0, 3.0, 4.0, 5.0]
        ALLOCATE(X3%E)
        X3%E=10.0
        .

        .
  !     X1 is not finalizable. So no routine is called

  !     Compiler generated call for finalization
  !     CALL FSECOND(X2)
  !     CALL FTHIRD(X3)
  !     CALL FSECOND(X3%SECOND)
        END SUBROUTINE
```

Just before the subroutine is exited, the compiler generated calls to the FINAL routines FSECOND and FTHIRD. In this case the FINAL routines deallocate the allocated variables. Note that, these calls are generated by the compiler. The NAG compiler does not support this feature.

26.16 VOLATILE

A variable may be declared with the volatile attribute can be modified by another program that is being executed in parallel. That is, the variable is available outside the scope of the present program.

```
        INTEGER, VOLATILE :: A
```
or,

```
        INTEGER  :: A
        VOLATILE :: A
```

For a pointer this refers to its association with the target and not with the content of the target. If an object is declared as VOLATILE, all its sub-objects becomes VOLATILE too.

As the volatile variable can be changed by other program(s), every reference to the variable should fetch its value from the main memory, rather than obtaining from the registers which may not contain the current value.

26.17 SAME_TYPE_AS(A,B)

This inquiry function takes two arguments A and B both of which are objects of extensible type. If they are pointers, their states should not be "undefined association". The function returns true if the dynamic type of A and the dynamic type of B are same; it returns false otherwise.

26.18 EXTENDS_TYPE_OF(A, MOLD)

This is also an inquiry function. It tests whether the dynamic type A is an extension of dynamic type MOLD and returns true or false accordingly. Both A and MOLD must be objects of extensible type and if they are pointers they should not have "undefined association".

Chapter 27

MISCELLANEOUS SYSTEM FUNCTIONS

This chapter contains a few system functions, which could not be accommodated in earlier chapters.

27.1 Timing Intrinsics

There are three intrinsics in this category: CPU_TIME, SYSTEM_CLOCK and DATE_AND_TIME.
CPU_TIME: It takes one real argument and the returns the CPU time (in seconds) used upto that point. If returns a negative number if there is no clock. The subroutine is called before and after an instruction or a group of instructions. The difference gives the actual CPU time taken to execute the instruction or the group of instructions.

```
REAL :: T1,T2
INTEGER :: I,J,K
CALL CPU_TIME(T1)
!    dummy loop just to kill some time.
DO I=1, 10000
DO J=1, 1000
DO K=1, 1000
ENDDO
ENDDO
ENDDO
CALL CPU_TIME(T2)
PRINT *, T2-T1
END
```

The subroutine is called before the loop. It returns T1 as the CPU time used upto that point. Similarly, a call to the subroutine after the loop gives T2 and the difference, in this case, 46.1 seconds is the CPU time required to execute the loop. Note that this number is machine dependent.
SYSTEM_CLOCK: This subroutine takes three arguments, COUNT, COUNT_RATE and COUNT_MAX. All of them are optional. COUNT is an integer and scalar. It contains a processor dependent value and is incremented for each 'clock tick' of the processor. It is set to zero when it reaches COUNT_MAX (integer, scalar). The second argument COUNT_RATE (integer or real scalar) is the number of 'clock-ticks' of the processor per second.

```
        INTEGER:: COUNT, COUNT_MAX, COUNT_RATE

        CALL SYSTEM_CLOCK(COUNT, COUNT_RATE, COUNT_MAX)
        PRINT *, COUNT
        PRINT *, COUNT_RATE
        PRINT *, COUNT_MAX
        END
```

When the program was executed in author's laptop the outputs were:

```
82983375
1000
86399999
```

DATE_AND_TIME

The subroutine takes four arguments – DATE, TIME, ZONE and VALUES; all of them are optional. Let us first write a program and try to understand the output from this program.

```
        CHARACTER (LEN=15):: DATE=" ", TIME=" ", ZONE=" "
        INTEGER,DIMENSION(8) :: VALUES
        CALL DATE_AND_TIME(DATE,TIME,ZONE,VALUES)
        PRINT *, DATE
        PRINT *, TIME
        PRINT *, ZONE
        PRINT *, VALUES
        END
```

The outputs from the program, when executed from the author's laptop, are:

20070701   ←——— Date (July 1, 2007)
230743.717 ←——— Time (23:07:43.717)
+0530   ←——— Indian Standard Time=GMT+05:30
2007 7 1 330 23 7 43 718←——— Year, Month, Day of the month, GMT+330 min, hh, mm, ss and millisecond.

DATE is a (scalar) character variable, which returns century (20), year (07), month (07) and day of the month (01). TIME is a (scalar) character variable, which returns time in hour (23), minutes (07), second (43) and millisecond (717). ZONE (scalar) is a character variable which gives difference (+ or -) between the zonal time and Co-coordinated Universal Time in the form of (plus or minus) hour:minute. The last argument (VALUES) is an integer array of rank 1 of size at least 8. The returned values are as hereunder:

VALUES(1)=year, VALUES(2)=month, VALUES(3)=day of the month, VALUES(4)=time difference with UTC, VALUES(5)=hour, VALUES(6)=minute, VALUES(7)=second and VALUES(8)=millisecond.

27.2 COMMAND_ARGUMENT_COUNT

This function returns the number of arguments (integer) in the command line excluding the name of the program.

```
INTEGER:: TOT
TOT=COMMAND_ARGUMENT_COUNT()
PRINT *, TOT
END
```

If the command line contains only the name of the executable program, the function returns zero as there is no argument in the command line. If the command line contains:

```
A.EXE  B  C  D
```

the function returns 3. In fact, it possible to extract the arguments from the command line and the program can process these arguments. This will be discussed in the subsequent sections.

27.3 GET_COMMAND

This subroutine takes three arguments all of them are optional. It returns the command line (COMMAND, character), number of characters in the command line (LENGTH, integer) and the STATUS (integer). The value of the STATUS is zero if the subroutine has been executed successfully, positive if for some reason the command line cannot be extracted and -1 if the length of the COMMAND character variable is insufficient to hold the complete command. If the name of the executable file of the following program:

```
CHARACTER(LEN=30) :: COMMAND = " "
INTEGER:: LENGTH, STATUS

CALL GET_COMMAND(COMMAND, LENGTH, STATUS)
PRINT *, COMMAND
PRINT *, LENGTH
PRINT *, STATUS
END
```

is A.EXE, the outputs will be:

```
A.EXE
5
0
```

If the first line is changed to :

```
CHARACTER(LEN=3):: COMMAND= " "
```

the output will be:

```
A.E
5
-1
```

The STATUS variable is -1 as the command line cannot be accommodated within the character variable COMMAND.

27.4 GET_COMMAND_ARGUMENT

This subroutine takes four arguments – the last three are optional. The first argument NUMBER (integer) is the position number of the argument to be returned. If NUMBER=4, fourth argument will be returned. VALUE is character variable of sufficient length to accommodate the argument specified by the number (the name of the executable program is not considered). LENGTH is the length of the indicated argument. STATUS returns zero if the subroutine is executed successfully; it returns -1 if the length of the character variable is insufficient to accommodate the complete argument and returns some positive number if the subroutine fails to retrieve the command line.

```
CHARACTER(LEN=30):: VALUE=" "
INTEGER:: NUMBER=4, LENGTH, STATUS
CALL GET_COMMAND_ARGUMENT(NUMBER, VALUE, LENGTH, STATUS)
PRINT *, NUMBER
PRINT *, VALUE
PRINT *, LENGTH
PRINT *, STATUS
END
```

If the name of the executable file of the above program is A.EXE and if the command line contains:

```
A.EXE ABC DEF PQR RSTUV
```

the output will be:

```
4
RSTUV
5
0
```

Note that as the variable NUMBER=4, the fourth argument, RSTUV, would be picked up. Because the number of characters of the argument is 5, LENGTH will be set to 5.

27.5 GET_ENVIRONMENT_VARIABLE

This intrinsic takes five arguments, the last four are optional. The first argument NAME (character) contains the name of the environment variable (say PROMPT). The next argument VALUE (character) is returned with the value of the environment variable supplied through the first argument. It may return blank if the environment variable does not exist or does not contain any value. The third argument (integer) returns the length of the variable VALUE (number of characters) if the environment variable exists and has a value; otherwise it returns zero. The fourth argument STATUS (integer) returns zero if the environment variable exists and has a value; it returns -1 if the variable (VALUE) cannot accommodate the returned value; it returns 1 if the environment variable does not exist; it returns 2 if the processor does not support the environment variable. The fifth and last argument TRIM_NAME is a logical variable. If it is false, the trailing blanks of the variable NAME are considered significant (if processor supports); otherwise (if true) trailing blanks of the environment variable are ignored.

```
CHARACTER (LEN=20):: NAME
CHARACTER (LEN=255):: VALUE
INTEGER:: LENGTH, STATUS
LOGICAL:: TRIM_NAME=.TRUE.
READ *, NAME
CALL GET_ENVIRONMENT_VARIABLE (NAME,VALUE,LENGTH,STATUS,&
             TRIM_NAME)
PRINT *, NAME
PRINT *, TRIM(VALUE)
PRINT *, LENGTH
PRINT *, STATUS
PRINT *, TRIM_NAME
END
```

In the above program if the supplied data is PROMPT, the outputs are:

```
PROMPT
$P$G
4
0
T
```

27.6 RANDOM_NUMBER

This subroutine is used to generate pseudo-random numbers in the range zero to one. It takes one argument, conventionally called HARVEST, but X here, which is either a real variable or a real array.

```
REAL:: X
INTEGER :: I
DO I=1,10
CALL RANDOM_NUMBER(X)
PRINT *, X
ENDDO
END
```

The above program will generate and print 10 random numbers within the range 0 and 1. In this case X is a real variable (scalar).

The argument of the next program is a rank 1 array of size 100. If the RANDOM_NUMBER is called with this argument, the subroutine will return 100 random numbers through the array Y.

```fortran
REAL, DIMENSION(100) :: Y

CALL RANDOM_NUMBER(Y)
PRINT *, Y

END
```

One can replace the call by:

```fortran
CALL RANDOM_NUMBER(HARVEST=Y)
```

to obtain the same result.

Random Numbers may be used to solve various problems. The simplest one is the flipping of a coin. It is expected that statistically 50% time the result is heads and 50% of the time result is tails. The following program can be used to test the result of RANDOM_NUMBER.

```fortran
INTEGER, PARAMETER::NUM=100000
REAL :: X
INTEGER:: I, HEAD=0, TAIL=0
DO I=1, NUM
CALL RANDOM_NUMBER(X)
IF(X<=0.5) THEN
  HEAD=HEAD+1
ELSE
  TAIL=TAIL+1
ENDIF
ENDDO
PRINT *, 'Percentage of Heads ',HEAD/FLOAT(NUM)*100.0
PRINT *, 'Percentage of Tails ',TAIL/FLOAT(NUM)*100.0

END
```

The RANDOM_NUMBER subroutine generates uniformly distributed random numbers between 0 and 1. In the program if the value is less than or equal to 0.5, head is assumed; tail is assumed otherwise. For 100000 random numbers the result will be around 50%. The library function FLOAT converts an integer into a real number. This was done in the program to avoid integer division.

The next program simulates flipping of two coins simultaneously. The possible results are: both head (head-head), both tail (tail-tail) and one head and the other tail. If we do not make any distinction between head-tail and tail-head, the expected results are 25%, 25% and 50%.

```fortran
INTEGER, PARAMETER::NUM=100000
REAL :: X1, X2
INTEGER:: I, BHEAD=0, BTAIL=0, HEADTAIL=0
DO I=1, NUM

CALL RANDOM_NUMBER(X1) ! first coin
CALL RANDOM_NUMBER(X2) ! second coin
```

```
IF(X1<=0.5.AND.X2<=0.5) THEN          ! both head
  BHEAD=BHEAD+1
ELSE IF(X1>=0.5.AND.X2>=0.5) THEN      ! both tail
      BTAIL=BTAIL+1
    ELSE
      HEADTAIL=HEADTAIL+1              ! head-tail or tail-head
ENDIF

ENDDO
PRINT *, 'Percentage of Head-Head ',BHEAD/FLOAT(NUM)*100.0
PRINT *, 'Percentage of Tail-Tail ',BTAIL/FLOAT(NUM)*100.0
PRINT *, 'Percentage of Head-Tail ',HEADTAIL/FLOAT(NUM)*100.0

END
```

A better way of writing these two programs is to define a real variable T=100.0 /FLOAT(NUM) and use this T instead of the expression. This avoids repetition of the same calculation.

Random numbers have applications in many branches of science and engineering. One of the applications of Random number is to evaluate multi-dimensional integrals when the conventional numerical methods take enormous amount computer time. We, however, illustrate this method with a single dimensional integral and this can be extended to evaluate the multi-dimensional integrals. The same integral was evaluated earlier by Simpson's method (section 4.7). The techniques used here are (a) change the limits of the integration to 0 and 1 by proper substitution (b) call the random number N times (c) evaluate the function at these values (d) add these values of the function (e) then divide the result by N.

```
INTEGER, PARAMETER::LIMIT=100000
INTEGER::I
REAL::Y, FN=0, T
DO I=1,LIMIT
CALL RANDOM_NUMBER(Y)
T=3.0*Y+1.0
FN=FN+T**3*EXP(-T**3)
ENDDO
PRINT *, 3.0*FN/LIMIT
END
```

Here X of article 4.7 is substituted by $(3Y+1)$ so that the limits of the integration become zero to one. The result of this computation with 100000 random numbers is 0.1519691. The program given in section 4.7 gives 0.1511160.

27.7 RANDOM_SEED

This subroutine is used to restart or to query the random number generator for the subroutine RANDOM_NUMBER.

This subroutine takes three arguments, SIZE, GET and PUT. All of them are optional. However, if used, only one argument can be used in a particular subroutine call. SIZE is an integer (scalar). The subroutine returns the number of N integers that are required to hold the seed. PUT is an integer array of rank 1 and size greater than or equal to N. The seed of the current generator is transferred from this array. GET is an integer array of rank 1 and size greater than or equal N. The seed of the current generator is transferred to it.

```
REAL :: X(5)
INTEGER:: Y(100),Z
CALL RANDOM_SEED(SIZE=Z)

CALL RANDOM_SEED(GET=Y(1:Z))

CALL RANDOM_NUMBER(X)

PRINT *, X
CALL RANDOM_SEED(PUT=Y(1:Z))
CALL RANDOM_NUMBER(X)
PRINT *, X
END
```

As the seed is stored in the Y-array before the RANDOM_NUMBER is called and subsequently the seed is again restored through the call to RANDOM_SEED(PUT=Y(1:Z)), both the calls to RANDOM_NUMBER would generate the same set of random numbers. However if the second call to RANDOM_SEED is removed, the second call to RANDOM_NUMBER would generate different sets of random numbers.

Appendix A

ASCII CHARACTER SET.

Dec	Octal	Hex	Symbol	Dec	Octal	Hex	Symbol	Dec	Octal	Hex	Symbol
0	000	00	^@	29	035	1d	^]	58	072	3a	:
1	001	01	^A	30	036	1e	^^	59	073	3b	;
2	002	02	^B	31	037	1f	^_	60	074	3c	<
3	003	03	^C	32	040	20	space	61	075	3d	=
4	004	04	^D	33	041	21	!	62	076	3e	>
5	005	05	^E	34	042	22	"	63	077	3f	?
6	006	06	^F	35	043	23	#	64	100	40	@
7	007	07	^G	36	044	24	$	65	101	41	A
8	010	08	^H	37	045	25	%	66	102	42	B
9	011	09	^I	38	046	26	&	67	103	43	C
10	012	0a	^J	39	047	27		68	104	44	D
11	013	0b	^K	40	050	28	(	69	105	45	E
12	014	0c	^L	41	051	29	)	70	106	46	F
13	015	0d	^M	42	052	2a	*	71	107	47	G
14	016	0e	^N	43	053	2b	+	72	110	48	H
15	017	0f	^O	44	054	2c		73	111	49	I
16	020	10	^P	45	055	2d	-	74	112	4a	J
17	021	11	^Q	46	056	2e	.	75	113	4b	K
18	022	12	^R	47	057	2f		76	114	4c	L
19	023	13	^S	48	060	30	0	77	115	4d	M
20	024	14	^T	49	061	31	1	78	116	4e	N
21	025	15	^U	50	062	32	2	79	117	4f	O
22	026	16	^V	51	063	33	3	80	120	50	P
23	027	17	^W	52	064	34	4	81	121	51	Q
24	030	18	^X	53	065	35	5	82	122	52	R
25	031	19	^Y	54	066	36	6	83	123	53	S
26	032	1a	^Z	55	067	37	7	84	124	54	T
27	033	1b	^[	56	070	38	8	85	125	55	U
28	034	1c	^\	57	071	39	9	86	126	56	V

Dec	Octal	Hex	Symbol		Dec	Octal	Hex	Symbol		Dec	Octal	Hex	Symbol
87	127	57	W		101	145	65	e		115	163	73	s
88	130	58	X		102	146	66	f		116	164	74	t
89	131	59	Y		103	147	67	g		117	165	75	u
90	132	5a	Z		104	150	68	h		118	166	76	v
91	133	5b	[		105	151	69	i		119	167	77	w
92	134	5c	\		106	152	6a	j		120	170	78	x
93	135	5d	]		107	153	6b	k		121	171	79	y
94	136	5e	^		108	154	6c	l		122	172	7a	z
95	137	5f	_		109	155	6d	m		123	173	7b	{
96	140	60	`		110	156	6e	n		124	174	7c	|
97	141	61	a		111	157	6f	o		125	175	7d	}
98	142	62	b		112	160	70	p		126	176	7e	~
99	143	63	c		113	161	71	q		127	177	7f	DEL
100	144	64	d		114	162	72	r					

EXECUTABLE AND NON-EXECUTABLE STATEMENTS

Statement Name	Executable Statement	Non-executable Statement
ABSTRACT *		X
ALLOCATABLE *		X
ALLOCATE	X	
ASSIGN	X	
ASSOCIATE *	X	
ASYNCHRONOUS *		X
BACKSPACE	X	
BIND *		X
BLOCKDATA		X
CALL	X	
CLASS *		X
CASE	X	
CHARACTER		X
CLOSE	X	
COMMON		X
COMPLEX		X
CONTAINS		X
CONTINUE	X	
CYCLE	X	
DATA		X
DEALLOCATE	X	
(Derived) TYPE		X
DIMENSION		X
DO	X	
DO WHILE	X	
DOUBLE COMPLEX		X
DOUBLE PRECISION		X
ELSE	X	
ELSE IF	X	

END	X	
END ASSOCIATE *	X	
END BLOCKDATA		X
END DO	X	
END ENUM *		X
END IF	X	
END FORALL	X	
END FUNCTION	X	
END INTERFACE		X
END MODULE		X
END PROGRAM	X	
END SELECT	X	
END SUBROUTINE	X	
END TYPE		X
END WHERE		X
ENDFILE	X	
ENTRY		X
ENUM *		X
ENUMERATOR *		X
EQUIVALENCE		X
EXIT	X	
EXTERNAL		X
FLUSH	X	
FORALL	X	
FORMAT		X
FUNCTION		X
GOTO (ASSIGNED)	X	
GOTO (COMPUTED)	X	
GOTO	X	
IF (all types)	X	
IMPLICIT		X
IMPORT *		X
INQUIRE	X	
INTEGER		X
INTENT		X
INTERFACE		X
INTRINSIC		X
LOGICAL		X
MODULE		X
MODULE PROCEDURE		X
NAMELIST		X
NULLIFY	X	
OPEN	X	
OPTIONAL		X
PARAMETER		X
PAUSE	X	
POINTER		X
PRINT	X	

Statement	Executable	Non-executable
PRIVATE		X
PROCEDURE *		X
PROGRAM		X
PROTECTED *		X
PUBLIC		X
READ	X	
RECORD		X
RETURN	X	
REWIND	X	
SAVE		X
SELECT CASE	X	
SELECT TYPE *	X	
SEQUENCE		X
STOP	X	
SUBROUTINE		X
TARGET		X
TYPE		X
TYPE DECLARATION		X
TYPE GUARD *+	X	
USE		X
VOLATILE *		X
WAIT	X	
WHERE	X	
WRITE	X	

* Fortran/2003 Statement
+Exact syntax is described in section 26.9

Appendix C

LIBRARY FUNCTIONS (INTRINSICS)

This Appendix contains a list of all the library functions available in Fortran/2003. Most of them were discussed in the text. The following abbreviations are used in this Appendix.

Arguments - if there is more than one argument, the arguments are separated by comma. Optional arguments are typed in italics.

Class of the Intrinsic: Elemental(E), Inquiry(I), Transformational(T), Subroutine(S), Pure Subroutine(P).

Argument Type: Integer (I), Real(R), Complex(Z), Character(C), String(S), Integer/ Real/ Complex(A), Pointer(P), Target(T), Double Precision(D), Logical(L), Array (Ar), Real Array (Ar(R)), Scalar(Sc), Scalar Real (Sc(R)), Same as X (S(X)). I, R, Z and L also stand for scalar for their respective argument.

Result: Same as first argument (S), Array same as S (As(S)), Same as X (S(X))

The Class, Argument and Result are separated by vertical bar as shown below:

Class | Argument | Result

For example, ABS(A): Absolute Value: E|A|S (except complex) indicates that the function ABS returns the absolute value of it argument A which may be an integer or a real or a complex. The returned value is the same as its argument except for complex argument, which is described separately.

Some times details are not given just to avoid the repetition; this can be found in the main text. These are indicated by bold type. Complete information may be found in the Fortran/2003 report.

ABS(A) : Absolute Value : E|A|S (except complex)
For Complex Number (X): SQRT(X**2+Y**2)

ACHAR(I, *KIND*) : Character from ASCII collating sequence corresponding to I: E|I, I|C

ACOS(X) : Cosine inverse: E|R|S: ABS(X) .LE. 1

ADJUSTL(STRING): Removes leading blanks and adds at the end: E|S|S

ADJUSTR(STRING): Remove trailing blanks and adds at the beginning: E|S|S

AIMAG(Z): Imaginary part of Z: E | Z | R

AINT(A, *KIND*): Truncates to a whole number: E | R, I | R

ALL(MASK, *DIM*): Tests whether all values are true along DIM: T | L, I | Same as MASK, see text.

ALLOCATED (ARRAY) or ALLOCATED(SCALAR): Test whether allocated: I | Ar or Sc | L: argument should be allocatable array/scalar.

AINT(A, *KIND*): Nearest whole number: E | R, I | R

ANY(MASK, *DIM*): Tests whether there is any true value in MASK along DIM: T | L, I | L (same kind type as MASK), see text

ASIN(X): Sine inverse: E | R | S: X is between -PI/2 and +PI/2

ASSOCIATED(POINTER, *TARGET*): Association status of POINTER: I | P, T | L

ATAN(X): Tangent inverse: E | R | S: Result is in radian and is between -PI/2 and +PI/2

ATAN2(Y, X): Tangent inverse, principal value of the non-zero complex number (X, Y): E | R, R | S

BIT_SIZE(I): Number of bits required for I: I | I | I

BTEST(I, POS): Tests a bit: E | I, I | L

CEILING(A, *KIND*): Least integer .GE. A: E | R, I | I

CHAR(I, *KIND*): Inverse of ICHAR: E | I, I | C

CMPLX(X, Y, KIND): Complex conversion: E | I/R/Z,I/R,I | Z: If Y is absent, it is taken as zero, the first two arguments may be BOZ literal constant.

COMMAND_ARGUMENT_COUNT(): Number of command arguments: I | No argument | I

CONJG(Z): Conjugate of Z: E | Z | Z

COS(X): Cosine: E | R / Z | S

COSH(X): Hyperbolic Cosine: E | R | S

COUNT(MASK, *DIM, KIND*): Counts number of true elements in MASK along DIM: T | L, I, I | I, see text

CPU_TIME(TIME): Processor time: S | R | R

CSHIFT(ARRAY, SHIFT, *DIM*): Circular shift: T | Ar, I / Ar(I), I | Ar(S)

DATE_AND_TIME(DATE, TIME, ZONE, VALUES): Returns date and time - For details see text

DBLE(A): Converts to Double precision: E | A | D

DIGITS(X): Returns number of significant digits: I | I / R/Ar | I

DIM(X, Y): X-Y if positive or zero: E | I / R, S(X) | S(X)

DOT_PRODUCT(VECTOR_A, VECTOR_B): Dot Product: T | Ar(I, R, C, L), Ar(VECTOR_A) | S

DPROD(X, Y): Double precision real product: E | R, R | D, Arguments X, Y must be of default real type

EOSHIFT(ARRAY, SHIFT, *BOUNDARY*, *DIM*): End of shift - See text

EPSILON(X): Returns a positive number negligible compared to 1: I | R/Ar(R) | S

EXP(X): E to the power X: E | R / Z | S

EXPONENT(X): Exponent part of the argument: E | R | I

EXTENDS_TYPE_OF(A, MOLD): Checks whether dynamic type of A is an Extension of MOLD: I | See text | L

FLOOR(A, *KIND*): Greatest integer .LE. A: E | R, I | I

FRACTION(X): Returns fractional part of X: E | R | S

GET_COMMAND(*COMMAND*, *LENGTH*, *STATUS*): Returns the command line: S | See text

GET_COMMAD_ARGUMENT(NUMBER, *VALUE*, *LENGTH*, *STATUS*):
Returns command argument: S | See text

GET_ENVIRONMENT_VARIABLE(NAME, *VALUE*, *LENGTH*, *STATUS*, *TRIM_NAME*):
Returns the value of an environment variable: S | See text

HUGE(X): Largest number: I | I /R/Sc(I)/Sc(R) | S

IACHAR(C, *KIND*): Position of C in ASCII collating sequence: E | C,I | I

IAND(I, J): Bitwise AND: E | I, I | S

IBCLR(I, POS): Clear bit: E | I, I | S

IBITS(I,POS, LEN): Extracts bits: E | I, I, I | S - See text; LEN must be non negative

IBSET(I, POS): Bit set: E | I, I | S - See text

ICHAR(C, *KIND*): character position in processor dependent collating sequence, inverse of CHAR:
E | C, I | I

IEOR(I, J): Bitwise exclusive OR: E | I, I | S

INDEX(STRING, SUBSTRING, *BACK*, *KIND*): Locates the starting position of a substring within a string:
E | See text | I

INT(A, *KIND*): Converts to integer: E | A,I | S (except complex) - for complex it takes the real part only.

IOR(I, J): Bitwise inclusive OR: E | I, I | I

ISHFT(I, SHIFT): Logical shift: E | I, I | S

ISHFTC(I, SHIFT, *SIZE*): Circular shift: E | I, I, I | I

IS_IOSTAT_END(I): Determines EOF condition: E | I | L

IS_IOSTAT_EOR(I): Determines EOR condition: E | I | L

KIND(X): Kind type parameter: I | A, Ar(any) | I

LBOUND(ARRAY, *DIM, KIND*): Returns Lower bound of an array: I | Ar(A), I, I | I

LEN(STRING, *KIND*): Length of the string: I | S, I | I

LEN_TRIM(STRING, *KIND*): Length of the string without the trailing blanks: I | S, I | I

LGE(STRING_A, STRING_B): Lexically greater or equal to : E | C, C | L

LGT(STRING_A, STRING_B): Lexically greater: E | C, C | L

LLE(STRING_A, STRING_B): Lexically less than or equal to: E | C, C | L

LLT(STRING_A, STRING_B): Lexically less: E | C, C | L

LOG(X): Natural logarithm: E | R/C | S: X>0 for real argument; X is not equal to 0 when X is complex

LOG10(X): Common logarithm: E | R | S: X>0

LOGICAL(L, *KIND*): Changes between kinds of logical: E | L, I | L

MATMUL(MATRIX_A, MATRIX_B): Matrix multiplication: T | A / L,A/L | S, input: array of rank 1 or 2

MAX(A1, A2, *A3,...*): Maximum value: E | I/R/C,... | S - See text

MAXEXPONENT(X): Maximum exponent: I | R / Arr | I

MAXLOC(ARRAY, DIM, *MASK, KIND*) or MAXLOC(ARRAY, *MASK, KIND*): Location containing maximum value: T | Ar(I / R/C), I, L, I | See text

MAXVAL(ARRAY, *DIM, MASK*) or MAXVAL(ARRAY, *MASK*): Maximum value of the elements: T | See text | See text

MERGE(TSOURCE, FSOURCE, MASK): Selects alternative according to the MASK: E | A, S(A), L | S

MIN(A1, A2, *A3,...*): Minimum value: E | I / R / C,... | S

MINEXPONENT(X): Most negative exponent: I | R/Ar | I

MINLOC(ARRAY, DIM, *MASK, KIND*) or MAXLOC(ARRAY, *MASK, KIND*): Location containing minimum value: T | Ar(I / R / C), I, L, I | See text

MINVAL(ARRAY, *DIM, MASK*) or MAXVAL(ARRAY, *MASK*): Minimum value of the elements: T | See text | See text

MOD(A, P): Reminder: E | I / R, same as A not zero | S: Result is A-INT(A/P)*P

MODULO(A, P): Modulo: E | I / R, same as A not zero | S: Result is A-FLOOR(A/P)*P

MOVE_ALLOC(FROM, TO): Move allocation: P | Ar(any), Ar(same as FROM) - FROM and TO should be allocatable.

MVBITS(FROM, FROMPOS, LEN, TO, TOPOS): Copies some bits, see text for details.

NEAREST(X, S): Nearest machine-representable number greater than or less a X: E | R, R | S : second argument not equal to zero.

NEW_LINE(A): Newline character: I | C | S

NINT(A, *KIND*): Nearest integer: E | R, I | I

NOT(I): Bitwise NOT operation: E | I | S

NULL(*MOLD*): Deassociates a pointer: T | P/allocatable | Same as MOLD if present, otherwise see the Fortran report

PACK(ARRAY, MASK, *VECTOR*): Packs an array: T | Ar, L, Same type Array of Rank 1 | See text

PRECISION(X): Returns the decimal precision: I | R / Z/ Arr | I

PRESENT(A): Checks whether an optional argument is present: I | see text | L

PRODUCT(ARRAY, DIM, *MASK*) or PRODUCT(ARRAY, *MASK*): Product of all the elements of the array or controlled by MASK and DIM: T | Ar(A), I, L | S, L conformable with ARRAY.

RADIX(X): Returns the base: I | I / R | I

RANDOM_NUMBER(HARVEST): Generates Pseudo random number: S | R | R

RANDOM_SEED(*SIZE, PUT, GET*): Can send request or query the random number generator: S | I, Ar(I), Ar(I) | - Details may be found in the text.

RANGE(X): Decimal range: I | A/Arr | I

REAL(A, *KIND*): Conversion to real: E | A, I | R

REPEAT(STRING, NCOPIES): Concatenates NCOPIES of the STRING: T | S, I | S: I > 0

RESHAPE(SOURCE, SHAPE, *PAD, ORDER*): Constructs array: T | See text | See text

RRSPACING(X): Reciprocal of relative spacing: E | R | S

SAME_TYPE_AS(A, B): Checks whether A and B are of same dynamic type: I | See text | L

SCALE(X, I): Returns X*b**I, where b is the base: E | R, I | S

SCAN(STRING, SET, *BACK, KIND*): Scans a string: E | S, C/ S, L, I | I

SELECTED_CHAR_KIND(NAME): Returns the kind type parameter of a character set: T | C | I

SELECTED_INT_KIND(R): Returns the kind type parameter of an integer: T | I | I

SELECTED_REAL_KIND(*P, R*): Returns the kind type parameter of a real: T | I, I | I

SET_EXPONENT(X, I): Number whose fractional part is same a X, exponent I: Ë | R, I | S - See text

SHAPE(SOURCE, *KIND*): Returns the shape of an array: I | Ar(any), I | Shape of SOURCE

SIGN(A, B): Returns A* Sign of B: E | I / R, same as A | same as A

SIN(X): Sine: E | R /C | S

SINH(X): Sine hyperbolic: E | R | S

SIZE(ARRAY, *DIM, KIND*): Returns the extent of an array: I | Arr(any), I,I | I

SPACING(X): Absolute spacing: E | R | S

SPREAD(SOURCE, *DIM, NCOPIES*): Replicates an array: T | Ar(any),I,I | See text

SQRT(X): Square root: E | R /Z | S : For real number R > =0.

SUM(ARRAY, *DIM, MASK*) or SUM(ARRAY, *MASK*): Sums the elements of the array: T | Ar(Any), I, L) | See text

SYSTEM_CLOCK(*COUNT, COUNT_RATE, COUNT_MAX*): Real time clock: S | I, I / R,I | See text

TAN(X): Tangent: E | R | S

TANH(X): Hyperbolic Tangent: E | R | S

TINY(X): Smallest positive number of the kind type of X: I | R /Arr | S

TRANSFER(SOURCE, MOLD, *SIZE*): Transfer and interpreting the source: T | A, A, I | See text

TRANSPOSE(MATRIX): Transpose of a matrix: T | Ar | Ar, Ar is rank 2.

TRIM(STRING): Removes trailing bank from a string: T | S | S

UBOUND(ARRAY, *DIM, KIND*): Returns the upper bound of the array: I | Ar(any), I, I | See text

UNPACK(VECTOR,MASK,FIELD): Unpacks an rank 1 array: T | Ar(any), Arr(L), Same type as vector | see text

VERIFY(STRING, SET, *BACK, KIND*): Verify the presence of a set of character: E | S, S, L, I | See text

IEEE modules have been discussed in details in chapter 20. A complete list of all the IEEE procedures are given in a classified manner.

Inquiry Functions:
IEEE_SUPPORT_FLAG(FLAG, *X*)
IEEE_SUPPORT_HALTING(FLAG)
IEEE_SUPPORT_DATATYPE(*X*)
IEEE_SUPPORT_DENORMAL(*X*)
IEEE_SUPPORT_DIVIDE(*X*)
IEEE_SUPPORT_INF(*X*)
IEEE_SUPPORT_IO(*X*)
IEEE_SUPPORT_NAN(*X*)
IEEE_SUPPORT_ROUNDING(ROUNDING_VALUE, *X*)
IEEE_SUPPORT_SQRT(*X*)
IEEE_SUPPORT_STANDARD(*X*)
IEEE_SUPPORT_UNDERFLOW_CONTROL(*X*)

Elemental Functions:
IEEE_CLASS(X)
IEEE_COPY_SIGN(X, Y)
IEEE_IS_FINITE(X)
IEEE_IS_NAN(X)
IEEE_IS_NORMAL(X)
IEEE_IS_NEGATIVE(X)
IEEE_LOGB(X)
IEEE_NEXT_AFTER(X, Y)
IEEE_REM(X, Y)
IEEE_RINT(X)
IEEE_SCALB(X, I)
IEEE_UNORDERED(X, Y)
IEEE_VALUE(X, CLASS)

Kind Function:
IEEE_SELECTED_REAL_KIND(*P, R*)

Elemental Subroutines
IEEE_GET_FLAG(FLAG, FLAG_VALUE)
IEEE_GET_HALTING_MODE(FLAG, HALTING)

Nonelemental Subroutines:
IEEE_GET_STATUS(STATUS, VALUE)
IEEE_SET_FLAG(FLAG, FLAG_VALUE)
IEEE_SET_HALTING_MODE(FLAG, HALTING)
IEEE_SET_STATUS(STATUS_VALUE)

IEEE_GET_ROUNDING_MODE(ROUND_VALUE)
IEEE_GET_UNDERFLOW_MODE(GRADUAL)
IEEE_SET_ROUNDING_MODE(ROUND_VALUE)
IEEE_SET_UNDERFLOW_MODE(GRADUAL)

The following procedures have been discussed in chapter 22 (Strings with Variable Length)

EXTRACT(STRING, START, FINISH)
GET(UNIT, SET, SEPARATOR,MAXLEN,IOSTAT)
PUT(UNIT, STRING, IOSTAT)
PUT_LINE(UNIT, STRING, IOSTAT)
REMOVE(STRING, START, FINISH)
REPLACE(STRING, START, FINISH)
SPLIT(STRING, WORD, SET)

Appendix D

ORDER AND EXECUTION SEQUENCE

1. Program, Function, Subroutine, Module or Block Data Statement	
2. USE statement	
3. IMPORT Statement	
4. DATA, FORMAT and ENTRY statement	5. Derived-Type definitions, Interface blocks, Type declaration, Enumeration definitions, Procedure declarations, Specification statements, IMPLICIT statements, PARAMETER statements
	6. Executable Statements
7. CONTAINS Statements	
8. Internal subprogram or Module subprograms	
9. END Statement	

TYPE OF OPERANDS AND THE RESULT OF INTRINSIC OPERATIONS

Intrinsic Operator (op)	Type of First Operand (x1)	Type of Second Operand (x2)	Type of [x1] op x2
Unary +, -		I, R, Z	I, R, Z
Binary +, -, *, /, **	I R Z	I, R, Z I, R, Z I, R, Z	I, R, Z R, R, Z Z, Z, Z
//	C	C	C
.EQ., .NE., ==, /=	I R Z C	I, R, Z I, R, Z I, R, Z C	L, L, L L, L, L L, L, L L
.GT., .GE., .LT., .LE. >, >=, <, <=	I R C	I, R I, R C	L, L L, L L
.NOT.		L	L
.AND., .OR., .EQV., .NEQV.	L	L	L

I, R, Z, L and C are respectively stand for Integer, Real, Complex, Logical and Character.

Appendix F

PRIORITY OF OPERATORS

Category of Operation	Operators	Precedence
Extension	Defined Unary Operator	High
Numeric	**	
Numeric	* or /	
Numeric	Unary + or -	
Numeric	Binary + or -	
Character	//	
Relational	EQ., .NE., GT., .GE., .LT., .LE. ==, /=, >, >=, <, <=	
Logical	.NOT.	
Logical	.AND.	
Logical	.OR.	
Logical	.EQV. or .NEQV.	
Extension	Defined Binary Operator	Low

STATEMENTS ALLOWED IN SCOPING UNITS

Type of Scoping Unit	Main Program	Module	Block Data	External Subprog	Module Subprog	Internal Subprog	Interface body
USE statement	Y	Y	Y	Y	Y	Y	Y
IMPORT statement	N	N	N	N	N	N	Y
ENTRY statement	N	N	N	Y	Y	N	N
FORMAT statement	Y	N	N	Y	Y	Y	N
Misc Declaration (*)	Y	Y	Y	Y	Y	Y	Y
DATA statement	Y	Y	Y	Y	Y	Y	N
Derived Type definition	Y	Y	Y	Y	Y	Y	Y
Interface Block	Y	Y	N	Y	Y	Y	Y
Executable statement	Y	N	N	Y	Y	Y	N
CONTAINS statement	Y	Y	N	Y	Y	N	N
Statement Function statement	Y	N	N	Y	Y	Y	N

(*) PARAMETER, IMPLICIT, Type Declaration, Enumeration Definition, Procedure Declaration and Specification Statements.

(1) Module subprogram is not included in the scoping unit of a Module.
(2) Y stands for Yes and N stands for No.

REFERENCES

1. Working Draft J3/04-007 May 10, 2004.

2. Fortran 95/2003 Explained - M Metcalf, J Reid and M Cohen - Oxford University Press.

3. Varying Length String : ISO/IEC 1539-2:2000.

4. Stream Input/Output in Fortran - http://www.star.le.ac.uk/~cgp/streamIO.html.

5. Introduction to Programming with Fortran with Coverage of Fortran 90, 95, 2003 and 77 - I Chivers and J Sleightholme - Springer.

6. Intel Fortran Language Reference - Document Number: 253261-003.

7. Programmers Guide to Fortran 90 - W S Brainerd, C H Goldberg, J C Adams - McGraw-Hill.

8. Numerical Methods with Fortran IV Case Studies - W S Dorn and D D McCracken - Wiley.

9. A Book on C - Al Kelly and Ira Pohl - Pearson.

10. IBM XL Fortran Advanced Edition for Linux, V11.1, Language Reference : SC23-5894-00.